NON-LEAGUE
FOOTBALL
TABLES
1889-2004

EDITOR
Michael Robinson

British Library Cataloguing in Publication Data
A catalogue record for this book is available from the British Library

ISBN 1-86223-105-2

Copyright © 2004,   Soccer Books Limited

Printed by The Cromwell Press

FOREWORD

In selecting the Leagues to be included in this third edition of Non-League Football Tables we have again chosen those forming the pinnacle of the Non-League Football Pyramid, i.e. The Football Conference and it's three direct feeders.

In addition we have once more included the briefly-lived Football Alliance which became, effectively, the 2nd Division of the Football League in 1892 together with the four leagues for the North-Eastern part of the country and three other important but short-lived competitions. In future editions we expect to include leagues for other parts of the country.

Furthermore, as league sponsors change frequently, we have not used sponsored names (eg. Rymans League) other than in an indicative way on the cover.

We are indebted to Mick Blakeman for providing tables for the four North-Eastern Leagues and the final three Leagues included in this publication.

CONTENTS

Football Alliance . . . . .Page 4

Southern League (current sponsors Dr. Martens) . . . . Pages 4-36

Football Conference (current sponsors Nationwide) . . . . Pages 36-40

Isthmian League (current sponsors Rymans) . . . . Pages 41-66

Northern Premier League (current sponsors Unibond) . . . . Pages 66-75

North Regional League . . . . Pages 76-78

North-Eastern League . . . . Pages 79-90

Northern Counties (East) League . . . . Pages 91-100

The Yorkshire League. . . . . Pages 101-118

Central Amateur League . . . . Pages 119-120

The Central Combination . . . . .Page 121

United League . . . . Pages 122-123

Other Publications . . . . Pages 124-125

FOOTBALL ALLIANCE

1889-90

Sheffield Wednesday	22	15	2	5	70	39	32
Bootle	22	13	2	7	66	39	28
Sunderland Albion	21	12	2	7	64	39	28
Grimsby Town	22	12	2	8	58	47	26
Crewe Alexandra	22	11	2	9	68	59	24
Darwen	22	10	2	10	70	75	22
Birmingham St George	21	9	3	9	62	49	21
Newton Heath	22	9	2	11	40	44	20
Walsall Town Swifts	22	8	3	11	44	59	19
Small Heath	22	6	5	11	44	67	17
Nottingham Forest	22	6	5	11	31	62	17
Long Eaton Rangers	22	4	2	16	35	73	10

Sunderland Albion record includes 2 points awarded when Birmingham St George refused to fulfil a fixture which the Alliance committee had ordered to be replayed.

1890-91

Stoke	22	13	7	2	57	39	33
Sunderland Albion	22	12	6	4	69	28	30
Grimsby Town	22	11	5	6	43	27	27
Birmingham St George	22	12	2	8	64	62	26
Nottingham Forest	22	9	7	6	66	39	25
Darwen	22	10	3	9	64	59	23
Walsall Town Swifts	22	9	3	10	34	61	21
Crewe Alexandra	22	8	4	10	59	67	20
Newton Heath	22	7	3	12	37	55	17
Small Heath	22	7	2	13	58	66	16
Bootle	22	3	7	12	40	61	13
Sheffield Wednesday	22	4	5	13	39	66	13

1891-92

Nottingham Forest	22	14	5	3	59	22	33
Newton Heath	22	12	7	3	69	33	31
Small Heath	22	12	5	5	53	36	29
Sheffield Wednesday	22	12	4	6	65	35	28
Burton Swifts	22	12	2	8	54	52	26
Grimsby Town	22	6	6	10	40	39	18
Crewe Alexandra	22	7	4	11	44	49	18
Ardwick	22	6	6	10	39	51	18
Bootle	22	8	2	12	42	64	18
Lincoln City	22	6	5	11	37	65	17
Walsall Town Swifts	22	6	3	13	33	59	15
Birmingham St George	22	5	3	14	34	64	13

SOUTHERN LEAGUE

1894-95

First Division

Millwall Athletic	16	12	4	0	68	19	28
Luton Town	16	9	4	3	36	22	22
Southampton St Mary's	16	9	2	5	34	25	20
Ilford	16	6	3	7	26	40	15
Reading	16	6	2	8	33	38	14
Chatham	16	4	5	7	22	25	13
Royal Ordnance Factories	16	3	6	7	20	30	12
Clapton	16	5	1	10	22	38	11
Swindon Town	16	4	1	11	24	48	9

Second Division

New Brompton	12	11	0	1	57	10	22
Sheppey United	12	6	1	5	25	23	13
Old St Stephen's	12	6	0	6	26	26	12
Uxbridge	12	4	3	5	14	20	11
Bromley	12	4	1	7	23	30	9
Chesham	12	3	3	6	20	42	9
Maidenhead	12	2	4	6	19	33	8

1895-96

First Division

Millwall Athletic	18	16	1	1	75	16	33
Luton Town	18	13	1	4	68	14	27
Southampton St Mary's	18	12	0	6	44	23	24
Reading	18	11	1	6	45	38	23
Chatham	18	9	2	7	43	45	20
New Brompton	18	7	4	7	30	37	18
Swindon Town	18	6	4	8	38	41	16
Clapton	18	4	2	12	30	67	10
Royal Ordnance Factories	18	3	3	12	23	44	9
Ilford	18	0	0	18	10	81	0

Second Division

Wolverton L & NW Railway	16	13	1	2	43	10	27
Sheppey United	16	11	3	2	60	19	25
1st Scots Guards	16	8	5	3	37	22	21
Uxbridge	16	9	1	6	28	23	19
Old St Stephen's	16	6	3	7	34	21	15
Guildford	16	7	1	8	29	41	15
Maidenhead	16	4	1	11	20	49	9
Chesham	16	2	3	11	15	48	7
Bromley	16	2	2	12	16	49	6

1896-97

First Division

Southampton St Mary's	20	15	5	0	63	18	35
Millwall Athletic	20	13	5	2	63	24	31
Chatham	20	13	1	6	54	29	27
Tottenham Hotspur	20	9	4	7	43	29	22
Gravesend United	20	9	4	7	35	34	22
Swindon Town	20	8	3	9	33	37	19
Reading	20	8	3	9	31	49	19
New Brompton	20	7	2	11	32	42	16
Northfleet	20	5	4	11	24	46	14
Sheppey United	20	5	1	14	34	47	11
Wolverton L & NW Railway	20	2	0	18	17	74	4

Second Division

Dartford	24	16	4	4	83	19	36
Royal Engineers Training Battalion	24	11	9	4	49	37	31
Freemantle	24	12	4	8	58	40	28
Uxbridge	24	11	5	8	62	37	27
Wycombe Wanderers	24	10	6	8	37	54	26
Chesham	24	11	3	10	41	55	25
Southall	24	9	6	9	55	52	24
1st Scot Guards	24	9	6	9	49	50	24
West Herts	24	11	1	12	41	49	23
Warmley (Bristol)	24	10	2	12	44	43	22
Old St Stephen's	24	5	7	12	36	52	17
Maidenhead	24	4	8	12	33	64	16
1st Coldstream Guards	24	3	6	15	30	66	12

1897-98

First Division

Southampton	22	18	1	3	53	18	37
Bristol City	22	13	7	2	67	33	33
Tottenham Hotspur	22	12	4	6	52	31	28
Chatham	22	12	4	6	50	34	28
Reading	22	8	7	7	39	31	23
New Brompton	22	9	4	9	37	37	22
Sheppey United	22	10	1	11	40	49	21
Gravesend United	22	7	6	9	28	39	20
Millwall Athletic	22	8	2	12	48	45	18
Swindon Town	22	7	2	13	36	48	16
Northfleet	22	4	3	15	29	60	11
Wolverton L & NW Railway	22	3	1	18	28	82	7

Second Division

Royal Artillery (Portsmouth)	22	19	1	2	75	22	39
Warmley (Bristol)	22	19	0	3	108	15	38
West Herts	22	11	6	5	50	48	28
Uxbridge	22	11	2	9	39	57	24
St Albans	22	9	5	8	47	41	23
Dartford	22	11	0	11	68	55	22
Southall	22	8	2	12	49	61	18
Chesham	22	8	2	12	38	48	18
Olsd St Stephen's	22	7	2	13	47	66	16
Wycombe Wanderers	22	7	2	13	37	55	16
Maidenhead	22	4	4	14	27	81	12
Royal Engineers Training Battalion	22	4	2	16	26	62	10

Second Division

Watford	20	14	2	4	57	25	30
Fulham	20	10	4	6	44	23	24
Chesham Town	20	11	2	7	43	37	24
Wolverton L & NW Railway	20	9	6	5	46	36	24
Grays United	20	8	6	6	63	29	22
Shepherds Bush	20	9	4	7	45	37	22
Dartford	20	8	3	9	36	44	19
Wycombe Wanderers	20	8	3	9	35	50	19
Brentford	20	5	7	8	31	48	17
Southall	20	6	3	11	21	44	15
Maidenhead	20	1	2	17	16	64	4

1898-99

First Division

Southampton	24	15	5	4	54	24	35
Bristol City	24	15	3	6	55	12	33
Millwall Athletic	24	12	6	6	59	35	30
Chatham	24	10	8	6	32	23	28
Reading	24	9	8	7	31	24	26
New Brompton	24	10	5	9	38	30	25
Tottenham Hotspur	24	10	4	10	40	36	24
Bedminster	24	10	4	10	35	39	24
Swindon Town	24	9	5	10	43	49	23
Brighton United	24	9	2	13	37	48	20
Gravesend United	24	7	5	12	42	52	19
Sheppey United	24	5	3	16	23	53	13
Royal Artillery (Portsmouth)	24	4	4	16	17	60	12

Second Division (London Section)

Thames Ironworks	22	19	1	2	64	16	39
Wolverton L & NW Railway	22	13	4	5	88	43	30
Watford	22	14	2	6	62	35	30
Brentford	22	11	3	8	59	39	25
Wycombe Wanderers	22	10	2	10	55	57	22
Southall	22	11	0	11	44	55	22
Chesham	22	9	2	11	45	62	20
St Albans	22	8	3	11	45	59	19
Shepherds Bush	22	7	3	12	37	53	17
Fulham	22	6	4	12	36	44	16
Uxbridge	22	7	2	13	29	48	16
Maidenhead	22	3	2	17	33	86	8

Second Division (South West Section)

Cowes	10	10	0	0	58	8	20
Ryde	10	7	0	3	30	11	14
Freemantle	10	4	1	5	18	31	9
Sandown	10	4	0	6	20	29	8
Eastleigh	10	2	1	7	17	37	5
Andover	10	2	0	8	14	41	4

1899-1900

First Division

Tottenham Hotspur	28	20	4	4	67	26	44
Portsmouth	28	20	1	7	58	27	41
Southampton	28	17	1	10	70	33	35
Reading	28	15	2	11	41	28	32
Swindon Town	28	15	2	11	50	42	32
Bedminster	28	13	2	13	44	45	28
Millwall Athletic	28	12	3	13	36	37	27
Queens Park Rangers	28	12	2	14	49	57	26
Bristol City	28	9	7	12	43	47	25
Bristol Rovers	28	11	3	14	46	55	25
New Brompton	28	9	6	13	39	49	24
Gravesend United	28	10	4	14	38	58	24
Chatham	28	10	3	15	38	58	23
Thames Ironworks	28	8	5	15	30	45	21
Sheppey United	28	3	7	18	24	66	13

1900-01

First Division

Southampton	28	18	5	5	58	26	41
Bristol City	28	17	5	6	54	27	39
Portsmouth	28	17	4	7	56	32	38
Millwall Athletic	28	17	2	9	55	32	36
Tottenham Hotspur	28	16	4	8	55	33	36
West Ham United	28	14	5	9	40	28	33
Bristol Rovers	28	14	4	10	46	35	32
Queens Park Rangers	28	11	4	13	43	48	26
Reading	28	8	8	12	24	25	24
Luton Town	28	11	2	15	43	49	24
Kettering	28	7	9	12	33	46	23
New Brompton	28	7	5	16	34	51	19
Gravesend United	28	6	7	15	32	85	19
Watford	28	6	4	18	24	52	16
Swindon Town	28	3	8	17	19	47	14

Second Division

Brentford	16	14	2	0	63	11	30
Grays United	16	12	2	2	62	12	26
Sheppey United	16	8	1	7	44	26	17
Shepherds Bush	16	8	1	7	30	30	17
Fulham	16	8	0	8	38	26	16
Chesham Town	16	5	1	10	26	39	11
Maidenhead	16	4	1	11	21	49	9
Wycombe Wanderers	16	4	1	11	23	68	9
Southall	16	4	1	11	22	68	9

1901-02

First Division

Portsmouth	30	20	7	3	67	24	47
Tottenham Hotspur	30	18	6	6	61	22	42
Southampton	30	18	6	6	71	28	42
West Ham United	30	17	6	7	45	28	40
Reading	30	16	7	7	57	24	39
Millwall Athletic	30	13	6	11	48	31	32
Luton Town	30	11	10	9	31	35	32
Kettering	30	12	5	13	44	39	29
Bristol Rovers	30	12	5	13	43	39	29
New Brompton	30	10	7	13	39	38	27
Northampton	30	11	5	14	53	64	27
Queens Park Rangers	30	8	7	15	34	56	23
Watford	30	9	4	17	36	60	22
Wellingborough	30	9	4	17	34	75	22
Brentford	30	7	6	17	34	61	20
Swindon Town	30	2	3	25	17	93	7

Second Division

Fulham	16	13	0	3	51	19	26
Grays United	16	12	1	3	49	14	25
Brighton & Hove Albion	16	11	0	5	34	17	22
Wycombe Wanderers	17	7	3	6	36	30	17
West Hampstead	16	6	4	6	39	29	16
Shepherds Bush	16	6	1	9	31	31	13
Southall	15	5	2	9	28	52	12
Maidenhead	16	3	1	12	23	59	7
Chesham Town	16	2	2	12	24	64	6

1902-03

First Division

Southampton	30	20	8	2	83	20	48
Reading	30	19	7	4	72	30	45
Portsmouth	30	17	7	6	69	32	41
Tottenham Hotspur	30	14	7	9	47	31	35
Bristol Rovers	30	13	8	9	46	34	34
New Brompton	30	11	11	8	37	35	33
Millwall Athletic	30	14	3	13	52	37	31
Northampton Town	30	12	6	12	39	48	30
Queens Park Rangers	30	11	6	13	34	42	28
West Ham United	30	9	10	11	35	49	28
Luton Town	30	10	7	13	43	44	27
Swindon Town	30	10	7	13	38	46	27
Kettering	30	8	11	11	33	40	27
Wellingborough	30	11	3	16	36	56	25
Watford	30	6	4	20	35	87	16
Brentford	30	2	1	27	16	84	5

Second Division

Fulham	10	7	1	2	27	7	15
Brighton & Hove Albion	10	7	1	2	34	11	15
Grays United	10	7	0	3	28	12	14
Wycombe Wanderers	10	3	3	4	13	19	9
Chesham Town	10	2	1	7	9	37	5
Southall	10	1	0	9	10	35	2

1903-04

First Division

Southampton	34	22	6	6	75	30	50
Tottenham Hotspur	34	16	11	7	54	37	43
Bristol Rovers	34	17	8	9	66	42	42
Portsmouth	34	17	8	9	41	38	42
Queens Park Rangers	34	15	11	8	53	37	41
Reading	34	14	13	7	48	35	41
Millwall	34	16	8	10	64	42	40
Luton Town	34	14	12	8	38	33	40
Plymouth Argyle	34	13	10	11	44	34	36
Swindon Town	34	10	11	13	30	42	31
Fulham	34	9	12	13	33	34	30
West Ham United	34	10	7	17	38	43	27
Brentford	34	9	9	16	34	48	27
Wellingborough	34	11	5	18	44	63	27
Northampton Town	34	10	7	17	36	69	27
New Brompton	34	6	13	15	26	43	25
Brighton & Hove Albion	34	6	12	16	45	79	24
Kettering	34	6	7	21	30	78	19

Second Division

Watford	20	18	2	0	70	15	38
Portsmouth Reserves	20	15	2	3	85	25	32
Millwall Reserves	20	9	4	7	35	39	22
Southampton Reserves	20	9	3	8	59	35	21
Grays United	20	9	3	8	25	55	21
Fulham Reserves	20	8	4	8	40	34	20
Swindon Town Reserves	20	8	3	9	50	44	19
Reading Reserves	20	8	2	10	43	42	18
Wycombe Wanderers	20	5	5	10	29	64	15
Southall	20	4	2	14	25	62	10
Chesham Town	20	1	2	17	19	65	4

1904-05

First Division

Bristol Rovers	34	20	8	6	74	36	48
Reading	34	18	7	9	57	38	43
Southampton	34	18	7	9	54	40	43
Plymouth Argyle	34	18	5	11	57	39	41
Tottenham Hotspur	34	15	8	11	53	34	38
Fulham	34	14	10	10	46	34	38
Queens Park Rangers	34	14	8	12	51	46	36
Portsmouth	34	16	4	14	61	56	36
New Brompton	34	11	11	12	40	41	33
West Ham United	34	12	8	14	48	42	32
Brighton & Hove Albion	34	13	6	15	44	45	32
Northampton Town	34	12	8	14	43	54	32
Watford	34	14	3	17	41	44	31
Brentford	34	10	9	15	33	38	29
Millwall	34	11	7	16	38	47	29
Swindon Town	34	12	5	17	41	59	29
Luton Town	34	12	3	19	45	54	27
Wellingborough	34	5	3	26	25	104	13

Second Division

Fulham Reserves	22	16	4	2	78	25	36
Portsmouth Reserves	22	14	2	6	75	28	30
Swindon Town Reserves	22	12	3	7	54	47	27
Grays United	22	11	3	8	61	40	25
Southampton Reserves	22	10	5	7	52	35	25
Brighton & Hove Albion	22	9	3	10	48	49	21
West Ham United Reserves	22	8	5	9	45	47	21
Clapton Orient	22	7	7	8	47	56	21
Watford Reserves	22	5	6	11	30	62	16
Southall	22	7	2	13	31	66	16
Wycombe Wanderers	22	6	2	14	37	70	14
Reading Reserves	22	4	4	14	24	57	12

1905-06

First Division

Fulham	34	19	12	3	44	15	50
Southampton	34	19	7	8	58	39	45
Portsmouth	34	17	9	8	61	35	43
Luton Town	34	17	7	10	64	40	41
Tottenham Hotspur	34	16	7	11	46	29	39
Plymouth Argyle	34	16	7	11	52	33	39
Norwich City	34	13	10	11	46	38	36
Bristol Rovers	34	15	5	14	56	56	35
Brentford	34	14	7	13	43	52	35
Reading	34	12	9	13	53	46	33
West Ham United	34	14	5	15	42	39	33
Millwall	34	11	11	12	38	41	33
Queens Park Rangers	34	12	7	15	58	44	31
Watford	34	8	10	16	38	57	26
Swindon Town	34	8	9	17	31	52	25
Brighton & Hove Albion	34	9	7	18	30	55	25
New Brompton	34	7	8	19	20	62	22
Northampton Town	34	8	5	21	32	79	21

Second Division

Crystal Palace	24	19	4	1	66	14	42
Leyton	24	16	6	2	61	18	38
Portsmouth Reserves	24	12	8	4	52	24	32
Fulham Reserves	24	11	6	7	52	39	28
Southampton Reserves	24	7	9	8	39	41	23
Southern United	24	8	7	9	45	49	23
St Leonard's United	24	9	4	11	54	50	22
Watford Reserves	24	8	5	11	43	47	21
West Ham United Reserves	24	7	5	12	46	48	19
Grays United	24	8	3	13	24	77	19
Reading Reserves	24	6	5	13	36	49	15
Swindon Town Reserves	24	5	5	14	36	51	15
Wycombe Wanderers	24	5	3	16	36	83	13

1906-07

First Division

Fulham	38	20	13	5	58	32	53
Portsmouth	38	22	7	9	64	36	51
Brighton & Hove Albion	38	18	9	11	53	43	45
Luton Town	38	18	9	11	52	52	45
West Ham United	38	15	14	9	60	41	44
Tottenham Hotspur	38	17	9	12	63	45	43
Millwall	38	18	6	14	71	50	42
Norwich City	38	15	12	11	57	48	42
Watford	38	13	16	9	46	43	42
Brentford	38	17	8	13	57	56	42
Southampton	38	13	9	16	49	56	35
Reading	38	14	6	18	57	47	34
Leyton	38	11	12	15	38	60	34
Bristol Rovers	38	12	9	17	55	54	33
Plymouth Argyle	38	10	13	15	43	50	33
New Brompton	38	12	9	17	47	59	33
Swindon Town	38	11	11	16	43	54	33
Queens Park Rangers	38	11	10	17	47	55	32
Crystal Palace	38	8	9	21	46	66	25
Northampton Town	38	5	9	24	29	88	19

Second Division

Southend United	22	14	5	3	58	23	33
West Ham United Reserves	22	14	3	5	64	30	31
Portsmouth Reserves	22	11	6	5	53	24	28
Fulham Reserves	22	11	4	7	47	32	26
Hastings & St Leonards	21	10	4	7	46	31	24
Tunbridge Wells Rangers	22	10	1	11	46	36	21
Salisbury City	22	9	2	11	40	42	20
Southampton Reserves	22	8	2	12	37	56	18
Swindon Town Reserves	22	7	3	12	35	43	17
Reading Reserves	22	6	4	12	32	47	16
Royal Engineers (Aldershot)	21	5	4	12	27	58	14
Wycombe Wanderers	22	4	6	12	28	68	14

The match between Tunbridge Wells Rangers and Royal Engineers (Aldershot) was not completed.

1907-08

First Division

Queens Park Rangers	38	21	9	8	82	57	51
Plymouth Argyle	38	19	11	8	50	31	49
Millwall	38	19	8	11	49	32	46
Crystal Palace	38	17	10	11	54	51	44
Swindon Town	38	16	10	12	55	40	42
Bristol Rovers	38	16	10	12	59	56	42
Tottenham Hotspur	38	17	7	14	59	48	41
Northampton Town	38	15	11	12	50	41	41
Portsmouth	38	17	6	15	63	52	40
West Ham United	38	15	10	13	47	48	40
Southampton	38	16	6	16	51	60	38
Reading	38	15	6	17	55	50	36
Bradford Park Avenue	38	12	12	14	53	54	36
Watford	38	12	10	16	47	49	34
Brentford	38	14	5	19	49	52	33
Norwich City	38	12	9	17	46	49	33
Brighton & Hove Albion	38	12	8	18	46	59	32
Luton Town	38	12	6	20	33	56	30
Leyton	38	8	11	19	51	73	27
New Brompton	38	9	7	22	44	75	25

Second Division

Southend	18	13	3	2	47	16	29
Portsmouth Reserves	18	10	5	3	39	22	25
Croydon Common	18	10	3	5	35	25	23
Hastings & St Leonard's	18	10	2	6	43	29	22
Southampton Reserves	18	7	4	7	54	46	18
Tunbridge Wells Rangers	18	7	3	8	42	38	17
Salisbury City	18	6	4	8	35	46	16
Swindon Town Reserves	18	5	5	8	36	40	15
Brighton & Hove Albion Reserves	18	4	4	10	34	47	12
Wycombe Wanderers	18	1	1	16	16	72	3

1908-09

First Division

Northampton Town	40	25	5	10	90	45	55
Swindon Town	40	22	5	13	96	55	49
Southampton	40	19	10	11	67	58	48
Portsmouth	40	18	10	12	68	60	46
Bristol Rovers	40	17	9	14	60	63	43
Exeter City	40	18	6	16	56	65	42
New Brompton	40	17	7	16	48	59	41
Reading	40	11	18	11	60	57	40
Luton Town	40	17	6	17	59	60	40
Plymouth Argyle	40	15	10	15	46	47	40
Millwall	40	16	6	18	59	61	38
Southend United	40	14	10	16	52	54	38
Leyton	40	15	8	17	52	55	38
Watford	40	14	9	17	51	64	37
Queens Park Rangers	40	12	12	16	52	50	36
Crystal Palace	40	12	12	16	62	62	36
West Ham United	40	16	4	20	56	60	36
Brighton & Hove Albion	40	14	7	19	60	61	35
Norwich City	40	12	11	17	59	75	35
Coventry City	40	15	4	21	64	91	34
Brentford	40	13	7	20	59	74	33

Second Division

Croydon Common	12	10	0	2	67	14	20
Hastings & St Leonard's	12	8	1	3	42	18	17
Depot Battalion Royal Engineers	12	8	1	3	23	22	17
2nd Grenadier Guards	12	5	0	7	21	33	10
South Farnborough Athletic	12	2	4	6	20	39	8
Salisbury City	12	3	1	8	24	36	7
Chesham Town	12	2	1	9	17	52	5

1909-10

First Division

Brighton & Hove Albion	42	23	13	6	69	28	59
Swindon Town	42	22	10	10	92	46	54
Queens Park Rangers	42	19	13	10	56	47	51
Northampton Town	42	22	4	16	90	44	48
Southampton	42	16	16	10	64	55	48
Portsmouth	42	20	7	15	70	63	47
Crystal Palace	42	20	6	16	69	50	46
Coventry City	42	19	8	15	71	60	46
West Ham United	42	15	15	12	69	56	45
Leyton	42	16	11	15	60	46	43
Plymouth Argyle	42	16	11	15	61	54	43
New Brompton	42	19	5	18	76	74	43
Bristol Rovers	42	16	10	16	37	48	42
Brentford	42	16	9	17	50	58	41
Luton Town	42	15	11	16	72	92	41
Millwall	42	15	7	20	45	59	37
Norwich City	42	13	9	20	59	78	35
Exeter City	42	14	6	22	60	69	34
Watford	42	10	13	19	51	76	33
Southend United	42	12	9	21	51	90	33
Croydon Common	42	13	5	24	52	96	31
Reading	42	7	10	25	38	73	24

Second Division - Section A

Stoke	10	10	0	0	48	9	20
Ton Pentre	10	4	2	4	17	21	10
Merthyr Town	9	4	1	4	16	21	9
Salisbury City	8	2	1	5	7	18	5
Burton United	6	2	0	4	8	21	4
Aberdare	7	1	0	6	6	11	2

Second Division - Section B

Hastings & St Leonard's	9	6	3	0	26	11	15
Kettering	10	6	0	4	34	19	12
Chesham Town	10	5	2	3	25	25	12
Peterborough City	10	4	2	4	16	23	10
South Farnborough Athletic	10	4	1	5	23	19	9
Romford	9	0	0	9	7	33	0

1910-11

First Divison

Swindon Town	38	24	5	9	80	31	53
Northampton Town	38	18	12	8	54	27	48
Brighton & Hove Albion	38	20	8	10	58	35	48
Crystal Palace	38	17	13	8	55	48	47
West Ham United	38	17	11	10	63	46	45
Queens Park Rangers	38	13	14	11	52	41	40
Leyton	38	16	8	14	57	52	40
Plymouth Argyle	38	15	9	14	54	55	39
Luton Town	38	15	8	15	67	63	38
Norwich City	38	15	8	15	46	48	38
Coventry City	38	16	6	16	65	68	38
Brentford	38	14	9	15	41	42	37
Exeter City	38	14	9	15	51	53	37
Watford	38	13	9	16	49	65	35
Millwall	38	11	9	18	42	54	31
Bristol Rovers	38	10	10	18	42	55	30
Southampton	38	11	8	19	42	67	30
New Brompton	38	11	8	19	34	65	30
Southend United	38	10	9	19	47	64	29
Portsmouth	38	8	11	19	34	53	27

Second Division

Reading	22	16	3	3	55	11	35
Stoke	22	17	1	4	72	21	35
Merthyr Town	22	15	3	4	52	22	33
Cardiff City	22	12	4	6	48	29	28
Croydon Common	22	11	3	8	61	26	25
Treharris	22	10	3	9	38	31	23
Aberdare	22	9	5	8	38	33	23
Ton Pentre	22	10	3	9	44	40	23
Walsall	22	7	4	11	37	41	18
Kettering	22	6	1	15	34	68	13
Chesham Town	22	1	3	18	16	93	5
Salisbury City	22	0	3	19	16	92	3

1911-12

First Division

Queens Park Rangers	38	21	11	6	59	35	53
Plymouth Argyle	38	23	6	9	63	31	52
Northampton Town	38	22	7	9	82	41	51
Swindon Town	38	21	6	11	82	50	48
Brighton & Hove Albion	38	19	9	10	73	35	47
Coventry City	38	17	8	13	66	54	42
Crystal Palace	38	15	10	13	70	46	40
Millwall	38	15	10	13	60	57	40
Watford	38	13	10	15	56	69	36
Stoke	38	13	10	15	51	63	36
Reading	38	11	14	13	43	69	36
Norwich City	38	10	14	14	40	60	34
West Ham United	38	13	7	18	64	69	33
Brentford	38	12	9	17	60	65	33
Exeter City	38	11	11	16	48	62	33
Southampton	38	10	11	17	46	63	31
Bristol Rovers	38	9	13	16	41	62	31
New Brompton	38	11	9	18	35	72	31
Luton Town	38	9	10	19	49	61	28
Leyton	38	7	11	20	27	62	25

Second Division

Merthyr Town	26	19	3	4	60	14	41
Portsmouth	26	19	3	4	73	20	41
Cardiff City	26	15	4	7	55	26	34
Southend United	26	16	1	9	73	24	33
Pontypridd	26	13	6	7	39	24	32
Ton Pentre	26	12	3	11	56	45	27
Walsall	26	13	1	11	44	41	27
Treharris	26	11	5	10	44	47	27
Aberdare	26	10	3	13	39	44	23
Kettering	26	11	0	15	37	62	22
Croydon Common	26	8	2	15	43	45	18
Mardy	26	6	6	12	37	51	18
Cwm Albion	26	5	1	16	27	70	11
Chesham Town	26	1	0	25	18	131	2

1912-13

First Division

Plymouth Argyle	38	27	6	10	77	36	50
Swindon Town	38	20	8	10	66	41	48
West Ham United	38	18	12	8	66	43	48
Queens Park Rangers	38	18	10	10	46	35	43
Crystal Palace	38	17	11	10	55	36	45
Millwall	38	19	7	12	62	43	45
Exeter City	38	18	8	12	48	44	44
Reading	38	17	8	13	59	55	42
Brighton & Hove Albion	38	13	12	13	48	47	38
Northampton Town	38	12	12	14	61	48	36
Portsmouth	38	14	8	16	41	49	36
Merthyr Town	38	12	12	14	42	60	36
Coventry City	38	13	8	17	53	59	34
Watford	38	12	10	16	43	50	34
Gillingham	38	12	10	16	36	53	34
Bristol Rovers	38	12	9	17	55	64	33
Southampton	38	10	11	17	40	72	31
Norwich City	38	10	9	19	39	50	29
Brentford	38	11	5	22	42	55	27
Stoke	38	10	4	24	39	75	24

Second Division

Cardiff City	24	18	5	1	54	15	41
Southend United	24	14	6	4	43	23	34
Swansea Town	24	12	7	5	29	23	31
Croydon Common	24	13	4	7	51	29	30
Luton Town	24	13	4	7	52	39	30
Llanelly	24	9	6	9	33	39	24
Pontypridd	24	6	11	7	30	28	23
Mid Rhondda	24	9	4	11	33	31	22
Aberdare	24	8	6	10	38	40	22
Newport County	24	7	5	12	29	36	19
Mardy	24	6	3	15	38	38	15
Treharris	24	5	2	17	18	60	12
Ton Pentre	24	3	3	18	22	69	9

1913-14

First Division

Swindon Town	38	21	8	9	81	41	50
Crystal Palace	38	17	16	5	60	32	50
Northampton Town	38	14	19	5	50	37	47
Reading	38	17	10	11	43	36	44
Plymouth Argyle	38	15	13	10	46	42	43
West Ham United	38	15	12	11	61	60	42
Brighton & Hove Albion	38	15	12	11	43	45	42
Queens Park Rangers	38	16	9	13	45	43	41
Portsmouth	38	14	12	12	57	48	40
Cardiff City	38	13	12	13	46	42	38
Southampton	38	15	7	16	55	54	37
Exeter City	38	10	16	12	39	38	36
Gillingham	38	13	9	16	48	49	35
Norwich City	38	9	17	12	49	51	35
Millwall	38	11	12	15	51	56	34
Southend Unied	38	10	12	16	41	66	32
Bristol Rovers	38	10	11	17	46	67	31
Watford	38	10	9	19	50	56	29
Merthyr Town	38	9	10	19	38	61	28
Coventry City	38	6	14	18	43	68	26

Second Division

Croydon Common	30	23	5	2	76	14	51
Luton Town	30	24	3	3	92	22	51
Brentford	30	20	4	6	80	18	44
Swansea Town	30	20	4	6	66	23	44
Stoke	30	19	2	9	71	34	40
Newport County	30	14	8	8	49	38	36
Mid Rhondda	30	13	7	10	55	37	33
Pontypridd	30	14	5	11	43	38	33
Llanelly	30	12	4	14	45	39	28
Barry	30	9	8	13	44	70	26
Abertillery	30	8	4	18	44	57	20
Ton Pentre	30	8	4	18	33	61	20
Mardy	30	6	6	18	30	60	18
Caerphilly	30	4	7	19	21	103	15
Aberdare	30	4	5	21	33	87	13
Treharris	30	2	4	24	19	106	8

1914-15

First Division

Watford	38	22	8	8	68	46	52
Reading	38	21	7	10	68	43	49
Cardiff City	38	22	4	12	72	38	48
West Ham United	38	18	9	11	58	47	45
Northampton Town	38	16	11	11	56	51	43
Southampton	38	19	5	14	78	74	43
Portsmouth	38	16	10	12	54	42	42
Millwall	38	16	10	12	50	51	42
Swindon Town	38	15	11	12	77	59	41
Brighton & Hove Albion	38	16	7	15	46	47	39
Exeter City	38	15	8	15	50	41	38
Queens Park Rangers	38	13	12	13	55	56	38
Norwich City	38	11	14	13	53	56	36
Luton Town	38	13	8	17	61	73	34
Crystal Palace	38	13	8	17	47	61	34
Bristol Rovers	38	14	3	21	53	75	31
Plymouth Argyle	38	8	14	16	51	61	30
Southend United	38	10	8	20	44	64	28
Croydon Common	38	9	9	20	47	63	27
Gillingham	38	6	8	24	43	82	20

Second Division

Stoke	24	17	4	3	62	15	38
Stalybridge Celtic	24	17	3	4	47	22	37
Merthyr Town	24	15	5	4	46	20	35
Swansea Town	24	16	1	7	48	21	33
Coventry City	24	13	2	9	56	33	28
Ton Pentre	24	11	6	7	42	43	28
Brentford	24	8	7	9	35	45	23
Llanelly	24	10	1	13	39	32	21
Barry	24	6	5	13	30	35	17
Newport County	24	7	3	14	27	42	17
Pontypridd	24	5	6	13	31	58	16
Mid Rhondda	24	3	6	15	17	40	12
Ebbw Vale	24	3	1	20	23	88	7

1919-20

First Division

Portsmouth	42	23	12	7	73	27	58
Watford	42	26	6	10	69	42	58
Crystal Palace	42	22	12	8	69	43	56
Cardiff City	42	18	17	7	70	43	53
Plymouth Argyle	42	20	10	12	57	29	50
Queens Park Rangers	42	18	10	14	62	50	46
Reading	42	16	13	13	51	43	45
Southampton	42	18	8	16	72	63	44
Swansea Town	42	16	11	15	53	45	43
Exeter City	42	17	9	16	57	51	43
Southend United	42	13	17	12	46	48	43
Norwich City	42	15	11	16	64	57	41
Swindon Town	42	17	7	18	65	68	41
Millwall	42	14	12	16	52	55	40
Brentford	42	15	10	17	52	59	40
Brighton & Hove Albion	42	14	8	20	60	72	36
Bristol Rovers	42	11	13	18	61	78	35
Newport County	42	13	7	22	45	70	33
Northampton Town	42	12	9	21	64	103	33
Luton Town	42	10	10	22	51	76	30
Merthyr Town	42	9	11	22	47	78	29
Gillingham	42	10	7	25	34	74	27

Second Division

Mid Rhondda	20	17	3	0	79	10	37
Ton Pentre	20	12	7	1	50	14	31
Llanelly	20	10	5	5	47	30	25
Pontypridd	20	10	3	7	33	29	23
Ebbw Vale	20	7	7	6	38	40	21
Barry	20	7	5	8	32	27	19
Mardy	20	7	5	8	29	30	19
Abertillery	20	6	5	9	29	40	17
Porth Athletic	20	4	4	12	30	74	12
Aberaman Athletic	20	4	3	13	28	48	11
Caerphilly	20	1	3	16	20	74	5

1920-21

English Section

Brighton & Hove Albion Reserves	24	16	3	5	65	29	35
Portsmouth Reserves	24	13	7	4	44	20	33
Millwall Reserves	24	12	4	8	46	24	28
Southampton Reserves	24	10	7	7	53	35	27
Boscombe	24	10	6	8	25	40	26
Reading Reserves	24	11	3	10	41	34	25
Luton Town Reserves	24	8	8	8	38	35	24
Charlton Athletic	24	8	8	8	41	41	24
Watford Reserves	24	9	4	11	43	45	22
Norwich City Reserves	24	7	7	10	31	39	21
Gillingham Reserves	24	6	5	13	32	47	17
Chatham	24	5	6	13	24	47	16
Thornycrofts	24	4	6	14	29	74	14

Welsh Section

Barry	20	13	4	3	35	12	30
Aberdare Athletic	20	12	3	5	29	23	27
Ebbw Vale	20	10	5	5	34	23	25
Pontypridd	20	10	3	7	34	23	23
Mid Rhondda	20	10	3	7	26	18	23
Abertillery Town	20	8	5	7	35	24	21
Ton Pentre	20	7	5	8	32	34	19
Aberaman Athletic	20	5	7	8	30	33	17
Llanelly	20	7	2	11	28	46	16
Mardy	20	2	6	12	18	39	10
Porth Athletic	20	3	3	14	28	54	9

1921-22

English Section

Plymouth Argyle Reserves	36	22	5	9	91	38	49
Bristol City Reserves	36	18	8	10	73	50	44
Portsmouth Reserves	36	17	10	9	63	41	44
Southampton Reserves	36	19	5	12	70	47	43
Gillingham Reserves	36	17	9	10	65	47	43
Charlton Athletic Reserves	36	18	6	12	69	54	42
Boscombe	36	17	5	14	38	55	39
Luton Town Reserves	36	17	4	15	50	54	38
Watford Reserves	36	15	7	14	65	53	37
Brighton & Hove Albion Reserves	36	12	13	11	60	52	37
Bath City	36	16	5	15	55	53	37
Swindon Town Reserves	36	14	7	15	59	46	35
Bristol Rovers Reserves	36	13	7	16	50	82	33
Millwall Reserves	36	13	4	19	49	53	30
Reading Reserves	36	11	7	18	46	59	29
Exeter City Reserves	36	10	9	17	42	63	29
Guildford United	36	11	6	19	44	56	28
Norwich City Reserves	36	10	6	20	47	86	26
Southend United Reserves	36	9	3	24	47	92	21

Welsh Section

Ebbw Vale	16	11	3	2	33	11	25
Ton Pentre	16	9	4	3	35	14	22
Aberaman Athletic	16	7	5	4	25	19	19
Porth Athletic	16	6	6	4	31	20	18
Pontypridd	16	7	4	5	28	19	18
Swansea Town Reserves	16	7	4	5	24	17	18
Barry	16	3	3	10	14	35	9
Abertillery Town	16	3	2	11	21	45	8
Mardy	16	2	3	11	14	43	7

1922-23

English Section

Bristol City Reserves	38	24	5	9	84	39	53
Boscombe	38	22	7	9	67	34	51
Portsmouth Reserves	38	23	3	12	93	51	49
Bristol Rovers Reserves	38	20	8	10	59	41	48
Plymouth Argyle Reserves	38	20	7	11	74	41	47
Torquay United	38	18	8	12	63	38	44
Brighton & Hove Albion Reserves	38	20	3	15	95	60	43
Luton Town Reserves	38	16	11	11	67	56	43
Southend United Reserves	38	18	6	14	69	68	42
Southampton Reserves	38	18	5	15	65	54	41
Millwall Reserves	38	15	10	13	61	55	40
Coventry City Reserves	38	15	8	15	56	61	38
Guildford Town Reserves	38	15	7	16	65	59	37
Swindon Town Reserves	38	13	6	19	54	73	32
Bath City	38	10	8	20	44	71	28
Watford Reserves	38	11	6	21	34	79	28
Yeovil & Petters United	38	10	6	22	56	104	26
Norwich City Reserves	38	9	7	22	42	68	25
Exeter City Reserves	38	10	5	23	43	81	25
Reading Reserves	38	7	6	25	43	95	20

Welsh Section

Ebbw Vale	12	6	5	1	22	15	17
Aberaman Athletic	12	7	2	3	30	19	16
Swansea Town Reserves	12	6	2	4	25	14	14
Pontypridd	12	6	2	4	18	18	14
Barry	12	4	3	5	15	11	11
Bridgend Town	12	4	2	6	15	21	10
Porth Athletic	12	0	2	10	18	24	2

1923-24

Eastern Section

Peterborough & Fletton United	30	20	2	8	54	31	42
Leicester City Reserves	30	19	3	8	72	30	41
Southampton Reserves	30	18	5	7	60	36	41
Millwall Reserves	30	18	3	9	56	38	39
Portsmouth Reserves	30	16	2	12	66	37	34
Brighton & Hove Albion Reserves	30	13	7	10	55	42	33
Norwich City Reserves	30	13	6	11	46	34	32
Folkestone	30	12	5	13	61	51	29
Coventry City Reserves	30	10	8	12	39	4	28
Watford Reserves	30	11	6	13	36	48	28
Reading Reserves	30	11	6	13	32	43	28
Northampton Town Reserves	30	9	10	11	32	47	28
Luton Town Reserves	30	10	7	13	40	49	27
Guildford United	30	7	5	18	38	72	19
Kettering	30	5	8	17	30	67	18
Bournemouth Reserves	30	4	5	21	40	85	13

Western Section

Yeovil & Petters United	34	25	3	6	71	30	53
Plymouth Argyle Reserves	34	21	5	8	74	37	47
Pontypridd	34	19	8	7	81	44	46
Torquay United	34	19	7	8	59	25	45
Bristol City Reserves	34	17	9	8	63	39	43
Swansea Town Reserves	34	19	5	10	62	38	43
Bristol Rovers Reserves	34	17	6	11	69	43	40
Cardiff City Reserves	34	15	4	15	55	31	34
Exeter City Reserves	34	11	11	12	48	47	33
Weymouth	34	15	3	16	48	60	33
Llanelly	34	14	5	15	47	62	33
Swindon Town Reserves	34	11	6	17	36	60	28
Bridgend Town	34	11	5	18	57	72	27
Newport County Reserves	34	10	7	17	57	79	27
Ebbw Vale	34	8	8	18	38	62	24
Bath City	34	6	9	19	32	71	21
Barry	34	6	7	21	36	74	19
Aberaman Athletic	34	6	4	24	41	87	16

1924-25

Eastern Section

Southampton Reserves	32	17	10	5	65	30	44
Kettering Town	32	17	6	9	67	39	40
Brighton & Hove Albion Reserves	32	15	10	7	68	42	40
Millwall Reserves	32	15	10	7	65	48	40
Peterborough & Fletton United	32	15	9	8	56	29	39
Bournemouth Reserves	32	15	9	8	66	48	39
Leicester City Reserves	32	15	7	10	61	45	37
Portsmouth Reserves	32	15	7	10	51	40	37
Folkestone	32	13	11	8	55	46	37
Norwich City Reserves	32	13	8	11	65	58	34
Coventry City Reserves	32	12	9	11	51	41	33
Luton Town Reserves	32	15	2	15	48	63	32
Northampton Town Reserves	32	10	5	17	38	59	25
Watford Reserves	32	7	7	18	44	71	21
Nuneaton Town	32	8	2	22	37	62	18
Reading Reserves	32	8	1	23	38	87	17
Guildford United	32	4	3	25	40	107	11

Western Section

Swansea Town Reserves	38	25	4	9	73	26	54
Plymouth Argyle Reserves	38	22	10	6	97	35	54
Pontypridd	38	24	4	10	81	39	52
Bridgend Town	38	20	11	7	74	52	51
Mid Rhondda United	38	21	6	11	79	48	48
Weymouth	38	21	4	13	77	50	46
Cardiff City Reserves	38	18	6	14	56	44	42
Newport County Reserves	38	17	8	13	71	60	42
Swindon Town Reserves	38	17	8	13	48	46	42
Bristol City Reserves	38	18	5	15	51	43	41
Yeovil & Petters United	38	15	10	13	49	50	40
Exeter City Reserves	38	16	6	16	78	55	38
Taunton Unied	38	15	6	17	55	51	36
Bristol Rovers Reserves	38	13	6	19	45	50	32
Torquay United	38	9	11	18	41	73	29
Llanelly	38	6	12	20	49	94	24
Ebbw Vale	38	9	6	23	40	91	24
Bath City	38	8	8	22	28	85	24
Barry	38	8	6	24	38	82	22
Aberaman Athletic	38	6	7	25	39	95	19

1925-26

Eastern Section

Millwall Reserves	34	24	6	4	106	37	54
Leicester City Reserves	34	23	2	9	105	60	48
Brighton & Hove Albion Reserves	34	21	4	9	105	69	46
Kettering Town	34	19	5	10	98	68	43
Peterborough & Fletton United	34	19	3	12	76	62	41
Portsmouth Reserves	34	17	5	12	76	67	39
Norwich City Reserves	34	17	4	13	85	90	38
Bournemouth Reserves	34	15	7	12	76	67	37
Southampton Reserves	34	14	7	13	65	72	35
Fulham Reserves	34	13	6	15	86	77	32
Grays Thurrock United	34	13	5	16	63	77	31
Guildford United	34	11	8	15	71	87	30
Watford Reserves	34	12	2	20	62	94	26
Luton Town Reserves	34	11	3	20	70	78	25
Folkestone	34	9	6	19	67	93	24
Reading Reserves	34	10	3	21	58	84	23
Coventry City Reserves	34	9	5	20	54	93	23
Nuneaton Town	34	7	3	24	61	113	17

Western Section

Plymouth Argyle Reserves	26	20	1	5	67	31	41
Bristol City Reserves	26	16	4	6	48	28	36
Bristol Rovers Reserves	26	13	4	9	51	35	30
Swindon Town Reserves	26	13	4	9	57	40	30
Ebbw Vale	26	13	3	10	60	46	29
Torquay United	26	12	5	9	59	46	29
Yeovil & Petters United	26	9	8	9	43	48	26
Mid Rhondda	26	12	1	13	47	49	25
Weymouth	26	10	3	13	64	60	23
Exeter City Reserves	26	8	5	13	40	49	21
Barry	26	8	4	14	47	55	20
Taunton United	26	9	2	15	44	60	20
Pontypridd	26	7	5	14	44	77	19
Bath City	26	7	1	18	38	86	15

1926-27

Eastern Section

Brighton & Hove Albion Reserves	32	21	6	5	86	47	48
Peterborough & Fletton United	32	18	9	5	80	39	45
Portsmouth Reserves	32	19	6	7	95	65	44
Kettering Town	32	15	10	7	66	41	40
Millwall Reserves	32	16	5	11	67	56	37
Bournemouth Reserves	32	14	6	12	69	64	34
Norwich City Reserves	32	14	5	13	79	74	33
Dartford	32	13	7	12	60	71	33
Reading Reserves	32	12	8	12	75	79	32
Luton Town Reserves	32	10	11	11	75	70	1
Leicester City Reserves	32	12	5	15	94	72	29
Watford Reserves	32	10	8	14	74	84	28
Southampton Reserves	32	10	6	16	57	77	26
Poole	32	9	6	17	55	86	24
Grays Thurrock United	32	10	3	19	49	66	23
Guildford United	32	6	7	19	57	106	19
Folkestone	32	7	4	21	57	98	18

Western Section

Torquay United	26	17	4	5	63	30	38
Bristol City Reserves	26	14	10	2	77	37	38
Plymouth Argyle Reserves	26	15	4	7	56	38	34
Ebbw Vale	26	14	2	10	67	45	30
Bristol Rovers Reserves	26	12	4	10	51	43	28
Swindon Town Reserves	26	11	5	10	60	57	27
Barry	26	11	4	11	65	50	26
Essex City Reserves	26	10	6	10	62	49	26
Weymouth	26	12	2	12	48	65	26
Newport County Reserves	26	9	6	11	57	53	24
Bath City	26	7	9	10	44	52	23
Yeovil & Petters United	26	9	5	12	49	66	23
Taunton United	26	4	4	18	36	83	12
Mid Rhondda United	26	2	5	19	22	89	9

1927-28

Easter Section

Kettering Town	34	23	6	5	90	39	52
Peterborough & Fletton United	34	21	3	10	73	43	45
Northfleet United	34	17	7	10	83	54	41
Brighton & Hove Albion Reserves	34	20	0	14	90	63	40
Norwich City Reserves	34	17	6	11	69	69	40
Southampton Reserves	34	16	7	11	92	70	39
Aldershot Town	34	17	5	12	85	66	39
Sittingbourne	34	16	5	13	64	70	37
Millwall Reserves	34	15	6	13	66	59	36
Poole	34	15	5	14	69	84	35
Folkestone	34	12	6	16	71	91	30
Guildford City	34	12	5	17	65	89	29
Dartford	34	12	4	18	46	49	28
Gillingham Reserves	34	10	7	17	72	84	27
Sheppey United	34	11	3	20	57	87	25
Chatham	34	10	4	20	49	70	24
Grays Thurrock United	34	10	3	21	48	88	23
Bournemouth Reserves	34	9	4	21	48	62	22

Western Section

Bristol City Reserves	30	20	3	7	95	51	43
Exeter City Reserves	30	18	4	8	104	56	40
Bristol Rovers Reserves	30	16	3	11	80	64	35
Plymouth Argyle Reserves	30	16	2	12	88	53	34
Newport County Reserves	30	13	8	9	99	70	34
Ebbw Vale	30	15	3	12	67	74	33
Swindon Town Reserves	30	13	4	13	80	74	30
Aberdare & Aberaman	30	12	6	12	62	68	30
Yeovil & Petters United	30	11	7	12	64	57	29
Torquay United Reserves	30	11	6	13	51	67	28
Bath City	30	12	3	15	64	68	27
Taunton Town	30	11	5	14	60	65	27
Weymouth	30	10	6	14	50	83	26
Merthyr Town Reserves	30	9	4	17	50	77	22
Barry	30	8	6	16	45	87	22
Mid Rhondda United	30	7	6	17	36	81	20

1928-29

Eastern Section

Kettering Town	36	24	4	8	96	46	52
Peterborough & Fletton United	36	21	5	10	86	44	47
Brighton & Hove Albion Reserves	36	19	9	8	91	56	47
Millwall Reserves	36	21	4	11	90	67	46
Bournemouth Reserves	36	20	5	11	82	58	45
Aldershot Town	36	18	5	13	68	52	41
Sheppey United	36	17	7	12	58	58	41
Folkestone	36	17	6	13	83	80	40
Northfleet United	36	17	4	15	87	65	38
Gillingham Reserves	36	15	8	13	68	70	38
Guildford City	36	13	11	12	85	78	37
Southampton Reserves	36	14	6	16	86	79	34
Poole	36	13	8	15	62	66	34
Thames Association	36	13	5	18	67	74	31
Dartford	36	10	6	20	55	106	26
Chatham	36	8	8	20	47	81	24
Sittingbourne	36	11	1	24	59	98	23
Norwich City Reserves	36	8	6	22	48	96	22
Grays Thurrock United	36	6	6	24	47	91	18

Western Section

Plymouth Argyle Reserves	26	15	6	5	69	27	36
Newport County Reserves	26	15	2	9	64	58	32
Bristol Rovers Reserves	26	14	3	9	54	45	31
Bristol City Reserves	26	14	2	10	70	46	30
Torquay United Reserves	26	13	4	9	52	42	30
Bath City	26	13	4	9	43	59	30
Exeter City Reserves	26	11	6	9	69	53	28
Lovells Athletic	26	11	6	9	54	48	28
Swindon Town Reserves	26	11	5	10	68	74	27
Yeovil & Petters United	26	11	2	13	49	57	24
Taunton Town	26	9	5	12	58	66	23
Ebbw Vale	26	9	5	12	56	66	23
Barry	26	6	3	17	38	66	15
Merthyr Town Reserves	26	3	1	22	37	92	7

1929-30

Eastern Section

Aldershot Town	32	21	6	5	84	39	48
Millwall Reserves	32	21	3	8	75	56	45
Thames Association	32	17	6	9	80	60	40
Peterborough & Fletton United	32	18	3	11	66	39	39
Northampton Town Reserves	32	17	4	11	86	60	38
Southampton Reserves	32	14	7	11	73	62	35
Sheppey United	32	15	5	12	76	69	35
Kettering Town	32	13	7	12	70	69	33
Dartford	32	14	5	13	57	59	33
Norwich City Reserves	32	14	3	15	69	69	31
Guildford City	32	13	2	17	65	97	28
Bournemouth Reserves	32	10	7	15	59	63	27
Brighton & Hove Albion Reserves	32	12	2	18	56	79	26
Folkestone	32	13	0	19	56	82	26
Sittingbourne	32	10	5	17	55	59	25
Northfleet United	32	6	7	19	53	77	19
Grays Thurrock United	32	7	2	23	54	101	16

Western Section

Bath City	28	16	6	6	85	52	38
Bristol Rovers Reserves	28	16	4	8	66	50	36
Taunton Town	28	14	7	7	50	40	35
Barry	28	15	3	10	65	55	33
Yeovil & Petters United	28	12	7	9	63	47	31
Plymouth Argyle Reserves	28	14	3	11	68	52	31
Newport County Reserves	28	13	4	11	68	76	30
Lovells Athletic	28	13	2	13	59	57	28
Exeter City Reserves	28	11	6	11	49	54	28
Bristol City Reserves	28	11	5	12	59	63	27
Swindon Town Reserves	28	10	6	12	69	67	26
Torquay United Reserves	28	10	6	12	76	77	26
Llanelly	28	10	4	14	55	52	24
Ebbw Vale	28	5	6	17	52	97	16
Merthyr Town Reserves	28	5	1	22	48	93	11

1930-31

Eastern Section

	P	W	D	L	F	A	Pts
Dartford	16	9	5	2	39	18	23
Aldershot Town	16	10	3	3	50	28	23
Norwich City Reserves	16	9	1	6	47	38	19
Peterborough & Fletton United	16	6	5	5	35	29	17
Thames Association Reserves	17	7	2	7	38	31	16
Millwall Reserves	17	7	0	9	47	40	14
Folkestone	16	4	3	9	31	46	11
Guildford City	16	5	1	10	28	53	11
Sheppey United	16	4	2	10	31	63	10

Western Section

	P	W	D	L	F	A	Pts
Exeter City Reserves	22	15	2	5	59	28	32
Llanelly	22	10	8	4	72	39	28
Merthyr Town	22	12	3	7	62	49	27
Plymouth Argyle Reserves	22	12	2	8	55	34	26
Bath City	22	10	6	6	47	39	26
Torquay United Reserves	22	9	5	8	66	49	23
Swindon Town Reserves	22	7	7	8	48	52	21
Bristol Rovers Reserves	22	7	6	9	58	64	20
Barry	22	7	5	10	29	39	19
Taunton Town	22	5	7	10	36	62	17
Newport County Reserves	22	6	2	14	36	66	14
Ebbw Vale	22	5	1	16	32	79	11

1931-32

Eastern Section

	P	W	D	L	F	A	Pts
Dartford	18	12	3	3	53	18	27
Folkestone	18	12	2	4	58	27	26
Guildford City	18	11	1	6	33	24	23
Norwich City Reserves	18	9	2	7	46	33	20
Millwall Reserves	18	9	2	7	41	39	20
Tunbridge Wells Rangers	18	7	5	6	23	25	19
Bournemouth Reserves	18	6	4	8	43	61	16
Peterborough & Fletton United	18	4	5	9	28	29	13
Aldershot Town	18	3	5	10	17	30	11
Sheppey United	18	2	1	15	16	72	5

Western Section

	P	W	D	L	F	A	Pts
Yeovil & Petters United	24	16	4	4	65	31	36
Plymouth Argyle Reserves	24	15	5	4	81	31	35
Bath City	24	12	7	5	50	33	31
Llanelly	24	12	4	8	65	46	28
Taunton Town	24	13	2	9	53	58	28
Newport County Reserves	24	10	6	8	70	51	26
Exeter City Reserves	24	9	7	8	59	43	25
Merthyr Town	24	9	4	11	66	73	22
Bristol Rovers Reserves	24	8	4	12	54	47	20
Swindon Town Reserves	24	8	4	12	54	95	20
Barry	24	7	3	14	58	76	17
Torquay United Reserves	24	5	6	13	43	66	16
Ebbw Vale	24	3	2	19	34	102	8

1932-33

Eastern Section

	P	W	D	L	F	A	Pts
Norwich City Reserves	14	9	2	3	34	22	20
Dartford	14	8	2	4	26	23	18
Folkestone	14	7	1	6	35	32	15
Bournemouth Reserves	14	5	4	5	36	33	14
Tunbridge Wells Rangers	14	5	2	7	23	24	12
Guildford City	14	5	2	7	22	28	12
Millwall Reserves	14	5	1	8	27	31	11
Aldershot Reserves	14	3	4	7	24	34	10

Western Section

	P	W	D	L	F	A	Pts
Bath City	20	13	4	3	62	34	30
Exeter City Reserves	20	12	3	5	62	46	27
Torquay United Reserves	20	12	1	7	56	37	25
Plymouth Argyle Reserves	20	11	2	7	68	38	24
Yeovil & Petters United	20	11	2	7	59	44	24
Llanelly	20	10	2	8	53	33	22
Bristol Rovers Reserves	20	7	3	10	53	65	17
Newport County Reserves	20	6	4	10	42	55	16
Merthyr Tydfil	20	7	1	12	39	58	15
Barry	20	3	4	13	30	72	10
Taunton Town	20	4	2	14	21	63	10

1933-34

Eastern Section

	P	W	D	L	F	A	Pts
Norwich City Reserves	16	9	4	3	41	15	22
Margate	16	8	3	5	23	20	19
Millwall Reserves	16	7	4	5	28	28	18
Clapton Orient Reserves	16	8	1	7	33	34	17
Bournemouth Reserves	16	6	3	7	28	30	15
Tunbridge Wells Rangers	16	6	2	8	25	36	14
Folkestone	15	5	3	8	26	26	13
Guildford City	16	5	3	8	27	33	13
Dartford	16	4	5	7	15	24	13

Western Section

	P	W	D	L	F	A	Pts
Plymouth Argyle Reserves	20	13	6	1	62	22	32
Bristol Rovers Reserves	20	14	3	3	56	27	31
Bath City	20	11	3	6	43	25	25
Torquay United Reserves	20	9	4	7	54	36	22
Yeovil & Petters United	20	10	1	9	35	39	21
Exeter City Reserves	20	8	3	9	54	47	19
Merthyr Town	20	8	2	10	39	50	18
Llanelly	20	8	1	11	25	39	17
Barry	20	4	5	11	37	64	13
Newport County Reserves	20	4	3	13	36	54	11
Taunton Town	20	5	1	14	27	65	11

Central Section

	P	W	D	L	F	A	Pts
Plymouth Argyle Reserves	18	16	1	1	47	14	33
Clapton Orient Reserves	18	9	3	6	35	25	21
Norwich City Reserves	18	8	4	6	41	27	20
Yeovil & Petters United	18	7	4	7	34	38	18
Bath City	18	7	3	8	31	36	17
Dartford	18	6	4	8	28	26	16
Tunbridge Wells Rangers	18	7	1	10	26	37	15
Llanelly	18	6	2	10	28	39	14
Folkestone	18	6	1	11	30	41	13
Guildford City	18	6	1	11	28	45	13

1934-35

Eastern Section

	P	W	D	L	F	A	Pts
Norwich City Reserves	18	12	1	5	52	21	25
Dartford	18	8	6	4	36	22	22
Margate	18	7	6	7	38	30	20
Bournemouth Reserves	18	8	3	8	34	26	19
Guildford City	18	7	5	6	41	34	19
Aldershot Reserves	18	7	3	8	29	43	17
Folkestone	18	5	6	7	30	39	16
Tunbridge Wells Rangers	18	6	4	8	32	56	16
Clapton Orient Reserves	18	5	4	9	33	35	14
Millwall Reserves	18	3	6	9	26	45	12

Western Section

	P	W	D	L	F	A	Pts
Yeovil & Petters United	16	11	2	3	49	18	24
Newport County Reserves	16	8	5	3	45	29	21
Plymouth Argyle Reserves	16	7	5	4	40	24	19
Exeter City Reserves	16	7	2	7	38	32	16
Bath City	16	6	4	6	35	32	16
Bristol Rovers Reserves	16	5	5	6	33	37	15
Barry	16	6	3	7	30	40	15
Torquay United Reserves	16	5	3	8	24	29	13
Taunton Town	16	1	3	12	13	66	5

Central Section

	P	W	D	L	F	A	Pts
Folkestone	20	11	4	5	43	31	26
Guildford City	20	11	4	5	43	39	26
Plymouth Argyle Reserves	20	6	9	5	40	28	21
Torquay United Reserves	20	7	6	7	34	35	20
Bristol Rovers Reserves	20	8	4	8	38	46	20
Margate	20	8	3	9	40	34	19
Dartford	20	8	3	9	43	38	19
Aldershot Reserves	20	8	3	9	33	44	19
Tunbridge Wells Rangers	20	8	2	10	33	37	18
Yeovil & Petters United	20	8	1	11	45	51	17
Bath City	20	6	3	11	34	43	15

1935-36

Eastern Section

Margate	18	13	2	3	49	16	28
Folkestone	18	11	3	4	46	23	25
Dartford	18	9	3	6	47	25	21
Tunbridge Wells Rangers	18	9	1	8	26	41	19
Clapton Orient Reserves	18	7	4	7	39	31	18
Millwall Reserves	18	7	3	8	42	39	17
Norwich City Reserves	18	8	0	10	39	38	16
Guildford City	18	6	3	9	32	52	15
Aldershot Reserves	18	6	1	11	24	45	13
Bournemouth Reserves	18	3	2	13	25	59	8

Western Section

Plymouth Argyle Reserves	16	12	3	1	51	18	27
Bristol Rovers Reserves	16	8	3	5	35	30	19
Newport County Reserves	16	8	3	5	29	30	19
Torquay United Reserves	16	7	1	8	25	28	15
Bath City	16	5	5	6	18	26	15
Cheltenham Town	16	6	2	8	32	28	14
Yeovil & Petters United	16	5	3	8	31	35	13
Barry	16	5	2	9	29	41	12
Exeter City Reserves	16	4	2	10	24	38	10

Central Section

Margate	20	14	3	3	57	18	31
Bristol Rovers Reserves	20	13	1	6	51	37	27
Plymouth Argyle Reserves	20	12	2	6	53	32	26
Aldershot Reserves	20	9	4	7	37	37	22
Folkestone	20	9	3	8	51	36	21
Tunbridge Wells Rangers	20	7	4	9	40	41	18
Dartford	20	7	3	10	34	42	17
Guildford City	20	7	3	10	33	47	17
Cheltenham Town	20	5	5	10	32	45	15
Bath City	20	5	5	10	34	52	15
Yeovil & Petters United	20	3	5	12	40	75	11

1936-37

Ipswich Town	30	19	8	3	68	35	46
Norwich City Reserves	30	18	5	7	70	35	41
Folkestone	30	17	4	9	71	62	38
Margate	30	15	4	11	64	49	34
Guildford City	30	15	4	11	54	60	34
Bath City	30	14	5	11	65	55	33
Yeovil & Petters United	30	15	3	12	77	69	33
Plymouth Argyle Reserves	30	11	8	11	64	58	30
Newport County Reserves	30	11	8	11	72	68	30
Barry	30	12	4	14	58	72	28
Cheltenham Town	30	10	4	16	61	70	24
Dartford	30	9	5	16	41	55	23
Exeter City Reserves	30	8	7	15	57	78	23
Tunbridge Wells Rangers	30	8	6	16	62	64	22
Torquay United Reserves	30	8	5	17	46	76	21
Aldershot Reserves	30	7	6	17	47	74	20

Midweek Section

Margate	18	12	1	5	48	24	25
Bath City	18	10	5	3	38	28	25
Norwich City Reserves	18	9	5	4	44	27	23
Folkestone	18	7	6	5	32	36	20
Millwall Reserves	18	8	3	7	44	47	19
Portsmouth Reserves	18	6	5	7	40	27	17
Tunbridge Wells Rangers	18	5	4	9	30	41	14
Aldershot Reserves	18	6	2	10	20	30	14
Guildford City	18	3	6	9	24	36	12
Dartford	18	4	3	11	19	43	11

1937-38

Guildford City	34	22	5	7	94	60	49
Plymouth Argyle Reserves	34	18	9	7	98	58	45
Ipswich Town	34	19	6	9	89	54	44
Yeovil & Petters United	34	14	14	6	72	45	42
Norwich City Reserves	34	15	11	8	77	55	41
Colchester United	34	15	8	11	90	58	38
Bristol Rovers Reserves	34	14	8	12	63	62	36
Swindon Town Reserves	34	14	7	13	70	76	35
Tunbridge Wells Rangers	34	14	6	14	68	74	34
Aldershot Reserves	34	10	12	12	42	55	32
Cheltenham Town	34	13	5	16	72	68	31
Exeter City Reserves	34	13	5	16	71	75	31
Dartford	34	9	11	14	51	70	29
Bath City	34	9	9	16	45	65	27
Folkestone	34	10	6	18	58	82	26
Newport County Reserves	34	10	6	18	56	86	26
Barry	34	8	7	19	50	88	23
Torquay United Reserves	34	8	7	19	46	81	23

Midweek Section

Millwall Reserves	18	13	3	2	59	21	29
Colchester United	18	13	1	4	42	23	27
Aldershot Reserves	18	11	3	4	38	29	25
Norwich City Reserves	18	9	1	8	45	39	19
Portsmouth Reserves	18	5	5	8	31	30	15
Dartford	18	6	3	9	32	35	15
Folkestone	18	6	3	9	34	38	15
Tunbridge Wells Rangers	18	5	4	9	28	36	14
Bath City	18	5	3	10	27	45	13
Guildford City	18	4	0	14	21	61	8

1938-39

Colchester United	44	31	5	8	110	37	67
Guildford City	44	30	6	8	126	52	66
Gillingham	44	29	6	9	104	57	64
Plymouth Argyle Reserves	44	26	5	13	128	63	57
Yeovil & Petters United	44	22	10	12	85	70	54
Arsenal Reserves	44	21	9	14	92	57	51
Cardiff City Reserves	44	24	3	17	105	72	51
Tunbridge Wells Rangers	44	22	6	16	93	76	50
Norwich City Reserves	44	23	4	17	86	76	50
Chelmsford City	44	18	8	18	74	73	44
Bath City	44	16	12	16	58	74	44
Barry	44	18	7	19	76	90	43
Cheltenham Town	44	16	9	19	76	105	41
Ipswich Town Reserves	44	14	12	18	64	76	40
Worcester City	44	13	14	17	72	90	40
Folkestone	44	16	6	22	74	85	38
Newport County Reserves	44	13	10	21	74	108	36
Exeter City Reserves	44	12	9	23	51	107	33
Torquay United Reserves	44	12	8	24	53	89	32
Swindon Town Reserves	44	11	9	24	66	101	31
Aldershot Reserves	44	12	6	26	69	92	30
Bristol Rovers Reserves	44	9	11	24	66	85	29
Dartford	44	8	5	31	53	119	21

Midweek Section

Tunbridge Wells Rangers	16	8	7	1	37	18	23
Colchester United	16	9	2	5	36	21	20
Norwich City Reserves	16	7	4	5	40	26	18
Millwall Reserves	16	7	4	5	33	23	18
Portsmouth Reserves	16	5	4	7	21	29	14
Guildford City	16	4	6	6	24	39	14
Aldershot Reserves	16	4	5	7	22	25	13
Folkestone	16	4	5	7	24	35	13
Dartford	16	4	3	9	24	45	11

1939-40

Eastern Section

Chelmsford City	7	5	0	2	29	9	10
Guildford City	8	4	1	3	26	13	9
Tunbridge Wells Rangers	7	2	3	2	21	16	7
Dartford	7	2	1	4	17	30	5
Norwich City Reserves	7	2	1	4	9	34	5

Western Section

	P	W	D	L	F	A	Pts
Lovells Athletic	14	11	1	2	53	22	23
Worcester City	14	9	2	3	55	30	20
Hereford United	14	8	0	6	45	31	16
Yeovil & Petters United	14	7	2	5	30	24	16
Gloucester City	14	5	0	9	35	49	10
Barry	14	4	1	9	31	56	9
Cheltenham Town	13	3	2	8	21	38	8
Bath City	13	3	2	8	21	41	8

1945-46

	P	W	D	L	F	A	Pts
Chelmsford City	18	15	1	2	66	23	34
Hereford United	20	13	3	4	59	31	29
Bath City	20	12	2	6	62	32	26
Cheltenham Town	18	9	1	8	35	54	22
Barry Town	20	8	4	8	42	42	20
Yeovil & Petters United	18	7	1	10	57	52	18
Worcester City	20	8	2	10	60	58	18
Colchester United	20	7	3	10	29	47	17
Bedford Town	16	4	1	11	30	49	15
Swindon Town Reserves	18	4	3	11	36	65	14
Cardiff City Reserves	20	4	5	11	39	60	13

1946-47

	P	W	D	L	F	A	Pts
Gillingham	31	20	6	5	103	45	47
Guildford City	32	21	4	7	86	39	46
Merthyr Tydfil	31	21	2	8	104	37	45
Yeovil Town	32	19	6	7	100	49	44
Chelmsford City	31	17	3	11	90	60	38
Gravesend & Northfleet	32	17	4	11	82	58	38
Barry Town	30	14	6	10	89	61	36
Colchester United	31	15	4	12	65	60	35
Cheltenham Town	31	14	3	14	68	75	32
Millwall	24	8	5	11	54	57	29
Dartford	32	10	5	17	71	100	25
Bedford Town	32	8	8	16	63	98	24
Hereford United	32	8	7	17	37	85	23
Worcester City	31	8	5	18	55	90	22
Exeter City Reserves	32	10	2	20	69	126	22
Bath City	32	7	7	18	52	93	21
Gloucester City	32	8	1	23	57	120	17

1947-48

	P	W	D	L	F	A	Pts
Merthyr Tydfil	34	23	7	4	84	38	53
Gillingham	34	21	5	8	81	43	47
Worcester City	34	21	3	10	74	45	45
Colchester United	34	17	10	7	88	41	44
Hereford United	34	16	10	8	77	53	42
Lovells Athletic	34	17	6	11	74	50	40
Exeter City Reserves	34	15	7	12	65	57	37
Yeovil Town	34	12	11	11	56	50	35
Chelmsford City	34	14	7	13	62	58	35
Cheltenham Town	34	13	9	12	71	71	35
Bath City	34	12	8	14	55	62	32
Barry Town	34	10	9	15	60	70	29
Gravesend & Northfleet	34	11	6	17	52	81	28
Guildford City	34	11	4	19	69	74	26
Dartford	34	10	6	18	35	62	26
Gloucester City	34	8	6	20	45	78	22
Torquay United Reserves	34	6	9	19	43	95	21
Bedford Town	34	6	3	25	41	104	15

1948-49

	P	W	D	L	F	A	Pts
Gillingham	42	26	10	6	104	48	62
Chelmsford City	42	27	7	8	115	54	61
Merthyr Tydfil	42	26	8	8	133	54	60
Colchester United	42	21	10	11	94	61	52
Worcester City	42	22	7	13	87	56	51
Dartford	42	21	9	12	73	53	51
Gravesend & Northfleet	42	20	9	13	60	46	49
Yeovil Town	42	19	9	14	90	53	47
Cheltenham Town	42	19	9	14	71	64	47
Kidderminster Harriers	42	19	6	17	77	96	44
Exeter City Reserves	42	18	7	17	83	73	43
Hereford United	42	17	6	19	83	84	40
Bath City	42	15	8	19	72	87	38
Hastings United	42	14	10	18	69	93	38
Torquay United Reserves	42	15	7	20	73	93	37
Lovells Athletic	42	14	8	20	73	74	36
Guildford City	42	12	12	18	58	85	36
Gloucester City	42	12	10	20	78	100	34
Barry Town	42	12	10	20	55	95	34
Tonbridge	42	9	7	26	54	105	25
Chingford Town	42	6	9	27	43	94	21
Bedford Town	42	5	8	29	32	101	18

1949-50

	P	W	D	L	F	A	Pts
Merthyr Tydfil	46	34	3	9	143	62	71
Colchester United	46	31	9	6	109	51	71
Yeovil Town	46	29	7	10	104	45	65
Chelmsford City	46	26	9	11	121	64	61
Gillingham	46	23	9	14	92	61	55
Dartford	46	20	9	17	70	65	49
Worcester City	46	21	7	18	85	80	49
Guildford City	46	18	11	17	79	73	47
Weymouth	46	19	9	18	80	81	47
Barry Town	46	18	10	18	78	72	46
Exeter City Reserves	46	16	14	16	73	83	46
Lovells Athletic	46	17	10	19	86	78	44
Tonbridge	46	16	12	18	65	76	44
Hastings United	46	17	8	21	92	450	42
Gravesend & Northfleet	46	16	9	21	88	81	41
Torquay United Reserves	46	14	12	20	80	89	40
Bath City	46	16	7	23	61	78	39
Gloucester City	46	14	11	21	72	101	39
Hereford United	46	15	8	23	74	76	38
Cheltenham Town	46	13	11	22	75	96	37
Headington United	46	15	7	24	72	97	37
Bedford Town	46	12	11	23	63	79	35
Kidderminster Harriers	46	12	11	23	64	108	35
Chingford Town	46	10	6	30	63	151	26

1950-51

	P	W	D	L	F	A	Pts
Merthyr Tydfil	44	29	8	7	156	66	66
Hereford United	44	27	7	10	110	69	61
Guildford City	44	23	8	13	88	60	54
Chelmsford City	44	21	12	11	84	58	54
Llanelly	44	19	13	12	89	73	51
Cheltenham Town	44	21	8	15	91	61	50
Headington United	44	18	11	15	84	83	47
Torquay United Reserves	44	20	6	18	93	79	46
Exeter City Reserves	44	16	12	16	90	94	44
Weymouth	44	16	12	16	82	88	44
Tonbridge	44	16	12	16	79	87	44
Gloucester City	44	16	11	17	81	76	43
Yeovil Town	44	13	15	16	72	72	41
Worcester City	44	15	11	18	69	78	41
Bath City	44	15	10	19	66	73	40
Dartford	44	14	11	19	61	70	39
Bedford Town	44	15	9	20	64	94	39
Gravesend & Northfleet	44	12	14	18	65	83	38
Kettering Town	44	13	11	20	87	87	37
Lovells Athletic	44	12	13	19	81	93	37
Kidderminster Harriers	44	13	9	22	58	103	35
Barry Town	44	13	7	24	54	104	33
Hastings United	44	11	6	27	91	143	28

1951-52

	P	W	D	L	F	A	Pts
Merthyr Tydfil	42	27	6	9	128	60	60
Weymouth	42	22	13	7	81	42	57
Kidderminster Harriers	42	22	10	10	70	40	54
Guildford City	42	18	16	8	66	47	52
Hereford United	42	21	9	12	80	59	51
Worcester City	42	23	4	15	86	73	50
Kettering Town	42	18	10	14	83	56	46
Lovells Athletic	42	18	10	14	87	68	46
Gloucester City	42	19	8	15	68	55	46
Bath City	42	19	6	17	75	67	44
Headington United	42	16	11	15	55	53	43
Bedford Town	42	16	10	16	75	64	42
Barry Town	42	18	6	18	84	89	42
Chelmsford City	42	15	10	17	67	80	40
Dartford	42	15	9	18	63	65	39
Tonbridge	42	15	6	21	63	84	36
Yeovil Town	42	12	11	19	56	76	35
Cheltenham Town	42	15	4	23	59	85	34
Exeter City Reserves	42	13	7	22	76	106	33
Llanelly	42	13	6	23	70	111	32
Gravesend & Northfleet	42	12	7	23	68	88	31
Hastings United	42	3	5	34	41	131	11

1952-53

	P	W	D	L	F	A	Pts
Headington United	42	23	12	7	93	50	58
Merthyr Tydfil	42	25	8	9	117	66	58
Bedford Town	42	24	8	10	91	61	56
Kettering Town	42	23	8	11	88	50	54
Bath City	42	22	10	10	71	46	54
Worcester City	42	20	11	11	100	66	51
Llanelly	42	21	9	12	95	72	51
Barry Town	42	22	3	17	89	69	47
Gravesend & Northfleet	42	19	7	16	83	76	45
Gloucester City	42	17	9	16	50	78	43
Guildford City	42	17	8	17	64	60	42
Hastings United	42	18	5	19	75	66	41
Cheltenham Town	42	15	11	16	70	89	41
Weymouth	42	15	10	17	70	75	40
Hereford United	42	17	5	20	76	73	39
Tonbridge	42	12	9	21	62	88	33
Lovells Athletic	42	12	8	22	68	81	32
Yeovil Town	42	11	10	21	75	99	32
Chelmsford City	42	12	7	23	58	92	31
Exeter City Reserves	42	13	4	25	71	94	30
Kidderminster Harriers	42	12	5	25	54	85	29
Dartford	42	6	5	31	40	121	17

1953-54

	P	W	D	L	F	A	Pts
Merthyr Tydfil	42	27	8	7	97	55	62
Headington United	42	22	9	11	68	43	53
Yeovil Town	42	20	8	14	87	76	48
Bath City	42	17	12	13	73	67	46
Kidderminster Harriers	42	18	9	15	62	59	45
Weymouth	42	18	8	16	83	72	44
Barry Town	42	17	9	16	108	91	43
Bedford Town	42	19	5	18	80	84	43
Gloucester City	42	16	11	15	69	77	43
Hastings United	42	16	10	16	73	67	42
Kettering Town	42	15	12	15	65	63	42
Hereford United	42	16	9	17	66	62	41
Llanelly	42	16	9	17	80	85	41
Guildford City	42	15	11	16	56	60	41
Gravesend & Northfleet	42	16	8	18	76	77	40
Worcester City	42	17	6	19	66	71	40
Lovells Athletic	42	14	11	17	62	60	39
Tonbridge	42	15	9	18	85	91	39
Chelmsford City	42	14	10	18	67	71	38
Exeter City Reserves	42	11	13	18	61	72	35
Cheltenham Town	42	11	12	19	56	83	34
Dartford	42	6	13	23	42	89	25

1954-55

	P	W	D	L	F	A	Pts
Yeovil Town	42	23	9	10	105	66	55
Weymouth	42	24	7	11	105	84	55
Hastings United	42	21	9	12	94	60	51
Cheltenham Town	42	21	8	13	85	72	50
Guildford City	42	20	8	14	72	59	48
Worcester City	42	19	10	13	80	73	48
Barry Town	42	16	15	11	82	87	47
Gloucester City	42	16	13	13	66	54	45
Bath City	42	18	9	15	73	80	45
Headington Town	42	18	7	17	82	62	43
Kidderminster Harriers	42	18	7	17	84	86	43
Merthyr Tydfil	42	17	8	17	97	94	42
Exeter City Reserves	42	19	4	19	67	78	42
Lovells Athletic	42	15	11	16	71	68	41
Kettering Town	42	15	11	16	70	69	41
Hereford United	42	17	5	20	91	72	39
Llanelly	42	16	7	19	78	81	39
Bedford Town	42	16	3	23	75	103	35
Tonbridge	42	11	8	23	68	91	30
Dartford	42	9	12	21	55	76	30
Chelmsford City	42	11	6	25	73	111	28
Gravesend & Northfleet	42	9	9	24	62	97	27

1955-56

	P	W	D	L	F	A	Pts
Guildford City	42	26	8	8	74	34	60
Cheltenham Town	42	25	6	11	82	53	56
Yeovil Town	42	23	9	10	98	55	55
Bedford Town	42	21	9	12	99	69	51
Dartford	42	20	9	13	78	62	49
Weymouth	42	19	10	13	83	63	48
Gloucester City	42	19	9	14	72	60	47
Lovells Athletic	42	19	9	14	91	78	47
Chelmsford City	42	18	10	14	67	55	46
Kettering Town	42	16	11	15	105	86	43
Exeter City Reserves	42	17	9	16	75	76	43
Gravesend & Northfleet	42	17	8	17	79	75	42
Hereford United	42	17	7	18	90	90	41
Hastings United	42	15	10	17	90	76	40
Headington United	42	17	6	19	82	86	40
Kidderminster Harriers	42	14	7	21	86	108	35
Llanelly	42	14	6	22	64	98	34
Barry Town	42	11	11	20	91	108	33
Worcester City	42	12	9	21	66	83	33
Tonbridge	42	11	11	20	53	74	33
Merthyr Tydfil	42	7	10	25	52	127	24
Bath City	42	7	10	25	43	107	24

1956-57

	P	W	D	L	F	A	Pts
Kettering Town	42	28	10	4	106	47	66
Bedford Town	42	25	8	9	89	52	58
Weymouth	42	22	10	10	92	71	54
Cheltenham Town	42	19	15	8	73	46	53
Gravesend & Northfleet	42	21	11	10	74	58	53
Lovells Athletic	42	21	7	14	99	84	49
Guildford City	42	18	11	13	68	49	47
Hereford United	42	19	8	15	96	60	46
Headington United	42	19	7	16	64	61	45
Gloucester City	42	18	8	16	74	72	44
Hastings United	42	17	9	16	70	58	43
Worcester City	42	16	10	16	81	80	42
Dartford	42	16	10	16	79	88	42
Chelmsford City	42	16	9	17	73	85	41
Tonbridge	42	14	12	16	74	65	40
Yeovil Town	42	14	11	17	83	85	39
Bath City	42	15	8	19	56	78	38
Exeter City Reserves	42	10	10	22	52	89	30
Merthyr Tydfil	42	9	11	22	72	95	29
Barry Town	42	6	11	25	39	84	23
Kidderminster Harriers	42	7	10	25	60	83	20
Llanelly	42	5	8	29	39	123	18

1957-58

	P	W	D	L	F	A	Pts
Gravesend & Northfleet	42	27	5	10	109	71	59
Bedford Town	42	25	7	10	112	64	57
Chelmsford City	42	24	9	9	93	57	57
Weymouth	42	25	5	12	90	61	55
Worcester City	42	23	7	12	95	59	53
Cheltenham Town	42	21	10	11	115	66	52
Hereford United	42	21	6	15	79	56	48
Kettering Town	42	18	9	15	99	76	45
Headington Town	42	18	7	17	90	83	43
Poole Town	42	17	9	16	82	81	43
Hasting United	42	13	15	14	78	77	41
Gloucester City	42	17	7	18	70	70	41
Yeovil Town	42	16	9	17	70	84	41
Dartford	42	14	9	19	66	92	37
Lovells Athletic	42	15	6	21	60	83	36
Bath City	42	13	9	20	65	64	35
Guildford City	42	12	10	20	58	92	34
Tonbridge	42	16	7	22	77	100	33
Exeter City Reserves	42	12	8	22	60	94	32
Barry Town	42	11	9	22	72	101	31
Kidderminster Harriers	42	10	10	22	60	101	30
Merthyr Tydfil	42	9	3	30	69	137	21

1958-59

North-Western Zone

	P	W	D	L	F	A	Pts
Hereford United	34	22	5	7	80	37	49
Kettering Town	34	20	7	7	83	63	47
Boston United	34	18	8	8	73	47	44
Cheltenham Town	34	20	4	10	65	47	44
Worcester City	34	19	4	11	74	47	42
Bath City	34	17	5	12	89	62	39
Wellington Town	34	15	9	10	74	58	39
Nuneaton Borough	34	17	5	12	66	66	39
Wisbech Town	34	16	5	13	77	54	37
Headington United	34	16	3	15	76	61	35
Barry Town	34	15	5	14	64	67	35
Merthyr Tydfil	34	16	3	15	54	59	35
Gloucester City	34	12	6	16	50	65	30
Corby Town	34	10	8	16	59	79	28
Lovells Athletic	34	10	3	21	51	70	23
Rugby Town	34	7	6	21	45	93	20
Kidderminster Harriers	34	7	3	24	42	94	17
Burton Albion	34	3	3	28	41	104	9

South-Eastern Zone

	P	W	D	L	F	A	Pts
Bedford Town	32	21	6	5	90	41	48
Gravesend & Northfleet	32	21	2	9	79	54	44
Dartford	32	20	3	9	77	41	43
Yeovil Town	32	17	8	7	60	41	42
Weymouth	32	13	11	8	61	43	37
Chelmsford City	32	12	12	8	74	53	36
King's Lynn	32	14	5	13	70	63	33
Poole Town	32	12	8	12	60	65	32
Cambridge City	32	12	7	13	61	54	31
Hastings United	32	13	5	14	60	59	31
Tonbridge	32	14	3	15	51	59	31
Cambridge United	32	11	8	13	55	77	30
Trowbridge Town	32	12	4	16	53	75	28
Exeter City Reserves	32	7	12	13	47	71	26
Guildford City	11	7	6	19	45	67	20
Clacton Town	32	6	7	19	44	81	19
Yiewsley	32	3	7	22	36	78	13

1959-60

Premier Division

	P	W	D	L	F	A	Pts
Bath City	42	32	3	7	116	50	67
Headington United	42	23	8	11	78	61	54
Weymouth	42	22	9	11	93	69	53
Cheltenham Town	42	21	6	15	82	68	48
Cambridge City	42	18	11	13	81	72	47
Chelmsford Town	42	19	7	16	90	70	45
Bedford Town	42	21	3	18	97	85	45
King's Lynn	42	17	11	14	89	78	45
Boston United	42	17	10	15	83	80	44
Wisbech Town	42	17	10	15	81	84	44
Yeovil Town	42	17	8	17	81	73	42
Hereford United	42	15	12	15	70	74	42
Tonbridge	42	16	8	18	79	73	40
Hastings United	42	16	8	18	63	77	40
Wellington Town	42	13	11	18	63	78	37
Dartford	42	15	7	20	64	82	37
Gravesend & Northfleet	42	14	8	20	69	84	36
Worcester City	42	13	10	19	72	89	36
Nuneaton Borough	42	11	11	20	64	78	33
Barry Town	42	14	5	23	78	103	33
Poole Town	42	10	8	24	69	96	28
Kettering Town	42	9	10	23	60	90	28

First Division

	P	W	D	L	F	A	Pts
Clacton Town	42	27	5	10	106	69	59
Romford	42	21	11	10	65	40	53
Folkestone Town	42	23	5	14	93	71	51
Exeter City Reserves	42	23	3	16	85	62	49
Guildford City	42	19	9	14	79	56	47
Sittingbourne	42	20	7	15	66	55	47
Margate	42	20	6	16	88	77	46
Trowbridge Town	42	18	9	15	90	78	45
Cambridge United	42	18	9	15	71	72	45
Yiewsley	42	17	10	15	83	69	44
Bexleyheath & Welling	42	16	11	15	85	77	43
Merthyr Tydfil	42	16	10	16	63	65	42
Ramsgate Athletic	42	16	8	18	83	84	40
Ashford Town	42	14	12	16	61	70	40
Tunbridge Wells United	42	17	5	20	77	73	39
Hinckley Athletic	42	14	8	20	62	75	36
Gloucester City	42	13	9	20	56	84	35
Dover	42	14	6	22	59	85	34
Kidderminster Harriers	42	14	6	22	59	97	34
Corby Town	42	15	3	24	75	91	33
Burton Albion	42	11	10	21	52	79	32
Rugby Town	42	10	11	21	67	91	31

1960-61

Premier Division

	P	W	D	L	F	A	Pts
Oxford United	42	27	10	5	104	43	64
Chelmsford City	42	23	11	8	91	55	57
Yeovil Town	42	23	9	10	109	54	55
Hereford United	42	21	10	11	83	67	52
Weymouth	42	21	9	12	78	63	51
Bath City	42	18	14	10	74	52	50
Cambridge City	42	16	12	14	101	71	44
Wellington Town	42	17	9	16	66	68	43
Bedford Town	42	18	7	17	94	97	43
Folkestone Town	42	18	7	17	75	86	43
King's Lynn	42	13	16	13	68	66	42
Worcester City	42	15	11	16	69	69	41
Clacton Town	42	15	11	16	82	83	41
Romford	42	13	15	14	66	69	41
Guildford City	42	14	11	17	65	62	39
Tonbridge	42	16	6	20	79	85	38
Cheltenham Town	42	15	7	20	81	81	37
Gravesend & Northfleet	42	15	7	20	75	101	37
Dartford	42	13	11	18	57	90	37
Hastings United	42	8	9	25	60	100	25
Wisbech Town	42	9	6	27	58	112	24
Boston United	42	6	8	28	62	123	20

Oxford United were previously known as Headington United.

First Division

Kettering Town	40	26	7	7	100	55	59
Cambridge United	40	25	5	10	100	53	55
Bexleyheath & Welling	40	22	8	10	93	46	52
Merthyr Tydfil	40	23	6	11	88	65	52
Sittingbourne	40	21	10	9	77	63	52
Hinckley Athletic	40	17	13	10	74	59	47
Ramsgate Athletic	40	19	7	14	77	56	45
Rugby Town	40	18	9	13	89	71	45
Corby Town	40	16	10	14	82	73	42
Poole Town	40	18	5	17	71	65	41
Barry Town	40	16	9	15	65	74	41
Yiewsley	40	17	7	16	65	76	41
Trowbridge Town	40	14	10	16	71	73	38
Ashford Town	40	14	8	18	61	67	36
Margate	40	11	12	17	62	75	34
Dover	40	12	7	21	67	74	31
Canterbury City	40	10	10	20	52	75	30
Nuneaton Borough	40	11	7	22	60	91	29
Burton Albion	40	12	4	24	63	85	28
Tunbridge Wells United	40	8	5	27	56	115	21
Gloucester City	40	7	7	26	40	102	21

1961-62

Premier Division

Oxford United	42	28	5	9	118	46	61
Bath City	42	25	7	10	102	70	57
Guildford City	42	24	8	10	79	49	56
Yeovil Town	42	23	8	11	97	59	54
Chelmsford City	42	19	12	11	74	60	50 `
Weymouth	42	20	7	15	80	64	47
Kettering Town	42	21	5	16	90	84	47
Hereford United	42	21	2	19	81	68	44
Cambridge City	42	18	8	16	70	71	44
Bexleyheath & Welling	42	19	5	18	69	75	43
Romford	42	15	9	18	63	70	39
Cambridge United	42	13	12	17	76	78	38
Wellington Town	42	14	10	18	75	78	38
Gravesend & Northfleet	42	17	4	21	59	92	38
Bedford Town	42	16	5	21	73	79	37
Worcester City	42	15	7	20	51	64	37
Merthyr Tydfil	42	13	11	18	62	80	37
Clacton Town	42	13	10	19	74	91	36
Tonbridge	42	10	14	18	71	92	34
King's Lynn	42	12	8	22	59	74	32
Folkestone Town	42	12	6	24	64	103	30
Cheltenham	42	9	7	26	48	86	25

First Division

Wisbech Town	38	21	11	6	76	42	53
Poole Town	38	23	6	9	81	47	52
Dartford	38	21	8	9	89	50	50
Rugby Town	38	20	9	9	82	49	49
Margate	38	20	6	12	73	55	46
Corby Town	38	19	6	13	82	60	44
Sittingbourne	38	16	12	10	69	51	44
Dover	38	19	6	13	66	55	44
Yiewsley	38	18	6	14	64	51	42
Barry Town	38	14	11	13	55	51	39
Ashford Town	38	14	11	13	66	70	39
Hinckley Athletic	38	15	8	15	75	65	38
Burton Albion	38	16	5	17	70	79	37
Nuneaton Borough	38	12	12	14	63	69	36
Tunbridge Wells United	38	12	7	19	60	85	31
Canterbury City	38	11	8	19	60	82	30
Ramsgate Athletic	38	10	9	19	48	70	29
Trowbridge Town	39	9	9	20	45	69	27
Gloucester City	38	6	4	28	46	104	16
Hastings United	38	5	4	29	45	115	14

1962-63

Premier Division

Cambridge City	40	25	6	9	99	64	56
Cambridge United	40	23	7	10	74	50	53
Weymouth	40	20	11	9	82	43	51
Guildford City	40	20	11	9	70	50	51
Kettering Town	40	22	7	11	66	49	51
Wellington Town	40	19	9	12	71	49	47
Dartford	40	19	9	12	61	54	47
Chelmsford City	40	18	10	12	63	50	46
Bedford Town	40	18	8	14	61	45	44
Bath City	40	18	6	16	58	56	42
Yeovil Town	40	15	10	15	64	54	40
Romford	40	14	11	15	73	68	39
Bexleyheath & Welling	40	13	11	16	55	63	37
Hereford United	40	14	7	19	56	66	35
Merthyr Tydfil	40	15	4	21	54	71	34
Rugby Town	40	14	5	21	65	76	33
Wisbech Town	40	15	3	22	64	84	33
Worcester City	40	12	9	19	47	65	33
Poole Town	40	10	12	18	54	66	32
Gravesend & Northfleet	40	10	3	27	62	91	23
Clacton Town	40	3	7	30	50	135	13

First Division

Margate	38	21	13	4	86	47	55
Hinckley Athletic	38	22	9	7	66	38	53
Hastings United	38	22	8	8	86	36	52
Nuneaton Borough	38	21	10	7	82	41	52
Tonbridge	38	22	8	8	81	51	52
Dover	38	22	7	9	78	56	51
Corby Town	38	19	8	11	79	50	46
King's Lynn	38	19	7	15	76	66	45
Cheltenham Town	38	18	7	13	83	52	43
Folkestone Town	38	15	10	13	79	57	40
Canterbury City	38	14	8	16	42	56	36
Yiewsley	38	11	10	17	63	71	32
Ramsgate Athletic	38	12	7	19	58	82	31
Trowbridge Town	38	11	9	18	50	81	31
Burton Albion	38	10	10	18	48	76	30
Gloucester City	38	9	11	18	42	78	29
Sittingbourne	38	12	3	23	56	75	27
Ashford Town	38	9	6	23	58	76	24
Barry Town	38	6	5	27	35	75	17
Tunbridge Wells United	38	6	2	30	43	118	14

1963-64

Premier Division

Yeovil Town	42	29	5	8	93	36	63
Chelmsford City	42	26	7	9	99	55	59
Bath City	42	24	9	9	88	51	57
Guildford City	42	21	9	12	90	55	51
Romford	42	20	9	13	71	58	49
Hastings United	42	20	8	14	75	61	48
Weymouth	42	20	7	15	65	53	47
Bedford Town	42	19	9	14	71	68	47
Cambridge United	42	17	9	16	92	77	43
Cambridge City	42	17	9	16	76	70	43
Wisbech Town	42	17	8	17	64	68	42
Bexley United	42	16	10	16	70	77	42
Dartford	42	16	8	18	56	71	40
Worcester City	42	12	15	15	70	74	39
Nuneaton Borough	42	15	8	19	58	61	38
Rugby Town	42	15	8	19	68	86	38
Margate	42	12	13	17	68	81	37
Wellington Town	42	12	9	21	73	85	33
Merthyr Tydfil	42	12	8	22	69	108	32
Hereford United	42	12	7	23	58	86	31
Kettering Town	42	10	5	27	49	89	25
Hinckley Athletic	42	7	6	29	51	104	20

First Division

Folkstone Town	42	28	7	7	82	38	63
King's Lynn	42	28	5	9	94	44	61
Cheltenham Town	42	25	10	7	92	49	60
Tonbridge	42	24	11	7	98	54	59
Corby town	42	24	7	11	114	56	55
Stevenage Town	42	21	6	15	70	59	48
Ashford Town	42	19	9	14	73	57	47
Burton Albion	42	19	8	15	76	70	46
Poole Town	42	17	11	14	75	61	45
Dover	42	18	9	15	86	75	45
Canterbury City	42	16	12	14	66	66	44
Crawley Town	42	20	2	20	81	71	42
Trowbridge Town	42	16	9	17	71	78	41
Clacton Town	42	19	1	22	76	88	39
Gloucester City	42	17	4	21	88	89	38
Yiewsley	42	15	8	19	63	77	38
Sittingbourne	42	15	8	19	52	70	38
Ramsgate Athletic	42	13	9	20	57	55	35
Tunbridge Wells Rangers	42	10	8	24	47	89	28
Gravesend & Northfleet	42	7	9	26	43	96	23
Deal Town	42	5	7	30	48	106	17
Barry Town	42	3	6	33	33	137	12

1964-65

Premier Division

Weymouth	42	24	8	10	99	50	56
Guildford City	42	21	12	9	73	49	54
Worcester City	42	22	6	14	100	62	50
Yeovil Town	42	18	14	10	76	55	50
Chelmsford City	42	21	8	13	86	77	50
Margate	42	20	9	13	88	79	49
Dartford	42	17	11	14	74	64	45
Nuneaton Borough	42	19	7	16	57	55	45
Cambridge United	42	16	11	15	78	66	43
Bedford Town	42	17	9	16	66	70	43
Cambridge City	42	16	9	17	72	69	41
Cheltenham Town	42	15	11	16	72	78	41
Folkestone Town	42	17	7	18	72	79	41
Romford	42	17	7	18	61	70	41
King's Lynn	42	13	13	16	56	79	39
Tonbridge	42	10	16	16	66	75	36
Wellington Town	42	13	10	19	63	78	36
Rugby Town	42	15	6	21	71	98	36
Wisbech Town	42	14	6	22	75	91	34
Bexley United	42	14	5	23	67	74	33
Hastings United	42	9	14	19	58	86	32
Bath City	42	13	3	26	60	86	29

First Division

Hereford United	42	34	4	4	124	39	72
Wimbledon	42	24	13	5	108	52	61
Poole Town	42	26	6	10	92	56	58
Corby Town	42	24	7	11	88	55	55
Stevenage Town	42	19	13	10	83	43	51
Hillingdon Borough	42	21	7	14	105	63	49
Crawley Town	42	22	5	15	83	52	49
Merthyr Tydfil	42	20	9	13	75	59	49
Gloucester City	42	19	10	13	68	65	48
Burton Albion	42	20	7	15	83	75	47
Canterbury City	42	13	16	13	73	53	42
Kettering Town	42	14	13	15	74	64	41
Ramsgate Athletic	42	16	8	18	51	59	40
Dover	42	14	10	18	54	59	38
Hinckley Athletic	42	13	9	20	56	81	35
Trowbridge Town	42	13	5	24	68	106	31
Ashford Town	42	11	8	23	60	98	30
Barry Town	42	11	7	24	47	103	29
Deal Town	42	7	13	22	61	127	27
Tunbridge Wells Rangers	42	10	6	26	51	107	26
Gravesend & Northfleet	42	9	7	26	57	101	25
Sittingbourne	42	8	5	29	58	103	21

1965-66

Premier Division

Weymouth	42	22	13	7	70	35	57
Chelmsford City	42	21	12	9	74	50	54
Hereford United	42	21	10	11	81	49	52
Bedford Town	42	23	6	13	80	57	52
Wimbledon	42	20	10	12	80	47	50
Cambridge City	42	19	11	12	67	52	49
Romford	42	21	7	14	87	72	49
Worcester City	42	20	8	14	69	54	48
Yeovil Town	42	17	11	14	91	70	45
Cambridge United	42	18	9	15	72	64	45
King's Lynn	42	18	7	17	75	72	43
Corby Town	42	16	9	17	66	73	41
Wellington Town	42	13	13	16	65	70	39
Nuneaton Borough	42	15	8	19	60	74	38
Folkestone Town	42	14	9	19	53	75	37
Guildford City	42	14	8	20	70	84	36
Poole Town	42	14	7	21	61	75	35
Cheltenham Town	42	13	9	20	69	99	35
Dartford	42	13	7	22	62	69	33
Rugby Town	42	11	10	21	67	95	32
Tonbridge	42	11	6	25	63	101	28
Margate	42	8	10	24	66	111	26

First Division

Barnet	46	30	9	7	114	49	69
Hillingdon Borough	46	27	10	9	101	46	64
Burton Albion	46	28	8	10	121	60	64
Bath City	46	25	13	8	88	50	63
Hastings United	46	25	10	11	104	59	60
Wisbech Town	46	25	9	12	98	54	59
Canterbury City	46	25	8	13	89	66	58
Stevenage Town	46	23	9	14	86	49	55
Kettering Town	46	22	9	15	77	74	53
Merthyr Tydfil	46	22	6	18	95	68	50
Dunstable Town	46	15	14	17	76	72	44
Crawley Town	46	17	10	19	72	71	44
Bexley United	46	20	4	22	65	71	44
Trowbridge Town	46	16	11	19	79	81	43
Dover	46	17	8	21	59	62	42
Barry Town	46	16	10	20	72	94	42
Gravesend & Northfleet	46	16	9	21	84	86	41
Gloucester City	46	14	12	20	75	98	40
Sittingbourne	46	11	12	23	77	121	34
Ramsgate Athletic	46	9	15	22	35	76	33
Hinckley Athletic	46	10	12	24	59	93	32
Tunbridge Wells Rangers	46	12	8	26	47	88	32
Ashford Town	46	9	10	27	44	92	28
Deal Town	46	3	4	39	29	165	10

1966-67

Premier Division

Romford	42	22	8	12	80	60	52
Nuneaton Borough	42	21	9	12	82	54	51
Weymouth	42	18	14	10	64	40	50
Wimbledon	42	19	11	12	88	60	49
Barnet	42	18	13	11	86	66	49
Guildford City	42	19	10	13	65	51	48
Wellington Town	42	20	7	15	70	67	47
Cambridge United	42	16	13	13	75	67	45
Chelmsford City	42	15	15	12	66	59	45
Hereford United	42	16	12	14	79	61	44
King's Lynn	42	15	14	13	78	72	44
Cambridge City	42	15	13	14	66	70	43
Cheltenham Town	42	16	11	15	60	71	43
Yeovil Town	42	14	14	14	66	72	42
Burton Albion	42	17	5	20	63	71	39
Corby Town	42	15	9	18	60	75	39
Poole Town	42	14	11	17	52	65	39
Hillingdon Borough	42	11	13	18	49	70	35
Bath City	42	11	12	19	51	74	34
Worcester City	42	11	8	23	59	79	30
Bedford Town	42	8	13	21	54	72	29
Folkestone Town	42	6	15	21	44	81	27

First Division

Dover	46	29	12	5	92	35	70
Margate	46	31	7	8	127	54	69
Stevenage Town	46	29	8	9	90	32	66
Hastings United	46	25	16	5	89	45	66
Kettering Town	46	27	9	10	105	62	63
Canterbury City	46	26	8	12	81	48	60
Ramsgate Athletic	46	23	8	15	79	62	54
Dartford	46	19	15	12	92	67	53
Tonbridge	46	21	10	15	91	69	52
Trowbridge Town	46	20	12	14	73	60	52
Ashford Town	46	18	8	20	74	68	44
Merthyr Tydfil	46	17	9	20	81	71	43
Gloucester City	46	18	6	22	69	83	42
Canterbury City	46	17	8	21	57	75	42
Wisbech Town	46	16	9	21	87	93	41
Bexley United	46	13	15	18	53	69	41
Banbury United	46	13	14	19	88	100	40
Rugby Town	46	15	7	24	57	77	37
Dunstable Town	46	14	6	26	55	87	34
Barry Town	46	11	11	24	62	89	33
Gravesend & Northfleet	46	11	9	26	63	106	31
Hinckley Athletic	46	10	8	28	44	100	28
Tunbridge Wells Rangers	46	4	15	27	31	96	23
Sittingbourne	46	5	10	31	44	136	20

1967-68

Premier Division

Chelmsford City	42	25	7	10	85	50	57
Wimbledon	42	24	7	11	85	47	55
Cambridge United	42	20	13	9	73	42	53
Cheltenham Town	42	23	7	12	97	67	53
Guildford City	42	18	13	11	56	43	49
Romford	42	20	8	14	72	60	48
Barnet	42	20	8	14	81	71	48
Margate	42	19	8	15	80	71	46
Wellington Town	42	16	13	13	70	66	45
Hillingdon Borough	42	18	9	155	53	54	45
King's Lynn	42	18	8	16	66	57	44
Yeovil Town	42	16	12	14	45	43	44
Weymouth	42	17	8	17	65	62	42
Hereford United	42	17	7	18	58	62	41
Nuneaton Borough	42	13	14	15	62	64	40
Dover	42	17	6	19	54	56	40
Poole Town	42	13	10	19	55	74	36
Stevenage Town	42	13	9	20	57	75	35
Burton Albion	42	14	6	22	51	73	34
Corby Town	42	7	13	22	40	77	27
Cambridge City	42	10	6	26	51	81	26
Hastings United	42	4	8	30	33	94	16

First Division

Worcester City	42	23	14	5	92	35	60
Kettering Town	42	24	10	8	88	40	58
Bedford Town	42	24	7	11	101	40	55
Rugby Town	42	20	15	7	72	44	55
Dartford	42	23	9	10	70	48	55
Bath City	42	21	12	9	78	51	54
Banbury United	42	22	9	11	79	59	53
Ramsgate Athletic	42	17	7	8	70	37	51
Merthyr Tydfil	42	18	13	11	80	66	49
Tonbridge	42	18	9	15	76	71	45
Canterbury City	42	16	11	15	66	63	43
Ashford Town	42	18	6	18	73	78	42
Brentwood Town	42	16	9	17	63	73	41
Bexley United	42	12	13	17	56	64	37
Trowbridge Town	42	12	11	19	64	70	35
Gloucester City	42	12	9	21	54	68	33
Wisbech Town	42	11	10	21	43	78	32
Crawley Town	42	10	8	24	54	85	28
Folkestone Town	42	10	7	25	49	80	27
Dunstable Town	42	8	10	24	44	94	26
Barry Town	42	7	12	23	36	81	26
Gravesend & Northfleet	42	6	7	29	28	112	19

1968-69

Premier Division

Cambridge United	42	27	5	10	72	39	59
Hillingdon Borough	42	24	10	8	68	47	58
Wimbledon	42	21	12	9	66	48	54
King's Lynn	42	20	9	13	68	60	49
Worcester City	42	19	11	12	53	47	49
Romford	42	18	12	12	58	52	48
Weymouth	42	16	15	11	52	41	47
Yeovil Town	42	16	13	13	52	50	45
Kettering Town	42	18	8	16	51	55	44
Dover	42	17	9	16	66	61	43
Nuneaton Borough	42	17	7	18	74	58	41
Barnet	42	15	10	17	72	66	40
Chelmsford City	42	17	6	19	56	58	40
Hereford United	42	15	9	18	66	62	39
Telford United	42	14	10	18	62	61	38
Poole Town	42	16	6	20	75	76	38
Burton Albion	42	16	5	21	55	71	37
Margate	42	14	7	21	79	90	35
Cheltenham Town	42	15	5	22	55	64	35
Bedford Town	42	11	12	19	46	63	34
Rugby Town	42	10	6	26	38	83	26
Guildford City	42	7	11	24	41	73	25

First Division

Brentwood Town	42	26	12	4	44	37	64
Bath City	42	26	10	6	96	40	62
Gloucester City	42	25	9	8	100	53	59
Crawley Town	42	21	13	8	65	32	55
Corby Town	42	22	6	14	81	65	50
Dartford	42	20	8	14	79	51	48
Ramsgate Athletic	42	19	9	14	72	57	47
Salisbury	42	20	6	16	69	52	46
Cambridge City	42	18	10	14	73	63	46
Banbury United	42	16	12	14	67	72	44
Trowbridge Town	42	15	8	19	70	60	44
Folkestone Town	42	19	5	18	53	59	43
Canterbury City	42	17	7	18	67	63	41
Ashford Town	42	16	8	18	72	73	40
Bexley United	42	15	9	18	62	75	39
Hastings United	42	15	9	18	58	69	39
Wisbech Town	42	11	13	18	57	70	35
Dunstable Town	42	14	6	22	73	99	34
Merthyr Tydfil	42	10	7	25	49	101	27
Barry Town	42	8	10	24	39	78	26
Gravesend & Northfleet	42	8	9	25	51	79	25
Tonbridge	42	2	6	34	36	137	10

1969-70

Premier Division

Cambridge United	42	26	6	10	86	49	58
Yeovil Town	42	25	7	10	78	48	57
Chelmsford City	42	20	11	11	76	58	51
Weymouth	42	18	14	10	59	37	50
Wimbledon	42	19	12	11	64	52	50
Hillingdon Borough	42	19	12	11	56	50	50
Barnet	42	16	15	11	71	54	47
Telford United	42	18	10	14	61	62	46
Brentwood Town	42	16	13	13	61	38	45
Hereford United	42	18	9	15	74	65	45
Bath City	42	18	8	16	63	55	44
King's Lynn	42	16	11	15	72	68	43
Margate	42	17	8	17	70	64	42
Dover	42	15	10	17	51	50	40
Kettering Town	42	18	3	21	64	75	39
Worcester City	42	14	10	18	35	44	38
Romford	42	13	11	18	50	62	37
Poole Town	42	8	19	15	48	57	35
Gloucester City	42	12	9	21	53	73	33
Nuneaton Borough	42	11	10	21	52	74	32
Crawley Town	42	6	15	21	53	101	27
Burton Albion	42	3	9	30	24	82	15

First Division

Bedford Town	42	26	9	7	93	37	61
Cambridge City	42	26	8	8	104	43	60
Dartford	42	24	11	7	33	46	58
Ashford Town	42	19	15	8	71	43	53
Rugby Town	42	20	10	12	82	66	50
Trowbridge Town	42	20	8	14	72	65	48
Hastings United	42	18	11	13	67	51	47
Guildford City	42	19	9	14	68	58	47
Cheltenham Town	42	20	5	17	78	81	45
Canterbury City	42	15	13	14	61	57	43
Corby Town	42	14	15	13	58	53	43
Folkestone Town	42	19	5	18	57	55	43
Ramsgate Athletic	42	14	13	15	53	57	41
Salisbury	42	13	13	16	48	53	39
Gravesend & Northfleet	42	13	11	18	62	71	37
Bexley United	42	10	11	21	58	76	31
Dunstable Town	42	11	9	22	52	82	31
Merthyr Tydfil	42	9	11	22	40	80	29
Barry Town	42	11	6	25	39	76	28
Wisbech Town	42	8	9	25	58	116	25
Tonbridge	42	4	10	28	46	101	18

1971-72

Premier Division

Chelmsford City	42	28	6	8	109	46	62
Hereford United	42	24	12	6	68	30	60
Dover	42	20	11	11	67	45	51
Barnet	42	21	7	14	80	57	49
Dartford	42	20	8	14	75	68	48
Weymouth	42	21	5	16	69	43	47
Yeovil Town	42	18	11	13	67	51	47
Hillingdon Borough	42	20	6	16	64	58	46
Margate	42	19	8	15	74	68	46
Wimbledon	42	19	7	16	75	64	45
Romford	42	16	13	13	54	49	45
Guildford City	42	20	5	17	71	65	45
Telford United	42	18	7	17	83	68	43
Nuneaton Borough	42	16	10	16	46	47	42
Bedford Town	42	16	9	17	59	66	41
Worcester City	42	17	7	18	46	57	41
Cambridge City	42	12	14	16	68	71	38
Folkestone	42	14	7	21	58	64	35
Poole Town	42	9	11	22	43	72	29
Bath City	42	11	4	27	45	86	26
Merthyr Tydfil	42	7	8	27	29	93	22
Gravesend & Northfleet	42	5	6	31	30	110	16

1970-71

Premier Division

Yeovil Town	42	25	7	10	66	31	57
Cambridge City	42	22	11	9	67	38	55
Romford	42	23	9	10	63	42	55
Hereford United	42	23	8	11	71	53	54
Chelmsford City	42	20	11	11	61	32	51
Barnet	42	18	14	10	69	49	50
Bedford Town	42	20	10	12	62	46	50
Wimbledon	42	20	8	14	72	54	48
Worcester City	42	20	8	14	61	46	48
Weymouth	42	14	16	12	64	48	44
Dartford	42	15	12	15	53	51	42
Dover	42	16	9	17	64	63	41
Margate	42	15	10	17	64	70	40
Hillingdon Borough	42	17	6	19	61	68	40
Bath City	42	13	12	17	48	68	38
Nuneaton Borough	42	12	12	18	43	66	36
Telford United	42	13	8	21	64	70	34
Poole Town	42	14	6	22	57	75	34
King's Lynn	42	11	7	24	44	67	29
Ashford Town	42	8	13	21	52	86	29
Kettering Town	42	8	11	23	48	84	27
Gloucester City	42	6	10	26	34	81	21

First Division

Guildford City	38	22	10	6	76	36	54
Merthyr Tydfil	38	19	12	7	52	33	50
Gravesend & Northfleet	38	19	10	9	74	42	48
Folkestone	38	20	8	10	83	53	48
Burton Albion	38	19	10	9	56	37	48
Rugby Town	38	17	14	7	58	40	48
Ramsgate Athletic	38	20	5	13	83	54	45
Trowbridge Town	38	19	7	12	78	55	45
Bexley United	38	17	11	10	57	45	45
Crawley Town	38	15	11	12	84	68	41
Hastings United	38	13	12	13	51	50	38
Banbury United	38	13	11	14	58	53	37
Corby Town	38	14	8	16	57	60	36
Salisbury	38	13	7	18	56	60	33
Cheltenham Town	38	8	15	15	44	58	31
Stevenage Athletic	38	12	7	19	55	79	31
Tonbridge	38	8	8	22	48	83	24
Barry Town	38	9	6	23	35	82	24
Dunstable Town	38	8	4	26	32	81	20
Canterbury City	38	5	4	29	37	105	14

First Division (North)

Kettering Town	34	23	6	5	70	27	52
Burton Albion	34	18	13	3	58	27	49
Cheltenham Town	34	20	4	10	72	51	44
Rugby Town	34	18	7	9	52	36	43
Wellingborough Town	34	15	10	9	73	44	40
Stourbridge	34	13	14	7	59	42	40
King's Lynn	34	14	11	9	62	45	39
Corby Town	34	15	9	10	47	35	39
Ilkeston Town	34	14	11	9	44	38	39
Banbury United	34	14	5	15	54	46	33
Bury Town	34	14	5	15	44	44	33
Wealdstone	34	14	5	15	51	58	33
Lockheed Leamington	34	15	3	16	41	52	33
Gloucester City	34	8	8	18	46	61	24
Stevenage Athletic	34	8	8	18	41	69	24
Bletchley	34	7	7	20	36	70	21
Dunstable Town	34	5	7	22	29	75	17
Barry Town	34	1	7	26	22	84	9

First Division (South)

Waterlooville	30	15	9	6	40	22	39
Ramsgate Athletic	30	14	11	5	42	27	39
Maidstone United	30	14	10	6	48	28	38
Crawley Town	30	15	5	10	67	55	35
Metropolitan Police	30	15	3	12	48	41	33
Tonbridge	30	12	9	9	37	34	33
Bexley United	30	14	4	12	52	46	32
Basingstoke Town	30	14	4	12	37	36	32
Andover	30	11	9	10	32	34	31
Ashford Town	30	12	4	14	43	48	28
Salisbury	30	10	7	13	45	44	27
Winchester City	30	10	7	13	40	47	27
Hastings United	30	10	7	13	28	42	27
Trowbridge Town	30	8	7	15	41	49	23
Canterbury City	30	7	8	15	39	56	22
Woodford Town	30	4	6	20	22	52	14

1972-73

Premier Division

Kettering Town	42	20	17	5	74	44	57
Yeovil Town	42	21	14	7	67	61	56
Dover	42	23	9	10	61	68	55
Chelmsford City	42	23	7	12	75	43	53
Worcester City	42	20	13	9	68	47	53
Weymouth	42	20	12	10	72	51	52
Margate	42	17	15	10	80	60	49
Bedford Town	42	16	15	11	43	36	47
Nuneaton Borough	42	16	14	12	51	41	46
Telford United	42	12	20	10	57	47	44
Cambridge City	42	14	15	13	64	53	43
Wimbledon	42	14	14	14	50	50	42
Barnet	42	15	11	16	60	59	41
Romford	42	17	5	20	51	65	39
Hillingdon Borough	42	16	6	20	52	58	38
Dartford	42	12	11	19	49	63	35
Folkestone	42	11	11	20	41	72	33
Guildford City	42	10	11	21	59	84	31
Ramsgate	42	9	13	20	35	61	31
Poole Town	42	10	10	22	50	88	30
Burton Albion	42	9	7	26	43	81	25
Waterlooville	42	4	16	22	33	63	24

First Division (North)

Grantham	42	29	8	5	113	41	66
Atherstone Town	42	23	11	8	82	48	57
Cheltenham Town	42	24	8	10	87	47	56
Rugby Town	42	20	10	12	60	47	50
Kidderminster Harriers	42	19	12	11	67	56	50
Merthyr Tydfil	42	17	12	13	51	40	46
Corby Town	42	14	16	12	62	56	44
Stourbridge	42	16	11	15	70	64	43
Gloucester City	42	18	7	17	55	64	43
Bromsgrove Rovers	42	17	8	17	63	54	42
Redditch United	42	18	6	18	58	59	42
Banbury United	42	18	5	19	60	53	41
Wellingborough Town	42	17	7	18	58	71	41
King's Lynn	42	14	12	16	45	49	40
Lockheed Leamington	42	13	12	17	51	58	38
Enderby Town	42	12	14	16	50	61	38
Stevenage Athletic	42	12	13	17	50	63	37
Tamworth	42	14	8	20	45	65	36
Bury Town	42	13	9	20	52	69	35
Barry Town	42	11	10	21	45	71	32
Ilkeston Town	42	9	6	27	35	68	24
Bedworth United	42	10	3	29	42	94	23

First Division (South)

Maidstone United	42	25	12	5	90	38	62
Tonbridge	42	26	7	9	70	44	59
Ashford Town	42	24	7	11	90	40	55
Bideford	42	19	14	9	70	43	52
Minehead	42	20	12	10	65	47	52
Gravesend & Northfleet	42	22	7	13	81	55	51
Bath City	42	18	11	13	56	54	47
Wealdstone	42	16	12	14	81	61	44
Bletchley Town	42	14	13	15	54	51	41
Hastings United	42	14	13	15	53	53	41
Andover	42	15	11	16	62	70	41
Canterbury City	42	14	12	16	51	59	40
Basingstoke Town	42	14	12	16	48	57	40
Crawley Town	42	14	11	17	59	76	39
Metropolitan Police	42	15	8	19	82	75	38
Trowbridge Town	42	15	8	19	65	77	38
Bexley United	42	12	14	16	54	64	38
Salisbury	42	14	10	18	49	60	38
Bognor Regis Town	42	12	9	21	41	66	33
Dorchester Town	42	10	12	20	47	73	32
Winchester City	42	7	11	24	41	79	25
Dunstable Town	42	4	10	28	38	105	18

1973-74

Premier Division

Dartford	42	22	13	7	67	37	57
Grantham	42	18	13	11	70	49	49
Chelmsford City	42	19	10	13	62	49	48
Kettering Town	42	16	16	10	62	51	48
Maidstone United	42	16	14	12	54	43	46
Yeovil Town	42	13	20	9	45	39	46
Weymouth	42	19	7	16	60	41	45
Barnet	42	18	9	15	55	46	45
Nuneaton Borough	42	13	19	10	54	47	45
Cambridge City	42	15	12	15	45	54	42
Atherstone Town	42	16	9	17	61	59	41
Wimbledon	42	15	11	16	50	56	41
Telford United	42	12	16	14	51	57	40
Dover	42	11	17	14	41	46	39
Tonbridge	42	12	15	15	38	45	39
Romford	42	11	17	14	39	52	39
Margate	42	15	8	19	56	63	38
Guildford City	42	13	11	18	48	67	37
Worcester City	42	11	14	17	53	67	36
Bedford Town	42	11	14	17	38	51	36
Folkestone	42	11	12	19	56	65	34
Hillingdon Borough	42	9	15	18	44	65	33

First Division (North)

Stourbridge	42	29	11	2	103	36	69
Burton Albion	42	27	9	6	88	32	63
Cheltenham Town	42	24	9	10	75	51	56
AP Leamington	42	21	12	9	82	45	54
Enderby Town	42	19	14	9	60	36	52
Witney Town	42	20	10	12	69	55	50
Stevenage Athletic	42	19	11	12	65	46	49
Banbury United	42	19	11	12	69	57	49
King's Lynn	42	19	10	13	65	50	48
Kidderminster Harriers	42	15	14	13	67	53	44
Merthyr Tydfil	42	16	12	14	70	61	44
Redditch United	42	14	11	17	56	73	39
Bromsgrove Rovers	42	14	10	18	54	61	38
Bedworth United	42	14	10	18	50	77	38
Tamworth	42	13	11	18	42	51	37
Corby Town	42	12	11	19	40	57	35
Bletchley Town	42	10	15	17	47	71	35
Barry Town	42	10	8	24	53	85	29
Bury Town	42	10	6	26	57	84	26
Gloucester City	42	10	6	26	52	81	26
Wellingborough Town	42	7	9	26	42	87	23
Dunstable Town	42	5	11	26	26	83	21

First Division (South)

Wealdstone	38	26	7	5	75	35	59
Bath City	38	20	8	10	55	34	48
Waterlooville	38	16	15	7	55	38	47
Minehead	38	16	15	7	69	52	47
Bideford	38	17	12	9	61	51	46
Poole Town	38	18	9	11	67	47	45
Bexley United	38	18	7	13	50	42	43
Hastings United	38	16	9	13	45	36	41
Basingstoke Town	38	14	11	13	55	44	39
Gravesend & Northfleet	38	13	13	12	58	52	39
Bognor Regis Town	38	13	12	13	48	54	38
Ashford Town	38	14	8	16	41	42	36
Ramsgate	38	13	9	16	44	44	35
Dorchester Town	38	10	13	15	40	48	33
Canterbury City	38	9	12	17	37	46	30
Trowbridge Town	38	8	14	16	44	61	30
Salisbury	38	10	9	19	40	60	29
Metropolitan Police	38	9	11	18	37	61	29
Andover	38	11	3	24	38	70	25
Crawley Town	38	6	9	23	35	79	21

1974-75

Premier Division

Team	P	W	D	L	F	A	Pts
Wimbledon	42	25	7	10	63	33	57
Nuneaton Borough	42	23	8	11	56	37	54
Yeovil Town	42	21	9	12	64	34	51
Kettering United	42	20	10	12	73	41	50
Burton Albion	42	18	13	11	54	48	49
Bath City	42	20	8	14	63	50	48
Margate	42	17	12	13	64	64	46
Wealdstone	42	17	11	14	62	61	45
Telford United	42	16	13	13	55	56	45
Chelmsford City	42	16	12	14	62	51	44
Grantham	42	16	11	15	70	62	43
Dover	42	15	13	14	43	53	43
Maidstone United	42	15	12	15	52	50	42
Atherstone Town	42	14	14	14	48	53	42
Weymouth	42	13	13	16	66	58	39
Stourbridge	42	13	12	17	56	70	38
Cambridge	42	11	14	17	51	56	36
Tonbridge	42	11	12	19	44	66	34
Romford	42	10	13	19	46	62	33
Dartford	42	9	13	20	52	70	31
Barnet	42	10	9	23	44	76	29
Guildford & Dorking United	42	10	5	27	45	82	25

First Division (North)

Team	P	W	D	L	F	A	Pts
Bedford Town	42	28	9	5	85	33	65
Dunstable Town	42	25	8	9	105	61	58
AP Leamington	42	25	7	10	68	48	57
Redditch United	42	22	12	8	76	40	56
Worcester City	42	24	8	10	84	50	56
Cheltenham Town	42	21	9	12	72	53	51
Tamworth	42	21	8	13	74	53	50
King's Lynn	42	19	10	13	71	64	48
Enderby Town	42	17	12	13	61	48	46
Banbury United	42	18	10	14	52	51	46
Stevenage Athletic	42	16	13	13	62	48	45
Bromsgrove Rovers	42	18	9	15	63	52	45
Merthyr Tydfil	42	11	15	16	53	64	37
Witney Town	42	16	4	22	57	76	36
Corby Town	42	11	13	18	60	57	35
Kidderminster Harriers	42	12	11	19	50	66	35
Gloucester City	42	13	8	21	55	75	34
Wellingborough Town	42	9	13	20	42	61	31
Barry Town	42	10	10	22	49	73	30
Bedworth United	42	9	9	24	60	91	27
Milton Keynes City	42	7	5	30	48	100	19
Bury Town	42	5	7	30	36	119	17

First Division (South)

Team	P	W	D	L	F	A	Pts
Gravesend & Northfleet	38	24	12	2	70	30	60
Hillingdon Borough	38	22	8	8	87	45	52
Minehead	38	21	9	8	74	33	51
Ramsgate	38	19	11	8	70	37	49
Bexley United	38	19	7	12	61	44	45
Waterlooville	38	17	11	10	67	49	45
Ashford Town	38	16	12	10	64	55	44
Basingstoke Town	38	16	11	11	64	50	43
Canterbury City	38	16	9	13	54	43	41
Hastings United	38	13	14	11	54	45	40
Poole Town	38	11	13	14	50	60	35
Metropolitan Police	38	11	13	14	54	66	35
Folkestone & Shepway	38	10	14	14	53	57	34
Andover	38	12	8	18	52	71	32
Bognor Regis Town	38	10	11	17	49	64	31
Salisbury	38	9	11	18	45	66	29
Trowbridge Town	38	10	9	19	48	76	29
Bideford	38	10	8	20	40	71	28
Dorchester Town	38	8	10	20	40	63	26
Crawley Town	38	3	5	30	31	102	11

1975-76

Premier Division

Team	P	W	D	L	F	A	Pts
Wimbledon	42	26	10	6	74	29	62
Yeovil Town	42	21	12	9	68	35	54
Atherstone Town	42	18	15	9	56	55	51
Maidstone United	42	17	16	9	52	39	50
Nuneaton Borough	42	16	18	8	41	33	50
Gravesend & Northfleet	42	16	18	8	49	47	50
Grantham	42	15	14	13	56	47	44
Dunstable Town	42	17	9	16	52	43	43
Bedford Town	42	13	17	12	55	51	43
Burton Albion	42	17	9	16	52	53	43
Margate	42	15	12	15	62	60	42
Hillingdon Borough	42	13	14	15	61	54	40
Telford United	42	14	12	16	54	51	40
Chelmsford City	42	13	14	15	52	57	40
Kettering Town	42	11	17	14	48	52	39
Bath City	42	11	16	15	62	57	38
Weymouth	42	13	9	20	51	67	35
Dover	42	8	18	16	51	60	34
Wealdstone	42	12	9	21	61	82	33
Tonbridge AFC	42	11	11	20	45	70	33
Cambridge City	42	8	15	19	41	67	31
Stourbridge	42	10	9	23	38	72	29

First Division (North)

Team	P	W	D	L	F	A	Pts
Redditch United	42	29	11	2	101	39	69
AP Leamington	42	27	10	5	85	31	64
Witney Town	42	24	9	9	66	40	57
Worcester City	42	24	8	10	90	49	56
Cheltenham Town	42	20	10	12	87	55	50
Barry Town	42	19	10	13	52	47	48
King's Lynn	42	17	14	11	52	48	48
Tamworth	42	18	11	13	65	43	47
Barnet	42	15	12	15	56	56	42
Oswestry Town	42	16	8	18	63	71	40
Enderby Town	42	16	6	20	48	51	38
Banbury United	42	15	8	19	58	67	38
Merthyr Tydfil	42	11	15	16	59	67	37
Bromsgrove Rovers	42	13	11	18	49	65	37
Milton Keynes City	42	15	6	21	51	63	36
Bury Town	42	12	11	19	52	72	35
Gloucester City	42	13	9	20	49	78	35
Kidderminster Harriers	42	13	8	21	54	70	34
Bedworth United	42	8	18	16	41	66	34
Corby Town	42	11	10	21	50	65	32
Wellingborough Town	42	9	11	22	42	68	29
Stevenage Athletic	42	6	6	30	46	105	18

First Division (South)

Team	P	W	D	L	F	A	Pts
Minehead	38	27	8	3	102	35	62
Dartford	38	26	4	8	84	46	56
Romford	38	21	9	8	66	37	51
Salisbury	38	17	11	10	73	53	45
Hastings United	38	15	15	8	67	51	45
Poole United	38	20	2	16	57	57	42
Bexley United	38	14	13	11	62	53	41
Waterlooville	38	13	13	12	62	54	39
Basingstoke Town	38	13	12	13	69	71	38
Ashford Town	38	14	8	16	67	73	36
Canterbury City	38	11	13	14	53	60	35
Folkestone & Shepway	38	10	14	14	36	51	34
Metropolitan Police	38	9	14	15	46	58	32
Trowbridge Town	38	11	10	17	48	75	32
Guildford & Dorking United	38	9	13	16	43	50	31
Bognor Regis Town	38	6	17	15	44	72	29
Ramsgate	38	9	10	19	57	76	28
Crawley Town	38	9	10	19	46	66	28
Andover	38	9	10	19	42	62	28
Dorchester Town	38	11	6	21	45	69	28

1976-77

Premier Division

Wimbledon	42	28	7	7	64	22	63
Minehead	42	23	12	7	73	39	58
Kettering Town	42	20	16	6	66	46	56
Bath City	42	20	15	7	51	30	55
Nuneaton Borough	42	20	11	11	52	35	51
Bedford Town	42	17	14	11	54	47	48
Yeovil Town	42	15	16	11	54	42	46
Dover	42	13	16	13	46	43	42
Grantham	42	14	12	16	55	50	40
Maidstone United	42	13	14	15	46	50	40
Gravesend & Northfleet	42	13	13	16	38	43	39
AP Leamington	42	12	15	15	44	53	39
Redditch United	42	12	14	16	45	54	38
Wealdstone	42	13	12	17	54	66	38
Hillingdon Borough	42	14	10	18	45	59	38
Atherstone Town	42	14	9	19	41	49	37
Weymouth	42	16	5	21	53	73	37
Dartford	42	13	10	19	52	57	36
Telford United	42	11	12	19	36	50	34
Chelmsford City	42	9	13	20	56	68	31
Burton Albion	42	10	10	22	41	52	30
Margate	42	9	10	23	47	85	28

First Division (North)

Worcester City	38	32	5	1	97	22	69
Cheltenham Town	38	23	8	7	85	35	54
Witney Town	38	21	8	9	48	31	50
Bromsgrove Rovers	38	20	8	10	61	37	48
Barry Town	38	19	8	11	62	45	46
Cambridge City	38	17	10	11	68	43	44
Stourbridge	38	17	9	12	48	35	43
Kidderminster Harriers	38	17	6	15	74	65	40
Banbury United	38	15	10	13	51	47	40
Gloucester City	38	18	4	16	70	81	40
Enderby Town	38	15	9	14	50	44	39
King's Lynn	38	13	11	14	47	53	37
Corby Town	38	11	13	14	56	64	35
Tamworth	38	11	13	14	49	58	35
Merthyr Tydfil	38	12	6	20	60	69	30
Oswestry Town	38	8	10	20	30	60	26
Wellingborough Town	38	8	7	23	37	73	23
Dunstable	38	7	7	24	38	84	21
Bedworth United	38	5	10	23	28	68	20
Milton Keynes City	38	7	6	25	31	76	20

First Division (South)

Barnet	34	23	8	3	65	25	54
Hastings United	34	18	11	5	47	18	47
Waterlooville	34	19	6	9	50	25	44
Dorchester Town	34	16	11	7	48	30	43
Salisbury	34	15	11	8	57	39	41
Romford	34	18	5	11	47	32	41
Poole Town	34	17	7	10	40	35	41
Trowbridge Town	34	15	8	11	47	39	38
Crawley Town	34	14	9	11	53	42	37
Folkestone & Shepway	34	12	11	11	39	42	35
Basingstoke Town	34	12	10	12	51	43	34
Canterbury City	34	6	16	12	36	46	28
Bognor Regis Town	34	9	9	16	33	50	27
Tonbridge AFC	34	9	9	16	33	50	27
Metropolitan Police	34	5	12	17	37	61	22
Andover	34	4	11	19	17	49	19
Ashford Town	34	5	8	21	32	65	18
Aylesbury United	34	5	6	23	27	68	16

1977-78

Premier Division

Bath City	42	22	18	2	83	32	62
Weymouth	42	21	16	5	64	36	58
Maidstone United	42	20	11	11	59	41	51
Worcester City	42	20	11	11	67	50	51
Gravesend & Northfleet	42	19	11	12	57	42	49
Kettering Town	42	18	11	13	58	48	47
Barnet	42	18	11	13	63	58	47
Wealdstone	42	16	14	12	54	48	46
Telford United	42	17	11	14	52	45	45
Nuneaton Borough	42	15	14	13	38	36	44
Dartford	42	14	15	13	57	65	43
Yeovil Town	42	14	14	14	57	49	42
Hastings United	42	15	9	18	49	60	39
Cheltenham Town	42	12	14	16	43	52	38
Hillingdon Borough	42	13	9	20	45	54	35
Atherstone Town	42	10	15	17	41	56	35
Redditch United	42	15	5	22	40	55	35
AP Leamington	42	11	13	18	34	57	35
Minehead	42	11	12	19	43	48	34
Dover	42	9	13	20	41	63	31
Bedford Town	42	8	13	21	51	75	29
Grantham	42	11	6	25	40	66	28

First Division (North)

Witney Town	38	20	15	3	54	27	55
Bridgend Town	38	20	9	9	59	45	49
Burton Albion	38	17	11	10	48	32	45
Enderby Town	38	17	10	11	59	44	44
Bromsgrove Rovers	38	16	12	10	56	41	44
Banbury United	38	17	10	11	52	47	44
Kidderminster Harriers	38	16	11	11	58	41	43
Merthyr Tydfil	38	18	6	14	85	62	42
Cambridge City	38	14	12	12	56	45	40
Barry Town	38	14	11	13	58	48	39
Wellingborough Town	38	11	15	12	47	43	37
King's Lynn	38	12	13	13	55	55	37
Gloucester City	38	14	8	16	68	75	36
Corby Town	38	9	17	12	46	48	35
Dunstable Town	38	11	13	14	49	59	35
Stourbridge	38	9	15	14	52	53	33
Tamworth	38	10	11	17	37	48	31
Bedworth United	38	8	14	16	36	58	30
Milton Keynes City	38	5	11	22	26	74	21
Oswestry Town	38	6	8	24	29	85	20

First Division (South)

Margate	38	24	10	4	92	32	58
Dorchester Town	38	23	10	5	67	31	56
Salisbury	38	21	10	7	60	27	52
Waterlooville	38	19	13	6	66	36	51
Romford	38	17	15	6	58	37	49
Aylesbury United	38	20	7	11	56	42	47
Trowbridge Town	38	16	11	11	65	59	43
Chelmsford City	38	15	11	12	58	46	41
Folkestone & Shepway	38	16	9	13	64	56	41
Taunton Town	38	15	10	13	57	54	40
Addlestone	38	14	10	14	57	60	38
Crawley Town	38	14	9	15	61	60	37
Basingstoke Town	38	11	11	16	44	50	33
Tonbridge AFC	38	13	5	20	64	77	31
Ashford Town	38	9	13	16	39	60	31
Hounslow	38	10	10	18	43	62	30
Bognor Regis Town	38	9	8	21	52	69	26
Poole Town	38	8	10	20	43	68	26
Andover	38	4	12	22	30	68	20
Canterbury City	38	2	6	30	31	113	10

1978-79

Premier Division

Worcester City	42	27	11	4	92	33	65
Kettering Town	42	27	7	8	109	43	61
Telford United	42	22	10	10	60	39	54
Maidstone United	42	18	18	6	55	35	54
Bath City	42	17	19	6	59	41	53
Weymouth	42	18	15	9	71	51	51
AP Leamington	42	19	11	12	65	53	49
Redditch United	42	19	10	13	70	57	48
Yeovil Town	42	15	16	11	59	49	46
Witney Town	42	17	10	15	53	52	44
Nuneaton Borough	42	13	17	12	59	50	43
Gravesend & Northfleet	42	15	12	15	56	55	42
Barnet	42	16	10	16	52	64	42
Hillingdon Borough	42	12	16	14	50	41	40
Wealdstone	42	12	12	18	51	59	36
Atherstone Town	42	9	17	16	46	65	35
Dartford	42	10	14	18	40	56	34
Cheltenham Town	42	11	10	21	38	72	32
Margate	42	10	9	23	44	75	29
Dorchester Town	42	7	11	24	46	86	25
Hastings United	42	5	13	24	37	85	23
Bridgend Town	42	6	6	30	39	90	18

First Division (North)

Grantham	38	21	10	7	70	45	52
Merthyr Tydfil	38	22	7	9	90	53	51
Alvechurch	38	20	10	8	70	42	50
Bedford Town	38	19	9	10	74	49	47
King's Lynn	38	17	11	10	57	46	45
Oswestry Town	38	18	8	12	63	43	44
Gloucester City	38	18	8	12	76	59	44
Burton Albion	38	16	10	12	51	40	42
Kidderminster Harriers	38	13	14	11	70	60	40
Bedworth United	38	13	14	11	41	34	40
Tamworth	38	15	8	15	47	45	38
Stourbridge	38	15	7	16	64	61	37
Barry Town	38	14	9	15	51	53	37
Enderby Town	38	14	8	16	46	55	36
Banbury United	38	10	13	15	42	58	33
Wellingborough Town	38	13	6	19	50	71	32
Cambridge City	38	9	9	20	37	62	27
Bromsgrove Rovers	38	6	14	18	33	61	26
Milton Keynes City	38	7	9	22	37	87	23
Corby Town	38	5	6	27	40	85	16

First Division (South)

Dover	40	28	9	3	88	20	65
Folkestone & Shepway	40	22	6	12	84	50	50
Gosport Borough	40	19	11	10	62	47	49
Chelmsford City	40	20	7	13	65	61	47
Minehead	40	16	13	11	58	39	45
Poole Town	40	15	15	10	48	44	45
Hounslow	40	16	12	12	56	45	44
Waterlooville	40	17	10	13	52	43	44
Trowbridge Town	40	15	12	13	65	61	42
Aylesbury United	40	16	9	15	54	52	41
Taunton Town	40	16	9	15	53	51	41
Bognor Regis Town	40	17	7	16	58	58	41
Dunstable	40	18	4	18	57	55	40
Tonbridge AFC	40	15	10	15	43	47	40
Salisbury	40	13	10	17	47	51	36
Basingstoke Town	40	12	11	17	49	62	35
Addlestone	40	12	9	19	56	64	33
Andover	40	12	6	22	47	69	30
Ashford Town	40	10	10	20	28	53	30
Crawley Town	40	9	9	22	44	75	27
Canterbury City	40	6	3	31	31	98	15

1979-80

Midland Division

Bridgend Town	42	28	6	8	85	39	62
Minehead	42	22	15	5	70	42	59
Bedford Town	42	20	12	10	71	42	52
Kidderminster Harriers	42	23	6	13	81	59	52
Merthyr Tydfil	42	20	11	11	70	47	51
Enderby Town	42	21	8	13	62	50	50
Stourbridge	42	19	11	12	67	49	49
Alvechurch	42	17	14	11	78	60	48
Trowbridge Town	42	19	9	14	62	61	47
Bromsgrove Rovers	42	18	10	14	67	56	46
Barry Town	42	15	12	15	64	58	42
King's Lynn	42	15	11	16	48	55	41
Banbury United	42	13	14	15	56	56	40
Taunton Town	42	16	8	18	55	62	40
Witney Town	42	10	19	13	43	45	39
Bedworth United	42	12	15	15	40	42	39
Milton Keynes City	42	15	7	20	46	59	37
Gloucester City	42	10	14	18	55	68	32
Cheltenham Town	42	13	5	24	49	70	31
Wellingborough Town	42	9	7	26	54	106	25
Cambridge City	42	6	9	27	30	73	21
Corby Town	42	5	9	28	40	94	19

Southern Division

Dorchester Town	46	25	12	9	81	53	62
Aylesbury United	46	25	11	10	73	40	61
Dover	46	22	13	11	78	47	57
Gosport Borough	46	21	15	10	70	50	57
Dartford	46	21	14	11	66	45	56
Bognor Regis Town	46	20	15	11	66	38	55
Hillingdon Borough	46	19	16	11	64	41	54
Dunstable	46	17	19	10	93	64	53
Addlestone	46	20	13	13	72	57	53
Hastings United	46	19	15	12	74	65	53
Fareham Town	46	16	16	14	61	53	48
Waterlooville	46	17	12	17	67	64	46
Andover	46	16	13	17	65	65	45
Poole Town	46	16	13	17	49	64	45
Canterbury City	46	15	15	17	56	60	44
Hounslow	46	14	14	17	44	57	43
Margate	46	17	8	21	51	62	42
Folkestone & Shepway	46	14	11	21	54	63	39
Ashford Town	46	12	14	20	54	71	38
Crawley Town	46	13	11	22	55	72	37
Chelmsford City	46	9	18	19	47	69	36
Basingstoke Town	46	9	15	22	48	79	33
Salisbury	46	10	12	24	47	59	32
Tonbridge AFC	46	3	9	34	30	128	15

1980-81

Midland Division

Alvechurch	42	26	9	7	76	40	61
Bedford Town	42	25	11	6	63	32	61
Trowbridge Town	42	24	9	9	69	39	57
Kidderminster Harriers	42	23	9	10	67	41	55
Barry Town	42	21	9	12	60	40	51
Stourbridge	42	17	16	9	75	49	50
Enderby Town	42	21	8	13	71	47	50
Cheltenham Town	42	18	12	12	70	59	48
Bromsgrove Rovers	42	19	9	14	65	50	47
Corby Town	42	19	7	16	69	58	45
Bridgend Town	42	19	7	16	74	64	45
Minehead	42	19	7	16	54	60	45
Gloucester City	42	19	6	17	82	72	44
Merthyr Tydfil	42	15	12	15	60	50	42
Bedworth United	42	14	12	16	49	46	40
Banbury United	42	11	11	20	51	65	33
Taunton Town	42	10	9	23	48	68	29
Cambridge City	42	8	12	22	46	87	28
Witney Town	42	9	9	24	44	65	27
Wellingborough Town	42	10	7	25	43	91	27
Redditch United	42	11	4	27	54	92	26
Milton Keynes City	42	3	7	32	28	103	13

Southern Division

Dartford	46	26	14	6	76	39	66
Bognor Regis Town	46	25	13	8	95	43	63
Hastings United	46	24	14	8	87	43	62
Gosport Borough	46	24	12	10	84	52	60
Waterlooville	46	19	21	6	67	50	59
Dorchester Town	46	21	13	12	84	56	55
Dover	46	22	10	14	70	50	54
Poole Town	46	19	14	13	70	56	52
Addlestone & Weybridge	46	21	9	16	66	57	51
Dunstable	46	19	13	14	73	68	51
Aylesbury United	46	20	10	16	66	60	50
Hounslow	46	17	13	16	65	55	47
Hillingdon Borough	46	16	15	15	50	49	47
Basingstoke Town	46	16	14	16	69	58	46
Crawley Town	46	18	4	24	64	78	40
Ashford Town	46	12	15	19	55	76	39
Tonbridge AFC	46	12	15	19	44	68	39
Chelmsford City	46	13	12	21	54	78	38
Canterbury City	46	12	13	21	40	59	37
Salisbury	46	14	8	24	57	76	36
Folkestone	46	11	11	24	47	65	33
Margate	46	11	7	28	65	117	29
Fareham Town	46	5	18	23	31	73	28
Andover	46	6	10	30	41	94	22

1981-82

Midland Division

Nuneaton Borough	42	27	11	4	88	32	65
Alvechurch	42	26	10	6	79	34	62
Kidderminster Harriers	42	22	12	8	71	40	56
Stourbridge	42	21	10	11	69	47	52
Gloucester City	42	21	9	12	64	48	51
Bedworth United	42	20	10	12	59	40	50
Enderby Town	42	20	10	12	79	66	50
Witney Town	42	19	8	15	71	49	46
Barry Town	42	16	14	12	59	46	46
Corby Town	42	19	8	15	70	59	46
Merthyr Tydfil	42	16	12	14	63	54	44
Wellingborough Town	42	15	12	15	50	45	42
Bridgend Town	42	13	13	16	50	62	39
Bromsgrove Rovers	42	15	8	19	57	63	38
Bedford Town	42	12	13	17	45	54	37
Cheltenham Town	42	11	14	17	65	68	36
Taunton Town	42	12	8	22	46	76	32
Banbury United	42	11	8	23	63	91	30
Minehead	42	12	6	24	38	69	30
Cambridge City	42	10	8	24	38	80	28
Milton Keynes City	42	6	11	25	34	70	23
Redditch United	42	8	5	29	37	103	21

Southern Division

Wealdstone	46	32	8	6	100	32	72
Hastings United	46	31	9	6	79	34	71
Dorchester Town	46	21	18	7	76	41	60
Gosport Borough	46	26	8	12	76	45	60
Fareham Town	46	20	14	12	58	48	54
Poole Town	46	19	15	12	92	63	53
Waterlooville	46	22	9	15	75	53	53
Welling United	46	19	13	14	70	48	51
Addlestone & Weybridge	46	17	17	12	71	53	51
Chelmsford City	46	20	11	15	64	53	51
Aylesbury United	46	19	12	15	79	61	50
Basingstoke Town	46	18	12	16	75	61	48
Dover	46	19	8	19	61	63	46
Ashford Town	46	14	14	16	52	56	46
Tonbridge AFC	46	19	7	20	62	70	45
Dunstable	46	18	8	20	63	68	44
Salisbury	46	16	10	20	64	81	42
Hounslow	46	15	11	20	59	83	41
Hillingdon Borough	46	14	10	22	46	58	38
Canterbury City	46	10	16	20	49	78	36
Crawley Town	46	9	12	25	46	81	30
Folkestone	46	10	6	30	49	101	26
Andover	46	4	11	31	39	100	19
Thanet United	46	5	7	34	37	110	17

1982-83

Premier Division

AP Leamington	38	25	4	9	78	50	79
Kidderminster Harriers	38	23	7	8	69	40	76
Welling United	38	21	6	11	63	40	69
Chelmsford City	38	16	11	11	57	40	59
Bedworth United	38	16	11	11	47	39	59
Dartford	38	16	8	14	48	38	56
Gosport Borough	38	14	13	11	47	43	55
Fareham Town	38	16	7	15	73	82	55
Dorchester Town	38	14	12	12	52	50	54
Gravesend & Northfleet	38	14	12	12	49	50	54
Gloucester City	38	13	12	13	61	57	51
Witney Town	38	12	13	13	60	48	47
Alvechurch	38	13	8	17	60	66	47
Stourbridge	38	12	11	15	48	54	47
Corby Town	38	12	11	15	58	67	47
Hastings United	38	11	11	16	48	61	44
Enderby Town	38	11	9	18	44	62	42
Waterlooville	38	10	9	19	62	83	39
Poole Town	39	9	9	20	57	73	36
Addlestone & Weybridge	38	5	10	23	24	62	25

Midland Division

Cheltenham Town	32	22	5	5	65	29	71
Sutton Coldfield Town	32	21	7	4	62	24	70
Forest Green Rovers	32	21	3	8	68	32	66
Merthyr Tydfil	32	17	7	8	64	45	58
Willenhall Town	32	17	6	9	74	49	57
Oldbury United	32	16	6	10	52	49	54
Banbury United	32	15	3	14	59	55	48
Bridgend Town	32	12	11	9	46	37	47
Wellingborough Town	32	13	7	12	49	37	46
Bromsgrove Rovers	32	13	5	14	47	47	44
Dudley Town	32	12	7	13	40	45	43
Bridgwater Town	32	12	6	14	42	43	42
Aylesbury United	32	12	5	15	37	51	41
Redditch United	32	8	6	18	51	73	30
Taunton Town	32	5	7	20	30	64	22
Minehead	32	5	7	20	24	62	22
Milton Keynes City	32	0	4	28	22	90	4

Southern Division

Fisher Athletic	34	23	5	6	79	34	74
Folkestone	34	22	6	6	79	41	72
RS Southampton	34	21	7	6	66	30	70
Dunstable	34	19	5	10	57	39	62
Hillingdon Borough	34	14	11	9	41	30	53
Salisbury	34	14	10	10	59	49	52
Crawley Town	34	14	9	11	51	43	51
Ashford Town	34	13	10	11	51	41	49
Tonbridge AFC	34	14	5	15	57	57	47
Hounslow	34	11	12	11	46	47	45
Canterbury City	34	12	9	13	52	63	45
Cambridge City	34	12	5	17	56	63	41
Dover	34	11	7	16	35	52	40
Thanet United	34	10	5	19	30	61	35
Basingstoke Town	34	8	10	16	37	56	34
Woodford Town	34	6	9	19	29	57	27
Andover	34	6	8	20	28	53	26
Erith & Belvedere	34	5	9	20	26	62	24

1983-84

Premier Division

Dartford	38	23	9	6	67	32	78
Fisher Athletic	38	22	9	7	80	42	75
Chelmsford City	38	19	9	10	67	45	66
Gravesend & Northfleet	38	18	9	11	50	38	63
Witney Town	38	18	6	14	75	50	60
King's Lynn	38	18	6	14	42	45	60
Folkestone	38	16	9	13	60	56	57
Cheltenham Town	38	16	7	15	63	56	55
Gloucester City	38	13	15	10	55	50	54
Hastings United	38	15	9	14	55	57	54
Bedworth United	38	15	9	14	51	55	54
Welling United	38	15	7	16	61	61	52
AP Leamington	38	14	9	15	73	83	51
Corby Town	38	12	14	12	55	54	50
Fareham Town	38	13	11	14	65	70	50
Alvechurch	38	12	12	14	56	62	48
Sutton Coldfield Town	38	10	14	14	49	53	44
Gosport Borough	38	6	15	17	31	64	33
Dorchester Town	38	4	8	26	40	69	20
Stourbridge	38	4	7	27	30	82	19

Midland Division

Willenhall Town	38	27	4	7	100	44	85
Shepshed Charterhouse	38	25	5	8	88	37	80
Bromsgrove Rovers	38	20	8	10	73	43	68
Dudley Town	38	18	13	7	71	43	67
Aylesbury United	38	17	15	6	62	35	66
Moor Green	38	18	12	8	63	44	66
Rushden Town	38	17	12	9	68	42	63
Merthyr Tydfil	38	18	8	12	63	44	62
Redditch United	38	17	9	12	67	67	60
VS Rugby	38	15	12	11	68	51	57
Forest Green Rovers	38	15	12	11	67	51	57
Bridgnorth Town	38	16	9	13	64	52	57
Leicester United	38	12	9	17	58	58	45
Oldbury United	38	10	13	15	53	51	43
Coventry Sporting	38	11	7	20	40	67	40
Bridgwater Town	38	10	8	20	39	65	38
Wellingborough Town	38	7	9	22	43	80	30
Banbury United	38	6	11	21	37	78	29
Milton Keynes City	38	3	9	26	31	110	18
Tamworth	38	2	7	29	25	118	13

Southern Division

RS Southampton	38	26	6	6	83	35	84
Crawley Town	38	22	9	7	68	28	75
Basingstoke Town	38	20	9	9	54	36	69
Tonbridge AFC	38	20	9	9	61	44	69
Addlestone & Weybridge	38	19	11	8	58	34	68
Poole Town	38	20	7	11	68	42	67
Hillingdon Borough	38	18	11	9	43	20	65
Ashford Town	38	19	5	14	65	47	62
Salisbury	38	17	8	13	61	48	59
Cambridge City	38	13	9	16	43	53	48
Canterbury City	38	12	9	17	44	52	45
Waterlooville	38	12	9	17	56	69	45
Dover Athletic	38	12	9	17	51	74	45
Chatham Town	38	11	10	17	46	56	43
Andover	38	12	6	20	35	54	42
Erith & Belvedere	38	11	9	18	43	68	42
Dunstable	38	10	8	20	38	65	38
Thanet United	38	9	8	21	40	65	35
Woodford Town	38	7	8	23	30	69	29
Hounslow	38	4	12	22	30	58	24

1984-85

Premier Division

Cheltenham Town	38	24	5	9	83	41	77
King's Lynn	38	23	6	9	73	48	75
Crawley Town	38	22	8	8	76	52	74
Willenhall Town	38	20	8	10	57	38	68
RS Southampton	38	21	4	13	76	52	67
Welling United	38	18	11	9	55	38	65
Folkestone	38	19	6	13	70	54	63
Fisher Athletic	38	19	5	14	67	57	62
Chelmsford City	38	17	10	11	52	50	61
Shepshed Charterhouse	38	18	5	15	67	50	59
Corby Town	38	15	6	17	56	54	51
Bedworth United	38	14	8	16	48	52	50
Gravesend & Northfleet	38	12	12	14	46	46	48
Fareham Town	38	13	8	17	52	55	47
Alvechurch	38	11	7	20	53	59	40
Hastings United	38	11	7	20	46	71	40
Witney Town	38	9	12	17	51	58	39
Gloucester City	38	10	6	22	49	74	36
Trowbridge	38	10	5	23	45	83	35
AP Leamington	38	2	5	31	22	112	11

Midland Division

Dudley Town	34	21	8	5	70	36	71
Aylesbury United	34	20	7	7	62	30	67
Hednesford Town	34	18	7	9	58	42	61
Moor Green	34	17	9	8	63	43	60
VS Rugby	34	17	9	8	59	41	60
Bromsgrove Rovers	34	16	10	8	53	42	58
Stourbridge	34	15	11	8	52	45	56
Redditch United	34	12	11	11	68	57	47
Sutton Coldfield Town	34	13	6	15	50	56	45
Bridgnorth Town	34	13	5	16	67	65	44
Coventry Sporting	34	11	9	14	45	52	42
Merthyr Tydfil	34	10	11	13	43	46	41
Rushden Town	34	10	7	17	42	52	37
Forest Green Rovers	34	9	10	15	49	65	37
Wellingborough Town	34	10	7	17	39	63	37
Oldbury United	34	10	6	18	52	66	36
Banbury United	34	9	5	20	33	59	32
Leicester United	34	3	6	25	17	62	15

Southern Division

Basingstoke Town	38	24	9	5	61	22	81
Gosport Borough	38	22	6	10	78	41	72
Poole Town	38	20	12	6	69	38	72
Hillingdon	38	19	10	9	51	23	67
Thanet United	38	19	9	10	63	47	66
Salisbury	38	19	5	14	55	54	62
Sheppey United	38	18	6	14	49	45	60
Addlestone & Weybridge	38	16	9	13	68	54	57
Waterlooville	38	15	10	13	71	63	55
Canterbury City	38	15	7	16	61	64	52
Woodford Town	38	13	13	12	46	53	52
Tonbridge AFC	38	16	3	19	59	62	51
Andover	38	15	5	18	42	54	50
Dorchester Town	38	13	7	18	45	60	46
Cambridge City	38	11	11	16	59	71	44
Chatham Town	38	12	8	18	44	66	44
Ashford Town	38	10	9	19	54	69	69
Dunstable	38	8	10	20	35	56	64
Dover Athletic	38	7	7	24	39	78	28
Erith & Belvedere	38	6	8	24	36	65	26

1985-86

Premier Division

Team	P	W	D	L	F	A	Pts
Welling United	38	29	6	3	95	31	93
Chelmsford City	38	20	10	8	68	41	70
Fisher Athletic	38	20	7	11	67	45	67
Alvechurch	38	19	9	10	71	56	66
Worcester City	38	19	9	10	64	50	66
Crawley Town	38	18	5	15	76	59	59
Shepshed Charterhouse	38	19	1	18	51	52	58
Aylesbury United	38	14	10	14	52	49	52
Folkestone	38	14	10	14	56	56	52
Bedworth United	38	14	8	16	44	49	50
Willenhall Town	38	12	13	13	51	44	49
Dudley Town	38	15	4	19	58	62	49
Corby Town	38	14	7	17	61	67	49
King's Lynn	38	12	10	16	39	42	46
Basingstoke Town	38	13	4	21	36	67	43
RS Southampton	38	11	9	18	44	61	42
Witney Town	38	11	6	21	44	74	39
Gosport Borough	38	10	8	20	42	66	38
Fareham Town	38	8	13	17	40	62	37
Gravesend & Northfleet	38	9	9	20	29	55	36

Midland Division

Team	P	W	D	L	F	A	Pts
Bromsgrove Rovers	40	29	5	6	95	44	92
Redditch United	40	23	6	11	70	42	75
Merthyr Tydfil	40	21	10	9	60	40	73
VS Rugby	40	17	14	9	41	31	65
Stourbridge	40	15	14	11	62	49	59
Rusden Town	40	17	7	16	69	74	58
Bilston Town	40	15	12	13	60	48	57
Bridgnorth Town	40	13	18	9	56	45	57
Gloucester City	40	15	12	13	61	57	57
Grantham	40	16	7	17	46	59	55
Wellingborough Town	40	15	9	16	56	56	54
Sutton Coldfield Town	40	13	14	13	60	45	53
Hednesford Town	40	14	9	17	67	70	51
Forest Green Rovers	40	14	9	17	52	56	51
Mile Oak Rovers	40	14	8	18	56	73	50
Leicester United	40	13	10	17	41	48	49
Banbury United	40	13	8	19	38	55	47
Coventry Sporting	40	10	15	15	42	48	45
Moor Green	40	12	6	22	63	91	42
Leamington	40	10	6	24	40	77	36
Oldbury United	40	8	7	25	50	87	31

Southern Division

Team	P	W	D	L	F	A	Pts
Cambridge City	40	23	11	6	87	41	80
Salisbury	40	24	8	8	84	51	80
Hastings Town	40	23	9	8	83	51	78
Dover Athletic	40	23	6	11	89	53	75
Corinthian	40	20	9	11	79	45	69
Tonbridge AFC	40	17	13	10	65	51	64
Dunstable	40	17	11	12	70	61	62
Ruislip	40	17	6	17	67	66	57
Erith & Belvedere	40	14	12	14	35	40	54
Waterlooville	40	16	6	18	52	58	54
Burnham & Hillingdon	40	16	6	18	44	59	54
Canterbury City	40	13	13	14	58	58	52
Trowbridge Town	40	13	13	14	57	63	52
Sheppey United	40	14	10	16	43	53	52
Thanet United	40	13	7	20	58	63	46
Woodford Town	40	12	10	18	49	62	46
Poole Town	40	12	7	21	55	63	43
Ashford Town	40	10	12	18	45	65	42
Chatham Town	40	8	15	17	53	70	39
Andover	40	10	8	22	52	92	38
Dorchester Town	40	5	8	27	35	94	23

1986-87

Premier Division

Team	P	W	D	L	F	A	Pts
Fisher Athletic	42	25	11	6	72	29	86
Bromsgrove Rovers	42	24	11	7	82	41	83
Aylesbury United	42	24	11	7	72	40	83
Dartford	42	19	12	11	76	43	69
Chelmsford City	42	17	13	12	48	45	64
Cambridge City	42	14	20	8	68	52	62
Redditch United	42	16	14	12	59	54	62
Alvechurch	42	18	8	16	66	62	62
Corby Town	42	14	17	11	65	51	59
Worcester City	42	16	11	15	62	55	59
Shepshed Charterhouse	42	16	10	16	59	59	58
Bedworth United	42	15	12	15	55	51	57
Crawley Town	42	14	11	17	59	60	53
Fareham Town	42	11	17	14	58	49	50
Willenhall Town	42	13	11	18	48	57	50
Basingstoke Town	42	12	12	18	53	78	48
Witney Town	42	12	12	18	29	56	48
Gosport Borough	42	11	13	18	42	57	46
Salisbury	42	12	7	23	52	82	43
King's Lynn	42	9	13	20	48	72	40
Dudley Town	42	9	9	24	39	76	36
Folkestone	42	8	11	23	36	79	35

Midland Division

Team	P	W	D	L	F	A	Pts
VS Rugby	38	25	5	8	81	43	80
Leicester United	38	26	1	11	89	49	79
Merthyr Tydfil	38	23	6	9	95	54	75
Moor Green	38	22	6	10	73	55	72
Halesowen Town	38	19	12	7	72	50	69
Hednesford Town	38	21	5	12	84	56	68
Gloucester City	38	19	5	14	77	59	62
Coventry Sporting	38	17	8	13	55	54	59
Forest Green Rovers	38	16	9	13	65	53	57
Stourbridge	38	16	7	15	56	56	55
Grantham	38	15	9	14	74	54	54
Banbury United	38	14	7	17	55	65	49
Buckingham Town	38	13	9	16	55	59	48
Bridgnorth Town	38	12	9	17	59	63	45
Wellingborough Town	38	13	6	19	55	76	45
Mile Oak Rovers	38	11	10	17	50	63	43
Sutton Coldfield Town	38	8	10	20	56	78	34
Bilston Town	38	8	7	23	37	76	31
Leamington	38	4	13	21	37	80	25
Rushden Town	38	1	10	27	42	124	13

Southern Division

Team	P	W	D	L	F	A	Pts
Dorchester Town	38	23	8	7	83	42	77
Ashford Town	38	23	7	8	63	32	76
Woodford Town	38	22	6	10	72	44	72
Hastings Town	38	20	10	8	74	54	70
Dover Athletic	38	20	6	12	66	43	66
Gravesend & Northfleet	38	18	7	13	67	46	61
Tonbridge AFC	38	16	10	12	73	67	58
Erith & Belvedere	38	15	12	11	57	50	57
Chatham Town	38	16	9	13	53	46	57
Thanet United	38	14	14	10	56	50	56
Waterlooville	38	16	8	14	66	65	56
Trowbridge Town	38	15	9	14	77	65	54
Dunstable	38	13	9	16	60	57	48
Corinthian	38	11	12	15	56	65	45
Sheppey United	38	9	12	17	43	65	39
Andover	38	9	9	20	51	80	36
Burnham & Hillingdon	38	7	11	20	32	62	32
Poole Town	38	8	6	24	50	90	30
Ruislip	38	6	12	20	35	75	30
Canterbury City	38	8	5	25	46	82	29

1987-88

Premier Division

Aylesbury United	42	27	8	7	79	35	89
Dartford	42	27	8	7	79	39	89
Cambridge City	42	24	8	10	84	43	80
Bromsgrove Rovers	42	22	11	9	65	39	77
Worcester City	42	22	6	14	58	48	72
Crawley Town	42	17	14	11	73	63	65
Alvechurch	42	17	13	12	54	52	64
Leicester United	42	15	14	13	68	59	59
Fareham Town	42	16	11	15	51	59	59
Corby Town	42	16	8	18	61	64	56
Dorchester Town	42	14	14	14	51	57	56
Ashford Town	42	12	16	14	45	54	52
Shepshed Charterhouse	42	13	11	18	53	62	50
Bedworth United	42	12	14	16	49	64	50
Gosport Borough	42	10	17	15	39	49	47
Burton Albion	42	11	14	17	62	74	47
VS Rugby	42	10	16	16	52	57	46
Redditch United	42	10	13	19	55	63	43
Chelmsford City	42	11	10	21	60	75	43
Willenhall Town	42	9	12	21	39	76	39
Nuneaton Borough	42	8	13	21	58	77	37
Witney Town	42	8	11	23	45	71	35

Midland Division

Merthyr Tydfil	42	30	4	8	102	40	94
Moor Green	42	26	8	8	91	49	86
Grantham Town	42	27	4	11	97	53	85
Atherstone United	42	22	10	10	93	56	76
Sutton Coldfield Town	42	22	6	14	71	47	72
Halesowen Town	42	18	15	9	75	59	69
Gloucester City	42	18	14	10	86	62	68
Dudley Town	42	20	5	17	64	55	65
Forest Green Rovers	42	14	16	12	67	54	58
Banbury United	42	17	7	18	48	46	58
Bridgnorth Town	42	16	7	19	59	75	55
Buckingham Town	42	15	9	18	74	75	54
King's Lynn	42	16	6	20	53	63	54
Wellingborough Town	42	14	10	18	67	70	52
Rushden Town	42	14	9	19	69	85	51
Trowbridge Town	42	14	3	25	53	82	45
Bilston Town	42	12	8	22	52	87	44
Hednesford Town	42	11	10	21	50	81	43
Mile Oak Rovers	42	9	14	19	43	65	41
Coventry Sporting	42	11	8	23	46	83	41
Stourbridge	42	10	10	22	46	79	40
Paget Rangers	42	10	9	23	49	89	39

Southern Division

Dover Athletic	40	28	10	2	81	28	94
Waterlooville	40	27	10	3	88	33	91
Salisbury	40	24	11	5	71	33	83
Gravesend & Northfleet	40	20	12	8	60	32	72
Thanet United	40	17	13	10	60	38	64
Andover	40	17	13	10	64	58	64
Dunstable	40	17	12	11	78	56	63
Burnham	40	17	10	13	61	45	61
Bury Town	40	17	7	16	80	67	58
Erith & Belvedere	40	16	9	15	52	56	57
Sheppey United	40	14	10	16	58	52	52
Hastings Town	40	14	10	16	62	70	52
Tonbridge AFC	40	14	8	18	51	56	50
Poole Town	40	13	10	17	69	70	49
Baldock Town	40	12	12	16	44	53	48
Hounslow	40	11	8	21	41	76	41
Folkestone	40	9	11	20	47	76	38
Corinthian	40	9	10	21	49	67	37
Ruislip	40	5	13	22	33	80	28
Canterbury City	40	7	6	27	33	87	27
Chatham Town	40	7	5	28	39	88	26

1988-89

Premier Division

Merthyr Tydfil	42	26	7	9	104	58	85
Dartford	42	25	7	10	79	33	82
VS Rugby	42	24	7	11	64	43	79
Worcester City	42	20	13	9	72	49	73
Cambridge City	42	20	10	12	72	51	70
Dover Athletic	42	19	12	11	65	47	69
Gosport Borough	42	18	12	12	73	57	66
Burton Albion	42	18	10	14	79	68	64
Bath City	42	15	13	14	66	51	59
Bromsgrove Rovers	42	14	16	12	68	56	59
Wealdstone	42	16	10	16	60	53	59
Crawley Town	42	14	16	12	61	56	59
Dorchester Town	42	14	16	12	56	61	59
Alvechurch	42	16	8	18	56	59	56
Moor Green	42	14	13	15	58	70	55
Corby Town	42	14	11	17	55	59	53
Waterlooville	42	13	13	16	61	63	52
Ashford Town	42	13	13	16	59	76	52
Fareham Town	42	15	6	21	43	68	51
Leicester United	42	6	11	25	46	84	29
Redditch United	42	5	7	30	36	105	22
Bedworth United	42	4	7	31	36	102	19

Midland Division

Gloucester City	42	28	8	6	95	37	92
Atherstone United	42	26	9	7	85	38	87
Tamworth	42	26	9	7	85	45	87
Halesowen Town	42	25	10	7	85	42	85
Grantham Town	42	23	11	8	66	37	80
Nuneaton Borough	42	19	9	14	71	58	66
Rushden Town	42	19	8	15	71	50	65
Spalding United	42	17	13	12	72	64	64
Dudley Town	42	16	13	13	73	62	61
Sutton Coldfield Town	42	18	7	17	56	56	61
Willenhall Town	42	16	12	14	65	71	60
Forest Green Rovers	42	12	16	14	64	67	52
Bilston Town	42	15	7	20	63	71	52
Ashtree Highfield	42	12	15	15	57	62	51
Hednesford Town	42	12	15	15	49	57	51
Banbury United	42	10	14	18	53	74	44
Bridgnorth Town	42	12	7	23	59	77	43
Stourbridge	41	11	10	21	37	65	43
King's Lynn	42	7	13	22	31	67	34
Coventry Sporting	42	6	13	23	39	91	31
Wellingborough Town	42	5	15	22	39	72	30
Mile Oak Rovers	42	5	10	27	46	98	25

Southern Division

Chelmsford City	42	30	5	7	106	38	95
Gravesend & Northfleet	42	27	6	9	70	40	87
Poole Town	42	24	11	7	98	48	83
Bury Town	42	25	7	10	75	34	82
Burnham	42	22	13	7	78	47	79
Baldock Town	42	23	5	14	69	40	74
Hastings Town	42	21	11	10	75	48	74
Hounslow	42	21	6	15	75	60	69
Salisbury	42	20	5	17	79	58	65
Trowbridge Town	42	19	7	16	59	52	64
Folkestone	42	17	8	17	62	65	59
Corinthian	42	13	13	16	59	69	52
Canterbury City	42	14	8	20	52	60	50
Witney Town	42	13	11	18	61	71	50
Dunstable	42	11	14	17	42	57	47
Buckingham Town	42	12	10	20	56	79	46
Erith & Belvedere	42	11	10	21	48	63	43
Andover	42	11	9	22	56	90	42
Sheppey United	42	10	8	24	50	90	38
Thanet United	42	7	15	20	47	95	36
Tonbridge AFC	42	7	6	29	50	98	27
Ruislip	42	6	8	28	47	112	26

1989-90

Premier Division

Dover Athletic	42	32	6	4	87	27	102
Bath City	42	30	8	4	81	28	98
Dartford	42	26	9	7	80	35	87
Burton Albion	42	20	12	10	64	40	72
VS Rugby	42	19	12	11	51	35	69
Atherstone United	42	19	10	13	60	52	67
Gravesend & Northfleet	42	18	12	12	44	50	66
Cambridge City	42	17	11	14	76	56	62
Gloucester City	42	17	11	14	80	68	62
Bromsgrove Rovers	42	17	10	15	56	48	61
Moor Green	42	18	7	17	62	59	61
Wealdstone	42	16	9	17	55	54	57
Dorchester Town	42	16	7	19	52	67	55
Worcester City	42	15	10	17	62	63	54
Crawley Town	42	13	12	17	53	57	51
Waterlooville	42	13	10	19	63	81	49
Weymouth	42	11	13	18	50	70	46
Chelmsford City	42	11	10	21	52	72	43
Ashford Town	42	10	7	25	43	75	37
Corby Town	42	10	6	26	57	77	36
Alvechurch	42	7	5	30	46	95	26
Gosport Borough	42	6	5	31	28	93	23

Midland Division

Halesowen Town	42	28	8	6	100	49	92
Rushden Town	42	28	5	9	82	39	89
Nuneaton Borough	42	26	7	9	81	47	85
Tamworth	42	22	8	12	82	70	74
Barry Town	42	21	8	13	67	53	71
Spalding United	42	20	7	15	73	63	67
Sutton Coldfield Town	42	18	10	14	72	69	64
Stourbridge	42	17	12	13	73	61	63
Dudley Town	42	18	9	15	69	64	63
Stroud	42	16	13	13	75	62	61
Leicester United	42	17	5	20	66	77	56
Bridgnorth Town	42	13	14	15	68	73	53
King's Lynn	42	16	5	21	57	69	53
Grantham Town	42	14	10	18	57	63	52
Bedworth United	42	14	9	19	50	60	51
Hednesford Town	42	11	14	17	50	62	47
Bilston Town	42	11	14	17	40	54	47
Redditch United	42	11	13	18	57	64	46
Racing Club Warwick	42	11	11	20	45	66	44
Willenhall Town	42	9	9	24	37	66	36
Banbury United	42	9	9	24	46	83	34
Sandwell Borough	42	6	12	24	46	79	30

Southern Division

Bashley	42	25	7	10	80	47	82
Poole Town	42	23	8	11	85	60	77
Buckingham Town	42	22	10	10	67	46	76
Dunstable	42	20	14	8	56	38	74
Salisbury	42	21	9	12	72	50	72
Hythe Town	42	20	12	10	69	48	72
Trowbridge Town	42	20	9	13	79	64	69
Hastings Town	42	20	9	13	64	54	69
Bury Town	42	18	12	12	76	62	66
Baldock Town	42	18	11	13	69	52	65
Burnham	42	17	11	14	77	52	62
Fareham Town	42	14	14	14	49	53	56
Yate Town	42	16	6	20	53	52	54
Witney Town	42	16	6	20	54	56	54
Canterbury City	42	14	10	18	52	52	52
Margate	42	12	15	15	46	45	51
Folkestone	42	14	9	19	61	83	51
Andover	42	13	11	18	54	70	50
Hounslow	42	11	5	26	39	82	38
Erith & Belvedere	42	8	11	23	34	73	35
Corinthian	42	6	10	26	44	93	28
Sheppey United	42	6	7	29	35	83	25

1990-91

Premier Division

Farnborough Town	42	26	7	9	79	43	85
Gloucester City	42	23	14	5	86	49	83
Cambridge City	42	21	14	7	63	43	77
Dover Athletic	42	21	11	10	56	37	74
Bromsgrove Rovers	42	20	11	11	68	49	71
Worcester City	42	18	12	12	55	42	66
Burton Albion	42	15	15	12	59	48	60
Halesowen Town	42	17	9	16	73	67	60
VS Rugby	42	16	11	15	56	46	59
Bashley	42	15	12	15	56	52	57
Dorchester Town	42	15	12	15	47	54	57
Wealdstone	42	16	8	18	57	58	56
Dartford	42	15	9	18	61	64	54
Rushden Town	42	14	11	17	64	66	53
Atherstone United	42	14	10	18	55	58	52
Moor Green	42	15	6	21	64	75	51
Poole Town	42	12	13	17	56	69	49
Chelmsford City	42	11	15	16	37	68	48
Crawley Town	42	12	12	18	45	67	48
Waterlooville	42	11	13	18	51	70	46
Gravesend & Northfleet	42	9	7	26	46	91	34
Weymouth	42	4	12	26	50	88	24

Midland Division

Stourbridge	42	28	6	8	80	48	90
Corby Town	42	27	4	11	99	48	85
Hednesford Town	42	25	7	10	79	47	82
Tamworth	42	25	5	12	84	45	80
Nuneaton Borough	42	21	11	10	74	51	70
Barry Town	42	20	7	15	61	48	67
Newport AFC	42	19	6	17	54	46	63
King's Lynn	42	17	9	16	53	62	60
Grantham Town	42	17	7	18	62	56	56
Redditch United	42	16	10	16	66	75	58
Hinckley Town	42	16	9	17	72	68	57
Sutton Coldfield Town	42	15	11	16	56	65	56
Bedworth United	42	15	9	18	57	73	54
Bilston Town	42	14	9	19	69	79	51
Leicester United	42	14	10	18	65	77	51
Racing Club Warwick	42	12	13	17	56	65	49
Bridgnorth Town	42	13	9	20	62	74	48
Stroud	42	11	14	17	51	64	47
Dudley Town	42	11	13	18	48	73	46
Alvechurch	42	10	8	24	54	92	38
Willenhall Town	42	10	10	22	58	69	37
Spalding United	42	8	9	25	35	70	33

Southern Division

Buckingham Town	40	25	8	7	73	38	83
Trowbridge Town	40	22	12	6	67	31	78
Salisbury	40	22	11	7	63	39	77
Baldock Town	40	21	9	10	66	52	72
Ashford Town	40	22	5	13	82	52	71
Yate Town	40	21	8	11	76	48	71
Hastings Town	40	18	11	11	66	46	65
Hythe Town	40	17	9	14	55	44	59
Andover	40	16	6	18	69	76	54
Margate	40	14	11	15	52	55	53
Burnham	40	12	16	12	57	49	52
Bury Town	40	15	5	20	58	74	50
Sudbury Town	40	13	10	17	60	68	49
Newport IOW	40	13	9	18	56	62	48
Gosport Borough	40	12	11	17	47	58	47
Witney Town	40	12	11	17	57	75	47
Dunstable	40	9	15	16	48	63	42
Canterbury City	40	12	6	22	60	83	42
Erith & Belvedere	40	10	0	24	46	73	36
Fareham Town	40	9	9	22	46	74	36
Corinthian	40	5	12	23	34	78	27

1991-92

Premier Division

Bromsgrove Rovers	42	27	9	6	78	34	90
Dover Athletic	42	23	15	4	66	30	84
VS Rugby	42	23	11	8	70	44	80
Bashley	42	22	8	12	70	44	74
Cambridge City	42	18	14	10	71	53	68
Dartford	42	17	15	10	62	45	66
Trowbridge Town	42	17	10	15	69	51	61
Halesowen Town	42	15	15	12	61	49	60
Moor Green	42	15	11	16	61	59	56
Burton Albion	42	15	10	17	59	61	55
Dorchester Town	42	14	13	15	66	73	55
Gloucester City	42	15	9	18	67	70	54
Atherstone United	42	15	8	19	54	66	53
Corby Town	42	13	12	17	66	81	51
Waterlooville	42	13	11	18	43	56	50
Worcester City	42	12	13	17	56	59	49
Crawley Town	42	12	12	18	62	67	48
Chelmsford City	42	12	12	18	49	56	48
Wealdstone	42	13	7	22	52	69	46
Poole Town	42	10	13	19	46	77	43
Fisher Athletic	42	9	11	22	53	89	38
Gravesend & Northfleet	42	8	9	25	39	87	33

Midland Division

Solihull Borough	42	29	10	3	92	40	97
Hednesford Town	42	26	13	3	81	37	91
Sutton Coldfield Town	42	21	11	10	71	51	74
Barry Town	42	21	6	15	88	56	69
Bedworth United	42	16	15	11	67	63	63
Nuneaton Borough	42	17	11	14	68	53	62
Tamworth	42	16	12	14	66	52	60
Rushden Town	42	16	12	14	69	63	60
Stourbridge	42	17	8	17	85	62	59
Newport AFC	42	15	13	14	72	60	58
Yate Town	42	14	15	13	65	64	57
Bilston Town	42	15	10	17	56	67	55
Grantham Town	42	11	17	14	59	55	50
King's Lynn	42	13	11	18	61	68	50
Hinckley Town	42	14	8	20	61	87	50
Leicester United	42	12	13	17	56	63	49
Bridgnorth Town	42	12	12	18	61	74	48
Racing Club Warwick	42	11	14	17	45	61	47
Stroud	42	14	4	24	66	88	46
Redditch United	42	12	8	22	52	92	44
Alvechurch	42	11	10	21	54	88	43
Dudley Town	42	8	9	25	41	92	33

Southern Division

Hastings Town	42	28	7	7	80	37	91
Weymouth	42	22	12	8	64	35	78
Havant Town	42	21	12	9	67	46	75
Braintree Town	42	21	8	13	77	58	71
Buckingham Town	42	19	15	8	57	26	69
Andover	42	18	10	14	73	68	64
Ashford Town	42	17	12	13	66	57	63
Sudbury Town	42	18	9	15	70	66	63
Sittingbourne	42	19	10	13	63	41	61
Burnham	42	15	14	13	57	55	59
Baldock Town	42	16	10	16	62	67	58
Salisbury	42	13	16	13	67	51	55
Hythe Town	42	15	10	17	61	62	55
Margate	42	13	16	13	49	56	55
Newport IOW	42	13	10	19	58	63	49
Dunstable	42	12	12	18	55	67	48
Bury Town	42	14	4	24	52	94	46
Witney Town	42	11	12	19	55	76	45
Fareham Town	42	12	8	22	45	71	44
Erith & Belvedere	42	11	10	21	44	67	43
Canterbury City	42	8	14	20	43	69	38
Gosport Borough	42	6	9	27	32	65	27

1992-93

Premier Division

Dover Athletic	40	25	11	4	65	23	86
Cheltenham Town	40	21	10	9	76	40	73
Corby Town	40	20	12	8	68	43	72
Hednesford Town	40	21	7	12	72	52	70
Trowbridge Town	40	18	8	14	70	66	62
Crawley Town	40	16	12	12	68	59	60
Solihull Borough	40	17	9	14	68	59	60
Burton Albion	40	16	11	13	53	50	59
Bashley	40	18	8	14	60	60	59
Halesowen Town	40	15	11	14	67	54	56
Waterlooville	40	15	9	16	59	62	54
Chelmsford City	40	15	9	16	59	69	54
Gloucester City	40	14	11	15	66	68	53
Cambridge City	40	14	10	16	62	73	52
Atherstone United	40	13	14	13	56	60	50
Hastings Town	40	13	11	16	50	55	50
Worcester City	40	12	9	19	45	62	45
Dorchester Town	40	12	6	22	52	74	42
Moor Green	40	10	6	24	58	79	36
VS Rugby	40	10	6	24	40	63	36
Weymouth	40	5	10	25	39	82	23

Bashley had 3 points deducted

Midland Division

Nuneaton Borough	42	29	5	8	102	45	92
Gresley Rovers	42	27	6	9	94	55	87
Rushden & Diamonds	42	25	10	7	85	41	85
Barri	42	26	5	11	82	49	83
Newport AFC	42	23	8	11	73	58	77
Bedworth United	42	22	8	12	72	55	74
Stourbridge	42	17	9	16	93	79	60
Sutton Coldfield Town	42	17	9	16	82	78	60
Redditch United	42	18	6	18	75	79	60
Tamworth	42	16	11	15	65	51	59
Weston-super-Mare	42	17	7	18	79	86	58
Leicester United	42	16	9	17	67	67	57
Grantham Town	42	16	9	17	60	73	57
Bilston Town	42	15	10	17	74	69	55
Evesham United	42	15	8	19	67	83	53
Bridgnorth Town	42	15	7	20	61	68	52
Dudley Town	42	14	8	20	60	75	50
Yate Town	42	14	5	22	63	81	50
Forest Green Rovers	42	12	6	24	61	97	42
Hinckley Athletic	42	9	11	22	56	89	37
King's Lynn	42	10	6	26	45	90	36
Racing Club Warwick	42	3	7	32	40	88	16

Southern Division

Sittingbourne	42	26	12	4	102	43	90
Salisbury	42	27	7	8	87	50	88
Witney Town	42	25	9	8	77	37	84
Gravesend & Northfleet	42	25	4	13	99	63	79
Havant Town	42	23	6	13	78	55	75
Sudbury Town	42	20	11	11	89	54	71
Erith & Belvedere	42	22	5	15	73	66	71
Ashford Town	42	20	8	14	91	66	68
Braintree Town	42	20	6	16	95	65	66
Margate	42	19	7	16	65	58	64
Wealdstone	42	18	7	17	75	69	61
Buckingham Town	42	16	11	15	61	58	59
Baldock Town	42	15	9	18	59	63	54
Poole Town	42	15	7	20	61	69	52
Fareham Town	42	14	8	20	67	65	50
Burnham	42	14	8	20	53	77	50
Canterbury City	42	12	10	20	54	76	46
Newport IOW	42	9	16	17	44	56	43
Fisher Athletic	42	8	9	25	38	98	33
Andover	42	7	9	26	42	99	30
Dunstable	42	5	14	23	42	92	29
Bury Town	42	8	5	29	46	119	29

1993-94

Premier Division

Farnborough Town	42	25	7	10	74	44	82
Cheltenham Town	42	21	12	9	67	38	75
Halesowen Town	42	21	11	10	69	46	74
Atherstone United	42	22	7	13	57	43	73
Crawley Town	42	21	10	11	56	42	73
Chelmsford City	42	21	7	14	74	59	70
Trowbridge Town	42	16	17	9	52	41	65
Sittingbourne	42	17	13	12	65	48	64
Corby Town	42	17	8	17	52	56	59
Gloucester City	42	17	6	19	55	60	57
Burton Albion	42	15	11	10	57	49	56
Hastings Town	42	16	7	19	51	60	55
Hednesford Town	42	15	9	18	67	66	54
Gresley Rovers	42	14	11	17	61	72	53
Worcester City	42	14	9	19	61	70	51
Solihull Borough	42	13	11	18	52	57	50
Cambridge City	42	13	11	18	50	60	50
Dorchester Town	42	12	11	19	38	51	47
Moor Green	42	11	10	21	49	66	43
Waterlooville	42	11	10	21	47	69	43
Bashley	42	11	10	21	47	80	43
Nuneaton Borough	42	11	8	23	42	66	41

Midland Division

Rushden & Diamonds	42	29	11	2	109	37	98
VS Rugby	42	28	8	6	98	41	92
Weston-super-Mare	42	27	10	5	94	39	91
Newport AFC	42	26	9	7	84	37	87
Clevedon Town	42	24	10	8	75	46	82
Redditch United	42	19	11	12	79	62	68
Tamworth	42	19	7	16	82	68	64
Bilston Town	42	16	10	16	65	73	58
Stourbridge	42	17	6	19	71	75	57
Evesham United	42	16	8	18	50	60	56
Grantham Town	42	16	6	20	77	73	54
Bridgnorth Town	42	15	6	21	56	68	51
Racing Club Warwick	42	13	12	17	53	66	51
Dudley Town	42	13	10	19	64	61	49
Forest Green Rangers	42	12	12	18	61	84	48
Sutton Coldfield Town	42	12	8	22	53	75	44
Bedworth United	42	12	7	23	62	81	43
Hinckley Town	42	11	10	21	44	71	43
Leicester United	42	11	9	22	34	73	42
King's Lynn	42	9	11	22	47	72	38
Yate Town	42	10	6	26	48	86	36
Armitage	42	8	11	23	45	103	35

Southern Division

Gravesend & Northfleet	42	27	11	4	87	24	92
Sudbury Town	42	27	8	7	98	47	89
Witney Town	42	27	8	7	69	36	89
Salisbury City	42	26	10	6	90	39	88
Havant Town	42	27	4	11	101	41	85
Ashford Town	42	24	13	5	93	46	85
Baldock Town	42	26	7	9	76	40	85
Newport IOW	42	22	8	12	74	51	74
Margate	42	20	8	14	76	58	68
Weymouth	42	18	9	15	71	65	63
Tonbridge	42	19	5	18	59	62	62
Buckingham Town	42	14	14	14	43	42	56
Braintree Town	42	16	7	19	72	84	55
Fareham Town	42	12	12	18	54	75	48
Poole Town	42	13	6	23	54	86	45
Burnham	42	10	9	23	53	92	39
Fisher 93	42	9	10	23	52	81	37
Dunstable	42	9	7	26	50	91	34
Erith & Belvedere	42	9	5	28	40	72	32
Canterbury City	42	8	7	27	35	80	31
Wealdstone	42	6	7	29	45	95	25
Bury Town	42	3	5	34	36	121	14

1994-95

Premier Division

Hednesford Town	42	28	9	5	99	49	93
Cheltenham Town	42	25	11	6	87	39	86
Burton Albion	42	20	15	7	55	39	75
Gloucester City	42	22	8	12	76	48	74
Rushden & Diamonds	42	19	11	12	99	65	68
Dorchester Town	42	19	10	13	84	61	67
Leek Town	42	19	10	13	72	60	67
Gresley Rovers	42	17	12	13	70	63	63
Cambridge City	42	18	8	16	60	55	62
Worcester City	42	14	15	13	46	34	57
Crawley Town	42	15	10	17	64	71	55
Hastings Town	42	13	14	15	55	57	53
Halesowen Town	42	14	10	18	81	80	52
Gravesend & Northfleet	42	16	13	16	38	55	52
Chelmsford City	42	14	6	22	56	60	48
Atherstone United	42	12	12	18	51	67	48
VS Rugby	42	11	14	17	49	61	47
Sudbury Town	42	12	10	20	50	77	46
Solihull Borough	42	10	15	17	39	65	45
Sittingbourne	42	11	10	21	51	73	43
Trowbridge Town	42	9	13	20	43	69	40
Corby Town	42	4	10	28	36	113	21

Corby Town had 1 point deducted for fielding ineligible players

Midland Division

Newport AFC	42	29	8	5	106	39	95
Ilkeston Town	42	25	6	11	101	75	81
Tamworth	42	24	8	10	98	70	80
Moor Green	42	23	8	11	105	63	77
Bridgnorth Town	42	22	10	10	75	49	76
Buckingham Town	42	20	14	8	55	37	74
Nuneaton Borough	42	19	11	12	76	55	68
Rothwell Town	42	19	7	16	71	71	64
King's Lynn	42	18	8	16	76	64	62
Racing Club Warwick	42	17	11	14	68	63	62
Dudley Town	42	17	10	15	65	69	61
Bilston Town	42	17	8	17	73	64	59
Bedworth United	42	17	7	18	64	68	58
Evesham United	42	14	10	18	57	56	52
Hinckley Town	42	14	0	18	61	76	52
Stourbridge	42	15	7	20	59	77	52
Sutton Coldfield Town	42	12	10	20	62	72	46
Forest Green Rovers	42	11	13	18	56	76	46
Redditch United	42	8	14	20	47	64	38
Leicester United	42	10	8	24	51	99	38
Grantham Town	42	8	9	25	55	93	33
Armitage	42	2	5	35	35	116	11

Southern Division

Salisbury City	42	30	7	5	88	37	97
Baldock Town	42	28	10	4	92	44	94
Havant Town	42	25	10	7	81	34	85
Waterlooville	42	24	8	10	77	36	80
Ashford Town	42	21	12	9	106	72	75
Weston-super-Mare	42	18	13	11	82	54	67
Bashley	42	18	11	13	62	49	65
Weymouth	42	16	13	13	60	55	61
Newport IOW	42	17	10	15	67	67	61
Witney Town	42	14	14	14	57	57	56
Clevedon Town	42	14	13	15	73	64	55
Tonbridge Angels	42	14	12	16	74	87	54
Margate	42	15	7	20	60	72	52
Braintree Town	42	12	13	17	64	71	49
Wealdstone	42	13	8	21	76	94	47
Yate Town	42	11	13	18	57	75	46
Fisher 93	42	9	16	17	54	70	43
Bury Town	42	11	8	23	59	86	41
Erith & Belvedere	42	10	9	23	49	94	39
Poole Town	42	10	8	24	53	79	38
Fareham Town	42	10	8	24	46	91	38
Burnham	42	7	7	28	40	89	28

1995-96

Premier Division

Team	P	W	D	L	F	A	Pts
Rushden & Diamonds	42	29	7	6	99	41	94
Halesowen Town	42	27	11	4	70	36	92
Cheltenham Town	42	21	11	10	76	57	74
Gloucester City	42	21	8	13	65	47	71
Gresley Rovers	42	20	10	12	70	58	70
Worcester City	42	19	12	11	61	43	69
Merthyr Tydfil	42	19	6	17	67	59	63
Hastings Town	42	16	13	13	68	56	61
Crawley Town	42	15	13	14	57	56	58
Sudbury Town	42	15	10	17	69	71	55
Gravesend & Northfleet	42	15	10	17	60	62	55
Chelmsford City	42	13	16	13	46	53	55
Dorchester Town	42	15	8	19	62	57	53
Newport AFC	42	13	13	16	53	59	52
Salisbury City	42	14	10	18	57	69	52
Burton Albion	42	13	12	17	55	56	51
Atherstone United	42	12	12	18	58	75	48
Baldock Town	42	11	14	17	51	56	47
Cambridge City	42	12	10	20	56	68	46
Ilkeston Town	42	11	10	21	53	87	43
Stafford Rangers	42	11	4	27	58	90	37
VS Rugby	42	5	10	27	37	92	25

Midland Division

Team	P	W	D	L	F	A	Pts
Nuneaton Borough	42	30	5	7	82	35	95
King's Lynn	42	27	5	10	85	43	84
Bedworth United	42	24	10	8	76	42	81
Moor Green	42	22	8	12	81	47	74
Paget Rangers	42	21	9	12	70	45	72
Tamworth	42	22	3	17	97	64	69
Solihull Borough	42	19	9	14	77	64	66
Rothwell Town	42	17	14	11	79	62	65
Buckingham Town	42	18	9	15	74	62	63
Dudley Town	42	15	16	11	83	66	61
Stourbridge	42	17	8	17	60	63	59
Bilston Town	42	16	9	17	61	62	57
Sutton Coldfield Town	42	16	9	17	62	67	57
Grantham Town	42	17	5	20	71	83	56
Redditch United	42	14	11	17	57	77	53
Leicester United	42	13	13	16	58	72	52
Hinckley Town	42	14	7	21	62	83	49
Racing Club Warwick	42	10	13	19	67	90	43
Evesham United	42	11	6	25	59	94	39
Corby Town	42	9	7	26	52	95	34
Bury Town	42	8	8	26	57	95	32
Bridgnorth Town	42	7	6	29	53	112	27

Bedworth United 1 point deducted, King's Lynn had 2 points deducted

Southern Division

Team	P	W	D	L	F	A	Pts
Sittingbourne	42	28	4	10	102	44	88
Ashford Town	42	25	9	8	75	44	84
Waterlooville	42	24	8	10	87	44	80
Newport IOW	42	24	6	12	75	58	78
Braintree Town	42	24	8	10	93	70	77
Weymouth	42	24	4	14	75	55	76
Havant Town	42	23	11	8	73	42	74
Forest Green Rovers	42	22	8	12	85	55	74
Trowbridge Town	42	18	8	16	86	51	62
Yate Town	42	17	8	17	85	71	59
Margate	42	18	5	19	68	62	59
Witney Town	42	16	11	15	60	54	59
Weston-super-Mare	42	16	9	17	78	68	57
Cinderford Town	42	16	8	18	74	77	56
Fisher 93	42	14	13	15	58	59	55
Bashley	42	14	11	17	63	61	53
Clevedon Town	42	15	6	21	70	80	51
Tonbridge Angels	42	13	10	19	58	79	49
Fleet Town	42	14	5	23	58	79	47
Fareham Town	42	12	5	25	71	97	41
Erith & Belvedere	42	4	4	34	38	111	16
Poole Town	42	0	1	41	17	188	1

Braintree Town 3 points deducted, Havant Town had 6 points deducted

1996-97

Premier Division

Team	P	W	D	L	F	A	Pts
Gresley Rovers	42	25	10	7	75	40	85
Cheltenham Town	42	21	11	10	76	44	74
Gloucester City	42	21	10	11	81	56	73
Halesowen Town	42	21	10	11	77	54	73
King's Lynn	42	20	8	14	65	61	68
Burton Albion	42	18	12	12	70	53	66
Nuneaton Borough	42	19	9	14	61	52	66
Sittingbourne	42	19	7	16	76	65	64
Merthyr Tydfil	42	17	9	16	69	61	60
Worcester City	42	15	14	13	52	50	59
Atherstone United	42	15	13	14	46	47	58
Salisbury City	42	15	13	14	57	66	58
Sudbury Town	42	16	7	19	72	72	55
Gravesend & Northfleet	42	16	7	19	63	73	55
Dorchester Town	42	14	9	19	62	66	51
Hastings Town	42	12	15	15	49	60	51
Crawley Town	42	13	8	21	49	67	47
Cambridge City	42	11	13	18	57	65	46
Ashford Town	42	9	18	15	53	79	45
Baldock Town	42	11	8	23	52	90	41
Newport AFC	42	9	13	20	40	60	40
Chelmsford City	42	6	14	22	49	70	32

Midland Division

Team	P	W	D	L	F	A	Pts
Tamworth	40	30	7	3	90	28	97
Rothwell Town	40	20	11	9	82	54	71
Ilkeston Town	40	19	13	8	76	50	70
Grantham Town	40	22	4	14	65	46	70
Bedworth United	40	18	11	11	77	41	65
Solihull Borough	40	19	8	13	84	62	65
Bilston Town	40	18	10	12	74	57	64
Moor Green	40	18	7	15	88	68	61
Stafford Rangers	40	17	9	14	68	62	60
Raunds Town	40	16	11	13	61	66	59
Racing Club Warwick	40	16	10	14	70	72	58
Shepshed Dynamo	40	14	12	14	64	65	54
Redditch United	40	15	8	17	56	59	53
Paget Rangers	40	13	9	18	42	55	48
Dudley Town	40	12	10	18	70	89	46
Hinckley Town	40	11	11	18	39	63	44
Stourbridge	40	10	9	21	61	81	39
Evesham United	40	9	12	19	55	77	39
VS Rugby	40	9	9	22	49	81	36
Corby Town	40	8	8	24	49	88	32
Sutton Coldfield Town	40	7	9	24	29	85	30

Leicester United FC closed down and their record was expunged from the League table.

Southern Division

Team	P	W	D	L	F	A	Pts
Forest Green Rovers	42	27	10	5	87	40	91
St Leonards Stamcroft	42	26	9	7	95	48	87
Havant Town	42	23	10	9	81	49	79
Weston-super-Mare	42	21	13	8	82	43	76
Margate	42	21	9	12	70	47	72
Witney Town	42	20	11	11	71	42	71
Weymouth	42	20	10	12	82	51	70
Tonbridge Angels	42	17	15	10	56	44	66
Newport IOW	42	15	15	12	73	58	60
Fisher Athletic (London)	42	18	6	18	77	77	60
Clevedon Town	42	17	9	16	75	76	60
Fareham Town	42	14	12	16	53	70	54
Bashley	42	15	8	19	73	84	53
Dartford	42	14	10	18	59	64	52
Waterlooville	42	14	9	19	58	67	51
Cirencester Town	42	12	12	18	50	68	48
Cinderford Town	42	13	7	22	64	76	46
Trowbridge Town	42	11	11	20	50	61	44
Yate Town	42	12	8	22	55	87	44
Fleet Town	42	12	6	24	47	91	42
Erith & Belvedere	42	9	10	23	60	95	37
Buckingham Town	42	2	8	32	27	107	14

1997-98

Premier Division

Forest Green Rovers	42	27	8	7	93	55	89
Merthyr Tydfil	42	24	12	6	80	42	84
Burton Albion	42	21	8	13	64	43	71
Dorchester Town	42	19	13	10	63	38	70
Halesowen Town	42	18	15	9	70	38	69
Bath City	42	19	12	11	72	51	69
Worcester City	42	19	12	11	54	44	69
King's Lynn	42	18	11	13	64	65	65
Atherstone United	42	17	12	13	55	49	63
Crawley Town	42	17	8	17	63	60	59
Gloucester City	42	16	11	15	57	57	59
Nuneaton Borough	42	17	6	19	68	61	57
Cambridge City	42	16	8	18	62	70	56
Hastings Town	42	14	12	16	67	70	54
Tamworth	42	14	11	17	68	65	53
Rothwell Town	42	11	16	15	55	73	49
Gresley Rovers	42	14	6	22	59	77	48
Salisbury City	42	12	12	18	53	72	48
Bromsgrove Rovers	42	13	6	23	67	85	45
Sittingbourne	42	12	8	22	47	66	44
Ashford Town	42	8	5	29	34	85	29
St Leonards Stamcroft	42	5	10	27	48	97	25

Midland Division

Grantham Town	40	30	4	6	87	39	94
Ilkeston Town	40	29	6	5	123	39	93
Solihull Borough	40	22	9	9	81	48	75
Raunds Town	40	20	8	12	73	44	68
Wisbech Town	40	20	7	13	79	57	67
Moor Green	40	20	7	13	72	55	67
Bilston Town	40	20	5	15	69	57	65
Blakenall	40	17	13	10	66	55	64
Stafford Rangers	40	18	6	16	57	56	60
Redditch United	40	16	11	13	59	41	59
Stourbridge	40	16	9	15	57	55	57
Hinckley United	40	15	11	14	59	56	56
Brackley Town	40	15	7	18	45	57	52
Bedworth United	40	15	5	20	50	73	50
Racing Club Warwick	40	11	9	20	49	56	42
Shepshed Dynamo	40	9	14	17	55	74	41
Sutton Coldfield Town	40	9	12	19	42	68	39
Paget Rangers	40	9	12	19	40	75	39
VS Rugby	40	8	12	20	53	93	36
Evesham United	40	7	9	24	47	94	30
Corby Town	40	2	8	30	41	112	14

Southern Division

Weymouth	42	32	2	8	107	48	98
Chelmsford City	42	29	8	5	86	39	95
Bashley	42	29	4	9	101	59	91
Newport IOW	42	25	9	8	72	34	84
Fisher Athletic (London)	42	25	5	12	87	50	80
Margate	42	23	8	11	71	42	77
Newport AFC	42	21	6	15	83	65	69
Witney Town	42	20	9	13	74	58	69
Clevedon Town	42	20	7	15	57	55	67
Waterlooville	42	17	7	18	69	64	58
Dartford	42	17	7	18	60	60	58
Havant Town	42	13	14	16	65	70	53
Fleet Town	42	16	5	21	63	83	53
Tonbridge Angels	42	14	10	18	49	55	52
Trowbridge Town	42	14	6	22	55	69	48
Erith & Belvedere	42	11	13	18	47	68	46
Fareham Town	42	12	9	21	75	87	45
Cirencester Town	42	12	7	23	63	88	43
Weston-super-Mare	42	12	5	25	49	86	41
Baldock Town	42	10	5	27	53	81	35
Cinderford Town	42	6	5	31	40	112	23
Yate Town	42	5	7	30	44	97	22

1998-99

Premier Division

Nuneaton Borough	42	27	9	6	91	33	90
Boston United	42	17	16	9	69	51	67
Ilkeston Town	42	18	13	11	72	59	67
Bath City	42	18	11	13	70	44	65
Hastings Town	42	18	11	13	57	49	65
Gloucester City	42	18	11	13	57	52	65
Worcester City	42	18	9	15	58	54	63
Halesowen Town	42	17	11	14	72	60	62
Tamworth	42	19	5	18	62	67	62
King's Lynn	42	17	10	15	53	46	61
Crawley Town	42	17	10	15	57	58	61
Salisbury City	42	16	12	14	56	61	60
Burton Albion	42	17	7	18	58	52	58
Weymouth	42	14	14	14	56	55	56
Merthyr Tydfil	42	15	8	19	52	62	53
Atherstone United	42	12	14	16	47	52	50
Grantham Town	42	14	8	20	51	58	50
Dorchester Town	42	11	15	16	49	63	48
Rothwell Town	42	13	9	20	47	67	48
Cambridge City	42	11	12	19	47	68	45
Gresley Rovers	42	12	8	22	49	73	44
Bromsgrove Rovers	42	8	7	27	38	84	31

Hastings Town resigned from the League

Midland Division

Clevedon Town	42	28	8	6	83	35	92
Newport AFC	42	26	7	9	92	51	85
Redditch United	42	22	12	8	81	45	75
Hinckley United	42	20	12	10	58	40	72
Stafford Rangers	42	21	8	13	92	60	71
Bilston Town	42	20	11	11	79	69	71
Solihull Borough	42	19	12	11	76	53	69
Moor Green	42	20	7	15	71	61	67
Blakenall	42	17	14	11	65	54	65
Shepshed Dynamo	42	17	12	13	62	54	63
Sutton Coldfield Town	42	17	8	17	46	57	59
Stourbridge	42	16	10	16	60	55	58
Evesham United	42	16	9	17	63	63	57
Wisbech Town	42	16	9	17	59	66	57
Weston-super-Mare	42	15	10	17	59	56	55
Bedworth United	42	15	9	18	63	52	54
Cinderford Town	42	13	8	21	61	74	47
Stamford AFC	42	13	7	22	60	75	46
Paget Rangers	42	11	12	19	49	58	45
VS Rugby	42	12	9	21	53	74	45
Racing Club Warwick	42	5	8	29	38	93	23
Bloxwich Town	42	1	2	39	26	151	5

Southern Division

Havant & Waterlooville	42	29	7	6	86	32	94
Margate	42	27	8	7	84	33	89
Folkestone Invicta	42	26	8	8	92	47	86
Newport IOW	42	23	7	12	68	40	76
Chelmsford City	42	20	12	10	91	51	72
Raunds Town	42	19	13	10	87	50	70
Ashford Town	42	17	12	13	59	54	63
Baldock Town	42	17	9	16	60	59	60
Fisher Athletic (London)	42	16	11	15	58	54	59
Bashley	42	17	7	18	74	77	58
Witney Town	42	15	12	15	56	48	57
Cirencester Town	42	16	8	18	61	66	56
Sittingbourne	42	11	18	12	53	56	54
Dartford	42	14	10	18	48	53	52
Erith & Belvedere	42	15	7	20	48	64	52
Tonbridge Angels	42	12	15	15	48	59	51
St Leonards	42	14	8	20	57	72	50
Fleet Town	42	11	11	19	54	72	47
Corby Town	42	10	10	22	48	73	40
Yate Town	42	10	7	25	37	79	37
Andover	42	6	10	26	50	115	28
Brackley Town	42	6	8	28	41	105	26

1999-2000

Premier Division

Boston United	42	27	11	4	102	39	92
Burton Albion	42	23	9	10	73	43	78
Margate	42	23	8	11	64	43	77
Bath City	42	19	15	8	70	49	72
King's Lynn	42	19	14	9	59	43	71
Tamworth	42	20	10	12	80	51	70
Newport County	42	16	18	8	67	50	66
Clevedon Town	42	18	9	15	52	52	63
Ilkeston Town	42	16	12	14	77	69	60
Weymouth	42	14	16	12	60	51	58
Halesowen Town	42	14	14	14	52	54	56
Crawley Town	42	15	8	19	68	82	53
Havant & Waterlooville	42	13	13	16	63	68	52
Cambridge City	42	14	10	18	52	66	52
Worcester City	42	13	11	18	60	66	50
Salisbury City	42	14	8	20	70	84	50
Merthyr Tydfil	42	13	9	20	51	63	48
Dorchester Town	42	10	17	15	56	65	47
Grantham Town	42	14	5	23	63	76	47
Gloucester City	42	8	14	20	40	82	38
Rothwell Town	42	5	14	23	48	85	29
Atherstone United	42	5	13	24	30	76	28

Eastern Division

Fisher Athletic (London)	42	31	5	6	107	42	98
Folkestone Invicta	42	30	7	5	101	39	97
Newport IOW	42	25	7	10	74	40	82
Chelmsford City	42	24	8	10	74	38	80
Hastings Town	42	22	9	11	76	56	75
Ashford Town	42	21	9	12	70	49	72
Tonbridge Angels	42	20	10	12	82	60	70
Dartford	42	17	6	19	52	58	57
Burnham	42	15	9	18	55	64	54
Baldock Town	42	14	10	18	57	69	52
Erith & Belvedere	42	14	9	19	62	68	51
Witney Town	42	13	11	18	48	60	50
VS Rugby	42	13	11	18	58	79	50
Wisbech Town	42	14	7	21	58	66	49
Spalding United	42	14	6	22	52	71	48
Sittingbourne	42	13	7	22	48	75	46
Stamford	42	9	18	15	50	62	45
St Leonards	42	11	12	19	67	81	45
Raunds Town	42	11	12	19	44	63	45
Bashley	42	12	7	23	56	95	43
Corby Town	42	11	12	19	56	62	42
Fleet Town	42	8	8	26	54	104	32

Corby Town had 3 points deducted for fielding an ineligible player
Raunds Town gave notice to withdraw and take the place of the 2nd
relegated Club. They then unsuccessfully sought re-election

Western Division

Stafford Rangers	42	29	6	7	107	47	93
Moor Green	42	26	12	4	85	33	90
Hinckley United	42	25	12	5	89	47	87
Tiverton Town	42	26	7	9	91	44	85
Solihull Borough	42	20	11	11	85	66	71
Blakenall	42	19	12	11	70	46	69
Cirencester Town	42	20	8	14	72	64	68
Bilston Town	42	16	18	8	66	52	66
Cinderford Town	42	17	11	14	62	64	62
Redditch United	42	17	10	15	73	65	61
Gresley Rovers	42	14	15	13	54	49	57
Weston-super-Mare	42	16	9	17	55	55	57
Sutton Coldfield Town	42	13	17	12	49	52	56
Evesham Town	42	13	12	17	69	61	51
Bedworth Town	42	13	10	19	52	71	49
Rocester	42	12	12	18	63	78	48
Bromsgrove Rovers	42	13	7	22	59	72	46
Shepshed Dynamo	42	12	7	23	46	66	43
Paget Rangers	42	11	4	27	44	82	37
Racing Club Warwick	42	7	14	21	41	82	35
Stourbridge	42	10	3	29	45	101	33
Yate Town	42	3	3	36	28	108	12

2000-2001

Premier Division

Margate	42	28	7	7	75	27	91
Burton Albion	42	25	13	4	76	36	88
King's Lynn	42	18	11	13	67	58	65
Welling United	42	17	13	12	59	55	64
Weymouth	42	17	12	13	69	51	63
Havant & Waterlooville	42	18	9	15	65	53	63
Stafford Rangers	42	18	9	15	70	59	63
Worcester City	42	18	8	16	52	53	62
Moor Green	42	18	8	16	49	53	62
Newport County	42	17	10	15	70	61	61
Crawley Town	42	17	10	15	61	54	61
Tamworth	42	17	8	17	58	55	59
Salisbury City	42	17	8	17	64	69	59
Ilkeston Town	42	16	11	15	51	61	59
Bath City	42	15	13	14	67	68	55
Cambridge City	42	13	11	18	56	59	50
Folkestone Invicta	42	14	6	22	49	74	48
Merthyr Tydfil	42	11	13	18	49	62	46
Clevedon Town	42	11	7	24	61	74	40
Fisher Athletic (London)	42	12	6	24	51	85	39
Dorchester Town	42	10	8	24	40	70	38
Halesowen Town	42	8	13	21	47	69	37

Bath City and Fisher Athletic (London) both had 3 points deducted

Eastern Division

Newport IOW	42	28	10	4	91	30	94
Chelmsford City	42	27	9	6	102	45	90
Grantham Town	42	25	11	6	100	47	86
Histon	42	23	11	8	84	53	80
Baldock Town	42	23	10	9	81	44	79
Hastings Town	42	22	10	10	72	50	76
Stamford	42	20	11	11	69	59	71
Tonbridge Angels	42	18	11	13	79	58	65
Langney Sports	42	19	8	15	75	55	65
Rothwell Town	42	20	5	17	86	74	62
Corby Town	42	14	10	18	64	92	52
Ashford Town	42	15	4	23	53	83	49
Banbury United	42	12	11	19	57	54	47
Witney Town	42	12	11	19	55	71	47
Bashley	42	10	14	18	57	71	44
Dartford	42	11	11	20	49	67	44
Burnham	42	10	14	18	39	65	43
Wisbech Town	42	10	9	23	45	89	39
St Leonards	42	9	10	23	55	87	37
Erith & Belvedere	42	10	7	25	49	92	37
Sittingbourne	42	8	9	25	41	79	33
Spalding United	42	7	12	23	35	73	33

Burnham had 1 point deducted, Rothwell Town had 3 points deducted

Western Division

Hinckley United	42	30	8	4	102	38	98
Tiverton Town	42	28	7	7	97	36	91
Bilston Town	42	27	9	6	88	48	90
Evesham United	42	27	5	10	86	46	86
Mangotsfield United	42	25	9	8	91	45	84
Solihull Borough	42	22	12	8	73	43	78
Redditch United	42	17	13	12	76	69	64
Weston-super-Mare	42	17	10	15	68	58	61
Atherstone United	42	16	11	15	64	58	59
Rochester	42	18	5	19	57	77	59
Cirencester Town	42	14	15	13	65	74	57
Rugby United	42	13	10	19	51	68	49
Gloucester City	42	12	11	19	76	86	47
Blakenall	42	13	10	19	54	64	46
Shepshed Dynamo	42	12	9	21	56	73	45
Bedworth United	42	12	9	21	38	60	45
Racing Club Warwick	42	13	6	23	46	77	45
Gresley Rovers	42	11	8	23	46	65	41
Cinderford Town	42	11	8	23	56	84	41
Sutton Coldfield Town	42	7	14	21	45	66	35
Paget Rovers	42	9	4	29	38	93	31
Bromsgrove Rovers	42	7	9	26	47	92	30

Blakenall had 3 points deducted

2001-2002

Premier Division

Team	P	W	D	L	F	A	Pts
Kettering Town	42	27	6	9	80	41	87
Tamworth	42	24	13	5	81	41	85
Havant & Waterlooville	42	22	9	11	74	50	75
Crawley Town	42	21	10	11	67	48	73
Newport County	42	19	9	14	61	48	66
Tiverton Town	42	17	10	15	70	63	61
Moor Green	42	18	7	17	64	62	61
Worcester City	42	16	12	14	65	54	60
Stafford Rangers	42	17	9	16	70	62	60
Ilkeston Town	42	14	16	12	58	61	58
Weymouth United	42	15	11	16	59	67	56
Hinckley Town	42	14	13	15	64	62	55
Folkestone Invicta	42	14	12	16	51	61	54
Cambridge City	42	12	16	14	60	70	52
Welling United	42	13	12	17	69	66	51
Hednesford Town	42	15	6	21	59	70	51
Bath City	42	13	11	18	56	65	50
Chelmsford City	42	13	11	18	63	75	50
Newport IOW	42	12	12	18	38	61	48
King's Lynn	42	11	13	18	44	57	46
Merthyr Tydfil	42	12	8	22	53	71	44
Salisbury City	42	6	8	28	36	87	26

Eastern Division

Team	P	W	D	L	F	A	Pts
Hastings Town	42	29	8	5	85	38	95
Grantham Town	42	29	6	7	99	43	93
Dorchester Town	42	26	10	6	81	36	88
Histon	42	23	8	11	83	49	77
Stamford	42	24	4	14	76	61	76
Fisher Athletic (London)	42	20	10	12	83	56	70
Eastbourne Borough	42	21	6	15	63	46	69
Dartford	42	18	5	19	62	66	59
Erith & Belvedere	42	18	3	21	75	79	57
Bashley	42	15	11	16	71	63	56
Burnham	42	15	10	17	52	54	55
Rugby United	42	16	6	20	55	67	54
Rothwell Town	42	14	8	20	46	66	50
Ashford Town	42	14	6	22	58	78	48
Banbury United	42	13	9	20	53	66	47
Chatham Town	42	13	8	21	56	87	47
Sittingbourne	42	14	4	24	46	69	46
Spalding	42	13	6	23	72	84	45
Tonbridge Angels	42	13	6	23	65	80	45
St Leonards	42	14	3	25	52	88	45
Corby Town	42	10	13	19	54	82	43
Wisbech Town	42	11	8	23	56	84	41

Western Division

Team	P	W	D	L	F	A	Pts
Halesowen Town	40	27	9	4	85	24	90
Chippenham Town	40	26	9	5	81	28	87
Weston-super-Mare	40	22	10	8	70	38	76
Solihull Borough	40	20	11	9	75	42	71
Gresley Rovers	40	19	9	12	59	50	66
Sutton Coldfield Town	40	17	11	12	53	46	62
Mangotsfield United	40	17	10	13	74	54	61
Stourport Swifts	40	18	6	16	59	59	60
Atherstone United	40	16	8	16	61	59	56
Clevedon Town	40	15	11	14	57	58	56
Bedworth United	40	16	7	17	59	63	55
Evesham United	40	16	7	17	54	70	55
Cirencester Town	40	17	3	20	64	69	54
Gloucester City	40	14	10	16	48	63	52
Cinderford Town	40	14	9	17	54	67	51
Shepshed Dynamo	40	10	10	20	64	84	40
Bilston Town	40	11	7	22	50	72	40
Redditch United	40	11	6	23	47	77	39
Swindon Supermarine	40	11	4	25	52	76	37
Racing Club Warwick	40	8	11	21	38	63	35
Rocester	40	5	12	23	33	75	27

2002-2003

Premier Division

Team	P	W	D	L	F	A	Pts
Tamworth	42	26	10	6	73	32	88
Stafford Rangers	42	21	12	9	76	40	75
Dover Athletic	42	19	14	9	42	35	71
Tiverton Town	42	19	12	11	60	43	69
Chippenham Town	42	17	17	8	59	37	68
Worcester City	42	18	13	11	60	39	67
Crawley Town	42	17	13	12	64	51	64
Havant & Waterlooville	42	15	15	12	67	64	60
Chelmsford City	42	15	12	15	65	63	57
Newport County	42	15	11	16	53	52	56
Hednesford Town	42	14	13	15	59	60	55
Moor Green	42	13	14	15	49	58	53
Hinckley Town	42	12	16	14	61	64	52
Bath City	42	13	13	16	50	61	52
Welling United	42	13	12	17	55	58	51
Grantham Town	42	14	9	19	59	65	51
Weymouth	42	12	15	15	44	62	51
Cambridge City	42	13	10	19	54	56	49
Halesowen Town	42	12	13	17	52	63	49
Hastings United	42	10	13	19	44	57	43
Ilkeston Town	42	10	10	22	54	92	40
Folkestone Invicta	42	7	7	28	57	105	28

Eastern Division

Team	P	W	D	L	F	A	Pts
Dorchester Town	42	28	9	5	114	40	93
Eastbourne Borough	42	29	6	7	92	33	93
Stamford	42	27	6	9	80	39	87
Salisbury City	42	27	8	7	81	42	86
Bashley	42	23	12	7	90	44	81
King's Lynn	42	24	7	11	98	62	79
Rothwell Town	42	22	10	10	77	52	76
Banbury United	42	21	11	10	75	50	74
Tonbridge Angels	42	20	11	11	71	55	71
Histon	42	20	7	15	99	62	67
Ashford Town	42	18	9	15	63	57	63
Sittingbourne	42	15	8	19	57	69	53
Burnham	42	15	7	20	62	79	52
Fisher Athletic	42	15	5	22	57	80	50
Chatham Town	42	14	5	23	54	84	47
Newport IOW	42	12	6	24	53	87	42
Dartford	42	11	8	23	48	78	41
Erith & Belvedere	42	11	6	25	65	96	39
Corby Town	42	9	11	22	49	84	38
Fleet Town	42	8	8	26	34	80	32
Spalding United	42	4	6	32	40	108	18
St. Leonards	42	4	4	34	38	116	16

Western Division

Team	P	W	D	L	F	A	Pts
Merthyr Tydfil	42	28	8	6	78	32	92
Weston-super-Mare	42	26	7	9	77	42	85
Bromsgrove Rovers	42	23	7	12	73	41	76
Solihull Borough	42	21	13	8	77	48	76
Gloucester City	42	22	9	11	87	58	75
Mangotsfield United	42	21	10	11	106	53	73
Redditch United	42	22	6	14	76	42	72
Rugby United	42	20	9	13	58	43	69
Gresley Rovers	42	19	10	13	63	54	67
Taunton Town	42	20	7	15	76	78	67
Sutton Coldfield Town	42	18	10	14	63	53	64
Evesham United	42	19	6	17	76	72	63
Clevedon Town	42	14	13	15	54	60	55
Cirencester Town	42	15	7	20	62	82	52
Cinderford Town	42	13	12	17	50	67	51
Shepshed Dynamo	42	12	6	24	48	76	42
Stourport Swifts	42	10	11	21	48	66	41
Bedworth United	42	11	7	24	46	74	40
Swindon Supermarine	42	11	5	26	52	85	38
Atherstone United	42	9	10	23	45	78	37
Rocester	42	9	10	23	34	74	37
Racing Club Warwick	42	3	9	30	33	104	18

2003-2004
Premier Division

Crawley Town	42	25	9	8	77	43	84
Weymouth	42	20	12	10	76	47	72
Stafford Rangers	42	19	11	12	55	43	68
Nuneaton Borough	42	17	15	10	65	49	66
Worcester City	42	18	9	15	71	50	63
Hinckley United	42	15	14	13	55	46	59
Newport County	42	15	14	13	52	50	59
Cambridge City	42	14	15	13	54	53	57
Welling United	42	16	8	18	56	58	56
Weston-super-Mare	42	14	13	15	52	52	55
Eastbourne Borough	42	14	13	15	48	56	55
Havant & Waterlooville	42	15	10	17	59	70	55
Moor Green	42	14	12	16	42	54	54
Merthyr Tydfil	42	13	14	15	60	66	53
Tiverton Town	42	12	15	15	63	64	51
Bath City	42	13	12	17	49	57	51
Dorchester Town	42	14	9	19	56	69	51
Chelmsford City	42	11	16	15	46	53	49
Dover Athletic	42	12	13	17	50	59	49
Hednesford Town	42	12	12	18	56	69	48
Chippenham Town	42	10	17	15	51	63	47
Grantham Town	42	10	15	17	45	67	45

Eastern Division

King's Lynn	42	28	7	7	90	35	91
Histon	42	26	10	6	96	41	88
Tonbridge Angels	42	27	7	8	82	46	88
* Eastleigh	42	27	4	11	88	40	82
Folkestone Invicta	42	20	15	7	91	45	75
Salisbury City	42	21	11	10	73	45	74
Stamford	42	20	11	11	63	45	71
Banbury United	42	19	10	13	65	57	67
Burgess Hill Town	42	19	7	16	67	54	64
Sittingbourne	42	18	8	16	61	55	62
Bashley	42	18	7	17	66	58	61
Ashford Town	42	15	9	18	51	53	54
Chatham Town	42	13	10	19	49	67	49
Fisher Athletic	42	13	10	19	61	81	49
Corby Town	42	12	9	21	44	75	45
Dartford	42	13	6	23	48	81	45
* Burnham	42	12	11	19	52	76	44
Hastings United	42	12	7	23	60	91	43
Newport IOW	42	11	7	24	42	69	40
Rothwell Town	42	9	11	22	30	47	38
Erith & Belvedere	42	7	10	25	45	84	31
Fleet Town	42	5	7	30	35	114	22

* Eastleigh and Burnham both had 3 points deducted.

Western Division

Redditch United	40	25	9	6	75	30	84
Gloucester City	40	24	7	9	77	46	79
Cirencester Town	40	24	4	12	73	40	76
Halesowen Town	40	20	13	7	64	40	73
Rugby United	40	21	8	11	57	40	71
Team Bath	40	21	6	13	62	41	69
Solihull Borough	40	19	9	12	50	31	66
Sutton Coldfield	40	16	15	9	52	38	63
Bromsgrove Rovers	40	16	11	13	60	48	59
Ilkeston Town	40	16	10	14	58	59	58
Clevedon Town	40	16	5	19	55	59	53
Gresley Rovers	40	15	7	18	52	60	52
Mangotsfield United	40	14	8	18	70	70	50
Evesham United	40	15	5	20	56	57	50
Taunton Town	40	14	8	18	50	55	50
Yate Town	40	11	9	20	51	79	42
Swindon Supermarine	40	10	9	21	41	69	39
Stourport Swifts	40	9	11	20	43	62	38
Bedworth United	40	8	12	20	39	61	36
Cinderford Town	40	7	9	24	50	94	30
Shepshed Dynamo	40	5	13	22	31	87	28

FOOTBALL CONFERENCE

1979-80

Altrincham	38	24	8	6	79	35	56
Weymouth	38	22	10	6	73	37	54
Worcester City	38	19	11	8	53	36	49
Boston United	38	16	13	9	52	43	45
Gravesend & Northfleet	38	17	10	11	49	44	44
Maidstone United	38	16	11	11	54	37	43
Kettering Town	38	15	13	10	55	50	43
Northwich Victoria	38	16	10	12	50	38	42
Bangor City	38	14	14	10	41	46	42
Nuneaton Borough	38	13	13	12	58	44	39
Scarborough	38	12	15	11	47	38	39
Yeovil Town	38	13	10	15	46	49	36
Telford United	38	13	8	17	52	60	34
Barrow	38	14	6	18	47	55	34
Wealdstone	38	9	15	14	42	54	33
Bath City	38	10	12	16	43	69	32
Barnet	38	10	10	18	32	48	30
AP Leamington	38	7	11	20	32	63	25
Stafford Rangers	38	6	10	22	41	57	22
Redditch United	38	5	8	25	26	69	18

1980-81

Altrincham	38	23	8	7	72	41	54
Kettering Town	38	21	9	8	66	37	51
Scarborough	38	17	13	8	49	29	47
Northwich Victoria	38	17	11	10	53	40	45
Weymouth	38	19	6	13	54	40	44
Bath City	38	16	10	12	51	32	42
Maidstone United	38	16	9	13	64	53	41
Boston United	38	16	9	13	63	58	41
Barrow	38	15	8	15	50	49	38
Frickley Athletic	38	15	8	15	61	62	38
Stafford Rangers	38	11	15	12	56	56	37
Worcester City	38	14	7	17	47	54	35
Telford United	38	13	9	16	47	59	35
Yeovil Town	38	14	6	18	60	64	34
Gravesend & Northfleet	38	13	8	17	48	55	34
AP Leamington	38	10	11	17	47	66	31
Barnet	38	12	7	19	39	64	31
Nuneaton Borough	38	10	9	19	49	65	29
Wealdstone	38	9	11	18	37	56	29
Bangor City	38	6	12	20	35	68	24

1981-82

Runcorn	42	28	9	5	75	37	93
Enfield	42	26	8	8	90	46	86
Telford United	42	23	8	11	70	51	77
Worcester City	42	21	8	13	70	60	71
Dagenham	42	19	12	11	69	51	69
Northwich Victoria	42	20	9	13	56	46	69
Scarborough	42	19	11	12	65	52	68
Barrow	42	18	11	13	59	50	65
Weymouth	42	18	9	15	56	47	63
Boston United	42	17	11	14	61	57	62
Altrincham	42	14	13	15	66	56	55
Bath City	42	15	10	17	50	57	55
Yeovil Town	42	14	11	17	56	68	53
Stafford Rangers	42	12	16	14	48	47	52
Frickley Athletic	42	14	10	18	47	60	52
Maidstone United	42	11	15	16	55	59	48
Trowbridge Town	42	12	11	19	38	54	47
Barnet	42	9	14	19	36	52	41
Kettering Town	42	9	13	20	64	76	40
Gravesend & Northfleet	42	10	10	22	51	69	40
Dartford	42	10	9	23	47	69	39
AP Leamington	42	4	10	28	40	105	22

1982-83

Enfield	42	25	9	8	95	48	84
Maidstone United	42	25	8	9	83	34	83
Wealdstone	42	22	13	7	80	41	79
Runcorn	42	22	8	12	73	53	74
Boston United	42	20	12	10	77	57	72
Telford United	42	20	11	11	69	48	71
Weymouth	42	20	10	12	63	48	70
Northwich Victoria	42	18	10	14	68	63	64
Scarborough	42	17	12	13	71	58	63
Bath City	42	17	9	16	58	55	60
Nuneaton Borough	42	15	13	14	57	60	58
Altrincham	42	15	10	17	62	56	55
Bangor City	42	14	13	15	71	77	55
Dagenham	42	12	15	15	60	65	51
Barnet	42	16	3	23	55	78	51
Frickley Athletic	42	12	13	17	66	77	49
Worcester City	42	12	10	20	58	87	46
Trowbridge Town	42	12	7	23	56	88	43
Kettering Town	42	11	7	24	69	99	40
Yeovil Town	42	11	7	24	63	99	40
Barrow	42	8	12	22	46	74	36
Stafford Rangers	42	5	14	23	40	75	29

1983-84

Maidstone United	42	23	13	6	71	34	70
Nuneaton Borough	42	24	11	7	70	40	69
Altrincham	42	23	9	10	64	39	65
Wealdstone	42	21	14	7	75	36	62
Runcorn	42	20	13	9	61	45	62
Bath City	42	17	12	13	60	48	53
Northwich Victoria	42	16	14	12	54	47	51
Worcester City	42	15	13	14	64	55	49
Barnet	42	16	10	16	55	58	49
Kidderminster Harriers	42	14	14	14	54	61	49
Telford United	42	17	11	14	50	58	49
Frickley Athletic	42	17	10	15	68	56	48
Scarborough	42	14	16	12	52	55	48
Enfield	42	14	9	19	61	58	43
Weymouth	42	13	8	21	54	65	42
Gateshead	42	12	13	17	59	73	42
Boston United	42	13	12	17	66	80	41
Dagenham	42	14	8	20	57	69	40
Kettering Town	42	12	9	21	53	67	37
Yeovil Town	42	12	8	22	55	77	35
Bangor City	42	10	6	26	54	82	29
Trowbridge Town	42	5	7	30	33	87	19

2 points awarded for a Home win, 3 points awarded for an Away win, 1 point awarded for any Draw

1984-85

Wealdstone	42	20	10	12	64	54	62
Nuneaton Borough	42	19	14	9	85	53	58
Dartford	42	17	13	12	57	48	57
Bath City	42	21	9	12	52	49	57
Altrincham	42	21	6	15	63	47	56
Scarborough	42	17	13	12	69	62	54
Enfield	42	17	13	12	84	61	53
Kidderminster Harriers	42	17	8	17	79	77	51
Northwich Victoria	42	16	11	15	50	46	50
Telford United	42	15	14	13	59	54	49
Frickley Athletic	42	18	7	17	65	71	49
Kettering Town	42	15	12	15	68	59	48
Maidstone United	42	15	13	14	58	51	48
Runcorn	42	13	15	14	48	47	48
Barnet	42	15	11	16	59	52	47
Weymouth	42	15	13	14	70	66	45
Boston United	42	15	10	17	69	69	45
Barrow	42	11	16	15	47	57	43
Dagenham	42	13	10	19	47	67	41
Worcester City	42	12	9	21	55	84	38
Gateshead	42	9	12	21	51	82	33
Yeovil Town	42	6	11	25	44	87	25

2 points awarded for a Home win, 3 points awarded for an Away win, 1 point awarded for any Draw.   Gateshead had 1 point deducted

1985-86

Enfield	42	27	10	5	94	47	76
Frickley Athletic	42	25	10	7	78	50	69
Kidderminster Harriers	42	24	7	11	99	62	67
Altrincham	42	22	11	9	70	49	63
Weymouth	42	19	15	8	75	60	61
Runcorn	42	19	14	9	70	44	60
Stafford Rangers	42	19	13	10	61	54	60
Telford United	42	18	10	14	68	66	51
Kettering Town	42	15	15	12	55	53	49
Wealdstone	42	16	9	17	57	56	47
Cheltenham Town	42	16	11	15	69	69	46
Bath City	42	13	11	18	53	54	45
Boston United	42	16	7	19	66	76	44
Barnet	42	13	11	18	56	60	41
Scarborough	42	13	11	18	54	66	40
Northwich Victoria	42	10	12	20	42	54	37
Maidstone United	42	9	16	17	57	66	36
Nuneaton Borough	42	13	5	24	58	73	36
Dagenham	42	10	12	20	48	66	36
Wycombe Wanderers	42	10	13	19	55	84	36
Dartford	42	8	9	25	51	82	26
Barrow	42	7	8	27	41	86	24

2 points awarded for a Home win; 3 points awarded for an Away win; 1 point awarded for any Draw

1986-87

Scarborough	42	27	10	5	64	33	91
Barnet	42	25	10	7	86	39	85
Maidstone United	42	21	10	11	71	48	73
Enfield	42	21	7	14	66	47	70
Altrincham	42	18	15	9	66	53	69
Boston United	42	21	6	15	82	74	69
Sutton United	42	19	11	12	81	51	68
Runcorn	42	18	13	11	71	58	67
Telford United	42	18	10	14	69	59	64
Bath City	42	17	12	13	63	62	63
Cheltenham Town	42	16	13	13	64	50	61
Kidderminster Harriers	42	17	4	21	77	81	55
Stafford Rangers	42	14	11	17	58	60	53
Weymouth	42	13	12	17	68	77	51
Dagenham	42	14	7	21	56	72	49
Kettering Town	42	12	11	19	54	66	47
Northwich Victoria	42	10	14	18	53	69	44
Nuneaton Borough	42	10	14	18	48	73	44
Wealdstone	42	11	10	21	50	70	43
Welling United	42	10	10	22	61	84	40
Frickley Athletic	42	7	11	24	47	82	32
Gateshead	42	6	13	23	48	95	31

1987-88

Lincoln City	42	24	10	8	86	48	82
Barnet	42	23	11	8	93	45	80
Kettering Town	42	22	9	11	68	48	75
Runcorn	42	21	11	10	68	47	74
Telford United	42	20	10	12	65	50	70
Stafford Rangers	42	20	9	13	79	58	69
Kidderminster Harriers	42	18	15	9	75	66	69
Sutton United	42	16	18	8	77	54	66
Maidstone United	42	18	9	15	79	64	63
Weymouth	42	18	9	15	53	43	63
Macclesfield Town	42	18	9	15	64	62	63
Enfield	42	15	10	17	68	78	55
Cheltenham Town	42	11	20	11	64	67	53
Altrincham	42	14	10	18	59	59	52
Fisher Athletic	42	13	13	16	58	61	52
Boston United	42	14	7	21	60	75	49
Northwich Victoria	42	10	17	15	46	57	47
Wycombe Wanderers	42	11	13	18	50	76	46
Welling United	42	11	9	22	50	72	42
Bath City	42	9	10	23	48	76	37
Wealdstone	42	5	17	20	39	76	32
Dagenham	42	5	6	31	37	104	21

1988-89

	P	W	D	L	F	A	Pts
Maidstone United	40	25	9	6	92	46	84
Kettering Town	40	23	7	10	56	39	76
Boston United	40	22	8	10	61	51	74
Wycombe Wanderers	40	20	11	9	68	52	71
Kidderminster Harriers	40	21	6	13	68	57	69
Runcorn	40	19	8	13	77	53	65
Macclesfield Town	40	17	10	13	63	57	61
Barnet	40	18	7	15	64	69	61
Yeovil Town	40	15	11	14	68	67	56
Northwich Victoria	40	14	11	15	64	65	53
Welling United	40	14	11	15	45	46	53
Sutton United	40	12	15	13	64	54	51
Enfield	40	14	8	18	62	67	50
Altrincham	40	13	10	17	51	61	49
Cheltenham Town	40	12	12	16	55	58	48
Telford United	40	13	9	18	37	43	48
Chorley	40	13	6	21	57	71	45
Fisher Athletic	40	10	11	19	55	65	41
Stafford Rangers	40	11	7	22	49	74	40
Aylesbury United	40	9	9	22	43	71	36
Weymouth	40	7	10	23	37	70	31
Newport County	29	4	7	18	31	62	19

Newport County expelled from League – their record was deleted.

1989-90

	P	W	D	L	F	A	Pts
Darlington	42	26	9	7	76	25	87
Barnet	42	26	7	9	81	41	85
Runcorn	42	19	13	10	79	62	70
Macclesfield Town	42	17	15	10	56	41	66
Kettering Town	42	18	12	12	66	53	66
Welling United	42	18	10	14	62	50	64
Yeovil Town	42	17	12	13	62	54	63
Sutton United	42	19	6	17	68	64	63
Merthyr Tydfil	42	16	14	12	67	63	62
Wycombe Wanderers	42	17	10	15	64	56	61
Cheltenham Town	42	16	11	15	58	60	59
Telford United	42	15	13	14	56	63	58
Kidderminster Harriers	42	15	9	18	64	67	54
Barrow	42	12	16	14	51	67	52
Northwich Victoria	42	15	5	22	51	67	50
Altrincham	42	12	13	17	49	48	49
Stafford Rangers	42	12	12	18	50	62	48
Boston United	42	13	8	21	48	67	47
Fisher Athletic	42	13	7	22	55	78	46
Chorley	42	13	6	23	42	67	45
Farnborough Town	42	10	12	20	60	73	42
Enfield	42	10	6	26	52	89	36

1990-91

	P	W	D	L	F	A	Pts
Barnet	42	26	9	7	103	52	87
Colchester United	42	25	10	7	68	35	85
Altrincham	42	23	13	6	87	46	82
Kettering Town	42	23	11	8	67	45	80
Wycombe Wanderers	42	21	11	10	75	46	74
Telford United	42	20	7	15	62	52	67
Macclesfield Town	42	17	12	13	63	52	63
Runcorn	42	16	10	16	69	67	58
Merthyr Tydfil	42	16	9	17	62	61	57
Barrow	42	15	12	15	59	65	57
Welling United	42	13	15	14	55	57	54
Northwich Victoria	42	13	13	16	65	75	52
Kidderminster Harrier	42	14	10	18	56	67	52
Yeovil Town	42	13	11	18	58	58	50
Stafford Rangers	42	12	14	16	48	51	50
Cheltenham Town	42	12	12	18	54	72	48
Gateshead	42	14	6	22	52	92	48
Boston United	42	12	11	19	55	69	47
Slough Town	42	13	6	23	51	80	45
Bath City	42	10	12	20	55	61	42
Sutton United	42	10	9	23	62	82	39
Fisher Athletic	42	5	15	22	38	79	30

1991-92

	P	W	D	L	F	A	Pts
Colchester United	42	28	10	4	98	40	94
Wycombe Wanderers	42	30	4	8	84	35	94
Kettering Town	42	20	13	9	72	50	73
Merthyr Tydfil	42	18	14	10	59	56	68
Farnborough Town	42	18	13	12	68	53	66
Telford United	42	19	7	16	62	66	64
Redbridge Forest	42	18	9	15	69	56	63
Boston United	42	18	9	15	71	66	63
Bath City	42	16	12	14	54	51	60
Witton Albion	42	16	10	16	63	60	58
Northwich Victoria	42	16	6	20	63	58	54
Welling United	42	14	12	16	69	79	54
Macclesfield Town	42	13	13	16	50	50	52
Gateshead	42	12	13	18	49	57	48
Yeovil Town	42	11	14	17	40	49	47
Runcorn	42	11	13	18	50	63	46
Stafford Rangers	42	10	16	16	41	59	46
Altrincham	42	11	12	19	61	82	45
Kidderminster Harriers	42	12	9	21	56	77	45
Slough Town	42	13	6	23	56	82	45
Cheltenham Town	42	10	13	19	56	83	43
Barrow	42	8	14	20	52	72	38

1992-93

	P	W	D	L	F	A	Pts
Wycombe Wanderers	42	24	11	7	84	37	83
Bromsgrove Rovers	42	18	14	10	67	49	68
Dagenham & Redbridge	42	19	11	12	75	47	67
Yeovil Town	42	18	12	12	59	49	66
Slough Town	42	18	11	13	60	55	65
Stafford Rangers	42	18	10	14	55	47	64
Bath City	42	15	14	13	53	46	59
Woking	42	17	8	17	58	62	59
Kidderminster Harriers	42	14	16	12	60	60	58
Altrincham	42	15	13	14	52	52	58
Northwich Victoria	42	16	8	18	68	55	56
Stalybridge Celtic	42	13	17	12	48	55	56
Kettering Town	42	14	13	15	61	63	55
Gateshead	42	14	10	18	53	56	52
Telford United	42	14	10	18	55	60	52
Merthyr Tydfil	42	14	10	18	51	79	52
Witton Albion	42	11	17	14	62	65	50
Macclesfield	42	12	13	17	40	50	49
Runcorn	42	13	10	19	58	76	49
Welling United	42	12	12	18	57	72	48
Farnborough Town	42	12	11	19	68	87	47
Boston United	42	9	13	20	50	69	40

Dagenham & Redbridge had 1 point deducted

1993-94

	P	W	D	L	F	A	Pts
Kidderminster Harriers	42	22	9	11	63	35	75
Kettering Town	42	18	15	8	46	24	72
Woking	42	18	13	11	58	58	67
Southport	42	18	12	12	57	51	66
Runcorn	42	14	19	9	63	57	61
Dagenham & Redbridge	42	15	14	13	62	54	59
Macclesfield Town	42	16	11	15	48	49	59
Dover Athletic	42	17	7	18	48	49	58
Stafford Rangers	42	14	15	13	56	52	57
Altrincham	42	16	9	17	41	42	57
Gateshead	42	15	12	15	45	53	57
Bath City	42	13	17	12	47	38	56
Halifax Town	42	13	16	13	59	49	55
Stalybridge Celtic	42	14	12	16	54	55	54
Northwich Victoria	42	11	19	12	44	45	52
Welling United	42	13	12	17	47	49	51
Telford United	42	13	12	17	41	49	51
Bromsgrove Rovers	42	12	15	15	54	66	51
Yeovil Town	42	14	9	19	49	62	51
Merthyr Tydfil	42	12	15	15	60	61	49
Slough Town	42	11	14	17	44	58	47
Witton Albion	42	7	13	22	37	63	44

Merthyr Tydfil had 2 points deducted

1994-95

Team							
Macclesfield Town	42	24	8	10	70	40	80
Woking	42	21	12	9	76	54	75
Southport	42	21	9	12	68	50	72
Altrincham Town	42	20	8	14	77	60	68
Stevenage Borough	42	20	7	15	68	49	67
Kettering Town	42	19	10	13	73	56	67
Gateshead	42	19	10	13	61	53	67
Halifax Town	42	17	12	13	68	54	63
Runcorn	42	16	10	16	59	71	58
Northwich Victoria	42	14	15	13	77	66	57
Kidderminster Harriers	42	16	9	17	63	61	57
Bath City	42	15	12	15	55	56	57
Bromsgrove Rovers	42	14	3	15	66	69	55
Farnborough Town	42	15	10	17	45	64	55
Dagenham & Redbridge	42	13	13	16	56	69	52
Dover Athletic	42	11	16	15	48	55	49
Welling United	42	13	10	19	57	74	49
Stalybridge Celtic	42	11	14	17	52	72	47
Telford United	42	10	16	16	53	62	46
Merthyr Tydfil	42	11	11	20	53	63	44
Stafford Rangers	42	9	11	22	53	79	38
Yeovil Town	42	8	14	20	50	71	37

Yeovil Town had 1 point deducted for fielding an ineligible player

1995-96

Team							
Stevenage Borough	42	27	10	5	101	44	91
Woking	42	25	8	9	83	54	83
Hednesford Town	42	23	7	12	71	46	76
Macclesfield Town	42	22	9	11	66	49	75
Gateshead	42	18	13	11	58	46	67
Southport	42	18	12	12	77	64	66
Kidderminster Harriers	42	18	10	14	78	66	64
Northwich Victoria	42	16	12	14	72	64	60
Morecambe	42	17	8	17	78	72	59
Farnborough Town	42	15	14	13	63	58	59
Bromsgrove Rovers	42	15	14	13	59	57	59
Altrincham	42	15	13	14	59	64	58
Telford United	42	15	10	17	51	56	55
Stalybridge Celtic	42	16	7	19	59	68	55
Halifax Town	42	13	13	16	49	63	52
Kettering Town	42	13	9	20	68	84	48
Slough Town	42	13	8	21	63	76	47
Bath City	42	13	7	22	45	66	46
Welling United	42	10	15	17	42	53	45
Dover Athletic	42	11	7	24	51	74	40
Runcorn	42	9	8	25	48	87	35
Dagenham & Redbridge	42	7	12	23	43	73	33

1996-97

Team							
Macclesfield Town	42	27	9	6	80	30	90
Kidderminster Harriers	42	26	7	9	84	42	85
Stevenage Borough	42	24	10	8	87	53	82
Morecambe	42	19	9	14	69	56	66
Woking	42	18	10	14	71	63	64
Northwich Victoria	42	17	12	13	61	54	63
Farnborough Town	42	16	13	13	58	53	61
Hednesford Town	42	16	12	14	52	50	60
Telford United	42	16	10	16	46	56	58
Gateshead	42	15	11	16	59	63	56
Southport	42	15	10	17	51	61	55
Rushden & Diamonds	42	14	11	17	61	63	53
Stalybridge Celtic	42	14	10	18	53	58	52
Kettering Town	42	14	9	19	53	62	51
Hayes	42	12	14	16	54	55	50
Slough Town	42	12	14	16	62	65	50
Dover Athletic	42	12	14	16	57	68	50
Welling United	42	13	9	20	50	60	48
Halifax Town	42	12	12	18	55	74	48
Bath City	42	12	11	19	53	80	47
Bromsgrove Rovers	42	12	5	25	41	67	41
Altrincham	42	9	12	21	49	73	39

1997-98

Team							
Halifax Town	42	25	12	5	74	43	87
Cheltenham Town	42	23	9	10	63	43	78
Woking	42	22	8	12	72	46	74
Rushden & Diamonds	42	23	5	14	79	57	74
Morecambe	42	21	10	11	77	64	73
Hereford United	42	18	13	11	56	49	67
Hednesford Town	42	18	12	12	59	50	66
Slough Town	42	18	10	14	58	49	64
Northwich Victoria	42	15	15	12	63	59	60
Welling United	42	17	9	16	64	62	60
Yeovil Town	42	17	8	17	73	63	59
Hayes	42	16	10	16	62	52	58
Dover Athletic	42	15	10	17	60	70	55
Kettering Town	42	13	13	16	53	60	52
Stevenage Borough	42	13	12	17	59	63	51
Southport	42	13	11	18	56	58	50
Kidderminster Harriers	42	11	14	17	56	63	49
Farnborough Town	42	12	8	22	56	70	44
Leek Town	42	10	14	18	52	67	44
Telford United	42	10	12	20	53	76	42
Gateshead	42	8	11	23	51	87	35
Stalybridge Celtic	42	7	8	27	48	93	29

1998-99

Team							
Cheltenham Town	42	22	14	6	71	36	80
Kettering Town	42	22	10	10	58	37	76
Hayes	42	22	8	12	63	50	74
Rushden & Diamonds	42	20	12	10	71	42	72
Yeovil Town	42	20	11	11	68	54	71
Stevenage Borough	42	17	17	8	62	45	68
Northwich Victoria	42	19	9	14	60	51	66
Kingstonian	42	17	13	12	50	49	64
Woking	42	18	9	15	51	45	62
Hednesford Town	42	15	16	11	49	44	61
Dover Athletic	42	15	13	14	54	48	58
Forest Green Rovers	42	15	13	14	55	50	58
Hereford United	42	15	10	17	49	46	55
Morecambe	42	15	8	19	66	62	53
Kidderminster Harriers	42	14	9	19	56	52	51
Doncaster Rovers	42	12	12	18	51	55	48
Telford United	42	10	16	16	44	46	46
Southport	42	10	15	17	47	59	45
Barrow	42	11	10	21	40	63	43
Welling United	42	9	14	19	44	65	41
Leek Town	42	8	8	26	48	76	32
Farnborough United	42	7	11	24	41	89	32

1999-2000

Team							
Kidderminster Harriers	42	26	7	9	75	40	85
Rushden & Diamonds	42	21	13	8	71	42	76
Morecambe	42	18	16	8	70	48	70
Scarborough	42	19	12	11	60	35	69
Kingstonian	42	20	7	15	58	44	67
Dover Athletic	42	18	12	12	65	56	66
Yeovil Town	42	18	10	14	60	63	64
Hereford United	42	15	14	13	61	52	59
Southport	42	15	13	14	55	56	58
Stevenage Borough	42	16	9	17	60	54	57
Hayes	42	16	8	18	57	58	56
Doncaster Rovers	42	15	9	18	46	48	54
Kettering Town	42	12	16	14	44	50	52
Woking	42	13	13	16	45	53	52
Nuneaton Borough	42	12	15	15	49	53	51
Telford United	42	14	9	19	56	66	51
Hednesford Town	42	15	6	21	45	68	51
Northwich Victoria	42	13	12	17	53	78	51
Forest Green Rovers	42	13	8	21	54	63	47
Welling United	42	13	8	21	54	66	47
Altrincham	42	9	19	14	51	60	46
Sutton United	42	8	10	24	39	75	34

2000-2001

Rushden & Diamonds	42	25	11	6	78	36	86
Yeovil Town	42	24	8	10	73	50	80
Dagenham & Redbridge	42	23	8	11	71	54	77
Southport	42	20	9	13	58	46	69
Leigh RMI	42	19	11	12	63	57	68
Telford United	42	19	8	15	51	51	65
Stevenage Borough	42	15	18	9	71	61	63
Chester City	42	16	14	12	49	43	62
Doncaster Rovers	42	15	13	14	47	43	58
Scarborough	42	14	16	12	56	54	58
Hereford United	42	14	15	13	60	46	57
Boston United	42	13	17	12	74	63	56
Nuneaton Borough	42	13	15	14	60	60	54
Woking	42	13	15	14	52	57	54
Dover Athletic	42	14	11	17	54	56	53
Forest Green Rovers	42	11	15	16	43	54	48
Northwich Victoria	42	11	13	18	49	67	46
Hayes	42	12	10	20	44	71	46
Morecambe	42	11	12	19	64	66	45
Kettering Town	42	11	10	21	46	62	43
Kingstonian	42	8	10	24	47	73	34
Hednesford Town	42	5	13	24	46	86	28

2001-2002

Boston United	42	25	9	8	84	42	84
Dagenham & Redbridge	42	24	12	6	70	47	84
Yeovil Town	42	19	13	10	66	53	70
Doncaster Rovers	42	18	13	11	68	46	67
Barnet	42	19	10	13	64	48	67
Morecambe	42	17	11	14	63	67	62
Farnborough Town	42	18	7	17	66	54	61
Margate	42	14	16	12	59	53	58
Telford United	42	14	15	13	63	58	57
Nuneaton Borough	42	16	9	17	57	57	57
Stevenage Borough	42	15	10	17	57	60	55
Scarborough	42	14	14	14	55	63	55
Northwich Victoria	42	16	7	19	57	70	55
Chester City	42	15	9	18	54	51	54
Southport	42	13	14	15	53	49	53
Leigh RMI	42	15	8	19	56	58	53
Hereford United	42	14	10	18	50	53	52
Forest Green Rovers	42	12	15	15	54	76	51
Woking	42	13	9	20	59	70	48
Hayes	42	13	5	24	53	80	44
Stalybridge Celtic	42	11	10	21	40	69	43
Dover Athletic	42	11	6	25	41	65	39

2002-2003

Yeovil Town	42	28	11	3	100	37	95
Morecambe	42	23	9	10	86	42	78
Doncaster Rovers	42	22	12	8	73	47	78
Chester City	42	21	12	9	59	31	75
Dagenham & Redbridge	42	21	9	12	71	59	72
Hereford United	42	19	7	16	64	51	64
Scarborough	42	18	10	14	63	54	64
Halifax Town	42	18	10	14	50	51	64
Forest Green Rovers	42	17	8	17	61	62	59
Margate	42	15	11	16	60	66	56
Barnet	42	13	14	15	65	68	53
Stevenage Borough	42	14	10	18	61	55	52
Farnborough Town	42	13	12	17	57	56	51
Northwich Victoria	42	13	12	17	66	72	51
Telford United	42	14	7	21	54	69	49
Burton Albion	42	13	10	19	52	77	49
Gravesend & Northfleet	42	12	12	18	62	73	48
Leigh RMI	42	14	6	22	44	71	48
Woking	42	11	14	17	52	81	47
Nuneaton Borough	42	13	7	22	51	78	46
Southport	42	11	12	19	54	69	45
Kettering Town	42	8	7	27	37	73	31

2003-2004

Chester City	42	27	11	4	85	34	92
Hereford United	42	28	7	7	103	44	91
Shrewsbury Town	42	20	14	8	67	42	74
Barnet	42	19	14	9	60	46	71
Aldershot Town	42	20	10	12	80	67	70
Exeter City	42	19	12	11	71	57	69
Morecambe	42	20	7	15	66	66	67
Stevenage Borough	42	18	9	15	58	52	63
Woking	42	15	16	11	65	52	61
Accrington Stanley	42	15	13	14	68	61	58
Gravesend & Northfleet	42	14	15	13	69	66	57
Telford United	42	15	10	17	49	51	55
Dagenham & Redbridge	42	15	9	18	59	64	54
* Burton Albion	42	15	7	20	57	59	51
Scarborough	42	12	15	15	51	54	51
Margate	42	14	9	19	56	64	51
Tamworth	42	13	10	19	49	68	49
Forest Green Rovers	42	12	12	18	58	80	48
Halifax Town	42	12	8	22	43	65	44
Farnborough Town	42	10	9	23	53	74	39
Leigh RMI	42	7	8	27	46	97	29
Northwich Victoria	42	4	11	27	30	80	23

* Burton Albion had 1 point deducted.

ISTHMIAN LEAGUE

1905-06

London Caledonians	10	7	1	2	25	8	15
Clapton	10	6	1	3	11	13	13
Casuals	10	3	4	3	14	14	10
Civil Service	10	4	1	5	16	20	9
Ealing Association	10	3	2	5	15	19	8
Ilford	10	1	3	6	5	12	5

1906-07

Ilford	10	8	2	0	26	9	18
London Caledonians	10	6	0	4	19	14	12
Clapton	10	4	3	3	18	11	11
Civil Service	10	3	1	6	11	19	7
Ealing Association	10	3	1	6	12	22	7
Casuals	10	2	1	7	15	26	5

1907-08

London Caledonians	10	5	2	3	20	15	12
Clapton	10	4	3	3	24	14	11
Ilford	10	5	1	4	28	22	11
Oxford City	10	5	1	4	20	20	11
Dulwich Hamlet	10	3	2	5	15	18	8
West Norwood	10	3	1	6	13	31	7

1908-09

Bromley	18	11	1	6	42	29	23
Leytonstone	18	9	4	5	43	31	22
Ilford	18	9	4	5	37	36	22
Dulwich Hamlet	18	9	2	7	39	30	20
Clapton	18	8	4	6	34	32	20
Oxford City	18	6	4	8	29	32	16
Nunhead	18	7	2	9	31	35	16
Shepherd's Bush	18	6	3	9	26	44	15
London Caledonians	18	4	6	8	25	34	14
West Norwood	18	5	2	11	40	43	12

1909-10

Bromley	18	11	4	3	32	10	26
Clapton	18	10	4	4	56	19	24
Nunhead	18	10	4	4	49	26	24
Ilford	18	10	3	5	31	17	23
Dulwich Hamlet	18	8	4	6	26	26	20
Leytonstone	18	7	3	8	44	46	17
Oxford City	18	5	4	9	28	45	14
London Caledonians	18	5	3	10	19	40	13
West Norwood	18	5	2	11	28	54	12
Shepherd's Bush	18	2	3	13	23	55	7

1910-11

Clapton	18	11	4	3	39	19	26
Leytonstone	18	12	1	5	47	30	25
Dulwich Hamlet	18	8	5	5	28	22	21
Oxford City	18	7	4	7	32	43	18
Ilford	18	8	1	9	41	32	17
Shepherd's Bush	18	7	3	8	31	27	17
Bromley	18	8	4	6	32	27	16
Nunhead	18	5	4	9	32	36	14
West Norwood	18	4	5	9	24	43	13
London Caledonians	18	3	3	12	18	45	9

Bromley had 4 points deducted

1911-12

London Caledonians	20	11	7	2	39	25	29
Ilford	20	11	3	6	37	24	25
Nunhead	20	10	5	5	36	30	25
Dulwich Hamlet	20	8	5	7	33	23	21
West Norwood	20	9	3	8	38	38	21
Clapton	20	7	5	8	37	37	19
Woking	20	7	5	8	38	41	19
Shepherd's Bush	20	5	6	9	39	49	16
Leytonstone	20	5	6	9	28	38	16
Oxford City	20	5	5	10	33	36	15
Tunbridge Wells	20	5	4	11	23	40	14

1912-13

London Caledonians	20	14	5	1	38	12	33
Leytonstone	20	12	3	5	45	20	27
Nunhead	20	12	3	5	36	23	27
Clapton	20	7	7	6	23	20	21
Dulwich Hamlet	20	8	4	8	34	28	20
Woking	20	7	5	8	33	40	19
Oxford City	20	6	6	8	23	39	18
Ilford	20	6	5	9	27	37	17
Shepherd's Bush	20	5	5	10	26	38	15
Tunbridge Wells	20	5	4	11	22	36	14
West Norwood	20	3	3	14	23	37	9

1913-14

London Caledonians	20	12	6	2	55	23	30
Nunhead	20	11	6	3	49	27	28
Ilford	20	11	4	5	52	35	26
Dulwich Hamlet	20	10	4	6	34	22	24
New Crusaders	20	10	3	7	40	30	23
Oxford City	20	10	0	10	42	42	20
Leytonstone	20	8	4	8	29	32	20
Clapton	20	8	3	9	29	27	19
Shepherd's Bush	20	7	2	11	24	46	16
West Norwood	20	4	3	13	27	47	11
Woking	20	1	1	18	11	61	3

1919

Leytonstone	8	5	1	2	21	7	11
Ilford	8	4	2	2	22	16	10
Dulwich Hamlet	8	3	2	3	19	17	8
Nunhead	8	3	2	3	18	19	8
Clapton	8	0	3	5	14	35	3

1919-20

Dulwich Hamlet	22	15	3	4	58	16	33
Nunhead	22	14	5	3	48	26	33
Tufnell Park	22	12	4	6	45	32	28
Ilford	22	13	1	8	63	42	27
Oxford City	22	12	3	7	63	51	27
London Caledonians	22	10	3	9	32	30	23
Leytonstone	22	8	3	11	50	43	19
Clapton	22	8	3	11	38	44	19
Civil Service	22	7	4	11	35	40	18
Woking	22	6	3	13	36	42	15
West Norwood	22	5	4	13	19	53	14
Casuals	22	3	2	17	20	88	8

1920-21

Ilford	22	16	4	2	70	24	36
London Caledonians	22	13	5	4	45	17	31
Tufnell Park	22	14	3	5	43	24	31
Nunhead	22	12	5	5	53	33	29
Dulwich Hamlet	22	11	6	5	60	30	28
Oxford City	22	12	3	7	56	38	27
Leytonstone	22	8	6	8	36	29	22
Clapton	22	7	7	8	33	52	21
Civil Service	22	3	7	12	28	45	13
Woking	22	3	5	14	16	43	11
Casuals	22	3	3	16	31	87	9
West Norwood	22	2	2	18	18	67	6

1921-22

Ilford	26	17	4	5	66	34	38
Dulwich Hamlet	26	14	8	4	65	24	36
London Caledonians	26	16	4	6	41	21	36
Nunhead	26	12	5	9	65	41	29
Clapton	26	13	3	10	51	46	29
Tufnell Park	26	10	7	9	44	39	27
Oxford City	26	18	2	12	48	47	26
Wycombe Wanderers	26	18	2	12	61	64	26
Civil Service	26	9	8	9	60	48	26
Woking	26	10	6	10	39	49	26
Leytonstone	26	9	6	11	41	48	24
West Norwood	26	8	5	13	43	57	21
Wimbledon	26	7	4	15	52	56	18
Casuals	26	0	2	24	25	107	2

1922-23

Clapton	26	15	7	4	51	33	37
Nunhead	26	15	5	6	52	32	35
London Caledonians	26	13	7	6	43	26	33
Ilford	26	11	7	8	57	38	29
Casuals	26	12	5	9	68	51	29
Civil Service	26	9	10	7	39	36	28
Wycombe Wanderers	26	11	4	11	61	61	26
Dulwich Hamlet	26	9	7	10	60	44	25
Leytonstone	26	9	7	10	45	56	25
Tufnell Park	26	9	5	12	41	45	23
Wimbledon	26	10	2	14	49	50	22
Woking	26	7	6	13	42	67	20
Oxford City	26	6	5	15	45	68	17
West Norwood	26	5	5	16	25	71	15

1923-24

St Albans City	26	17	5	4	72	38	39
Dulwich Hamlet	26	15	6	5	49	28	36
Clapton	26	14	5	7	73	50	33
Wycombe Wanderers	26	14	5	7	88	65	33
London Caledonians	26	14	3	9	53	49	31
Civil Service	26	12	5	9	52	47	29
Casuals	26	13	1	12	65	54	27
Ilford	26	9	6	11	56	59	24
Nunhead	26	8	8	10	41	46	24
Wimbledon	26	8	4	14	43	62	20
Tufnell Park	26	8	2	16	38	53	18
Woking	26	5	8	13	31	62	18
Oxford City	26	7	2	17	53	74	16
Leytonstone	26	6	4	16	41	68	16

1924-25

London Caledonians	26	18	5	3	76	36	41
Clapton	26	19	1	6	64	34	39
St Albans City	26	16	2	8	69	39	34
Tufnell Park	26	11	4	11	47	41	26
Ilford	26	11	4	11	46	42	26
Leytonstone	26	12	2	12	55	63	26
The Casuals	26	12	1	13	55	58	25
Wycombe Wanderers	26	11	2	13	58	61	24
Civil Service	26	10	4	12	52	64	24
Nunhead	26	9	5	12	45	43	23
Wimbledon	26	10	2	14	50	54	22
Dulwich Hamlet	26	8	5	13	42	57	21
Oxford City	26	9	2	15	38	71	20
Woking	26	5	3	18	33	67	13

1925-26

Dulwich Hamlet	26	20	1	5	80	49	41
London Caledonians	26	18	1	7	81	44	37
Clapton	26	14	4	8	64	50	32
Wycombe Wanderers	26	14	3	9	97	83	31
St Albans City	26	12	6	8	76	54	30
Nunhead	26	13	4	9	49	43	30
Ilford	26	13	2	11	81	70	28
Leytonstone	26	12	1	13	75	63	25
Woking	26	8	6	12	56	73	22
Tufnell Park	26	8	5	13	36	53	21
The Casuals	26	8	4	14	48	61	20
Wimbledon	26	9	1	16	61	77	19
Oxford City	26	8	1	17	48	76	17
Civil Service	26	5	1	20	43	99	11

1926-27

St Albans City	26	20	1	5	96	34	41
Ilford	26	18	0	9	76	57	34
Wimbledon	26	15	3	8	72	45	33
Nunhead	26	11	8	7	51	33	30
Woking	26	12	6	8	68	60	30
London Caledonians	26	11	7	8	58	47	29
Clapton	26	11	4	11	58	60	26
Leytonstone	26	11	1	14	54	78	23
Dulwich Hamlet	26	9	4	13	60	58	22
Wycombe Wanderers	26	10	2	14	59	86	22
Tufnell Park	26	8	4	14	45	55	20
Oxford City	26	7	5	14	46	72	19
The Casuals	26	8	3	15	37	78	19
Civil Service	26	6	4	16	48	65	16

1927-28

St Albans City	26	15	5	6	86	50	35
London Caledonians	26	12	9	5	63	38	33
Ilford	26	14	4	8	72	54	32
Woking	26	13	5	8	72	56	31
Nunhead	26	13	2	11	57	54	28
Wimbledon	26	12	3	11	57	48	27
Leytonstone	26	13	1	12	53	56	27
Clapton	26	8	10	8	52	47	26
Dulwich Hamlet	26	8	9	9	56	49	25
The Casuals	26	8	8	10	54	58	24
Wycombe Wanderers	26	9	5	12	60	69	23
Oxford City	26	7	7	12	36	57	21
Civil Service	26	8	4	14	38	76	20
Tufnell Park	26	4	4	18	38	82	12

1928-29

Nunhead	26	15	6	5	47	35	36
London Caledonians	26	15	4	7	65	33	34
Dulwich Hamlet	26	14	6	6	65	34	34
Wimbledon	26	9	10	7	66	54	28
Ilford	26	12	3	11	67	52	27
Clapton	26	11	5	10	60	55	27
Tufnell Park	26	11	5	10	58	55	27
St Albans City	26	12	3	11	63	69	27
Leytonstone	26	11	3	12	56	79	25
Wycombe Wanderers	26	10	3	13	58	60	23
Oxford City	26	10	3	13	61	71	23
The Casuals	26	8	5	13	49	60	21
Woking	26	8	3	15	39	65	19
Civil Service	26	4	5	17	39	71	13

1929-30

Nunhead	26	19	3	4	69	36	41
Dulwich Hamlet	26	15	6	5	74	39	36
Kingstonian	26	15	4	7	57	37	34
Ilford	26	16	1	9	84	60	33
Woking	26	11	5	10	66	65	27
Wimbledon	26	11	2	13	64	66	24
Wycombe Wanderers	26	10	4	12	49	52	24
The Casuals	26	8	7	11	50	51	23
Oxford City	26	10	3	13	45	60	23
St Albans City	26	9	4	13	54	77	22
Clapton	26	8	4	14	47	57	20
London Caledonians	26	8	3	15	49	69	19
Leytonstone	26	8	3	15	48	68	19
Tufnell Park	26	6	7	13	35	54	19

1930-31

Wimbledon	26	18	6	2	69	37	42
Dulwich Hamlet	26	12	9	5	51	39	33
Wycombe Wanderers	26	12	6	8	67	45	30
The Casuals	26	12	6	8	71	56	30
St Albans City	26	11	7	8	67	66	29
Ilford	26	10	6	10	70	62	26
Oxford City	26	10	5	11	43	48	25
London Caledonians	26	8	8	10	43	53	24
Kingstonian	26	10	4	12	49	64	24
Tufnell Park	26	9	5	12	45	61	23
Nunhead	26	9	4	13	49	54	22
Woking	26	9	4	13	56	63	22
Clapton	26	7	4	15	62	75	18
Leytonstone	26	6	4	16	46	65	16

1931-32

Wimbledon	26	17	2	7	60	35	36
Ilford	26	13	9	4	71	45	35
Dulwich Hamlet	26	15	3	8	69	43	33
Wycombe Wanderers	26	14	5	7	72	50	33
Oxford City	26	15	2	9	63	49	32
Kingstonian	26	13	3	10	71	50	29
Tufnell Park	26	9	7	10	50	48	25
Nunhead	26	9	7	10	54	61	25
The Casuals	26	10	4	12	59	65	24
Clapton	26	9	5	12	50	57	23
Leytonstone	26	9	3	14	36	61	21
St Albans City	26	8	4	14	57	78	20
Woking	26	6	5	15	44	64	17
London Caledonians	26	2	7	17	24	74	11

1932-33

Dulwich Hamlet	26	15	6	5	71	45	36
Leytonstone	26	16	4	6	66	43	36
Kingstonian	26	15	2	9	77	49	32
Ilford	26	14	0	12	60	58	28
The Casuals	26	12	2	12	48	36	26
Tufnell Park	26	11	3	12	51	51	25
St Albans City	26	12	1	13	57	63	25
Clapton	26	10	5	11	51	65	25
Oxford City	26	9	6	11	49	54	24
Woking	26	10	4	12	53	61	24
Wycombe Wanderers	26	10	4	12	47	56	24
Nunhead	26	8	6	12	42	50	22
Wimbledon	26	8	5	13	55	67	21
London Caledonians	26	5	6	15	35	64	16

1933-34

Kingstonian	26	15	7	4	80	42	37
Dulwich Hamlet	26	15	5	6	68	36	35
Wimbledon	26	13	7	6	62	35	33
Tufnell Park	26	14	5	7	55	50	33
Ilford	26	15	2	9	60	56	32
The Casuals	26	13	5	8	47	32	31
Leytonstone	26	13	3	10	55	48	29
Nunhead	26	10	5	11	48	44	25
London Caledonians	26	7	8	11	29	51	22
Wycombe Wanderers	26	9	2	15	57	60	20
St Albans City	26	8	4	14	44	75	20
Oxford City	26	7	4	15	45	57	18
Clapton	26	5	6	15	35	62	16
Woking	26	6	1	19	43	81	13

1934-35

Wimbledon	26	14	7	5	63	30	35
Oxford City	26	14	4	8	69	50	32
Leytonstone	26	15	2	9	49	36	32
Dulwich Hamlet	26	11	7	8	66	45	29
Tufnell Park	26	11	7	8	53	44	29
Kingstonian	26	11	6	9	44	40	28
Nunhead	26	10	7	9	35	34	27
London Caledonians	26	9	7	10	40	41	25
St Albans City	26	9	6	11	61	80	24
Ilford	26	9	6	11	40	56	24
Clapton	26	7	7	12	46	48	21
Woking	26	9	3	14	44	68	21
Wycombe Wanderers	26	7	6	13	51	69	20
The Casuals	26	6	5	15	37	57	17

1935-36

Wimbledon	26	19	2	5	82	29	40
The Casuals	26	14	5	7	60	45	33
Ilford	26	13	3	10	67	47	29
Dulwich Hamlet	26	10	8	8	64	47	28
Nunhead	26	11	6	9	51	40	28
Wycombe Wanderers	26	13	2	11	60	68	28
Clapton	26	11	5	10	42	46	27
Oxford City	26	11	4	11	60	58	26
St Albans City	26	11	2	13	59	64	24
Woking	26	9	4	13	43	62	22
Tufnell Park	26	9	3	14	42	61	21
London Caledonians	26	9	3	14	35	52	21
Kingstonian	26	9	2	15	43	56	20
Leytonstone	26	7	3	16	34	67	17

1936-37

Kingstonian	26	18	3	5	63	43	39
Nunhead	26	17	3	6	77	32	37
Leytonstone	26	16	4	6	71	42	36
Ilford	26	14	5	7	86	39	33
Dulwich Hamlet	26	12	6	8	64	48	30
Wycombe Wanderers	26	10	5	11	55	52	25
Wimbledon	26	9	7	10	52	53	25
Clapton	26	10	5	11	42	51	25
The Casuals	26	10	3	13	46	58	23
Woking	26	9	4	13	53	69	22
Oxford City	26	8	5	13	56	89	21
St Albans City	26	7	5	14	44	62	19
Tufnell Park	26	4	7	15	43	74	15
London Caledonians	26	5	4	17	26	66	14

1937-38

Leytonstone	26	17	6	3	72	34	40
Ilford	26	17	3	6	70	39	37
Tufnell Park	26	15	2	9	62	47	32
Nunhead	26	14	3	9	52	44	31
Wycombe Wanderers	26	12	5	9	69	55	29
Dulwich Hamlet	26	13	3	10	57	46	29
Kingstonian	26	12	4	10	51	48	28
Clapton	26	9	6	11	49	53	24
Wimbledon	26	10	3	13	62	49	23
London Caledonians	26	9	4	13	44	55	22
Oxford City	26	7	7	12	35	71	21
The Casuals	26	8	3	15	51	74	19
Woking	26	7	2	17	41	72	16
St Albans City	26	4	5	17	31	60	13

1938-39

Leytonstone	26	18	4	4	68	32	40
Ilford	26	17	4	5	68	32	38
Kingstonian	26	17	3	6	62	39	37
Dulwich Hamlet	26	15	5	6	60	32	35
Wimbledon	26	14	3	9	88	56	31
Nunhead	26	11	6	9	54	44	28
The Casuals	26	11	6	9	54	51	28
Clapton	26	12	2	12	69	61	26
Wycombe Wanderers	26	10	6	10	62	62	26
St Albans City	26	8	5	13	44	50	21
Woking	26	9	2	15	35	56	20
Oxford City	26	4	4	18	44	84	12
Tufnell Park	26	4	4	18	33	87	12
London Caledonians	26	3	4	19	26	81	10

1945-46

Walthamstow Avenue	26	21	0	5	100	31	42
Oxford City	26	17	6	3	91	40	40
Romford	26	15	3	8	83	59	33
Dulwich Hamlet	26	14	2	10	63	59	30
Tufnell Park	26	12	4	10	70	55	28
Woking	26	10	7	9	56	54	27
Ilford	26	12	2	12	56	71	26
Leytonstone	26	11	3	12	61	75	25
Wycombe Wanderers	26	9	3	14	80	88	21
Wimbledon	26	7	6	13	52	72	20
Corinthian Casuals	26	8	4	14	58	83	20
Clapton	26	8	3	15	51	62	19
St Albans City	26	6	6	14	48	85	18
Kingstonian	26	6	3	17	48	86	15

1946-47

Leytonstone	26	19	2	5	92	36	40
Dulwich Hamlet	26	17	3	6	78	46	37
Romford	26	13	8	5	76	52	34
Walthamstow Avenue	26	13	4	9	64	37	30
Oxford City	26	12	6	8	70	51	30
Kingstonian	26	12	4	10	54	57	28
Wycombe Wanderers	26	9	8	9	62	62	26
Wimbledon	26	10	5	11	68	64	25
Ilford	26	7	7	12	66	78	21
Tufnell Park	26	8	5	13	45	69	21
Woking	26	7	7	12	34	62	21
Clapton	26	6	8	12	41	59	20
St Albans City	26	7	5	14	47	79	19
Corinthian Casuals	26	4	4	18	36	80	12

1947-48

Leytonstone	26	19	1	6	87	38	39
Kingstonian	26	16	6	4	74	39	38
Walthamstow Avenue	26	17	3	6	61	37	37
Dulwich Hamlet	26	17	2	7	71	39	36
Wimbledon	26	13	6	7	66	40	32
Romford	26	14	1	11	53	47	29
Oxford City	26	10	5	11	50	68	25
Woking	26	10	3	13	63	55	23
Ilford	26	7	8	11	51	59	22
St Albans City	26	9	2	15	43	56	20
Wycombe Wanderers	26	7	5	14	51	65	19
Tufnell Park	26	7	4	15	38	83	18
Clapton	26	5	4	17	35	69	14
Corinthian Casuals	26	5	2	19	33	81	12

1948-49

Dulwich Hamlet	26	15	6	5	60	31	36
Walthamstow Avenue	26	16	4	6	65	38	36
Wimbledon	26	15	4	7	64	41	34
Ilford	26	14	3	9	56	36	31
Oxford City	26	13	5	8	48	34	31
Leytonstone	26	12	6	8	49	41	30
Woking	26	14	1	11	64	59	29
Romford	26	11	3	12	47	54	25
Kingstonian	26	10	4	12	43	47	24
Corinthian Casuals	26	11	2	13	47	59	24
Wycombe Wanderers	26	11	2	13	49	61	24
St Albans City	26	6	6	14	40	60	16
Clapton	26	5	5	16	32	61	15
Tufnell Park	26	1	5	20	28	70	7

St Albans City had 2 points deducted

1949-50

Leytonstone	26	17	5	4	77	31	39
Wimbledon	26	18	2	6	72	51	38
Kingstonian	26	16	3	7	59	39	35
Walthamstow Avenue	26	14	6	6	73	42	34
Dulwich Hamlet	26	14	3	9	60	47	31
St Albans City	26	12	3	11	59	45	27
Woking	26	10	6	10	60	71	26
Wycombe Wanderers	26	9	7	10	51	52	25
Romford	26	10	4	12	45	49	24
Ilford	26	10	4	12	46	53	24
Clapton	26	8	6	12	51	59	22
Oxford City	26	6	6	14	35	54	18
Corinthian Casuals	26	4	5	17	41	69	13
Tufnell Park	26	3	2	21	24	91	8

1950-51

Leytonstone	26	20	3	3	72	26	43
Walthamstow Avenue	26	15	4	7	57	37	34
Romford	26	15	3	8	58	49	33
Wimbledon	26	13	5	8	58	39	31
Dulwich Hamlet	26	14	2	10	54	43	30
Woking	26	11	6	9	65	55	28
Ilford	26	12	4	10	44	45	28
Corinthian Casuals	26	13	0	13	62	60	26
St Albans City	26	11	4	11	32	36	26
Kingstonian	26	9	4	13	46	54	22
Wycombe Wanderers	26	8	3	15	46	64	19
Oxford City	26	7	4	15	47	65	18
Clapton	26	6	5	15	29	50	17
Tufnell Park Edmonton	26	4	1	21	24	73	9

1951-52

Leytonstone	26	13	9	4	63	36	35
Wimbledon	26	16	3	7	65	44	35
Walthamstow Avenue	26	15	4	7	71	43	34
Romford	26	14	4	8	64	42	32
Kingstonian	26	11	7	8	62	48	29
Wycombe Wanderers	26	12	5	9	64	59	29
Woking	26	11	5	10	60	71	27
Dulwich Hamlet	26	11	4	11	60	53	26
Corinthian Casuals	26	11	4	11	55	66	26
St Albans City	26	9	7	10	48	53	25
Ilford	26	8	5	13	32	47	21
Clapton	26	9	2	15	50	59	20
Oxford City	26	6	3	17	50	72	15
Tufnell Park Edmonton	26	2	6	18	25	73	10

1952-53

Walthamstow Avenue	28	19	6	3	53	25	44
Bromley	28	17	4	7	71	35	38
Leytonstone	28	14	6	8	60	38	34
Wimbledon	28	14	5	9	68	37	33
Kingstonian	28	13	6	9	62	50	32
Dulwich Hamlet	28	15	2	11	62	52	32
Romford	28	12	8	8	62	52	32
Wycombe Wanderers	28	14	2	12	54	62	30
St Albans City	28	11	6	11	43	57	28
Barking	28	9	7	12	42	51	25
Ilford	28	10	4	14	59	57	24
Woking	28	10	4	14	57	72	24
Corinthian Casuals	28	7	9	12	45	56	23
Oxford City	28	5	2	21	37	87	12
Clapton	28	2	5	21	27	71	9

1953-54

Bromley	28	18	3	7	76	45	39
Walthamstow Avenue	28	13	7	8	55	30	33
Wycombe Wanderers	28	15	3	10	65	44	33
Ilford	28	11	10	7	48	44	32
Corinthian Casuals	28	12	7	9	59	44	31
Woking	28	13	4	11	54	58	30
Leytonstone	28	12	5	11	58	48	29
St Albans City	28	11	6	11	54	55	28
Dulwich Hamlet	28	11	6	11	55	57	28
Romford	28	11	5	12	57	54	27
Clapton	28	11	5	12	42	56	27
Barking	28	11	2	15	59	84	24
Kingstonian	28	8	7	13	59	71	23
Wimbledon	28	7	8	13	43	59	22
Oxford City	28	4	6	18	49	84	14

1954-55

Walthamstow Avenue	28	21	1	6	80	38	43
St Albans City	28	18	3	7	61	41	39
Bromley	28	18	2	8	66	34	38
Wycombe Wanderers	28	16	3	9	68	43	35
Ilford	28	13	5	10	64	46	31
Barking	28	15	1	12	55	51	31
Woking	28	12	3	13	75	79	27
Kingstonian	28	10	7	11	47	57	27
Leytonstone	28	10	4	14	35	51	24
Oxford City	28	10	3	15	43	74	23
Clapton	28	9	4	15	41	50	22
Wimbledon	28	10	2	16	48	62	22
Corinthian Casuals	28	9	3	16	50	65	21
Dulwich Hamlet	28	7	5	16	48	60	19
Romford	28	4	10	14	43	73	18

1955-56

Wycombe Wanderers	28	19	5	4	82	36	43
Bromley	28	12	7	9	54	43	31
Leytonstone	28	12	7	9	50	44	31
Woking	28	14	3	11	62	60	31
Barking	28	12	7	9	41	45	31
Kingstonian	28	12	6	10	67	64	30
Walthamstow Avenue	28	13	3	12	61	45	29
Ilford	28	10	8	10	44	52	28
Oxford City	28	10	7	11	48	55	27
Clapton	28	9	8	11	45	48	26
Wimbledon	28	12	2	14	51	62	26
Corinthian Casuals	28	9	7	12	56	56	25
Dulwich Hamlet	28	9	6	13	55	67	24
Romford	28	9	6	13	42	55	24
St Albans City	28	2	10	16	36	62	14

1956-57

Wycombe Wanderers	30	18	6	6	86	53	42
Woking	30	20	1	9	104	47	41
Bromley	30	16	5	9	78	60	37
Oxford City	30	16	3	11	65	57	35
Ilford	30	12	8	10	59	65	32
Tooting & Mitcham United	30	10	11	9	53	48	31
Kingstonian	30	11	9	10	72	77	31
Walthamstow Avenue	30	11	8	11	48	46	30
Dulwich Hamlet	30	13	3	14	65	54	29
St Albans City	30	13	3	14	62	71	29
Leytonstone	30	11	6	13	50	50	28
Clapton	30	9	9	12	48	59	27
Wimbledon	30	10	5	15	47	66	25
Romford	30	10	5	15	53	81	25
Barking	30	7	6	17	48	72	20
Corinthian Casuals	30	7	4	19	46	78	18

1957-58

Tooting & Mitcham United	30	20	6	4	79	33	46
Wycombe Wanderers	30	19	4	7	78	42	42
Walthamstow Avenue	30	17	5	8	63	35	39
Bromley	30	13	9	8	66	51	35
Oxford City	30	13	6	11	59	48	32
Leytonstone	30	13	6	11	49	48	32
Wimbledon	30	15	2	13	64	66	32
Corinthian Casuals	30	12	8	10	62	68	32
Woking	30	12	7	11	70	58	31
Barking	30	10	6	14	49	61	26
St Albans City	30	11	3	16	56	76	25
Clapton	30	8	9	13	42	65	25
Kingstonian	30	7	8	15	45	66	22
Dulwich Hamlet	30	7	7	16	49	64	21
Ilford	30	8	4	18	46	70	20
Romford	30	6	8	16	45	71	20

1958-59

	P	W	D	L	F	A	Pts
Wimbledon	30	22	3	5	91	38	47
Dulwich Hamlet	30	18	5	7	68	44	41
Wycombe Wanderers	30	18	4	8	93	50	40
Oxford City	30	17	4	9	87	58	38
Walthamstow Avenue	30	16	5	9	59	40	37
Tooting & Mitcham United	30	15	4	11	84	55	34
Barking	30	14	2	14	59	53	30
Woking	30	12	6	12	66	66	30
Bromley	30	11	7	12	56	55	29
Clapton	30	10	6	14	55	67	26
Ilford	30	10	6	14	46	67	26
Kingstonian	30	9	4	17	54	72	22
St Albans City	30	8	6	16	53	89	22
Leytonstone	30	7	6	17	40	87	20
Romford	30	7	5	18	54	76	19
Corinthian Casuals	30	7	5	18	44	92	19

1959-60

	P	W	D	L	F	A	Pts
Tooting & Mitcham United	30	17	8	5	75	43	42
Wycombe Wanderers	30	19	3	8	84	46	41
Wimbledon	30	18	3	9	66	36	39
Kingstonian	30	18	3	9	76	51	39
Corinthian Casuals	30	18	1	11	69	61	37
Bromley	30	15	6	9	75	46	36
Dulwich Hamlet	30	14	6	10	65	47	34
Walthamstow Avenue	30	11	11	8	48	38	33
Oxford City	30	10	10	10	57	57	30
Leytonstone	30	10	8	12	43	46	28
Woking	30	10	6	14	54	61	26
St Albans City	30	10	6	14	50	65	26
Maidstone United	30	10	5	15	53	60	25
Barking	30	7	4	19	30	75	18
Ilford	30	5	6	19	34	86	16
Clapton	30	3	4	23	32	92	10

1960-61

	P	W	D	L	F	A	Pts
Bromley	30	20	6	4	89	42	46
Walthamstow Avenue	30	20	5	5	87	38	45
Wimbledon	30	18	6	6	72	43	42
Dulwich Hamlet	30	17	4	9	71	59	35
Maidstone United	30	14	8	8	63	39	36
Leytonstone	30	15	6	9	46	34	36
Tooting & Mitcham United	30	14	3	13	69	51	31
Wycombe Wanderers	30	12	5	13	63	61	29
St Albans City	30	12	4	14	45	72	28
Oxford City	30	10	7	13	59	59	27
Corinthian Casuals	30	9	9	12	49	59	27
Kingstonian	30	10	6	14	55	61	26
Woking	30	10	6	14	58	71	26
Ilford	30	5	8	17	30	69	18
Barking	30	3	8	19	30	76	14
Clapton	30	3	5	22	25	77	11

1961-62

	P	W	D	L	F	A	Pts
Wimbledon	30	19	6	5	68	24	44
Leytonstone	30	17	7	6	61	44	41
Walthamstow Avenue	30	14	8	8	51	31	36
Kingstonian	30	15	5	10	65	48	35
Tooting & Mitcham United	30	12	10	8	62	47	34
Oxford City	30	12	9	9	56	49	33
Wycombe Wanderers	30	12	7	11	57	51	31
Corinthian Casuals	30	12	7	11	45	51	31
St Albans City	30	10	9	11	55	55	29
Woking	30	9	9	12	51	60	27
Dulwich Hamlet	30	11	4	15	55	66	26
Barking	30	9	8	13	40	64	26
Ilford	30	7	10	13	50	59	24
Bromley	30	10	4	16	49	69	24
Clapton	30	6	8	16	45	67	20
Maidstone United	30	6	7	17	34	59	19

1962-63

	P	W	D	L	F	A	Pts
Wimbledon	30	19	8	3	84	33	46
Kingstonian	30	18	8	4	79	37	44
Tooting & Mitcham United	30	17	8	5	65	37	42
Ilford	30	19	3	8	70	44	41
Walthamstow Avenue	30	14	7	9	51	44	35
Maidstone United	30	13	8	9	56	45	34
Bromley	30	12	10	8	57	51	34
Leytonstone	30	12	7	11	48	50	31
Wycombe Wanderers	30	10	10	10	56	61	30
St Albans City	30	11	5	14	54	49	27
Barking	30	8	10	12	39	50	26
Oxford City	30	8	9	13	55	64	25
Woking	30	8	6	16	42	66	22
Clapton	30	7	4	19	30	71	18
Dulwich Hamlet	30	4	5	21	30	71	13
Corinthian Casuals	30	4	4	22	28	71	12

1963-64

	P	W	D	L	F	A	Pts
Wimbledon	38	27	6	5	87	44	60
Hendon	38	25	4	9	124	38	54
Kingstonian	38	24	4	10	100	62	52
Sutton United	38	23	5	10	99	64	51
Enfield	38	20	10	8	96	56	50
Oxford City	38	20	8	10	90	55	48
Tooting & Mitcham United	38	19	8	11	78	51	46
St Albans City	38	14	12	12	62	63	40
Ilford	38	16	8	14	75	79	40
Maidstone United	38	15	8	15	65	71	38
Walthamstow Avenue	38	15	6	17	70	66	36
Leytonstone	38	14	8	16	66	71	36
Wycombe Wanderers	38	13	6	19	74	80	32
Hitchin Town	38	14	4	20	67	100	32
Bromley	38	11	8	19	64	75	30
Barking	38	10	9	19	46	69	29
Woking	38	10	9	19	48	88	29
Corinthian Casuals	38	10	4	24	52	92	24
Dulwich Hamlet	38	6	12	20	47	97	24
Clapton	38	2	5	31	31	120	9

1964-65

	P	W	D	L	F	A	Pts
Hendon	38	28	7	3	123	49	63
Enfield	38	29	5	4	98	35	63
Kingstonian	38	24	8	6	86	44	56
Leytonstone	38	24	5	9	115	62	53
Oxford City	38	20	7	11	76	51	47
St Albans City	38	18	9	11	63	43	45
Sutton United	38	17	11	10	74	57	45
Wealdstone	38	19	6	13	93	68	44
Bromley	38	14	11	13	71	80	39
Tooting & Mitcham United	38	15	7	16	71	66	37
Hitchin Town	38	13	9	16	61	66	35
Walthamstow Avenue	38	15	5	18	63	82	35
Wycombe Wanderers	38	13	7	18	70	85	33
Corinthian Casuals	38	13	7	18	56	77	33
Barking	38	10	8	20	58	80	28
Ilford	38	8	8	22	43	89	24
Maidstone United	38	8	6	24	49	86	22
Dulwich Hamlet	38	8	5	25	45	79	21
Clapton	38	8	3	27	43	91	19
Woking	38	7	4	27	45	113	18

Hendon beat Enfield in a play-off to decide the Championship

1965-66

Leytonstone	38	27	7	4	98	33	63
Hendon	38	27	5	6	111	55	59
Enfield	38	24	8	6	104	54	56
Wycombe Wanderers	38	25	6	7	100	65	56
Kingstonian	38	24	5	9	94	55	53
Wealdstone	38	20	6	12	90	64	46
Maidstone United	38	19	6	13	74	61	44
St Albans City	38	19	5	14	57	56	43
Sutton United	38	17	7	14	83	72	41
Tooting & Mitcham United	38	16	7	15	65	58	39
Corinthian Casuals	38	17	5	16	74	67	39
Woking	38	12	10	16	60	83	34
Walthamstow Avenue	38	12	9	17	81	75	33
Oxford City	38	10	9	19	49	72	29
Barking	38	10	7	21	51	72	27
Bromley	38	10	5	23	69	101	25
Ilford	38	7	10	21	50	84	24
Hitchin Town	38	6	8	24	57	118	20
Clapton	38	5	6	27	46	103	16
Dulwich Hamlet	38	5	5	28	30	95	15

1968-69

22

Enfield	38	27	7	4	103	28	61
Hitchin Town	38	23	10	5	67	41	56
Sutton United	38	22	9	7	83	29	53
Wycombe Wanderers	38	23	6	9	70	37	52
Wealdstone	38	20	11	7	73	48	51
Hendon	38	22	5	11	69	47	49
St Albans City	38	17	13	8	75	44	47
Barking	38	20	7	11	69	46	47
Oxford City	38	18	8	12	76	64	44
Tooting & Mitcham United	38	16	10	12	68	55	42
Leytonstone	38	18	4	16	71	53	40
Kingstonian	38	15	8	15	62	56	38
Walthamstow Avenue	38	10	10	18	47	71	30
Maidstone United	38	10	8	20	47	75	28
Clapton	38	10	7	21	52	76	27
Woking	38	8	7	23	45	77	23
Bromley	38	8	7	23	52	95	23
Dulwich Hamlet	38	6	9	23	31	77	21
Ilford	38	6	8	24	33	77	20
Corinthian Casuals	38	2	4	32	23	120	8

1966-67

Sutton United	38	26	7	5	89	33	59
Walthamstow Avenue	38	22	12	4	89	47	56
Wycombe Wanderers	38	23	8	7	92	54	54
Enfield	38	25	2	11	87	33	52
Hendon	38	20	9	9	64	37	49
Tooting & Mitcham United	38	19	10	9	76	60	48
Leytonstone	38	19	9	10	67	38	47
St Albans City	38	16	12	10	59	45	44
Kingstonian	38	18	8	12	60	49	44
Oxford City	38	15	9	14	74	61	39
Woking	38	13	10	15	65	71	36
Wealdstone	38	13	8	17	72	73	34
Barking	38	11	12	15	56	61	34
Bromley	38	12	7	19	50	67	31
Clapton	38	10	8	20	49	92	28
Ilford	38	8	10	20	43	77	26
Corinthian Casuals	38	9	7	22	45	68	25
Maidstone United	38	6	10	22	43	90	22
Hitchin Town	38	8	6	24	39	89	22
Dulwich Hamlet	38	3	4	31	33	107	10

1969-70

Enfield	38	27	8	3	91	26	62
Wycombe Wanderers	38	25	11	2	85	24	61
Sutton United	38	24	9	5	75	35	57
Barking	38	21	9	8	93	47	51
Hendon	38	19	12	7	77	44	50
St Albans City	38	21	8	9	69	40	50
Hitchin Town	38	19	10	9	71	40	48
Tooting & Mitcham United	38	19	5	14	88	62	43
Leytonstone	38	17	7	14	57	41	41
Wealdstone	38	15	10	13	53	48	40
Oxford City	38	15	7	16	61	78	37
Kingstonian	38	13	9	16	55	57	35
Ilford	38	8	15	15	42	73	31
Dulwich Hamlet	38	8	12	18	46	66	28
Woking	38	10	7	21	46	69	27
Walthamstow Avenue	38	11	5	22	52	81	27
Clapton	38	9	7	22	45	87	25
Maidstone United	38	7	8	23	48	84	22
Corinthian Casuals	38	6	3	29	30	99	15
Bromley	38	3	4	31	28	111	10

1967-68

Enfield	38	28	8	2	85	22	64
Sutton United	38	22	11	5	89	27	55
Hendon	38	23	6	9	90	36	52
Leytonstone	38	21	10	7	78	41	52
St Albans City	38	20	8	10	78	41	48
Walthamstow Avenue	38	19	9	10	81	64	47
Wealdstone	38	19	8	11	80	45	46
Tooting & Mitcham United	38	19	5	14	57	45	43
Barking	38	17	8	13	75	57	42
Oxford City	38	17	4	17	59	58	38
Kingstonian	38	14	10	14	56	61	38
Hitchin Town	38	14	9	15	61	73	37
Bromley	38	12	10	16	58	80	34
Wycombe Wanderers	38	13	5	20	73	85	31
Dulwich Hamlet	38	10	7	21	39	66	27
Clapton	38	10	7	21	51	88	27
Woking	38	8	8	22	50	90	24
Corinthian Casuals	38	7	10	21	40	80	24
Ilford	38	7	7	24	41	77	21
Maidstone United	38	3	4	31	26	131	10

1970-71

Wycombe Wanderers	38	28	6	4	93	32	62
Sutton United	38	29	3	6	76	35	61
St Albans City	38	23	10	5	87	26	56
Enfield	38	24	7	7	67	24	55
Ilford	38	21	7	10	74	51	49
Hendon	38	18	11	9	81	37	47
Barking	38	20	4	14	89	59	44
Leytonstone	38	17	10	11	68	50	44
Woking	38	18	6	14	57	50	42
Walthamstow Avenue	38	14	11	13	63	52	39
Oxford City	38	13	10	15	51	48	36
Hitchin Town	38	12	9	17	46	60	33
Wealdstone	38	12	8	18	45	64	32
Tooting & Mitcham United	38	11	9	18	44	66	31
Kingstonian	38	11	8	19	53	71	30
Bromley	38	10	6	22	34	77	26
Dulwich Hamlet	38	7	10	21	30	66	24
Maidstone United	38	7	6	25	42	84	20
Clapton	38	5	7	26	33	101	17
Corinthian Casuals	38	2	8	28	23	103	12

1971-72

Wycombe Wanderers	40	31	3	6	102	20	65
Enfield	40	26	8	6	90	41	60
Walton & Hersham	40	24	8	8	69	25	56
Hendon	40	23	10	7	79	35	56
Bishop's Stortford	40	24	5	11	61	37	53
Sutton United	40	21	10	9	77	43	52
St Albans City	40	23	4	13	74	47	50
Ilford	40	17	11	12	62	52	45
Barking	40	20	4	16	65	61	44
Hitchin Town	40	17	10	13	68	66	44
Bromley	40	16	10	14	67	64	42
Hayes	40	14	12	14	50	48	40
Oxford City	40	13	9	18	67	74	35
Woking	40	11	10	19	52	58	32
Kingstonian	40	10	12	18	49	59	32
Walthamstow Avenue	40	12	8	20	58	71	32
Leytonstone	40	11	8	21	48	68	30
Tooting & Mitcham United	40	6	9	25	38	93	21
Clapton	40	7	7	26	45	118	21
Dulwich Hamlet	40	4	12	24	35	81	20
Corinthian Casuals	40	3	4	33	21	116	10

Second Division

Dagenham	30	22	4	4	68	23	70
Slough Town	30	18	6	6	46	23	60
Hertford Town	30	17	5	8	46	29	56
Chesham Town	30	16	6	8	61	43	54
Aveley	30	16	5	9	50	28	53
Tilbury	30	14	5	11	47	36	47
Maidenhead United	30	12	11	7	36	30	47
Horsham	30	12	9	9	47	35	45
Harwich & Parkeston	30	11	9	10	46	41	42
Staines Town	30	10	8	12	34	41	38
Carshalton Athletic	30	8	8	14	34	51	32
Hampton	30	6	10	14	33	51	28
Harlow Town	30	6	9	15	33	48	27
Finchley	30	6	7	17	29	52	25
Southall	30	3	10	17	17	52	19
Wokingham Town	30	3	8	19	30	74	17

1972-73

Hendon	42	34	6	2	88	18	74
Walton & Hersham	42	25	11	6	60	25	61
Leatherhead	42	23	10	9	76	32	56
Wycombe Wanderers	42	25	6	11	66	32	56
Walthamstow Avenue	42	20	12	10	66	48	52
Tooting & Mitcham United	42	20	11	11	73	39	51
Sutton United	42	21	9	12	69	48	51
Kingstonian	42	20	10	12	60	49	50
Enfield	42	20	8	14	90	54	48
Bishop's Stortford	42	18	12	12	58	51	48
Hayes	42	19	8	15	69	42	46
Dulwich Hamlet	42	18	9	15	59	52	45
Ilford	42	18	9	15	61	59	45
Leytonstone	42	17	11	14	55	54	45
Woking	42	18	8	16	61	56	44
Hitchin Town	42	15	9	18	52	64	39
Barking	42	8	7	27	45	88	23
St Albans City	42	5	12	25	34	76	22
Oxford City	42	6	7	29	30	101	19
Bromley	42	4	10	28	31	70	18
Clapton	42	3	11	28	31	100	17
Corinthian Casuals	42	3	8	31	30	106	14

1973-74

First Division

Wycombe Wanderers	42	27	9	6	96	34	90
Hendon	42	25	13	4	63	20	88
Bishop's Stortford	42	26	9	7	78	26	87
Dulwich Hamlet	42	22	11	9	71	38	77
Leatherhead	42	23	6	13	81	44	75
Walton & Hersham	42	20	12	10	68	50	72
Woking	42	22	6	14	63	55	72
Leytonstone	42	20	9	13	63	44	69
Ilford	42	20	8	14	60	44	68
Hayes	42	17	14	11	65	43	65
Oxford City	42	15	16	11	45	47	61
Sutton United	42	13	16	13	51	52	55
Hitchin Town	42	15	10	17	68	73	55
Barking	42	14	12	16	57	58	54
Kingstonian	42	12	15	15	47	46	51
Tooting & Mitcham United	42	14	9	19	57	62	51
Enfield	42	13	11	18	50	57	50
Walthamstow Avenue	42	11	13	18	46	62	46
Bromley	42	7	9	26	37	81	30
Clapton	42	8	3	31	36	128	27
St Albans City	42	4	7	31	30	92	19
Corinthian Casuals	42	3	4	35	31	107	13

1974-75

First Division

Wycombe Wanderers	42	28	11	3	93	30	95
Enfield	42	29	8	5	78	26	95
Dagenham	42	28	5	9	95	44	89
Tooting & Mitcham United	42	25	9	8	78	46	84
Dulwich Hamlet	42	24	10	8	75	38	82
Leatherhead	42	23	10	9	83	42	79
Ilford	42	23	10	9	98	51	79
Oxford City	42	17	9	16	63	56	60
Slough Town	42	17	6	19	68	52	57
Sutton United	42	17	6	19	68	63	57
Bishop's Stortford	42	17	6	19	56	64	57
Hitchin Town	42	15	10	17	57	71	55
Hendon	42	15	7	20	59	74	52
Walthamstow Avenue	42	13	9	20	56	62	48
Woking	42	12	10	20	53	73	46
Hayes	42	10	14	18	52	66	44
Barking	42	12	8	22	57	81	44
Leytonstone	42	12	7	23	42	61	43
Kingstonian	42	13	4	25	48	73	43
Clapton	42	12	4	26	46	96	40
Walton & Hersham	42	9	4	29	37	108	31
Bromley	42	6	3	33	25	110	21

Second Division

Staines Town	34	23	2	9	65	23	71
Southall	34	20	3	11	55	41	63
Tilbury	34	19	5	10	64	36	60
Harwich & Parkeston	34	18	4	12	52	44	58
Chesham United	34	17	6	11	59	39	57
St Albans City	34	15	11	8	42	37	56
Harlow Town	34	16	6	12	53	47	54
Horsham	34	16	5	13	59	49	53
Maidenhead United	34	13	7	14	38	40	46
Hampton	34	12	7	15	44	42	43
Croydon	34	11	10	13	48	55	43
Hertford Town	34	10	7	17	35	52	37
Boreham Wood	34	7	15	12	41	49	36
Wokingham Town	34	10	6	18	32	43	36
Finchley	34	9	9	16	36	53	36
Carshalton Athletic	34	9	9	16	38	58	36
Aveley	34	9	7	18	34	63	34
Corinthian Casuals	34	8	9	17	35	59	33

Tilbury had 2 points deducted

1975-76

First Division

	P	W	D	L	F	A	Pts
Enfield	42	26	9	7	83	38	87
Wycombe Wanderers	42	24	10	8	71	41	82
Dagenham	42	25	6	11	89	55	81
Ilford	42	22	10	10	58	39	76
Dulwich Hamlet	42	22	5	15	67	41	71
Hendon	42	20	11	11	60	41	71
Tooting & Mitcham United	42	19	11	12	73	49	68
Leatherhead	42	19	10	13	63	53	67
Staines Town	42	19	9	14	46	37	66
Slough Town	42	17	12	13	58	45	63
Sutton United	42	17	11	14	71	60	62
Bishop's Stortford	42	15	12	15	51	47	57
Walthamstow Avenue	42	14	11	17	47	60	53
Woking	42	14	9	19	58	62	51
Barking	42	15	6	21	57	70	51
Hitchin Town	42	13	11	18	45	57	50
Hayes	42	10	19	13	44	48	49
Kingstonian	42	13	8	21	53	87	47
Southall & Ealing Borough	42	11	9	22	56	69	42
Leytonstone	42	10	10	22	41	63	40
Oxford City	42	9	8	25	29	65	35
Clapton	42	3	3	36	19	112	12

Second Division

	P	W	D	L	F	A	Pts
Tilbury	42	32	6	4	97	30	102
Croydon	42	28	14	0	81	27	98
Carshalton Athletic	42	28	6	8	75	37	90
Chesham United	42	21	12	9	91	51	75
Harwich & Parkeston	42	21	11	10	78	56	74
Hampton	42	21	9	12	72	52	72
St Albans City	42	18	12	12	59	48	66
Boreham Wood	42	17	12	13	68	50	63
Harrow Borough	42	15	12	15	71	74	57
Hornchurch	42	15	11	16	61	61	56
Horsham	42	14	13	15	60	55	55
Wembley	42	14	13	15	51	54	55
Wokingham Town	42	13	16	13	45	52	55
Walton & Hersham	42	14	12	16	61	61	54
Finchley	42	14	11	17	52	53	53
Bromley	42	11	11	20	64	86	44
Aveley	42	11	9	22	34	51	42
Harlow Town	42	11	9	22	50	73	42
Maidenhead United	42	6	17	19	32	65	35
Ware	42	7	12	23	50	95	33
Hertford Town	42	5	9	28	32	87	24
Corinthian Casuals	42	4	7	31	42	113	19

1976-77

First Division

	P	W	D	L	F	A	Pts
Enfield	42	24	12	6	63	34	84
Wycombe Wanderers	42	25	8	9	71	34	83
Dagenham	42	23	10	9	80	39	79
Hendon	42	19	10	13	60	48	67
Tilbury	42	18	13	11	57	49	67
Tooting & Mitcham	42	18	10	14	85	72	64
Walthamstow Avenue	42	19	7	16	61	55	64
Slough Town	42	18	9	15	51	46	63
Hitchin Town	42	19	6	17	60	66	63
Leatherhead	42	18	7	17	61	47	61
Staines Town	42	16	13	13	52	48	61
Leytonstone	42	16	11	15	59	57	59
Barking	42	16	9	17	63	61	57
Southall & Ealing Borough	42	15	8	19	52	64	53
Croydon	42	13	10	19	38	52	49
Sutton United	42	14	7	21	40	55	49
Kingstonian	42	13	7	22	45	60	46
Hayes	42	12	10	20	49	69	46
Woking	42	11	12	19	47	61	45
Bishop's Stortford	42	11	11	20	51	71	44
Dulwich Hamlet	42	11	8	23	52	68	41
Ilford	42	10	8	24	32	73	38

Second Division

	P	W	D	L	F	A	Pts
Boreham Wood	42	33	4	5	80	26	103
Carshalton Athletic	42	25	12	5	80	33	87
Harwich & Parkeston	42	23	8	11	93	61	77
Wembley	42	23	8	11	82	58	77
Harrow Borough	42	21	12	9	78	44	75
Horsham	42	23	5	14	67	56	74
Bromley	42	20	10	12	71	46	70
Oxford City	42	20	8	14	73	55	68
Hampton	42	20	8	14	62	45	68
Wokingham Town	42	16	14	12	60	44	62
Hornchurch	42	18	7	17	62	53	61
Chesham United	42	17	10	15	63	66	61
St Albans City	42	16	12	14	59	53	60
Walton & Hersham	42	17	9	16	57	56	60
Aveley	42	14	8	20	49	62	50
Corinthian Casuals	42	13	6	23	52	75	45
Harlow Town	42	11	8	23	39	77	41
Hertford Town	42	9	9	24	45	80	36
Maidenhead United	42	8	8	26	36	73	32
Clapton	42	7	9	28	43	87	30
Finchley	42	5	13	24	36	82	28
Ware	42	5	8	29	43	98	23

1977-78

Premier Division

	P	W	D	L	F	A	Pts
Enfield	42	35	5	2	96	27	110
Dagenham	42	24	7	11	78	55	79
Wycombe Wanderers	42	22	9	11	66	41	75
Tooting & Mitcham United	42	22	8	12	64	49	74
Hitchin Town	42	20	9	13	69	53	69
Sutton United	42	18	12	12	66	57	66
Leatherhead	42	18	11	13	62	48	65
Croydon	42	18	10	14	61	52	64
Walthamstow Avenue	42	17	12	13	64	61	63
Barking	42	17	7	18	76	66	58
Carshalton Athletic	42	15	11	16	60	62	56
Hayes	42	15	11	16	46	53	56
Hendon	42	16	7	19	57	55	55
Woking	42	14	11	17	62	62	53
Boreham Wood	42	15	8	19	48	65	53
Slough Town	42	14	8	20	52	69	50
Staines Town	42	12	13	17	46	60	49
Tilbury	42	11	12	19	57	68	45
Kingstonian	42	8	13	21	43	65	37
Leytonstone	42	7	15	20	44	71	36
Southall & Ealing Borough	42	6	15	21	43	74	33
Bishop's Stortford	42	7	8	27	36	83	29

First Division

	P	W	D	L	F	A	Pts
Dulwich Hamlet	42	28	9	5	91	25	93
Oxford City	42	26	5	11	85	44	83
Bromley	42	23	13	6	74	41	82
Walton & Hersham	42	22	11	9	69	41	77
Ilford	42	21	14	7	57	47	77
St Albans City	42	22	10	10	83	46	76
Wokingham Town	42	19	12	11	69	48	69
Harlow Town	42	19	8	15	63	49	65
Harrow Borough	42	17	10	15	59	54	61
Maidenhead United	42	16	13	13	55	54	61
Hertford Town	42	15	14	13	57	51	59
Chesham United	42	14	13	15	69	70	55
Hampton	42	13	13	16	49	53	52
Harwich & Parkeston	42	12	13	17	68	79	49
Wembley	42	15	3	24	56	82	48
Horsham	42	12	10	20	41	57	46
Finchley	42	11	13	18	41	68	46
Aveley	42	13	7	22	47	75	46
Ware	42	8	13	21	61	95	37
Clapton	42	10	6	26	46	78	36
Hornchurch	42	8	10	24	47	81	34
Corinthian Casuals	42	3	10	29	40	88	19

Second Division

Epsom & Ewell	32	21	5	6	65	34	68
Metropolitan Police	32	19	6	7	53	30	63
Farnborough Town	32	19	4	9	68	40	61
Molesey	32	17	8	7	47	27	59
Egham Town	32	15	9	8	52	34	54
Tring Town	32	14	11	7	62	32	53
Letchworth Garden City	32	14	11	7	67	48	53
Lewes	32	13	7	12	52	51	46
Rainham Town	32	13	6	13	42	50	45
Worthing	32	11	9	12	40	45	42
Eastbourne United	32	10	8	14	40	50	38
Cheshunt	32	9	6	17	43	60	33
Feltham	32	7	9	16	30	49	30
Camberley Town	32	6	11	15	32	49	29
Hemel Hempstead	32	6	9	17	33	50	27
Epping Town	32	7	6	19	37	64	27
Willesden	32	7	3	22	38	88	24

Second Division

Farnborough Town	34	26	3	5	77	34	81
Camberley Town	34	21	8	5	71	32	71
Molesey	34	19	11	4	55	33	68
Lewes	34	19	6	9	66	50	63
Feltham	34	16	7	11	47	36	55
Letchworth Garden City	34	14	10	10	56	48	52
Eastbourne United	34	16	4	14	47	45	52
Hemel Hempstead	34	13	11	10	46	37	50
Epping Town	34	14	7	13	49	44	49
Rainham Town	34	13	10	11	42	41	49
Cheshunt	34	11	8	15	43	49	41
Hungerford Town	34	11	8	15	48	58	41
Worthing	34	9	8	17	40	50	35
Hornchurch	34	9	8	17	39	62	35
Egham Town	34	7	12	15	48	54	33
Tring Town	34	6	8	20	33	56	26
Willesden	34	6	8	20	41	77	26
Corinthian Casuals	34	4	7	23	23	65	19

1978-79

Premier Division

Barking	42	28	9	5	92	50	93
Dagenham	42	25	6	11	83	63	81
Enfield	42	22	11	9	69	37	77
Dulwich Hamlet	42	21	13	8	69	39	76
Slough Town	42	20	12	10	61	44	72
Wycombe Wanderers	42	20	9	13	59	44	69
Woking	42	18	14	10	79	59	68
Croydon	42	19	9	14	61	51	66
Hendon	42	16	14	12	55	48	62
Leatherhead	42	17	9	16	57	45	60
Sutton United	42	17	9	16	62	51	60
Tooting & Mitcham United	42	15	14	13	52	52	59
Walthamstow Avenue	42	15	6	21	61	69	51
Tilbury	42	13	1	18	60	76	50
Boreham Wood	42	13	10	19	50	67	49
Hitchin Town	42	12	11	19	59	71	47
Carshalton Athletic	42	10	16	16	49	69	46
Hayes	42	9	18	15	45	58	45
Oxford City	42	12	7	23	50	80	43
Staines Town	42	6	16	20	40	64	34
Leytonstone	42	8	7	27	36	75	31
Kingstonian	42	3	15	24	35	72	24

First Division

Harlow Town	42	31	7	4	93	32	100
Harrow Borough	42	26	8	8	85	49	86
Maidenhead United	42	25	6	11	72	50	81
Bishop's Stortford	42	22	11	9	68	40	77
Horsham	42	23	7	12	63	47	76
Hertford Town	42	21	11	10	62	41	74
Harwich & Parkeston	42	22	5	15	90	57	71
Bromley	42	18	12	12	76	50	66
Hampton	42	17	11	14	59	47	62
Epsom & Ewell	42	18	7	17	69	41	61
Wembley	42	15	14	13	57	57	59
Aveley	42	17	6	19	57	67	57
Wokingham Town	42	17	8	17	64	68	56
Clapton	42	15	8	19	67	80	53
Metropolitan Police	42	12	13	17	58	55	49
Walton & Hersham	42	12	9	21	47	71	45
Ilford	42	13	5	24	48	80	44
Ware	42	11	10	21	46	69	43
Chesham United	42	11	9	22	46	66	42
Finchley	42	7	15	20	43	75	36
St Albans City	42	7	7	28	43	90	28
Southall & Ealing Borough	42	5	5	32	41	114	20

Wokingham Town had 3 points deducted

1979-80

Premier Division

Enfield	42	25	9	8	74	32	84
Walthamstow Avenue	42	24	9	9	87	48	81
Dulwich Hamlet	42	21	16	5	66	37	79
Sutton United	42	20	13	9	67	40	73
Dagenham	42	20	13	9	82	56	73
Tooting & Mitcham United	42	21	6	15	62	59	69
Barking	42	19	10	13	72	51	67
Harrow Borough	42	17	15	10	64	51	66
Woking	42	17	13	12	78	59	64
Wycombe Wanderers	42	17	13	12	72	53	64
Harlow Town	42	14	12	16	55	61	54
Hitchin Town	42	13	15	14	55	69	54
Hendon	42	12	13	17	50	57	49
Slough Town	42	13	10	19	54	71	49
Boreham Wood	42	13	10	19	50	69	49
Staines Town	42	14	6	22	46	67	48
Hayes	42	12	9	21	48	68	45
Leatherhead	41	11	11	20	51	60	44
Carshalton Athletic	42	12	7	23	48	78	43
Croydon	42	10	10	22	51	59	40
Oxford City	42	10	9	23	49	87	39
Tilbury	42	7	11	24	41	90	30

Tilbury had 2 points deducted

First Division

Leytonstone & Ilford	42	31	6	5	83	35	99
Bromley	42	24	10	8	93	44	82
Maidenhead United	42	24	8	10	81	46	80
Bishop's Stortford	42	24	8	10	74	47	80
Kingstonian	42	22	8	12	59	44	74
Chesham United	42	18	13	11	68	56	67
St Albans City	42	17	13	12	65	47	64
Farnborough Town	42	19	7	16	70	57	64
Epsom & Ewell	42	18	7	17	62	57	61
Camberley Town	42	16	10	16	43	38	58
Walton & Hersham	42	15	12	15	61	50	57
Wembley	42	16	8	18	46	52	56
Wokingham Town	42	14	11	17	45	49	53
Hertford Town	42	13	11	18	71	74	50
Aveley	42	12	13	17	45	55	49
Hampton	42	14	7	21	57	74	49
Finchley	42	13	9	20	44	59	48
Metropolitan Police	42	13	8	21	46	67	47
Ware	42	11	12	19	45	61	45
Clapton	42	14	3	25	48	77	45
Harwich & Parkeston	42	11	6	25	51	84	38
Horsham	42	6	4	32	29	113	22

Harwich & Parkeston had 1 point deducted

Second Division

	P	W	D	L	F	A	Pts
Billericay Town	36	31	3	2	100	18	96
Lewes	36	24	7	5	82	33	79
Hungerford Town	36	21	8	7	78	36	71
Eastbourne United	36	21	6	9	77	45	69
Letchworth Garden City	36	21	6	9	63	32	69
Hornchurch	36	21	6	9	66	39	69
Molesey	36	15	9	12	67	60	54
Barton Rovers	36	15	7	14	49	49	52
Worthing	36	14	9	13	58	54	51
Cheshunt	36	13	7	16	47	52	46
Rainham Town	36	12	7	17	54	65	43
Egham Town	36	11	9	16	47	53	42
Southall & Ealing Borough	36	11	6	19	43	69	39
Feltham	36	8	11	17	23	49	35
Tring Town	36	7	13	16	38	55	34
Epping Town	36	10	4	22	44	69	34
Willesden	36	9	6	21	32	83	33
Hemel Hempstead	36	4	9	23	33	72	21
Corinthian Casuals	36	6	3	27	24	92	21

Second Division

	P	W	D	L	F	A	Pts
Feltham	38	24	10	4	65	30	82
Hornchurch	38	25	6	7	74	35	81
Hungerford Town	38	23	10	5	84	29	79
Barton Rovers	38	19	11	8	61	25	68
Worthing	38	19	11	8	74	43	68
Cheshunt	38	19	11	8	57	33	68
Letchworth Garden City	38	18	7	13	49	40	61
Southall	38	14	11	13	48	52	53
Dorking Town	38	13	12	13	47	45	51
Horsham	38	16	3	19	47	47	51
Hemel Hempstead	38	14	7	17	47	54	49
Egham Town	38	13	9	16	45	62	48
Harwich & Parkeston	38	12	11	15	57	58	47
Rainham Town	38	11	13	14	44	45	46
Epping Town	38	12	7	19	37	50	43
Eastbourne United	38	11	10	17	59	75	43
Willesden	38	11	8	19	57	68	41
Tring Town	38	11	6	21	40	71	39
Molesey	38	4	9	25	31	83	21
Corinthian Casuals	38	1	8	29	17	95	11

1980-81

Premier Division

	P	W	D	L	F	A	Pts
Slough Town	42	23	13	6	73	34	82
Enfield	42	23	11	8	81	43	80
Wycombe Wanderers	42	22	9	11	76	49	75
Leytonstone & Ilford	42	19	12	11	78	57	69
Sutton United	42	19	12	11	82	65	69
Hendon	42	18	10	14	66	58	64
Dagenham	42	17	11	14	79	66	62
Hayes	42	18	8	16	45	50	62
Harrow Borough	42	16	11	15	57	52	59
Bromley	42	16	9	17	63	69	57
Staines Town	42	15	9	18	60	61	54
Tooting & Mitcham United	42	15	8	19	49	53	53
Hitchin Town	42	14	10	18	64	62	52
Croydon	42	12	15	15	51	51	51
Dulwich Hamlet	42	13	12	17	62	67	51
Leatherhead	42	12	14	16	36	50	50
Carshalton Athletic	42	14	8	20	57	82	50
Barking	42	13	12	17	58	72	49
Harlow Town	42	11	15	16	53	66	48
Walthamstow Avenue	42	13	7	22	50	81	46
Boreham Wood	42	10	13	19	46	69	43
Woking	42	11	7	24	40	69	37

Barking had 1 point deducted
Woking had 3 points deducted

1981-82

Premier Division

	P	W	D	L	F	A	Pts
Leytonstone & Ilford	42	26	5	11	91	52	83
Sutton United	42	22	9	11	72	49	75
Wycombe Wanderers	42	21	10	11	63	48	73
Staines Town	42	21	9	12	58	45	72
Walthamstow Avenue	42	21	7	14	81	62	70
Harrow Borough	42	18	13	11	77	55	67
Tooting & Mitcham United	42	19	10	13	58	47	67
Slough Town	42	17	13	12	64	54	64
Leatherhead	42	16	12	14	57	52	60
Hayes	42	16	10	16	58	52	58
Croydon	42	16	9	17	59	57	57
Barking	42	14	14	14	53	51	56
Hendon	42	13	13	16	56	65	52
Dulwich Hamlet	42	14	10	18	47	59	52
Bishop's Stortford	42	15	5	22	50	70	50
Carshalton Athletic	42	14	8	20	58	86	50
Billericay Town	42	11	16	15	41	50	49
Hitchin Town	42	12	11	19	56	77	47
Bromley	42	13	7	22	63	79	46
Woking	42	11	13	18	57	75	46
Harlow Town	42	10	11	21	50	73	41
Boreham Wood	42	8	13	21	47	58	37

First Division

	P	W	D	L	F	A	Pts
Bishop's Stortford	42	30	6	6	84	28	96
Billericay Town	42	29	6	7	67	34	93
Epsom & Ewell	42	24	12	6	80	36	84
Farnborough Town	42	23	11	8	75	39	80
St Albans City	42	24	5	13	85	61	77
Kingstonian	42	20	9	13	63	52	66
Oxford City	42	18	9	15	71	48	63
Wokingham Town	42	16	15	11	70	56	63
Metropolitan Police	42	18	7	17	61	58	61
Chesham United	42	17	7	18	64	64	58
Lewes	42	17	7	18	72	83	58
Maidenhead United	42	16	7	19	58	62	55
Walton & Hersham	42	12	15	15	46	53	51
Hertford Town	42	13	11	18	46	65	50
Hampton	42	12	13	17	46	53	49
Aveley	42	13	9	20	54	55	48
Wembley	42	13	8	21	47	61	47
Clapton	42	12	8	22	53	86	44
Ware	42	9	13	20	50	69	40
Tilbury	42	10	8	24	42	84	35
Camberley Town	42	8	7	27	42	88	31
Finchley	42	6	11	25	36	77	29

Kingstonian and Tilbury both had 3 points deducted

First Division

	P	W	D	L	F	A	Pts
Wokingham Town	40	29	5	6	86	30	92
Bognor Regis Town	40	23	10	7	65	34	79
Metropolitan Police	40	22	11	7	75	48	77
Oxford City	40	21	11	8	82	47	74
Feltham	40	20	8	12	65	49	68
Lewes	40	19	7	14	73	66	64
Hertford Town	40	16	10	14	62	54	58
Wembley	40	14	15	11	69	55	57
Farnborough Town	40	15	11	14	71	57	56
Epsom & Ewell	40	16	8	16	52	44	56
Kingstonian	40	16	7	17	57	56	55
Hampton	40	15	9	16	52	52	54
Hornchurch	40	13	15	12	42	50	54
Aveley	40	14	10	16	46	58	54
St Albans City	40	14	9	17	55	55	51
Maidenhead United	40	11	10	19	49	70	43
Tilbury	40	9	15	16	49	66	42
Walton & Hersham	40	10	11	19	43	65	41
Chesham United	40	9	9	22	41	71	36
Clapton	40	9	7	24	44	75	34
Ware	40	5	2	33	29	105	17

Second Division

Team	P	W	D	L	F	A	Pts
Worthing	40	29	6	5	95	25	93
Cheshunt	40	25	7	8	79	33	82
Hungerford Town	40	22	10	8	89	42	74
Barton Rovers	40	22	8	10	65	32	74
Windsor & Eton	40	22	6	12	69	49	72
Corinthian Casuals	40	19	12	9	67	50	69
Harwich & Parkeston	40	19	12	9	64	47	69
Letchworth Garden City	40	15	11	14	67	55	56
Dorking Town	40	13	17	10	52	44	56
Hemel Hempstead	40	15	9	16	54	49	54
Basildon United	40	16	5	19	64	51	53
Finchley	40	14	9	17	57	68	51
Southall	40	12	14	14	36	42	50
Epping Town	40	12	11	17	48	62	47
Molesey	40	13	7	20	61	73	46
Egham Town	40	11	9	20	56	64	42
Rainham Town	40	11	9	20	53	83	42
Tring Town	40	9	13	18	49	78	40
Eastbourne United	40	9	12	19	51	73	39
Horsham	40	10	9	21	42	79	39
Camberley Town	40	3	2	35	21	140	11

Hungerford Town had 2 points deducted

Second Division

Team	P	W	D	L	F	A	Pts
Clapton	42	30	4	8	96	46	94
Windsor & Eton	42	27	7	8	98	43	88
Barton Rovers	42	26	6	10	86	48	84
Leyton Wingate	42	25	8	9	111	41	83
Basildon United	42	23	13	6	92	42	82
Uxbridge	42	22	12	8	80	42	78
Hungerford Town	42	22	10	10	82	39	76
Corinthian Casuals	42	23	6	13	95	48	75
Egham Town	42	21	8	13	77	67	71
Tring Town	42	20	10	12	86	59	70
Letchworth Garden City	42	18	13	11	68	53	66
Southall	42	18	7	17	81	80	61
Molesey	42	17	9	16	73	56	60
Dorking Town	42	15	9	18	56	75	54
Hemel Hempstead	42	12	14	16	53	59	50
Rainham Town	42	14	4	24	57	94	46
Eastbourne United	42	10	6	26	54	104	36
Epping Town	42	6	8	28	29	89	26
Ware	42	6	6	30	34	97	24
Finchley	42	4	12	26	28	92	24
Horsham	42	5	7	30	32	106	22
Harwich & Parkeston	42	5	7	30	42	130	22

Letchworth Garden City had 1 point deducted

1982-83

Premier Division

Team	P	W	D	L	F	A	Pts
Wycombe Wanderers	42	26	7	9	79	47	85
Leytonstone & Ilford	42	24	9	9	71	39	81
Harrow Borough	42	24	7	11	91	58	79
Hayes	42	23	9	10	63	41	78
Sutton United	42	20	8	14	96	71	68
Dulwich Hamlet	42	18	14	10	59	52	68
Slough Town	42	18	13	11	73	36	67
Bognor Regis Town	42	19	8	15	53	48	65
Tooting & Mitcham United	42	18	9	15	65	62	63
Billericay Town	42	17	10	15	54	51	61
Croydon	42	17	9	16	68	58	60
Hendon	42	18	6	18	68	61	60
Bishop's Stortford	42	17	9	16	61	58	60
Barking	42	14	14	14	47	55	56
Bromley	42	14	12	16	51	50	54
Carshalton Athletic	42	15	9	18	58	60	54
Wokingham Town	42	13	9	20	37	51	48
Walthamstow Avenue	42	12	11	19	48	64	47
Staines Town	42	12	11	19	62	79	47
Hitchin Town	42	11	9	22	49	77	42
Woking	42	6	6	30	30	79	24
Leatherhead	42	4	5	33	35	121	17

1983-84

Premier Division

Team	P	W	D	L	F	A	Pts
Harrow Borough	42	25	13	4	73	42	88
Worthing	42	20	11	11	89	72	71
Slough Town	42	20	9	13	73	56	69
Sutton United	42	18	12	12	67	45	66
Hayes	42	17	13	12	56	41	64
Hitchin Town	42	16	15	11	58	57	63
Wycombe Wanderers	42	16	14	12	63	52	62
Wokingham Town	42	18	10	14	78	55	61
Hendon	42	17	10	15	62	51	61
Dulwich Hamlet	42	16	11	15	61	64	59
Bishop's Stortford	42	15	13	14	56	57	58
Harlow Town	42	15	11	16	64	70	56
Bognor Regis Town	42	14	13	15	62	69	55
Staines Town	42	15	9	18	63	72	54
Billericay Town	42	15	8	19	53	73	53
Barking	42	13	13	16	60	64	52
Croydon	42	14	10	18	52	58	52
Walthamstow Avenue	42	13	10	19	53	67	49
Leytonstone & Ilford	42	13	9	20	54	67	48
Carshalton Athletic	42	11	10	21	59	72	43
Tooting & Mitcham United	42	10	13	19	50	63	43
Bromley	42	7	11	24	33	72	32

Wokingham Town had 3 points deducted

First Division

Team	P	W	D	L	F	A	Pts
Worthing	40	25	6	9	76	39	81
Harlow Town	40	21	11	8	84	55	74
Farnborough Town	40	20	13	7	69	39	73
Hertford Town	40	20	11	9	70	61	71
Oxford City	40	19	13	8	70	49	70
Boreham Wood	40	21	6	13	62	42	69
Metropolitan Police	40	19	9	12	77	57	66
Walton & Hersham	40	17	6	17	65	59	57
Hampton	40	15	10	15	62	60	55
Wembley	40	14	10	16	62	61	52
Aveley	40	15	7	18	52	62	52
Kingstonian	40	13	12	15	53	53	51
Tilbury	40	12	10	18	41	47	46
Feltham	40	11	12	17	45	54	45
Chesham United	40	13	6	21	43	70	45
Epsom & Ewell	40	10	14	16	44	49	44
Lewes	40	12	8	20	47	71	44
Cheshunt	40	10	13	17	41	49	43
Hornchurch	40	11	8	21	45	74	41
Maidenhead United	40	10	10	20	57	87	40
St Albans City	40	10	9	21	52	79	37

St Albans City had 2 points deducted

First Division

Team	P	W	D	L	F	A	Pts
Windsor & Eton	42	26	7	9	89	44	85
Epsom & Ewell	42	23	9	10	73	51	78
Wembley	42	21	11	10	65	32	74
Maidenhead United	42	22	8	12	67	42	74
Boreham Wood	42	22	7	13	74	43	73
Farnborough Town	42	18	12	12	78	60	66
Hampton	42	18	12	12	65	49	66
Metropolitan Police	42	20	5	17	79	64	65
Chesham United	42	18	8	16	64	57	62
Tilbury	42	17	10	15	54	64	61
Leatherhead	42	15	10	17	67	56	55
Aveley	42	15	10	17	49	53	55
Woking	42	16	7	19	66	73	55
Hertford Town	42	15	9	18	58	73	54
Oxford City	42	14	9	19	57	56	51
Lewes	42	13	12	17	49	65	51
Walton & Hersham	42	13	10	19	52	70	49
Hornchurch	42	13	10	19	43	65	49
Kingstonian	42	13	9	20	47	67	48
Clapton	42	12	11	19	49	67	47
Cheshunt	42	12	8	22	45	64	44
Feltham	42	7	4	31	31	106	25

Second Division

Basildon United	42	30	7	5	88	27	97
St Albans City	42	29	9	5	100	46	96
Leyton Wingate	42	29	4	9	97	41	91
Tring Town	42	23	11	8	89	44	80
Corinthian Casuals	42	23	11	8	75	47	80
Hungerford Town	42	21	12	9	94	47	75
Uxbridge	42	18	15	9	61	36	69
Grays Athletic	42	20	9	13	72	57	69
Dorking	42	21	5	16	66	54	68
Southall	42	20	8	14	79	60	65
Egham Town	42	16	15	11	59	49	63
Epping Town	42	15	16	11	61	50	61
Molesey	42	13	14	15	59	68	53
Barton Rovers	42	15	8	19	54	64	53
Letchworth Garden City	42	15	7	20	48	66	52
Newbury Town	42	14	5	23	60	82	47
Hemel Hempstead	42	12	9	21	63	69	45
Rainham Town	42	7	5	30	38	114	26
Finchley	42	5	9	28	28	78	24
Eastbourne United	42	7	3	32	36	98	24
Ware	42	6	6	30	48	114	24
Horsham	42	7	4	31	40	104	23

Southall had 2 points deducted
Horsham had 3 points deducted

1984-85

Premier Division

Sutton United	42	23	15	4	115	55	84
Worthing	42	24	8	10	89	59	80
Wycombe Wanderers	42	24	6	12	68	46	78
Wokingham Town	42	20	13	9	74	54	73
Windsor & Eton	42	19	10	13	65	55	67
Bognor Regis Town	42	20	6	16	67	58	66
Dulwich Hamlet	42	16	17	9	82	57	65
Harrow Borough	42	18	8	16	70	56	62
Hayes	42	17	8	17	60	56	59
Tooting & Mitcham United	42	16	11	15	64	66	59
Walthamstow Avenue	42	15	11	16	64	65	56
Croydon	42	15	12	15	62	63	54
Epsom & Ewell	42	13	14	15	65	62	53
Slough Town	42	13	12	17	69	74	51
Carshalton Athletic	42	14	8	20	55	68	50
Bishop's Stortford	42	12	12	18	48	67	48
Hendon	42	9	19	14	62	65	46
Billericay Town	42	11	14	17	53	74	46
Barking	42	13	7	22	43	75	46
Hitchin Town	42	10	15	17	55	70	45
Leytonstone & Ilford	42	11	10	21	37	72	43
Harlow Town	42	5	12	25	45	95	27

Billericay Town had 1 point deducted
Croydon had 3 points deducted

First Division

Farnborough Town	42	26	8	8	101	45	86
Kingstonian	42	23	10	9	67	39	79
Leatherhead	42	23	10	9	109	61	76
Chesham United	42	22	8	12	78	46	74
Wembley	42	20	10	12	59	40	70
St Albans City	42	19	10	13	79	60	67
Tilbury	42	18	13	11	86	68	67
Bromley	42	18	9	15	71	64	63
Hampton	42	17	11	14	75	62	62
Staines Town	42	16	11	15	59	53	59
Maidenhead United	42	17	8	17	65	64	59
Walton & Hersham	42	16	8	18	60	69	55
Aveley	42	16	7	19	62	78	55
Oxford City	42	14	12	16	62	53	54
Lewes	42	15	9	18	70	72	54
Basildon United	42	15	8	19	55	61	53
Boreham Wood	42	15	7	20	72	83	52
Hornchurch	42	15	6	21	55	74	51
Woking	42	15	6	21	60	91	51
Metropolitan Police	42	10	12	20	65	92	42
Clapton	42	5	11	26	50	124	26
Hertford Town	42	5	10	27	36	97	25

Walton & Hersham had 1 point deducted
Leatherhead had 3 points deducted

Second Division North

Leyton Wingate	38	24	9	5	98	50	81
Finchley	38	24	8	6	66	31	79
Heybridge Swifts	38	22	9	7	71	33	75
Stevenage Borough	38	23	6	9	79	49	75
Saffron Walden Town	38	22	8	8	73	31	74
Tring Town	38	19	11	8	76	41	68
Chalfont St Peter	38	17	10	11	72	41	61
Flackwell Heath	38	16	11	11	54	40	59
Berkhamsted Town	38	15	12	11	50	42	57
Letchworth Garden City	38	17	6	15	66	69	57
Royston Town	38	13	9	16	47	77	48
Cheshunt	38	14	5	19	52	57	47
Marlow	38	13	6	19	64	81	45
Hemel Hempstead	38	11	7	20	49	65	40
Barton Rovers	38	9	8	21	40	62	35
Wolverton Town	38	9	8	21	38	77	35
Kingsbury Town	38	9	7	22	53	72	34
Harefield United	38	7	9	22	51	81	30
Haringey Borough	38	6	12	20	38	79	30
Ware	38	7	5	26	40	100	26

Finchley had 1 point deducted
The record of Epping Town was expunged

Second Division South

Grays Athletic	36	24	9	3	84	25	81
Uxbridge	36	22	10	4	81	20	76
Molesey	36	20	5	11	62	42	65
Hungerford Town	36	18	9	9	71	49	63
Whyteleafe	36	17	10	9	66	34	61
Egham Town	36	17	7	12	54	42	58
Southall	36	18	3	15	54	57	57
Bracknell Town	36	15	7	14	54	48	52
Banstead Athletic	36	14	8	14	63	70	50
Horsham	36	13	10	13	44	39	49
Ruislip Manor	36	13	10	13	48	49	49
Dorking	36	12	11	13	45	50	47
Rainham Town	36	12	8	16	58	61	44
Feltham	36	10	13	13	44	58	43
Camberley Town	36	10	12	14	44	54	42
Eastbourne United	36	10	9	17	66	72	39
Petersfield Town	36	9	5	22	41	80	32
Newbury Town	36	8	7	21	35	69	16
Chertsey Town	36	2	3	31	23	118	6

Chertsey Town had 3 points deducted
Newbury Town had 15 points deducted

1985-86

Premier Division

Sutton United	42	29	8	5	109	39	95
Yeovil Town	42	28	7	7	92	48	91
Farnborough Town	42	23	8	11	90	50	77
Croydon	42	23	7	12	70	50	76
Harrow Borough	42	21	8	13	76	66	71
Slough Town	42	18	8	16	66	68	62
Bishop's Stortford	42	17	10	15	55	61	61
Kingstonian	42	15	15	12	57	56	60
Dulwich Hamlet	42	17	9	16	64	79	60
Wokingham Town	42	16	10	16	67	64	58
Windsor & Eton	42	17	7	18	58	75	58
Tooting & Mitcham United	42	14	11	17	65	76	53
Walthamstow Avenue	42	12	14	16	69	70	50
Worthing	42	13	10	19	72	82	49
Bognor Regis Town	42	15	6	21	63	70	48
Hayes	42	10	17	15	55	61	47
Hitchin Town	42	11	14	17	53	69	47
Barking	42	11	13	18	45	55	46
Hendon	42	10	13	19	59	77	43
Carshalton Athletic	42	9	13	20	56	79	40
Billericay Town	42	9	12	21	59	78	39
Epsom & Ewell	42	8	12	22	63	90	36

Bognor Regis Town had 3 points deducted

First Division

St Albans City	42	23	11	8	92	61	80
Bromley	42	24	8	10	68	41	80
Wembley	42	22	12	8	59	30	78
Oxford City	42	22	11	9	75	51	77
Hampton	42	21	11	10	63	45	74
Leyton Wingate	42	21	10	11	77	56	73
Uxbridge	42	20	8	14	64	49	68
Staines Town	42	18	10	14	69	66	64
Boreham Wood	42	15	16	11	62	54	61
Walton & Hersham	42	16	10	16	68	71	58
Lewes	42	16	8	18	61	75	56
Leytonstone & Ilford	42	13	15	14	57	67	54
Finchley	42	12	17	13	61	59	53
Grays Athletic	42	13	11	18	69	75	50
Leatherhead	42	14	8	20	62	68	50
Tilbury	42	13	11	18	60	66	50
Maidenhead United	42	13	7	22	61	67	46
Basildon United	42	12	9	21	52	72	45
Hornchurch	42	11	11	20	44	59	44
Chesham United	42	12	6	24	51	87	42
Harlow Town	42	8	14	20	53	70	38
Aveley	42	8	6	28	59	98	30

Second Division North

Stevenage Borough	38	26	6	6	71	24	84
Kingsbury Town	38	25	8	5	84	35	83
Heybridge Swifts	38	20	8	10	65	46	68
Cheshunt	38	18	10	10	60	40	64
Hertford Town	38	17	7	14	60	50	58
Chalfont St Peter	38	15	11	12	53	50	56
Tring Town	38	14	13	11	58	46	55
Royston Town	38	13	13	12	59	57	52
Saffron Walden Town	38	13	12	13	61	65	51
Berkhamsted Town	38	14	8	16	45	52	50
Haringey Borough	38	14	7	17	49	51	49
Letchworth Garden City	38	13	8	17	46	52	47
Rainham Town	38	14	4	20	54	91	46
Hemel Hempstead	38	12	9	17	50	66	45
Ware	38	11	11	16	56	61	44
Vauxhall Motors	38	11	10	17	58	62	43
Barton Rovers	38	12	7	19	50	60	43
Harefield United	38	9	12	17	56	72	39
Clapton	38	10	7	21	51	90	37
Wolverton Town	38	8	11	19	42	58	35

Second Division South

Southwick	38	25	8	5	86	34	83
Bracknell Town	38	24	9	5	80	23	81
Woking	38	23	9	6	94	45	78
Newbury Town	38	22	7	9	86	53	73
Whyteleafe	38	21	10	7	61	41	73
Molesey	38	21	8	9	59	39	71
Metropolitan Police	38	20	6	12	72	48	66
Southall	38	19	7	12	76	58	64
Dorking	38	18	10	10	70	57	64
Feltham	38	16	7	15	65	60	55
Banstead Athletic	38	15	8	15	60	66	53
Petersfield United	38	12	9	17	61	71	45
Hungerford Town	38	11	6	21	57	78	39
Flackwell Heath	38	11	6	21	46	72	39
Eastbourne United	38	9	8	21	51	81	35
Camberley Town	38	9	7	22	53	64	34
Egham Town	38	7	8	23	41	83	29
Horsham	38	6	10	22	33	74	28
Ruislip Manor	38	5	12	21	44	87	27
Marlow	38	6	5	27	47	108	23

1986-87

Premier Division

Wycombe Wanderers	42	32	5	5	103	32	101
Yeovil Town	42	28	8	6	71	27	92
Slough Town	42	23	8	11	70	44	77
Hendon	42	22	7	13	67	53	73
Bognor Regis Town	42	20	10	12	85	61	70
Harrow Borough	42	20	10	12	68	44	70
Croydon	42	18	10	14	51	48	64
Barking	42	16	14	12	76	56	62
Farnborough Town	42	17	11	14	66	72	62
Bishop's Stortford	42	15	15	12	62	57	60
Bromley	42	16	11	15	63	72	59
Kingstonian	42	16	9	17	58	50	57
Windsor & Eton	42	13	15	14	47	52	54
St Albans City	42	14	9	19	61	70	51
Carshalton Athletic	42	13	9	20	55	68	48
Wokingham Town	42	14	6	22	47	61	48
Hayes	42	12	12	18	45	68	48
Dulwich Hamlet	42	12	10	20	62	71	46
Tooting & Mitcham United	42	12	9	21	51	53	45
Hitchin Town	42	13	5	24	56	69	44
Worthing	42	8	9	25	58	107	33
Walthamstow Avenue	42	4	6	32	36	113	18

First Division

Leytonstone & Ilford	42	30	5	7	78	29	95
Leyton Wingate	42	23	13	6	68	31	82
Bracknell Town	42	24	9	9	92	48	81
Southwick	42	23	7	12	80	66	76
Wembley	42	21	9	12	61	47	72
Grays Athletic	42	19	10	13	76	64	67
Kingsbury Town	42	20	7	15	69	67	67
Boreham Wood	42	20	6	16	59	52	66
Uxbridge	42	18	9	15	60	59	63
Leatherhead	42	17	11	14	45	48	62
Hampton	42	18	5	19	57	55	59
Basildon United	42	16	10	16	58	60	58
Billericay Town	42	14	12	16	57	52	54
Staines Town	42	13	13	16	40	51	52
Lewes	42	15	6	21	55	65	51
Stevenage Borough	42	12	11	19	61	67	47
Oxford City	42	11	10	21	64	72	43
Walton & Hersham	42	11	10	21	53	74	43
Tilbury	42	12	7	23	46	70	43
Epsom & Ewell	42	12	7	23	44	68	43
Maidenhead United	42	11	4	27	44	76	37
Finchley	42	6	11	25	44	90	29

Second Division North

Chesham United	42	28	6	8	81	48	90
Wolverton Town	42	23	14	5	74	32	83
Haringey Borough	42	22	13	7	86	40	79
Heybridge Swifts	42	21	11	10	81	54	74
Aveley	42	19	13	10	68	50	70
Letchworth Garden City	42	19	11	12	77	62	68
Barton Rovers	42	18	11	13	49	39	65
Tring Town	42	19	7	16	69	49	64
Collier Row	42	19	5	18	67	65	62
Ware	42	17	8	17	51	50	59
Saffron Walden Town	42	14	14	14	56	54	56
Wivenhoe Town	42	15	11	16	61	61	56
Vauxhall Motors	42	15	10	17	61	57	55
Hornchurch	42	13	16	13	60	60	55
Hertford Town	42	14	13	15	52	53	55
Berkhamsted Town	42	12	16	14	62	64	52
Harlow Town	42	13	11	18	45	55	50
Rainham Town	42	12	11	19	53	70	47
Clapton	42	10	11	21	45	63	41
Hemel Hempstead	42	9	12	21	48	77	39
Royston Town	42	4	12	26	37	109	24
Cheshunt	42	5	6	31	43	114	21

Second Division South

Woking	40	27	7	6	110	32	88
Marlow	40	28	4	8	78	36	88
Dorking	40	24	12	4	78	30	84
Feltham	40	25	3	12	79	34	78
Ruislip Manor	40	22	10	8	85	47	76
Chertsey Town	40	18	11	11	56	44	65
Metropolitan Police	40	16	13	11	70	61	61
Chalfont St Peter	40	17	10	13	60	55	61
Hungerford Town	40	14	14	12	55	48	56
Harefield United	40	14	14	12	53	47	56
Eastbourne United	40	15	10	15	72	59	55
Whyteleafe	40	12	15	13	52	63	51
Horsham	40	14	8	18	54	61	50
Egham Town	40	14	6	20	45	77	48
Camberley Town	40	13	3	24	62	89	42
Flackwell Heath	40	9	11	20	34	63	38
Banstead Athletic	40	7	15	18	44	61	36
Petersfield United	40	9	8	23	45	84	34
Molesey	40	7	12	21	37	89	33
Newbury Town	40	6	14	20	51	83	32
Southall	40	6	6	28	28	85	24

1987-88

Premier Division

Yeovil Town	42	24	9	9	66	34	81
Bromley	42	23	7	12	68	40	76
Slough Town	42	21	9	12	67	41	72
Leytonstone & Ilford	42	20	11	11	59	43	71
Wokingham Town	42	21	7	14	62	52	70
Hayes	42	20	9	13	62	48	69
Windsor & Eton	42	16	17	9	59	43	65
Farnborough Town	42	17	11	14	63	60	62
Carshalton Athletic	42	16	13	13	49	41	61
Hendon	42	16	12	14	62	58	60
Tooting & Mitcham United	42	15	14	13	57	59	59
Harrow Borough	42	15	11	16	53	58	56
Bishop's Stortford	42	15	10	17	55	58	55
Kingstonian	42	14	12	16	47	53	54
St Albans City	42	15	6	21	60	69	51
Bognor Regis Town	42	14	9	19	41	57	51
Leyton Wingate	42	14	8	20	58	64	50
Croydon	42	11	13	18	40	52	46
Barking	42	11	12	19	44	57	45
Dulwich Hamlet	42	10	11	21	46	64	41
Hitchin Town	42	10	8	24	46	79	38
Basingstoke Town	42	6	17	19	37	71	35

First Division

Marlow	42	32	5	5	100	44	101
Grays Athletic	42	30	10	2	74	25	100
Woking	42	25	7	10	91	52	82
Boreham Wood	42	21	9	12	65	45	72
Staines Town	42	19	11	12	71	48	68
Wembley	42	18	11	13	54	46	65
Basildon United	42	18	9	15	65	58	63
Walton & Hersham	42	15	16	11	53	44	61
Hampton	42	17	10	15	59	54	61
Leatherhead	42	16	11	15	64	53	59
Southwick	42	13	12	17	59	63	51
Oxford City	42	13	12	17	70	77	51
Worthing	42	14	8	20	67	73	50
Kingsbury Town	42	11	17	14	62	69	50
Walthamstow Avenue	42	13	11	18	53	63	50
Lewes	42	12	13	17	83	77	49
Uxbridge	42	11	16	15	41	47	49
Chesham United	42	12	10	20	69	77	46
Bracknell Town	42	12	9	21	54	80	45
Billericay Town	42	11	11	20	58	88	44
Stevenage Borough	42	11	9	22	36	64	42
Wolverton Town	42	3	3	36	23	124	12

Second Division North

Wivenhoe Town	42	26	10	6	105	42	88
Collier Row	42	22	13	7	71	39	79
Tilbury	42	18	15	9	61	40	69
Berkhamsted Town	42	19	12	11	71	53	69
Harlow Town	42	17	16	9	67	36	67
Ware	42	17	15	10	63	58	66
Witham Town	42	17	14	11	69	47	65
Vauxhall Motors	42	16	17	9	56	42	65
Heybridge Swifts	42	17	13	12	56	50	64
Tring Town	42	18	6	18	69	67	60
Letchworth Garden City	42	18	5	19	59	64	59
Finchley	42	16	10	16	67	54	58
Clapton	42	14	15	13	50	62	57
Hornchurch	42	13	15	14	56	65	54
Barton Rovers	42	13	10	19	43	60	49
Rainham Town	42	12	12	18	63	66	48
Royston Town	42	13	8	21	49	70	47
Saffron Walden Town	42	13	7	22	34	67	46
Hemel Hempstead	42	11	12	19	38	71	45
Haringey Borough	42	11	8	23	54	78	41
Aveley	42	8	13	21	42	65	37
Hertford Town	42	8	4	30	45	92	28

Second Division South

Chalfont St Peter	42	26	9	7	81	35	87
Metropolitan Police	42	23	17	2	80	32	86
Dorking	42	25	11	6	86	39	86
Feltham	42	21	12	9	74	41	75
Epsom & Ewell	42	21	11	10	71	49	74
Chertsey Town	42	22	7	13	63	47	73
Whyteleafe	42	20	11	11	84	55	71
Hungerford Town	42	21	7	14	66	54	70
Ruislip Manor	42	21	5	16	74	57	68
Yeading	42	19	10	13	83	56	67
Maidenhead United	42	18	12	12	69	54	66
Eastbourne United	42	18	10	14	67	57	64
Harefield United	42	18	6	18	59	60	60
Egham Town	42	12	12	18	45	55	48
Horsham	42	12	10	20	45	66	46
Southall	42	13	7	22	45	72	46
Molesey	42	11	11	20	42	63	44
Newbury Town	42	8	13	21	40	81	37
Camberley Town	42	9	9	24	51	94	36
Flackwell Heath	42	6	8	28	42	96	26
Banstead Athletic	42	6	7	29	34	81	25
Petersfield United	42	6	7	29	45	102	25

1988-89

Premier Division

Leytonstone & Ilford	42	26	11	5	76	36	89
Farnborough Town	42	24	9	9	85	61	81
Slough Town	42	24	6	12	72	42	78
Carshalton Athletic	42	19	15	8	59	36	72
Grays Athletic	42	19	13	10	62	47	70
Kingstonian	42	19	11	12	54	37	68
Bishop's Stortford	42	20	6	16	70	56	66
Hayes	42	18	12	12	61	47	66
Bognor Regis Town	42	17	11	14	38	49	62
Barking	42	16	13	13	49	45	61
Wokingham Town	42	15	11	16	60	54	56
Hendon	42	13	17	12	51	68	56
Windsor & Eton	42	14	13	15	52	50	55
Bromley	42	13	15	14	61	48	54
Leyton Wingate	42	13	15	14	55	56	54
Dulwich Hamlet	42	12	12	18	58	57	48
St Albans City	42	12	9	21	51	59	45
Dagenham	42	11	12	19	53	68	45
Harrow Borough	42	9	13	20	53	75	40
Marlow	42	9	11	22	48	83	38
Tooting & Mitcham United	42	10	6	26	41	81	36
Croydon	42	4	9	29	27	81	21

First Division

Staines Town	40	26	9	5	79	29	87
Basingstoke Town	40	25	8	7	85	36	83
Woking	40	24	10	6	72	30	82
Hitchin Town	40	21	11	8	60	32	74
Wivenhoe Town	40	22	6	12	62	44	72
Lewes	40	21	8	11	72	54	71
Walton & Hersham	40	21	7	12	56	36	70
Kingsbury Town	40	20	7	13	65	41	67
Uxbridge	40	19	7	14	60	54	64
Wembley	40	18	6	16	45	58	60
Boreham Wood	40	16	9	15	57	52	57
Leatherhead	40	14	8	18	56	58	50
Metropolitan Police	40	13	9	18	52	68	48
Chesham United	40	12	9	19	54	67	45
Southwick	40	9	15	16	44	58	42
Chalfont St Peter	40	11	9	20	56	82	42
Hampton	40	7	14	19	37	62	35
Worthing	40	8	10	22	49	80	32
Collier Row	40	8	7	25	37	82	31
Bracknell Town	40	8	6	26	38	70	30
Basildon Town	40	6	7	27	34	77	25

Worthing had 2 points deducted.

Second Division North

Harlow Town	42	27	9	6	83	38	90
Purfleet	42	22	12	8	60	42	78
Tring Town	42	22	10	10	65	44	76
Stevenage Borough	42	20	13	9	84	55	73
Heybridge Swifts	42	21	9	12	64	43	72
Billericay Town	42	19	11	12	65	52	68
Clapton	42	18	11	13	65	56	65
Barton Rovers	42	18	11	13	58	50	65
Aveley	42	18	10	14	54	54	64
Hertford Town	42	16	13	13	62	49	59
Ware	42	17	8	17	60	65	59
Hemel Hempstead	42	16	10	16	55	58	58
Witham Town	42	16	7	19	69	67	55
Vauxhall Motors	42	15	9	18	53	57	54
Berkhamsted Town	42	14	10	18	57	70	52
Hornchurch	42	11	16	15	59	61	49
Tilbury	42	13	10	19	53	60	49
Royston Town	42	12	7	23	46	72	43
Rainham Town	42	9	15	18	49	62	42
Saffron Walden Town	42	8	16	18	54	72	40
Letchworth Garden City	42	4	18	20	34	71	30
Wolverton Town	42	5	7	30	42	95	13

Hertford Town 2 points deducted, Wolverton Town 9 points deducted.

Second Division South

Dorking	40	32	4	4	109	35	100
Whyteleafe	40	25	9	6	86	41	84
Finchley	40	21	9	10	70	45	72
Molesey	40	19	13	8	58	42	70
Harefield United	40	19	7	14	56	45	64
Hungerford Town	40	17	13	10	55	45	64
Ruislip Manor	40	16	9	15	56	43	57
Feltham	40	16	9	15	58	53	57
Epsom & Ewell	40	16	8	16	55	55	56
Egham Town	40	16	7	17	54	58	55
Eastbourne United	40	15	9	16	68	61	54
Chertsey Town	40	13	14	13	55	58	53
Flackwell Heath	40	13	11	16	51	49	50
Camberley Town	40	15	5	20	51	71	50
Yeading	40	13	9	18	47	63	46
Banstead Athletic	40	12	8	20	50	65	44
Maidenhead United	40	10	13	17	44	61	43
Southall	40	11	10	19	41	73	43
Newbury Town	40	11	8	21	47	65	41
Horsham	40	7	14	19	36	68	35
Petersfield United	40	5	7	28	36	87	22

Yeading had 2 points deducted.

1989-90

Premier Division

Slough Town	42	27	11	4	85	38	92
Wokingham Town	42	26	11	5	67	34	89
Aylesbury United	42	25	9	8	86	30	84
Kingstonian	42	24	9	9	87	51	81
Grays Athletic	42	19	13	10	59	44	70
Dagenham	42	17	15	10	54	43	66
Leyton Wingate	42	20	6	16	54	48	66
Basingstoke Town	42	18	9	15	65	55	63
Bishop's Stortford	42	19	6	17	60	59	63
Carshalton Athletic	42	19	5	18	63	59	59
Redbridge Forest	42	16	11	15	65	62	59
Hendon	42	15	10	17	54	63	55
Windsor & Eton	42	13	15	14	51	47	54
Hayes	42	14	11	17	61	59	53
St Albans City	42	13	10	19	49	59	49
Staines Town	42	14	6	22	53	69	48
Marlow	42	11	13	18	42	59	46
Harrow Borough	42	11	10	21	51	79	43
Bognor Regis Town	42	9	14	19	37	67	41
Barking	42	7	11	24	53	86	32
Bromley	42	7	11	24	32	69	32
Dulwich Hamlet	42	6	8	28	32	80	26

Carshalton Athletic had 3 points deducted.

First Division

Wivenhoe Town	42	31	7	4	94	36	100
Woking	42	30	8	4	102	29	98
Southwick	42	23	15	4	68	30	84
Hitchin Town	42	22	13	7	60	30	79
Walton & Hersham	42	20	10	12	68	50	70
Dorking	42	19	12	11	66	41	69
Boreham Wood	42	17	13	12	60	59	64
Harlow Town	42	16	13	13	60	53	61
Metropolitan Police	42	16	11	15	54	59	59
Chesham United	42	15	12	15	46	49	57
Chalfont St Peter	42	14	13	15	50	59	55
Tooting & Mitcham United	42	14	13	15	42	51	55
Worthing	42	15	8	19	56	63	53
Whyteleafe	42	11	16	15	50	65	49
Lewes	42	12	11	19	55	65	47
Wembley	42	11	10	21	57	68	43
Croydon	42	9	16	17	43	57	43
Uxbridge	42	11	10	21	52	75	43
Hampton	42	8	13	21	28	51	37
Leatherhead	42	7	10	25	34	77	31
Purfleet	42	7	8	27	33	78	29
Kingsbury Town	42	8	10	24	45	78	25

Kingsbury Town had 9 points deducted

Second Division North

Heybridge Swifts	42	26	9	7	79	29	87
Aveley	42	23	16	3	68	24	85
Hertford Town	42	24	11	7	92	51	83
Stevenage Borough	42	21	16	5	70	31	79
Barton Rovers	42	22	6	14	60	45	72
Tilbury	42	20	9	13	68	54	69
Basildon United	42	13	20	9	50	44	59
Collier Row	42	15	13	14	43	45	58
Royston Town	42	15	11	16	63	72	56
Saffron Walden Town	42	15	11	16	60	73	56
Vauxhall Motors	42	14	13	15	55	54	55
Clapton	42	13	16	13	50	46	54
Ware	42	14	11	17	53	59	53
Hemel Hempstead	42	12	15	15	58	70	51
Billericay Town	42	13	11	18	49	58	50
Hornchurch	42	12	12	18	49	64	48
Berkhamsted Town	42	9	16	17	44	68	43
Finchley	42	11	10	21	50	75	43
Tring Town	42	10	9	23	48	70	39
Witham Town	42	8	14	20	44	56	38
Rainham Town	42	9	11	22	48	75	38
Letchworth Garden City	42	7	12	23	30	68	33

Clapton had 1 point deducted

Second Division South

Yeading	40	29	4	7	86	37	91
Molesey	40	24	11	5	76	30	83
Abingdon Town	40	22	9	9	64	39	75
Ruislip Manor	40	20	12	8	60	32	72
Maidenhead United	40	20	12	8	66	39	72
Southall	40	22	5	13	56	33	71
Newbury Town	40	21	7	12	50	36	70
Flackwell Heath	40	16	11	13	69	65	59
Hungerford Town	40	14	16	10	54	51	58
Egham Town	40	12	14	14	39	38	50
Banstead Athletic	40	14	8	18	46	47	50
Harefield United	40	13	9	18	44	46	48
Chertsey Town	40	13	9	18	53	58	48
Epsom & Ewell	40	13	9	18	49	54	48
Malden Vale	40	13	7	20	36	67	46
Eastbourne United	40	11	10	19	47	65	43
Camberley Town	40	11	9	20	44	66	42
Feltham	40	11	7	22	47	80	40
Bracknell Town	40	10	9	21	40	57	39
Petersfield United	40	10	8	22	48	93	38
Horsham	40	4	8	28	29	70	20

Second Division North

Stevenage Borough	42	34	5	3	122	29	107
Vauxhall Motors	42	24	10	8	82	50	82
Billericay Town	42	22	8	12	70	41	74
Ware	42	22	8	12	78	51	74
Berkhamsted Town	42	19	11	12	60	51	68
Witham Town	42	19	10	13	70	59	67
Purfleet	42	17	14	11	68	57	65
Rainham Town	42	19	7	16	57	46	64
Hemel Hempstead	42	16	14	12	62	56	62
Barton Rovers	42	17	10	15	61	58	61
Saffron Walden Town	42	16	13	13	72	77	61
Collier Row	42	16	11	15	63	63	59
Kingsbury Town	42	17	8	17	64	72	59
Edgware Town	42	17	7	18	73	65	58
Hertford Town	42	16	10	16	69	70	58
Royston Town	42	14	15	13	78	62	57
Tilbury	42	14	6	22	70	79	48
Basildon United	42	11	10	21	61	90	43
Hornchurch	42	10	9	23	53	87	39
Clapton	42	9	10	23	54	93	34
Finchley	42	6	7	29	50	112	24
Tring Town	42	1	9	32	30	99	12

Finchley had 1 point deducted
Clapton had 3 points deducted

1990-91

Premier Division

Redbridge Forest	42	29	6	7	74	43	93
Enfield	42	26	11	5	83	30	89
Aylesbury United	42	24	11	7	90	47	83
Woking	42	24	10	8	84	39	82
Kingstonian	42	21	12	9	86	57	75
Grays Athletic	42	20	8	14	66	53	68
Marlow	42	18	13	11	72	49	67
Hayes	42	20	5	17	60	57	65
Carshalton Athletic	42	19	7	16	80	67	64
Wivenhoe Town	42	16	11	15	69	66	59
Wokingham Town	42	15	13	14	58	54	58
Windsor & Eton	42	15	10	17	48	63	55
Bishop's Stortford	42	14	12	16	54	49	54
Dagenham	42	13	11	18	62	68	50
Hendon	42	12	10	20	48	62	46
St Albans City	42	11	12	19	60	74	45
Bognor Regis Town	42	12	8	22	44	71	44
Basingstoke Town	42	12	7	23	57	95	43
Staines Town	42	10	10	22	46	79	39
Harrow Borough	42	10	8	24	57	84	38
Barking	42	8	10	24	41	85	34
Leyton Wingate	42	7	7	28	44	91	28

Staines Town had 1 point deducted

First Division

Chesham United	42	27	8	7	102	37	89
Bromley	42	22	14	6	62	37	80
Yeading	42	23	8	11	75	45	77
Aveley	42	21	9	12	76	43	72
Hitchin Town	42	21	9	12	78	50	72
Tooting & Mitcham United	42	20	12	10	71	48	72
Walton & Hersham	42	21	8	13	73	48	71
Molesey	42	22	5	15	65	46	71
Whyteleafe	42	21	6	15	62	53	69
Dorking	42	20	5	17	78	67	65
Chalfont St Peter	42	19	5	18	56	63	62
Dulwich Hamlet	42	16	11	15	67	54	59
Harlow Town	42	17	8	17	73	64	59
Boreham Wood	42	15	8	19	46	53	53
Wembley	42	13	12	17	62	59	51
Uxbridge	42	15	5	22	45	61	50
Croydon	42	15	5	22	44	85	50
Heybridge Swifts	42	13	10	19	46	59	49
Southwick	42	13	8	21	49	75	47
Lewes	42	10	8	24	49	82	38
Metropolitan Police	42	9	6	27	55	76	33
Worthing	42	2	4	36	28	157	10

Second Division South

Abingdon Town	42	29	7	6	95	28	94
Maidenhead United	42	28	8	6	85	33	92
Egham Town	42	27	6	9	100	46	87
Malden Vale	42	26	5	11	72	44	83
Ruislip Manor	42	25	5	12	93	44	80
Southall	42	23	10	9	84	43	79
Harefield United	42	23	10	9	81	56	79
Newbury Town	42	23	8	11	71	45	77
Hungerford Town	42	16	13	13	84	69	61
Leatherhead	42	17	9	16	82	55	60
Banstead Athletic	42	15	13	14	58	62	58
Hampton	42	14	15	13	62	43	57
Epsom & Ewell	42	15	12	15	49	50	57
Chertsey Town	42	15	9	18	76	72	54
Horsham	42	14	7	21	58	67	49
Flackwell Heath	42	11	11	20	56	78	44
Bracknell Town	42	11	7	24	60	97	40
Feltham	42	10	8	24	45	80	38
Cove	42	10	7	25	51	94	37
Eastbourne United	42	10	7	25	53	109	37
Petersfield United	42	6	3	33	35	119	21
Camberley Town	42	1	6	35	27	143	9

1991-92

Premier Division

Woking	42	30	7	5	96	25	97
Enfield	42	24	7	11	59	45	79
Sutton United	42	19	13	10	88	51	70
Chesham United	42	20	10	12	67	48	70
Wokingham Town	42	19	10	13	73	58	67
Marlow	42	20	7	15	56	50	67
Aylesbury United	42	16	17	9	69	46	65
Carshalton Athletic	42	18	8	16	64	67	62
Dagenham	42	15	16	11	70	59	61
Kingstonian	42	17	8	17	71	65	59
Windsor & Eton	42	15	11	16	56	56	56
Bromley	42	14	12	16	51	57	54
St Albans City	42	14	11	17	66	70	53
Basingstoke Town	42	14	11	17	56	65	53
Grays Athletic	42	14	11	17	53	68	53
Wivenhoe Town	42	16	4	22	56	81	52
Hendon	42	13	9	20	59	73	48
Harrow Borough	42	11	13	18	58	78	46
Hayes	42	10	14	18	52	63	44
Staines Town	42	11	10	21	43	73	43
Bognor Regis Town	42	9	11	22	51	89	38
Bishop's Stortford	42	7	12	23	41	68	33

First Division

Stevenage Borough	40	30	6	4	95	37	96
Yeading	40	24	10	6	83	34	82
Dulwich Hamlet	40	22	9	9	71	40	75
Boreham Wood	40	22	7	11	65	40	73
Wembley	40	21	6	13	54	43	69
Abingdon Town	40	19	8	13	60	47	65
Tooting & Mitcham United	40	16	13	11	57	45	61
Hitchin Town	40	17	10	13	55	45	61
Walton & Hersham	40	15	13	12	62	50	58
Molesey	40	16	9	15	55	61	57
Dorking	40	16	7	17	68	65	55
Barking	40	14	11	15	51	54	53
Chalfont St Peter	40	15	6	19	62	70	51
Leyton Wingate	40	13	11	16	53	56	50
Uxbridge	40	13	8	19	47	62	47
Maidenhead United	40	13	7	20	52	61	46
Harlow Town	40	11	9	20	50	70	42
Croydon	40	11	6	23	44	68	39
Heybridge Swifts	40	8	9	23	33	71	33
Whyteleafe	40	7	10	23	42	78	31
Aveley	40	8	3	29	33	95	27

Second Division

Purfleet	42	27	8	7	97	48	89
Lewes	42	23	14	5	74	36	83
Billericay Town	42	24	8	10	75	44	80
Leatherhead	42	23	6	13	68	40	75
Ruislip Manor	42	20	9	13	74	51	69
Egham Town	42	19	12	11	81	62	69
Metropolitan Police	42	20	9	13	76	58	69
Saffron Walden Town	42	19	11	12	86	67	68
Hemel Hempstead	42	18	10	14	63	50	64
Hungerford Town	42	18	7	17	53	58	61
Barton Rovers	42	17	8	17	61	64	59
Worthing	42	17	8	17	67	72	59
Witham Town	42	16	11	15	56	61	59
Banstead Athletic	42	16	10	16	69	58	58
Malden Vale	42	15	12	15	63	48	57
Rainham Town	42	14	13	15	53	48	55
Ware	42	14	9	19	58	62	51
Berkhamsted Town	42	13	11	18	56	57	50
Harefield United	42	11	7	24	47	66	40
Southall	42	8	7	27	39	93	31
Southwick	42	6	2	34	29	115	20
Newbury Town	42	4	8	30	30	117	20

Third Division

Edgware Town	40	30	3	7	106	44	93
Chertsey Town	40	29	4	7	115	44	91
Tilbury	40	26	9	5	84	40	87
Hampton	40	26	5	9	93	35	83
Horsham	40	23	8	9	92	51	77
Cove	40	21	9	10	74	49	72
Flackwell Heath	40	19	12	9	78	50	69
Thame United	40	19	7	14	73	46	64
Epsom & Ewell	40	17	11	12	55	50	62
Collier Row	40	17	9	14	67	59	60
Royston Town	40	17	7	16	59	58	58
Kingsbury Town	40	12	10	18	54	61	46
Hertford Town	40	12	10	18	55	73	46
Petersfield United	40	12	9	19	45	67	45
Camberley Town	40	11	8	21	52	69	41
Feltham & Hounslow	40	11	2	22	53	78	40
Bracknell Town	40	10	7	23	48	90	37
Hornchurch	40	8	7	25	40	87	31
Tring Town	40	9	4	27	35	94	31
Clapton	40	9	3	28	47	92	30
Eastbourne United	40	5	5	30	34	121	20

1992-93

Premier Division

Chesham United	42	30	8	4	104	34	98
St Albans City	42	28	9	5	103	50	93
Enfield	42	25	6	11	94	48	81
Carshalton Athletic	42	22	10	10	96	56	76
Sutton United	42	18	14	10	74	57	68
Grays Athletic	42	18	11	13	61	64	65
Stevenage Borough	42	8	8	16	62	60	62
Harrow Borough	42	16	14	12	59	60	62
Hayes	42	16	13	13	64	59	61
Aylesbury United	42	18	6	18	70	77	60
Hendon	42	12	18	12	52	54	54
Basingstoke Town	42	12	17	13	49	45	53
Kingstonian	42	14	10	18	59	58	52
Dulwich Hamlet	42	12	14	16	52	66	50
Marlow	42	12	11	19	72	73	47
Wokingham Town	42	11	13	18	62	81	46
Bromley	42	11	13	18	51	72	46
Wivenhoe Town	42	13	7	22	41	75	46
Yeading	42	11	12	19	58	66	45
Staines Town	42	10	13	19	59	77	43
Windsor & Eton	42	8	7	27	40	90	31
Bognor Regis Town	42	5	10	27	46	106	25

First Division

Hitchin Town	40	25	7	8	67	29	82
Molesey	40	23	11	6	81	38	80
Dorking	40	23	9	8	73	40	78
Purfleet	40	19	12	9	67	42	69
Bishop's Stortford	40	19	10	11	63	42	67
Abingdon Town	40	17	13	10	65	47	64
Tooting & Mitcham United	40	17	12	11	68	46	63
Billericay Town	40	18	6	16	67	61	60
Wembley	40	14	15	11	44	34	57
Walton & Hersham	40	14	12	14	58	54	54
Boreham Wood	40	12	14	14	44	43	50
Maidenhead United	40	10	18	12	45	50	48
Leyton	40	11	14	15	56	61	47
Whyteleafe	40	12	10	18	63	71	46
Uxbridge	40	11	13	16	50	59	46
Heybridge Swifts	40	11	9	20	47	65	42
Croydon	40	11	9	20	54	82	42
Chalfont St Peter	40	7	17	16	48	70	38
Barking	40	10	8	22	47	80	38
Lewes	40	9	10	21	34	80	37
Aveley	40	9	7	24	45	87	34

Second Division

Worthing	42	28	7	7	105	50	91
Ruislip Manor	42	25	12	5	78	33	87
Berkhamsted Town	42	24	8	10	77	55	80
Hemel Hempstead	42	22	12	8	84	52	78
Metropolitan Police	42	22	6	14	84	51	72
Malden Vale	42	20	9	13	78	54	69
Chertsey Town	42	20	7	15	84	60	67
Saffron Walden Town	42	19	10	13	63	49	67
Newbury Town	42	14	18	10	53	51	60
Hampton	42	16	11	15	59	59	59
Edgware Town	42	16	10	16	84	75	58
Egham Town	42	16	9	17	60	71	57
Banstead Athletic	42	14	13	15	67	52	55
Leatherhead	42	14	11	17	66	61	53
Ware	42	12	11	19	68	76	47
Witham Town	42	10	16	16	54	65	46
Tilbury	42	12	8	22	55	101	44
Barton Rovers	42	9	14	19	40	66	41
Hungerford Town	42	11	8	23	37	93	41
Rainham Town	42	9	10	23	56	80	37
Harefield United	42	10	7	25	37	72	37
Southall	42	7	7	28	43	106	28

Third Division

	P	W	D	L	F	A	Pts
Aldershot Town	38	28	8	2	90	35	92
Thame United	38	21	11	6	84	38	74
Collier Row	38	21	11	6	68	30	74
Leighton Town	38	21	10	7	89	47	73
Cove	38	21	8	9	69	42	71
Northwood	38	19	11	8	84	68	68
Royston Town	38	17	8	13	59	42	59
East Thurrock United	38	17	7	14	69	58	58
Kingsbury Town	38	15	9	14	62	59	54
Hertford Town	38	14	10	14	61	64	52
Flackwell Heath	38	15	6	17	82	76	51
Tring Town	38	12	11	15	59	63	47
Hornchurch	38	11	13	14	53	52	46
Horsham	38	12	7	19	63	72	43
Epsom & Ewell	38	10	11	17	52	67	41
Bracknell Town	38	7	13	18	52	94	34
Clapton	38	8	7	23	46	74	31
Camberley Town	38	8	7	23	37	72	31
Petersfield United	38	6	12	20	36	90	30
Feltham & Hounslow	38	5	4	29	47	119	19

Second Division

	P	W	D	L	F	A	Pts
Newbury Town	42	32	7	3	115	36	103
Chertsey Town	42	33	3	6	121	48	102
Aldershot Town	42	30	7	5	78	27	97
Barton Rovers	42	25	8	9	68	37	83
Witham Town	42	21	10	11	68	51	73
Malden Vale	42	20	10	12	70	49	70
Thame United	42	19	12	11	87	51	69
Metropolitan Police	42	20	9	13	75	54	69
Banstead Athletic	42	19	9	14	56	53	66
Aveley	42	19	5	18	60	66	62
Edgware Town	42	16	10	16	88	75	58
Saffron Walden Town	42	17	7	18	61	62	58
Hemel Hempstead	42	14	11	17	47	43	53
Egham Town	42	14	8	20	48	65	50
Ware	42	14	7	21	48	76	49
Hungerford Town	42	13	7	22	56	66	46
Tilbury	42	13	3	26	59	81	42
Hampton	42	12	5	25	42	70	41
Leatherhead	42	10	6	26	46	92	36
Lewes	42	8	11	24	38	85	34
Collier Row	42	7	8	27	37	88	29
Rainham Town	42	4	2	36	24	116	14

1993-94

Premier Division

	P	W	D	L	F	A	Pts
Stevenage Borough	42	31	4	7	88	39	97
Enfield	42	28	8	6	80	28	92
Marlow	42	25	7	10	90	67	82
Chesham United	42	24	8	10	73	45	80
Sutton United	42	23	10	9	77	31	79
Carshalton Athletic	42	22	7	13	81	53	73
St Albans City	42	21	10	11	81	54	73
Hitchin Town	42	21	7	14	81	56	70
Harrow Borough	42	18	11	13	54	56	65
Kingstonian	42	18	9	15	101	64	63
Hendon	42	18	9	15	61	51	63
Aylesbury United	42	17	7	18	64	67	58
Hayes	42	15	8	19	63	72	53
Grays Athletic	42	15	5	22	56	69	50
Bromley	42	14	7	21	56	69	49
Dulwich Hamlet	42	13	8	21	52	74	47
Yeading	42	11	13	18	58	66	46
Molesey	42	11	11	20	44	62	44
Wokingham Town	42	11	6	25	38	67	39
Dorking	42	9	4	29	58	104	31
Basingstoke Town	42	5	12	25	38	86	27
Wivenhoe Town	42	5	3	34	38	152	18

Third Division

	P	W	D	L	F	A	Pts
Bracknell Town	40	25	8	7	78	29	83
Cheshunt	40	23	12	5	62	34	81
Oxford City	40	24	6	10	94	55	78
Harlow Town	40	22	11	7	61	36	77
Southall	40	17	12	11	66	53	63
Camberley Town	40	18	7	15	56	50	61
Hertford Town	40	18	6	16	67	65	60
Royston Town	40	15	11	14	44	41	56
Northwood	40	15	11	14	78	77	56
Epsom & Ewell	40	15	9	16	63	62	54
Harefield United	40	12	15	13	45	55	51
Cove	40	15	6	19	59	74	51
Kingsbury Town	40	12	14	14	57	54	50
Feltham & Hounslow	40	14	7	19	60	63	49
Leighton Town	40	12	11	17	51	64	47
East Thurrock Town	40	10	15	15	65	64	45
Clapton	40	12	9	19	51	65	45
Hornchurch	40	12	8	20	42	60	44
Tring Town	40	10	11	19	48	64	41
Flackwell Heath	40	9	11	20	44	83	38
Horsham	40	6	8	26	43	86	26

First Division

	P	W	D	L	F	A	Pts
Bishop's Stortford	42	24	13	5	83	31	85
Purfleet	42	22	12	8	70	44	78
Walton & Hersham	42	22	11	9	81	53	77
Tooting & Mitcham United	42	21	12	9	66	37	75
Heybridge Swifts	42	20	11	11	72	45	71
Billericay Town	42	20	11	11	70	51	71
Abingdon Town	42	20	10	12	61	50	70
Worthing	42	19	11	12	79	46	68
Leyton	42	20	8	14	88	66	68
Boreham Wood	42	17	15	10	69	50	66
Staines Town	42	18	9	15	85	56	63
Bognor Regis Town	42	15	14	13	57	48	59
Wembley	42	16	10	16	66	52	58
Barking	42	15	11	16	63	69	56
Uxbridge	42	15	8	19	57	58	53
Whyteleafe	42	15	6	21	71	90	51
Maidenhead United	42	12	13	17	52	48	49
Berkhamsted Town	42	12	9	21	65	77	45
Ruislip Manor	42	10	8	24	42	79	38
Chalfont St Peter	42	7	10	25	40	79	31
Windsor & Eton	42	8	7	27	47	94	31
Croydon	42	3	3	36	37	198	12

1994-95

Premier Division

	P	W	D	L	F	A	Pts
Enfield	42	26	9	5	106	43	93
Slough Town	42	22	13	7	82	56	79
Hayes	42	20	14	8	66	47	74
Aylesbury United	42	21	6	15	86	59	69
Hitchin Town	42	18	12	12	68	59	66
Bromley	42	18	11	13	76	67	65
St Albans City	42	17	13	12	96	81	64
Molesey	42	18	8	16	65	61	62
Yeading	42	14	15	13	60	59	57
Harrow Borough	42	17	6	19	64	67	57
Dulwich Hamlet	42	16	9	17	70	82	57
Carshalton Athletic	42	16	9	17	69	84	57
Kingstonian	42	16	8	18	62	57	56
Walton & Hersham	42	14	11	17	75	73	53
Sutton United	42	13	12	17	74	69	51
Purfleet	42	13	12	17	76	90	51
Hendon	42	12	14	16	57	65	50
Grays Athletic	42	11	16	15	57	61	49
Bishop's Stortford	42	12	11	19	53	76	47
Chesham United	42	12	9	21	60	87	45
Marlow	42	10	9	23	52	84	39
Wokingham Town	42	6	9	27	39	86	27

First Division

Boreham Wood	42	31	5	6	90	38	98
Worthing	42	21	13	8	93	49	76
Chertsey Town	42	21	11	10	109	57	74
Aldershot Town	42	23	5	14	80	53	74
Billericay Town	42	20	9	13	68	52	69
Staines Town	42	17	12	13	83	65	63
Basingstoke Town	42	17	10	15	81	71	61
Tooting & Mitcham United	42	15	14	13	58	48	59
Wembley	42	16	11	15	70	61	59
Abingdon Town	42	16	11	15	67	69	59
Whyteleafe	42	17	7	18	70	78	58
Maidenhead United	42	15	12	15	73	76	57
Uxbridge	42	15	11	16	54	62	56
Leyton	42	15	10	17	67	66	55
Barking	42	16	7	19	74	77	55
Heybridge Swifts	42	16	6	20	73	78	54
Ruislip Manor	42	14	11	17	70	75	53
Bognor Regis Town	42	13	14	15	57	63	53
Berkhamsted Town	42	14	10	18	54	70	52
Newbury Town	42	12	15	15	58	71	51
Wivenhoe Town	42	8	7	27	47	94	31
Dorking	42	3	3	36	40	163	12

Second Division

Thame United	42	30	3	9	97	49	93
Barton Rovers	42	25	7	10	93	51	82
Oxford City	42	24	8	10	86	47	80
Bracknell Town	42	23	9	10	86	47	78
Metropolitan Police	42	19	12	11	81	65	69
Hampton	42	20	9	13	79	74	69
Croydon	42	20	5	17	85	65	65
Banstead Athletic	42	18	10	14	73	59	64
Saffron Walden Town	42	17	13	12	64	59	64
Chalfont St Peter	42	17	12	13	67	54	63
Witham Town	42	18	9	15	75	64	63
Leatherhead	42	16	12	14	71	75	60
Edgware Town	42	16	10	16	70	66	58
Tilbury	42	15	9	18	62	82	54
Cheshunt	42	13	13	16	66	81	52
Ware	42	14	7	21	61	81	49
Egham Town	42	11	14	17	60	65	47
Hemel Hempstead	42	10	11	21	45	76	41
Hungerford Town	42	11	7	24	55	81	40
Windsor & Eton	42	10	8	24	58	84	38
Aveley	42	9	5	28	48	95	32
Malden Vale	42	5	9	28	46	108	24

Third Division

Collier Row	40	30	5	5	86	23	95
Canvey Island	40	28	4	8	88	42	88
Bedford Town	40	22	11	7	90	50	77
Northwood	40	22	8	10	80	47	74
Horsham	40	22	6	12	84	61	72
Southall	40	21	8	11	87	59	71
Leighton Town	40	20	8	12	66	43	68
Camberley Town	40	19	8	13	59	39	65
Kingsbury Town	40	18	11	1	72	54	65
Hornchurch	40	17	8	15	64	63	59
Clapton	40	14	11	15	69	61	53
Tring Town	40	13	12	15	68	69	51
East Thurrock United	40	14	8	18	60	79	50
Epsom & Ewell	40	13	10	17	58	62	49
Harlow Town	40	13	8	19	53	83	47
Harefield United	40	12	8	20	51	79	44
Hertford Town	40	11	10	19	56	78	43
Feltham & Hounslow	40	13	4	23	64	87	43
Flackwell Heath	40	8	4	28	50	99	28
Lewes	40	6	5	29	34	104	23
Cove	40	3	5	32	37	94	14

1995-96

Premier Division

Hayes	42	24	14	4	76	32	86
Enfield	42	26	8	8	78	35	86
Boreham Wood	42	24	1	7	69	29	83
Yeovil Town	42	23	11	8	83	51	80
Dulwich Hamlet	42	23	11	8	85	59	80
Carshalton Athletic	42	22	8	12	68	49	74
St Albans City	42	20	12	10	70	41	72
Kingstonian	42	20	11	11	62	38	71
Harrow Borough	42	19	10	13	70	56	67
Sutton United	42	17	14	11	71	56	65
Aylesbury United	42	17	12	13	71	58	63
Bishop's Stortford	42	16	9	17	61	62	57
Yeading	42	11	14	17	48	60	47
Hendon	42	12	10	20	52	65	46
Chertsey Town	42	13	6	23	45	71	45
Purfleet	42	12	8	22	48	67	44
Grays Athletic	42	11	11	20	43	63	44
Hitchin Town	42	10	10	22	41	74	40
Bromley	42	10	7	25	52	91	37
Molesey	42	9	9	24	46	81	36
Walton & Hersham	42	9	7	26	42	79	34
Worthing	42	4	7	31	42	106	19

First Division

Oxford City	42	28	7	7	98	60	91
Heybridge Swifts	42	27	7	8	97	43	88
Staines Town	42	23	11	8	82	59	80
Leyton Pennant	42	22	7	13	77	57	73
Aldershot Town	42	21	9	12	81	46	72
Billericay Town	42	19	9	14	58	58	66
Bognor Regis Town	42	18	11	13	71	53	65
Marlow	42	19	5	18	72	75	62
Basingstoke Town	42	16	13	13	70	60	61
Uxbridge	42	16	12	14	46	49	60
Wokingham Town	42	16	10	16	62	65	58
Chesham United	42	15	12	15	51	44	57
Thame United	42	14	13	15	64	73	55
Maidenhead United	42	12	14	16	50	63	50
Whyteleafe	42	12	13	17	71	81	49
Abingdon Town	42	13	9	20	63	80	48
Barton Rovers	42	12	10	20	69	87	46
Berkhamsted Town	42	11	11	20	52	68	44
Tooting & Mitcham United	42	11	10	21	45	64	43
Ruislip Manor	42	11	9	22	55	77	42
Wembley	42	11	8	23	49	66	41
Barking	42	4	12	26	35	90	24

Second Division

Canvey Island	40	25	12	3	91	36	87
Croydon	40	25	6	9	78	42	81
Hampton	40	23	10	7	74	44	79
Banstead Athletic	40	21	11	8	72	36	74
Collier Row	40	21	11	8	73	41	74
Wivenhoe Town	40	21	8	11	82	57	71
Metropolitan Police	40	18	10	12	57	45	64
Bedford Town	40	18	10	12	69	59	64
Bracknell Town	40	18	8	14	69	50	62
Edgware Town	40	16	9	15	72	67	57
Tilbury	40	12	11	17	52	62	47
Ware	40	13	8	19	55	80	47
Chalfont St Peter	40	11	13	16	58	63	46
Leatherhead	40	12	10	18	71	77	46
Saffron Walden Town	40	11	12	17	56	58	45
Cheshunt	40	10	12	18	56	90	42
Hemel Hempstead	40	10	10	20	46	62	40
Egham Town	40	12	3	25	42	74	39
Witham Town	40	8	10	22	35	68	34
Hungerford Town	40	9	7	24	44	79	34
Dorking	40	8	5	27	44	104	29

Third Division

	P	W	D	L	F	A	Pts
Horsham	40	29	5	6	95	40	92
Leighton Town	40	28	5	7	95	34	89
Windsor & Eton	40	27	6	7	117	46	87
Wealdstone	40	23	8	9	104	39	77
Harlow Town	40	22	10	8	85	62	76
Northwood	40	20	9	11	76	56	69
Epsom & Ewell	40	18	14	8	95	57	68
Kingsbury Town	40	15	16	9	61	48	61
East Thurrock United	40	17	8	15	61	50	59
Aveley	40	16	10	14	62	53	58
Wingate & Finchley	40	16	7	17	74	70	55
Lewes	40	14	7	19	56	72	49
Flackwell Heath	40	14	5	21	60	84	47
Hornchurch	40	11	8	21	55	77	41
Harefield United	40	11	7	22	49	89	40
Tring Town	40	10	8	22	40	78	38
Camberley Town	40	9	9	22	45	81	36
Hertford Town	40	10	5	25	72	103	35
Cove	40	8	10	22	37	89	34
Clapton	40	9	6	25	48	89	33
Southall	40	9	5	26	34	104	32

1996-97

Premier Division

	P	W	D	L	F	A	Pts
Yeovil Town	42	31	8	3	83	34	101
Enfield	42	28	11	3	91	29	98
Sutton United	42	18	13	11	87	70	67
Dagenham & Redbridge	42	18	11	13	57	43	65
Yeading	42	17	14	11	58	47	65
St Albans City	42	18	11	13	65	55	65
Aylesbury United	42	18	11	13	64	54	65
Purfleet	42	17	11	14	67	63	62
Heybridge Swifts	42	16	14	12	62	62	62
Boreham Wood	42	15	13	14	56	52	58
Kingstonian	42	16	8	18	79	79	56
Dulwich Hamlet	42	14	13	15	57	57	55
Carshalton Athletic	42	14	11	17	51	56	53
Hitchin Town	42	15	7	20	67	73	52
Oxford City	42	14	10	18	67	83	52
Hendon	42	13	12	17	53	59	51
Harrow Borough	42	12	14	16	58	62	50
Bromley	42	13	9	20	67	72	48
Bishop's Stortford	42	10	13	19	43	64	43
Staines Town	42	10	8	24	46	71	38
Grays Athletic	42	8	9	25	43	78	33
Chertsey Town	42	8	7	27	40	98	31

First Division

	P	W	D	L	F	A	Pts
Chesham United	42	27	6	9	80	46	87
Basingstoke Town	42	22	13	7	81	38	79
Walton & Hersham	42	21	13	8	67	41	76
Hampton	42	21	12	9	62	39	75
Billericay Town	42	21	12	9	69	49	75
Bognor Regis Town	42	21	9	12	63	44	72
Aldershot Town	42	19	14	9	67	45	71
Uxbridge	42	15	17	10	65	48	62
Whyteleafe	42	18	7	17	71	68	61
Molesey	42	17	9	16	50	53	60
Abingdon Town	42	15	11	16	44	42	56
Leyton Pennant	42	14	14	16	71	72	54
Maidenhead United	42	15	10	17	57	57	52
Wokingham Town	42	14	10	18	41	45	52
Thame United	42	13	10	19	57	69	49
Worthing	42	11	11	20	58	77	44
Barton Rovers	42	11	11	20	61	58	44
Croydon	42	11	10	21	40	57	43
Berkhamsted Town	42	11	9	22	47	66	42
Canvey Island	42	9	14	19	52	71	41
Marlow	42	11	6	25	41	84	39
Tooting & Mitcham United	42	8	8	26	40	85	32

Maidenhead United had 3 points deducted

Second Division

	P	W	D	L	F	A	Pts
Collier Row & Romford	42	28	12	2	93	33	96
Leatherhead	42	30	5	7	116	45	95
Wembley	42	23	11	8	92	45	80
Barking	42	22	13	7	69	40	79
Horsham	42	22	11	9	78	48	77
Edgware Town	42	20	14	8	74	50	74
Bedford Town	42	21	8	13	77	43	71
Banstead Athletic	42	21	5	16	75	52	68
Windsor & Eton	42	17	13	12	65	62	64
Leighton Town	42	17	12	13	64	52	63
Bracknell Town	42	17	9	16	78	71	60
Wivenhoe Town	42	17	9	16	69	62	60
Chalfont St Peter	42	14	13	15	53	61	55
Hungerford Town	42	14	13	15	68	77	55
Metropolitan Police	42	14	7	21	72	75	49
Tilbury	42	14	7	21	68	77	49
Witham Town	42	11	10	21	39	67	43
Egham Town	42	10	9	23	47	86	39
Cheshunt	42	9	3	30	37	101	30
Ware	42	7	8	27	44	80	29
Dorking	42	7	6	29	40	100	27
Hemel Hempstead	42	5	6	31	34	125	21

Third Division

	P	W	D	L	F	A	Pts
Wealdstone	32	24	3	5	72	24	75
Braintree Town	32	23	5	4	99	29	74
Northwood	32	18	10	4	60	31	64
Harlow Town	32	19	4	9	60	41	61
Aveley	32	17	6	9	64	39	57
East Thurrock United	32	16	6	10	58	51	54
Camberley Town	32	15	6	11	55	44	51
Wingate & Finchley	32	11	7	14	52	63	40
Hornchurch	32	11	6	15	35	51	39
Clapton	32	11	6	15	31	49	39
Lewes	32	10	8	14	45	53	38
Kingsbury Town	32	11	4	17	41	54	37
Hertford Town	32	10	6	16	55	65	36
Epsom & Ewell	32	8	5	19	62	78	29
Flackwell Heath	32	8	5	19	36	71	29
Tring Town	32	7	3	22	33	74	24
Southall	32	6	4	22	28	69	22

1997-98

Premier Division

	P	W	D	L	F	A	Pts
Kingstonian	42	25	12	5	84	35	87
Boreham Wood	42	23	11	8	81	42	80
Sutton United	42	22	12	8	83	56	78
Dagenham & Redbridge	42	21	10	11	73	50	73
Hendon	42	21	10	11	69	50	73
Heybridge Swifts	42	18	11	13	74	62	65
Enfield	42	18	8	16	66	58	62
Basingstoke Town	42	17	11	14	56	60	62
Walton & Hersham	42	18	6	18	50	70	60
Purfleet	42	15	13	14	57	58	58
St Albans City	42	17	7	18	54	59	58
Harrow Borough	42	15	10	17	60	67	55
Gravesend & Northfleet	42	15	8	19	65	67	53
Chesham United	42	14	10	18	71	70	52
Bromley	42	13	13	16	53	53	52
Dulwich Hamlet	42	13	11	18	56	67	50
Carshalton Athletic	42	13	9	20	54	77	48
Aylesbury United	42	13	8	21	55	70	47
Bishop's Stortford	42	14	5	23	53	69	47
Yeading	42	12	11	19	49	65	47
Hitchin Town	42	8	15	19	45	62	39
Oxford City	42	7	9	26	35	76	30

First Division

Team	P	W	D	L	F	A	Pts
Aldershot Town	42	28	8	6	89	36	92
Billericay Town	42	25	6	11	78	44	81
Hampton	42	22	15	5	75	47	81
Maidenhead United	42	25	5	12	76	37	80
Uxbridge	42	23	6	13	66	59	75
Grays Athletic	42	21	10	11	79	49	73
Romford	42	21	8	13	92	59	71
Bognor Regis Town	42	20	9	13	77	45	69
Leatherhead	42	18	11	13	70	51	65
Leyton Pennant	42	17	11	14	66	58	62
Chertsey Town	42	16	13	13	83	70	61
Worthing	42	17	6	19	64	71	57
Berkhamsted Town	42	15	8	19	59	69	53
Staines Town	42	13	10	19	54	74	49
Croydon	42	13	10	19	47	64	49
Barton Rovers	42	11	13	18	53	72	46
Wembley	42	10	15	17	38	61	45
Molesey	42	10	11	21	47	65	41
Whyteleafe	42	10	10	22	48	83	40
Wokingham Town	42	7	10	25	41	74	31
Abingdon Town	42	9	4	29	47	101	31
Thame United	42	7	9	25	33	96	30

Second Division

Team	P	W	D	L	F	A	Pts
Canvey Island	42	30	8	4	116	41	98
Braintree Town	42	29	11	2	117	45	98
Wealdstone	42	24	11	7	81	46	83
Bedford Town	42	22	12	8	55	25	78
Metropolitan Police	42	21	8	13	80	65	71
Wivenhoe Town	42	18	12	12	84	66	66
Edgware Town	42	18	10	14	81	65	64
Chalfont St Peter	42	17	13	12	63	60	64
Northwood	42	17	11	14	65	69	62
Windsor & Eton	42	17	7	18	75	72	58
Tooting & Mitcham United	42	16	9	17	58	56	57
Barking	42	15	12	15	62	75	57
Banstead Athletic	42	15	9	18	60	63	54
Marlow	42	16	5	21	64	78	53
Horsham	42	13	9	20	67	75	48
Bracknell Town	42	13	8	21	68	93	47
Leighton Town	42	13	6	23	45	78	45
Hungerford Town	42	11	11	20	66	77	44
Witham Town	42	9	13	20	55	68	40
Tilbury	42	9	12	21	57	88	39
Egham Town	42	9	5	28	47	101	32
Cheshunt	42	4	10	28	31	90	32

Third Division

Team	P	W	D	L	F	A	Pts
Hemel Hempstead	38	27	6	5	86	28	87
Hertford Town	38	26	5	7	77	31	83
Harlow Town	38	24	11	3	81	43	83
Camberley Town	38	24	7	7	93	43	79
Ford United	38	23	9	6	90	34	78
East Thurrock United	38	23	7	8	70	40	76
Epsom & Ewell	38	17	6	15	69	57	57
Ware	38	17	6	15	69	57	57
Aveley	38	16	7	15	65	57	55
Corinthian Casuals	38	16	6	16	59	57	54
Hornchurch	38	12	9	17	55	68	45
Clapton	38	13	6	19	46	61	45
Flackwell Heath	38	12	9	17	50	76	45
Croydon Athletic	38	12	7	19	58	63	43
Tring Town	38	12	7	19	51	69	43
Southall	38	10	6	22	41	85	46
Dorking	38	9	6	23	49	94	33
Wingate & Finchley	38	7	8	23	46	80	29
Lewes	38	7	5	26	34	88	26
Kingsbury Town	38	5	3	30	35	93	18

1998-99

Premier Division

Team	P	W	D	L	F	A	Pts
Sutton United	42	27	7	8	89	39	88
Aylesbury United	42	23	8	11	67	38	77
Dagenham & Redbridge	42	20	13	9	71	44	73
Purfleet	42	22	7	13	71	54	73
Enfield	42	21	9	12	73	49	72
St Albans City	42	17	17	8	71	52	68
Aldershot Town	42	16	14	12	83	48	62
Basingstoke Town	42	17	10	15	63	53	61
Harrow Borough	42	17	9	16	72	66	60
Gravesend & Northfleet	42	18	6	18	54	53	60
Slough Town	42	16	11	15	60	53	59
Billericay Town	42	15	13	14	54	56	58
Hendon	42	16	9	17	70	71	57
Boreham Wood	42	14	15	13	59	63	57
Chesham United	42	15	9	18	58	79	54
Dulwich Hamlet	42	14	8	20	53	63	50
Heybridge Swifts	42	13	9	20	51	85	48
Walton & Hersham	42	12	7	23	50	77	43
Hampton	42	10	12	20	41	71	42
Carshalton Athletic	42	10	10	22	47	82	40
Bishops Stortford	42	9	10	23	49	90	37
Bromley	42	8	11	23	50	72	35

First Division

Team	P	W	D	L	F	A	Pts
Canvey Island	42	28	6	8	76	41	90
Hitchin Town	42	25	10	7	75	38	85
Wealdstone	42	26	6	10	75	48	84
Braintree Town	42	20	10	12	75	48	70
Bognor Regis Town	42	20	8	14	63	44	68
Grays Athletic	42	19	11	12	56	42	68
Oxford City	42	16	14	12	58	51	62
Croydon	42	16	13	13	53	53	61
Chertsey Town	42	14	16	12	57	57	58
Romford	42	14	15	13	58	63	57
Maidenhead United	42	13	15	14	50	46	54
Worthing	42	13	13	16	47	61	52
Leyton Pennant	42	13	12	17	62	70	51
Uxbridge	42	13	11	18	54	51	50
Barton Rovers	42	11	15	16	43	49	48
Yeading	42	12	10	20	51	85	46
Leatherhead	42	12	9	21	48	59	45
Whyteleafe	42	13	6	23	51	72	45
Staines Town	42	10	15	17	33	57	45
Molesey	42	8	20	14	35	52	44
Wembley	42	10	10	22	36	71	40
Berkhamsted Town	42	10	7	25	53	81	37

Second Division

Team	P	W	D	L	F	A	Pts
Bedford Town	42	29	7	6	89	31	94
Harlow Town	42	27	8	7	100	47	89
Thame United	42	26	8	8	89	50	86
Hemel Hempstead	42	21	12	9	90	50	75
Windsor & Eton	42	22	6	14	87	55	72
Banstead Athletic	42	21	8	13	83	62	71
Northwood	42	20	7	15	68	67	67
Tooting & Mitcham United	42	19	9	14	63	62	66
Chalfont St Peter	42	16	12	14	70	71	60
Metropolitan Police	42	17	8	17	61	58	59
Leighton Town	42	16	10	16	60	64	58
Horsham	42	17	6	19	74	67	57
Marlow	42	16	9	17	72	68	57
Edgware Town	42	14	10	18	65	68	52
Witham Town	42	12	15	15	64	64	51
Hungerford Town	42	13	12	17	59	61	51
Wivenhoe Town	42	14	8	20	71	83	50
Wokingham Town	42	14	4	24	44	79	46
Barking	42	10	11	21	50	75	41
Hertford Town	42	11	2	29	44	96	35
Bracknell Town	42	7	10	25	48	92	31
Abingdon Town	42	6	6	30	48	124	24

Third Division

Ford United	38	27	5	6	110	42	86
Wingate & Finchley	38	25	5	8	79	38	80
Cheshunt	38	23	10	5	70	41	79
Lewes	38	25	3	10	86	45	78
Epsom & Ewell	38	19	5	14	61	51	62
Ware	38	19	4	15	79	60	61
Tilbury	38	17	8	13	74	52	59
Croydon Athletic	38	16	10	12	82	59	58
East Thurrock United	38	15	13	10	74	56	58
Egham Town	38	16	8	14	65	58	56
Corinthian Casuals	38	16	7	15	70	71	55
Southall	38	14	9	15	68	66	51
Camberley Town	38	14	8	16	66	77	50
Aveley	38	12	7	19	50	67	43
Flackwell Heath	38	11	9	18	59	70	42
Hornchurch	38	10	9	19	48	73	39
Clapton	38	11	6	21	48	89	39
Dorking	38	8	7	23	52	98	31
Kingsbury Town	38	6	3	29	40	98	21
Tring Town	38	5	6	27	38	108	21

1999-2000

Premier Division

Dagenham & Redbridge	42	32	5	5	97	35	101
Aldershot Town	42	24	5	13	71	51	77
Chesham United	42	20	10	12	64	50	70
Purfleet	42	18	15	9	70	48	69
Canvey Island	42	21	6	15	70	53	69
St Albans City	42	19	10	13	75	55	67
Billericay Town	42	18	12	12	62	62	66
Hendon	42	18	8	16	61	64	62
Slough Town	42	17	9	16	61	59	60
Dulwich Hamlet	42	17	5	20	62	68	56
Gravesend & Northfleet	42	15	10	17	66	67	55
Farnborough Town	42	14	11	17	52	55	53
Hampton & Richmond Borough	42	13	13	16	49	57	52
Enfield	42	13	11	18	64	68	50
Heybridge Swifts	42	13	11	18	57	65	50
Hitchin Town	42	13	11	18	59	72	50
Carshalton Athletic	42	12	12	18	55	65	48
Basingstoke Town	42	13	9	20	56	71	48
Harrow Borough	42	14	6	22	54	70	48
Aylesbury United	42	13	9	20	64	81	48
Boreham Wood	42	11	10	21	44	71	43
Walton & Hersham	42	11	8	23	44	70	41

First Division

Croydon	42	25	9	8	85	47	84
Grays Athletic	42	21	12	9	80	44	75
Maidenhead United	42	20	15	7	72	45	75
Thame United	42	20	13	9	61	38	73
Worthing	42	19	12	11	80	60	69
Staines Town	42	19	12	11	63	52	69
Whyteleafe	42	20	9	13	60	49	69
Bedford Town	42	17	12	13	59	52	63
Bromley	42	17	9	16	63	65	60
Uxbridge	42	15	13	14	60	44	58
Bishop's Stortford	42	16	10	16	57	62	58
Barton Rovers	42	16	8	18	64	83	56
Oxford City	42	17	4	21	57	55	55
Braintree Town	42	15	10	17	65	74	55
Yeading	42	12	18	12	53	54	54
Wealdstone	42	13	12	17	51	58	51
Bognor Regis Town	42	12	13	17	47	53	49
Harlow Town	42	11	13	18	62	76	46
Romford	42	12	9	21	51	70	45
Leatherhead	42	9	13	20	47	70	40
Chertsey Town	42	9	5	28	50	84	32
Leyton Pennant	42	7	9	26	34	85	30

Second Division

Hemel Hempstead	42	31	8	3	98	27	101
Northwood	42	29	9	4	109	40	96
Ford United	42	28	8	6	108	41	92
Berkhamsted Town	42	22	8	12	75	52	74
Windsor & Eton	42	20	13	9	73	53	73
Wivenhoe Town	42	20	9	13	61	47	69
Barking	42	18	13	11	70	51	67
Marlow	42	20	4	18	86	66	64
Metropolitan Police	42	18	7	17	75	71	61
Banstead Athletic	42	16	11	15	55	56	59
Tooting & Mitcham United	42	16	7	19	72	74	55
Wokingham Town	42	15	9	18	58	80	54
Wembley	42	14	11	17	47	53	53
Edgware Town	42	13	11	18	72	71	50
Hungerford Town	42	13	10	19	61	78	49
Cheshunt	42	12	12	18	53	65	48
Horsham	42	13	8	21	66	81	47
Leighton Town	42	13	8	21	65	84	47
Molesey	42	10	12	20	54	69	42
Wingate & Finchley	42	11	7	24	54	97	40
Witham Town	42	7	9	26	39	110	30
Chalfont St Peter	42	2	8	32	39	124	14

Third Division

East Thurrock United	40	26	7	7	89	42	85
Great Wakering Rovers	40	25	7	8	81	41	82
Tilbury	40	21	12	7	67	39	75
Hornchurch	40	19	12	9	72	57	69
Croydon Athletic	40	19	11	10	85	52	68
Epsom & Ewell	40	18	12	10	67	46	66
Lewes	40	18	10	12	73	51	64
Bracknell Town	40	15	16	9	81	64	61
Aveley	40	17	10	13	73	64	61
Corinthian Casuals	40	16	10	14	59	51	58
Flackwell Heath	40	17	6	17	74	76	57
Ware	40	16	8	16	74	62	56
Egham Town	40	14	13	13	48	43	55
Hertford Town	40	15	10	15	63	60	55
Abingdon Town	40	10	12	18	48	64	42
Kingsbury Town	40	11	8	21	55	86	41
Camberley Town	40	11	7	22	44	79	40
Tring Town	40	10	9	21	37	64	39
Dorking	40	9	10	21	53	69	37
Clapton	40	9	7	24	50	93	34
Southall	40	3	5	32	33	123	14

2000-2001

Premier Division

Farnborough Town	42	31	6	5	86	27	99
Canvey Island	42	27	8	7	79	41	89
Basingstoke Town	42	22	13	7	73	40	79
Aldershot Town	41	21	11	9	73	39	74
Chesham United	42	22	6	14	78	52	72
Gravesend & Northfleet	42	22	5	15	62	45	71
Heybridge Swifts	42	18	13	11	74	60	67
Billericay Town	41	18	13	10	62	54	67
Hampton & Richmond Borough	42	18	12	12	73	60	66
Hitchin Town	42	18	5	19	72	69	59
Purfleet	42	14	13	15	55	55	55
Hendon	42	16	6	18	62	62	54
Sutton United	41	14	11	16	74	70	53
St Albans City	42	15	5	22	50	69	50
Grays Athletic	42	14	8	20	49	68	50
Maidenhead United	42	15	2	25	47	63	47
Croydon	42	12	10	20	55	77	46
Enfield	42	12	9	21	48	74	45
Harrow Borough	41	10	11	20	61	90	41
Slough Town	42	10	9	23	40	62	39
Carshalton Athletic	42	10	6	26	40	85	36
Dulwich Hamlet	42	4	10	28	33	84	22

First Division

Team	P	W	D	L	F	A	Pts
Boreham Wood	42	26	7	9	82	49	85
Bedford Town	42	22	16	4	81	40	82
Braintree Town	42	25	6	11	112	60	81
Bishop's Stortford	42	24	6	12	103	76	78
Thame United	42	22	8	12	86	54	74
Ford United	42	19	12	11	70	58	69
Uxbridge	42	21	5	16	73	55	68
Northwood	42	20	8	14	89	81	68
Whyteleafe	42	20	6	16	62	69	66
Oxford City	42	16	13	13	64	49	61
Harlow Town	42	15	16	11	70	66	61
Worthing	42	16	9	17	69	69	57
Staines Town	42	16	8	18	60	66	56
Aylesbury United	42	17	4	21	65	55	55
Yeading	42	15	9	18	72	74	54
Bognor Regis Town	42	13	11	18	71	71	50
Walton & Hersham	42	14	8	20	59	80	50
Bromley	42	14	6	22	63	86	48
Wealdstone	42	12	9	21	54	73	45
Leatherhead	42	12	4	26	37	87	40
Romford	42	9	4	29	53	113	31
Barton Rovers	42	2	9	31	30	94	15

Second Division

Team	P	W	D	L	F	A	Pts
Tooting & Mitcham United	42	26	11	5	92	35	89
Windsor	42	24	10	8	70	40	82
Barking	42	23	13	6	82	54	82
Berkhamsted Town	42	24	8	10	99	49	80
Wivenhoe Town	42	23	11	8	78	52	80
Hemel Hempstead	42	22	10	10	74	44	76
Horsham	42	19	9	14	84	61	66
Chertsey Town	42	18	9	15	59	59	63
Great Wakering Rovers	42	16	13	13	69	59	61
Tilbury	42	18	6	18	61	67	60
Banstead Athletic	42	17	8	17	69	58	59
East Thurrock United	42	16	11	15	72	64	59
Metropolitan Police	42	18	4	20	64	77	58
Marlow	42	15	11	16	62	61	56
Molesey	42	14	9	19	53	61	51
Wembley	42	12	10	20	39	63	46
Hungerford Town	42	11	9	22	40	73	42
Leyton Pennant	42	10	11	21	47	74	41
Cheshunt	42	11	6	25	48	77	39
Edgware Town	42	9	9	24	41	77	36
Leighton Town	42	8	10	24	44	87	34
Wokingham Town	42	3	12	27	39	94	20

Wokingham Town had 1 point deducted

Third Division

Team	P	W	D	L	F	A	Pts
Arlesey Town	42	34	6	2	138	37	108
Lewes	41	25	11	5	104	34	86
Ashford Town	42	26	7	9	102	49	85
Flackwell Heath	42	24	10	8	93	51	82
Corinthian Casuals	42	24	10	8	83	50	82
Aveley	42	24	3	15	85	61	75
Epsom & Ewell	42	23	4	15	76	52	73
Witham Town	42	21	7	12	76	57	72
Bracknell Town	41	19	10	12	90	70	67
Croydon Athletic	41	15	12	14	78	63	57
Ware	42	17	6	19	75	76	57
Tring Town	42	16	9	17	60	71	57
Egham Town	42	15	11	16	60	60	56
Hornchurch	42	14	13	15	73	60	55
Wingate & Finchley	42	15	7	20	75	75	52
Kingsbury Town	42	11	8	23	74	100	41
Abingdon Town	42	12	7	23	53	102	40
Dorking	42	10	9	23	59	99	39
Hertford Town	41	9	8	24	57	97	35
Camberley Town	42	8	8	26	53	107	32
Clapton	42	5	9	28	48	121	24
Chalfont St Peter	42	4	1	37	30	150	13

Abingdon Town had 3 points deducted

2001-2002

Premier Division

Team	P	W	D	L	F	A	Pts
Gravesend & Northfleet	42	31	6	5	90	33	99
Canvey Island	42	30	5	7	107	41	95
Aldershot Town	42	22	7	13	76	51	73
Braintree Town	42	23	4	15	66	61	73
Purfleet	42	19	15	8	67	44	72
Grays Athletic	42	20	10	12	65	55	70
Chesham United	42	19	10	13	69	53	67
Hendon Town	42	19	5	18	66	54	62
Billericay Town	42	16	13	13	59	60	61
St Albans City	42	16	9	17	71	60	57
Hitchin Town	42	15	10	17	73	81	55
Sutton Albion	42	13	15	14	62	62	54
Heybridge Swifts	42	15	9	18	68	85	54
Kingstonian	42	13	13	16	50	56	52
Boreham Wood	42	15	6	21	49	62	51
Maidenhead United	42	15	5	22	51	63	50
Bedford Town	42	12	12	18	64	69	48
Basingstoke Town	42	11	15	16	50	68	48
Enfield	42	11	9	22	48	77	42
Hampton & Richmond Borough	42	9	13	20	51	71	40
Harrow Borough	42	8	10	24	50	89	34
Croydon	42	7	5	30	36	93	26

First Division

Team	P	W	D	L	F	A	Pts
Ford United	42	27	7	8	92	56	88
Bishop's Stortford	42	26	9	7	104	51	87
Aylesbury United	42	23	10	9	96	64	79
Bognor Regis Town	42	20	13	9	74	55	73
Northwood	42	19	11	12	92	64	68
Carshalton Athletic	42	17	16	9	64	53	67
Harlow Town	42	19	9	14	77	65	66
Slough Town	42	17	11	14	68	51	62
Uxbridge	42	18	6	18	68	65	60
Oxford City	42	17	9	16	59	66	60
Thame United	42	15	14	13	75	61	59
Tooting & Mitcham United	42	16	11	15	70	70	59
Walton & Hersham	42	16	10	16	75	70	58
Yeading	42	16	10	16	84	90	58
Worthing	42	15	8	19	69	65	53
Staines Town	42	12	11	19	45	60	47
Dulwich Hamlet	42	11	13	18	64	76	46
Wealdstone	42	11	12	19	60	82	45
Bromley	42	10	11	21	44	74	41
Whyteleafe	42	10	11	21	46	86	41
Barking & East Ham United	42	8	7	27	61	123	31
Windsor & Eton	42	7	5	30	53	93	26

Second Division

Team	P	W	D	L	F	A	Pts
Lewes	42	29	9	4	108	31	96
Horsham	42	27	9	6	104	44	90
Berkhamstead Town	42	23	10	9	82	51	79
Arlesey Town	42	23	6	13	89	55	75
Banstead Athletic	42	22	8	12	83	54	74
Leyton Pennant	42	22	8	12	84	60	74
Great Wakering Rovers	42	21	8	13	64	37	71
East Thurrock United	42	21	8	13	67	59	71
Marlow	42	18	13	11	73	63	67
Hemel Hempstead Town	42	18	10	14	82	66	64
Leatherhead	42	17	6	19	72	62	57
Ashford Town	42	15	11	16	58	71	56
Metropolitan Police	42	16	7	19	84	84	55
Barton Rovers	42	15	9	18	54	60	54
Hungerford Town	42	14	9	19	56	75	51
Tilbury	42	15	6	21	55	74	51
Chertsey Town	42	10	14	18	79	112	44
Wembley	42	9	10	23	51	82	37
Molesey	42	10	6	26	40	93	36
Cheshunt	42	7	13	22	51	84	34
Wivenhoe Town	42	8	9	25	55	111	33
Romford	42	4	7	31	42	105	19

Third Division

Croydon Athletic	42	30	5	7	138	41	95
Hornchurch	42	25	11	6	96	46	86
Aveley	42	26	6	10	109	55	84
Bracknell Town	42	25	8	9	96	54	83
Epsom & Ewell	42	20	15	7	79	51	75
Egham Town	42	21	11	10	72	59	74
Wingate & Finchley	42	20	9	13	80	60	69
Dorking	42	18	14	10	77	66	68
Tring Town	42	19	11	12	64	62	68
Corinthian-Casuals	42	18	13	11	69	44	67
Hertford Town	42	20	7	15	88	74	67
Witham Town	42	15	10	17	66	72	55
Ware	42	14	10	18	74	76	52
Chalfont St Peter	42	15	4	23	69	92	49
Wokingham Town	42	14	6	22	79	105	48
Abingdon Town	42	13	7	22	61	75	46
Leighton Town	42	8	12	22	56	95	36
Kingsbury Town	42	8	11	23	58	91	35
Edgware Town	42	9	7	26	65	101	34
Flackwell Heath	42	9	8	25	53	99	32
Clapton	42	9	4	29	45	118	31
Camberley Town	42	7	9	26	37	95	30

2002-2003

Premier Division

Aldershot Town	46	33	6	7	81	36	105
Canvey Island	46	28	8	10	112	56	92
Hendon	46	22	13	11	70	56	79
St. Albans City	46	23	8	15	73	65	77
Basingstoke Town	46	23	7	16	80	60	76
Sutton United	46	22	9	15	77	62	75
Hayes	46	20	13	13	67	54	73
Purfleet	46	19	15	12	68	48	72
Bedford Town	46	21	9	16	66	58	72
Maidenhead United	46	16	17	13	75	63	65
Kingstonian	46	16	17	13	71	64	65
Billericay Town	46	17	11	18	46	44	62
Bishop's Stortford	46	16	11	19	74	72	59
Hitchin Town	46	15	13	18	69	67	58
Ford United	46	15	12	19	78	84	57
Braintree Town	46	14	12	20	59	71	54
Aylesbury United	46	13	15	18	62	75	54
Harrow Borough	46	15	9	22	54	75	54
Grays Athletic	46	14	11	21	53	59	53
Heybridge Swifts	46	13	14	19	52	80	53
Chesham United	46	14	10	22	56	81	52
Boreham Wood	46	11	15	20	50	58	48
Enfield	46	9	11	26	47	101	38
Hampton & Richmond Borough	46	3	14	29	35	86	23

Division One (North)

Northwood	46	28	7	11	109	56	91
Hornchurch	46	25	15	6	85	48	90
Hemel Hempstead Town	46	26	7	13	70	55	85
Slough Town	46	22	14	10	86	59	80
Uxbridge	46	23	10	13	62	41	79
Aveley	46	21	14	11	66	48	77
Berkhamsted Town	46	21	13	12	92	68	76
Thame United	46	20	12	14	84	51	72
Wealdstone	46	21	9	16	85	69	72
Harlow Town	46	20	12	14	66	53	72
Marlow	46	19	10	17	74	63	67
Barking & East Ham United	46	19	9	18	73	76	66
Yeading	46	18	11	17	77	69	65
Great Wakering Rovers	46	17	14	15	64	70	65
Oxford City	46	17	13	16	55	51	64
Arlesey Town	46	17	12	17	69	71	63
East Thurrock United	46	17	10	19	75	79	61
Wingate & Finchley	46	15	11	20	70	74	56
Barton Rovers	46	15	7	24	53	65	52
Tilbury	46	14	7	25	55	96	49
Wivenhoe Town	46	9	11	26	56	94	38
Leyton Pennant	46	9	7	30	38	81	34
Wembley	46	7	11	28	57	111	32
Hertford Town	46	6	6	34	46	119	24

Division One (South)

Carshalton Athletic	46	28	8	10	73	44	92
Bognor Regis Town	46	26	10	10	92	34	88
Lewes	46	24	16	6	106	50	88
Dulwich Hamlet	46	23	12	11	73	49	81
Whyteleafe	46	21	13	12	74	51	76
Bromley	46	21	13	12	70	53	76
Walton & Hersham	46	20	13	13	87	63	73
Horsham	46	21	9	16	80	58	72
Epsom & Ewell	46	19	12	15	67	66	69
Egham Town	46	19	10	17	62	71	67
Tooting & Mitcham United	46	18	9	19	83	78	63
Worthing	46	17	12	17	78	75	63
Windsor & Eton	46	18	9	19	66	65	63
Leatherhead	46	16	13	17	71	66	61
Staines Town	46	14	16	16	57	63	58
Banstead Athletic	46	14	15	17	58	59	57
Ashford Town (Middlesex)	46	14	11	21	47	70	53
Croydon	46	15	8	23	56	87	53
Croydon Athletic	46	13	13	20	52	66	52
Bracknell Town	46	12	16	18	57	74	52
Corinthian Casuals	46	12	14	20	50	68	50
Molesey	46	13	9	24	52	79	48
Metropolitan Police	46	12	10	24	50	76	46
Chertsey Town	46	3	7	36	43	139	16

Division Two

Cheshunt	30	25	3	2	91	29	78
Leyton	30	21	5	4	77	22	68
Flackwell Heath	30	17	3	10	52	44	54
Abingdon Town	30	14	11	5	65	42	53
Hungerford Town	30	12	12	6	49	36	48
Leighton Town	30	14	3	13	61	43	45
Witham Town	30	12	8	10	40	43	44
Ware	30	12	5	13	47	53	41
Clapton	30	12	5	13	40	47	41
Tring Town	30	11	5	14	49	58	38
Kingsbury Town	30	9	11	10	38	48	38
Edgware Town	30	10	3	17	49	65	33
Wokingham Town	30	7	7	16	34	81	28
Dorking	30	6	6	18	49	63	24
Chalfont St. Peter	30	6	5	19	34	63	23
Camberley Town	30	4	4	22	23	61	16

2003-2004

Premier Division

Canvey Island	46	32	8	6	106	42	104
Sutton United	46	25	10	11	94	56	85
Thurrock	46	24	11	11	87	45	83
Hendon	46	25	8	13	68	47	83
* Hornchurch	46	24	11	11	63	35	82
Grays Athletic	46	22	15	9	82	39	81
Carshalton Athletic	46	24	9	13	66	55	81
Hayes	46	21	11	14	56	46	74
Kettering Town	46	20	11	15	63	63	71
Bognor Regis Town	46	20	10	16	69	67	70
Bishop's Stortford	46	20	9	17	78	61	69
Maidenhead United	46	18	9	19	60	68	63
Ford United	46	16	14	16	69	63	62
Basingstoke Town	46	17	9	20	58	64	60
Bedford Town	46	14	13	19	62	63	55
Heybridge Swifts	46	14	11	21	57	78	53
Harrow Borough	46	12	14	20	47	63	50
Kingstonian	46	12	13	21	40	56	49
St. Albans City	46	12	12	22	55	83	48
Hitchin Town	46	13	8	25	55	89	47
Northwood	46	12	9	25	65	95	45
Billericay Town	46	11	11	24	51	66	44
Braintree Town	46	11	6	29	41	88	39
Aylesbury United	46	5	14	27	41	101	29

* Hornchurch had 1 point deducted

Division One (North)

Yeading	46	32	7	7	112	54	103
Leyton	46	29	9	8	90	53	96
Cheshunt	46	27	10	9	119	54	91
Chesham United	46	24	9	13	104	60	81
Dunstable Town	46	23	9	14	86	61	78
Hemel Hempstead Town	46	22	12	12	75	72	78
Wealdstone	46	23	7	16	81	51	76
Arlesey Town	46	23	7	16	95	70	76
Boreham Wood	46	20	13	13	82	59	73
Harlow Town	46	20	10	16	75	51	70
Wingate & Finchley	46	19	13	14	68	63	70
East Thurrock United	46	19	11	16	62	54	68
Uxbridge	46	15	14	17	59	57	59
Aveley	46	15	14	17	67	71	59
Thame United	46	16	9	21	72	83	57
* Waltham Forest	46	15	13	18	62	60	55
Wivenhoe Town	46	15	10	21	79	104	55
Barton Rovers	46	16	6	24	52	80	54
Oxford City	46	14	11	21	55	65	53
Berkhamstead Town	46	12	10	24	66	88	46
Great Wakering Rovers	46	10	13	23	47	97	43
Tilbury	46	10	9	27	56	100	39
Barking & East Ham United	46	8	7	31	37	100	31
Enfield	46	5	7	34	44	138	22

* Waltham Forest had 3 points deducted.

Division One (South)

Lewes	46	29	7	10	113	61	94
Worthing	46	26	14	6	87	46	92
Windsor & Eton	46	26	13	7	75	39	91
Slough Town	46	28	6	12	103	63	90
Hampton & Richmond Borough	46	26	11	9	82	45	89
Staines Town	46	26	9	11	85	52	87
Dulwich Hamlet	46	23	15	8	77	57	84
Bromley	46	22	10	14	80	58	76
Walton & Hersham	46	20	14	12	76	55	74
Croydon Athletic	46	20	10	16	70	54	70
Tooting & Mitcham United	46	20	9	17	82	68	69
Ashford Town (Middlesex)	46	18	13	15	69	62	67
Leatherhead	46	19	9	18	83	88	66
Bracknell Town	46	19	6	21	81	87	63
Horsham	46	16	11	19	71	69	59
Marlow	46	16	11	19	50	64	59
Whyteleafe	46	17	4	25	66	93	55
Banstead Athletic	46	15	8	23	56	73	53
Molesey	46	12	6	28	45	84	42
Metropolitan Police	46	9	14	23	58	84	41
Croydon	46	10	10	26	57	88	40
Egham Town	46	8	8	30	55	92	32
Corinthian Casuals	46	6	6	34	48	110	24
Epsom & Ewell	46	5	8	33	40	117	23

Division Two

Leighton Town	42	28	7	7	111	36	91
Dorking	42	27	8	7	87	47	89
Hertford Town	42	24	9	9	74	35	81
Chertsey Town	42	22	9	11	75	53	75
Flackwell Heath	42	22	5	15	71	53	71
Witham Town	42	20	10	12	75	54	70
Kingsbury Town	42	14	11	17	60	64	53
Ware	42	14	10	18	67	60	52
Abingdon Town	42	15	6	21	83	81	51
Camberley Town	42	15	6	21	51	71	51
Wembley	42	13	9	20	46	67	48
Wokingham Town	42	12	7	23	55	94	43
Edgware Town	42	12	6	24	62	88	42
Chalfont St. Peter	42	12	6	24	57	89	42
Clapton	42	8	5	29	47	129	29

NORTHERN PREMIER LEAGUE

1968-69

Macclesfield Town	38	27	6	5	82	38	60
Wigan Athletic	38	18	12	8	59	41	48
Morecambe	38	16	14	8	64	37	46
Gainsborough Trinity	38	19	8	11	64	43	46
South Shields	38	19	8	11	78	56	46
Bangor City	38	18	9	11	102	64	45
Hyde United	38	16	10	12	71	65	42
Goole Town	38	15	10	13	80	78	40
Altrincham	38	14	10	14	69	52	38
Fleetwood	38	16	6	16	58	58	38
Gateshead	38	14	9	15	42	48	37
South Liverpool	38	12	13	13	56	66	37
Northwich Victoria	38	16	5	17	59	82	37
Boston United	38	14	8	16	59	65	36
Runcorn	38	12	11	15	59	63	35
Netherfield	38	12	4	22	51	69	28
Scarborough	38	9	10	19	49	68	28
Ashington	38	10	8	20	48	74	28
Chorley	38	8	9	21	46	75	25
Worksop Town	38	6	8	24	34	88	20

1969-70

Macclesfield Town	38	22	8	8	72	41	52
Wigan Athletic	38	20	12	6	56	32	52
Boston United	38	21	8	9	65	33	50
Scarborough	38	20	10	8	74	39	50
South Shields	38	19	7	12	66	43	45
Gainsborough Trinity	38	16	11	11	64	49	43
Stafford Rangers	38	16	7	15	59	52	39
Bangor City	38	15	9	14	68	63	39
Northwich Victoria	38	15	8	15	60	66	38
Netherfield	38	14	9	15	56	54	37
Hyde United	38	15	7	16	59	59	37
Altrincham	38	14	8	16	62	65	36
Fleetwood	38	13	10	15	53	60	36
Runcorn	38	11	13	14	57	72	35
Morecambe	38	10	13	15	41	51	33
South Liverpool	38	11	11	16	44	55	33
Great Harwood	38	10	9	19	63	92	29
Matlock Town	38	8	12	18	52	67	28
Goole Town	38	10	6	22	50	71	26
Gateshead	38	5	12	21	37	94	22

1970-71

Wigan Athletic	42	27	13	2	91	32	67
Stafford Rangers	42	27	7	8	87	51	61
Scarborough	42	23	12	7	83	40	58
Boston United	42	22	12	8	69	31	56
Macclesfield Town	42	23	10	9	84	45	56
Northwich Victoria	42	22	5	15	71	55	49
Bangor City	42	19	10	13	72	61	48
Altrincham	42	19	10	13	80	76	48
South Liverpool	42	15	15	12	67	57	45
Chorley	42	14	14	14	58	61	42
Gainsborough Trinity	42	15	11	16	65	63	41
Morecambe	42	14	11	17	67	79	39
South Shields	42	12	14	16	66	66	38
Bradford Park Avenue	42	15	8	19	54	73	38
Lancaster City	42	12	12	18	53	76	36
Netherfield	42	13	9	20	59	57	35
Matlock Town	42	10	13	19	58	80	33
Fleetwood	42	10	11	21	56	90	31
Great Harwood	42	8	13	21	66	98	29
Runcorn	42	10	5	27	58	84	25
Kirkby Town	42	6	13	23	57	93	25
Goole Town	42	10	4	28	44	98	24

1971-72

Stafford Rangers	46	30	11	5	91	32	71
Boston United	46	28	13	5	87	37	69
Wigan Athletic	46	27	10	9	70	43	64
Scarborough	46	21	15	10	75	46	57
Northwich Victoria	46	20	14	12	65	59	54
Macclesfield Town	46	18	15	13	61	50	51
Gainsborough Trinity	46	21	9	16	93	79	51
South Shields	46	18	14	14	75	57	50
Bangor City	46	20	8	18	93	74	48
Altrincham	46	18	11	17	72	58	47
Skelmersdale United	46	19	9	18	61	58	47
Matlock Town	46	20	7	19	67	75	47
Chorley	46	17	12	17	66	59	46
Lancaster City	46	15	14	17	84	84	44
Great Harwood	46	15	14	17	60	74	44
Ellesmere Port Town	46	17	9	20	67	71	43
Morecambe	46	15	10	21	51	64	40
Bradford Park Avenue	46	13	13	20	54	71	39
Netherfield	46	16	5	25	51	73	37
Fleetwood	46	11	15	20	43	67	37
South Liverpool	46	12	12	22	61	73	36
Runcorn	46	8	14	24	48	80	30
Goole Town	46	9	10	27	51	97	28
Kirkby Town	46	6	12	28	38	104	24

1972-73

Boston United	46	27	16	3	88	34	70
Scarborough	46	26	9	11	72	39	61
Wigan Athletic	46	23	14	9	69	38	60
Altrincham	46	22	16	8	75	55	60
Bradford Park Avenue	46	19	17	10	63	50	55
Stafford Rangers	46	20	11	15	63	46	51
Gainsborough Trinity	46	18	13	15	70	50	49
Northwich Victoria	46	17	15	14	74	62	49
Netherfield	46	20	9	17	68	65	49
Macclesfield Town	46	16	16	14	58	47	48
Ellesmere Port Town	46	18	11	17	52	56	47
Skelmersdale United	46	15	16	15	58	59	46
Bangor City	46	16	13	17	70	60	45
Mossley	46	17	11	18	70	73	45
Morecambe	46	17	11	18	62	70	45
Great Harwood	46	14	15	17	63	74	43
South Liverpool	46	12	19	15	47	57	43
Runcorn	46	15	12	19	75	78	42
Goole Town	46	13	13	20	64	73	39
South Shields	46	17	4	25	64	81	38
Matlock Town	46	11	11	24	42	80	33
Lancaster City	46	10	11	25	53	78	31
Barrow	46	12	6	28	52	101	30
Fleetwood	46	5	15	26	31	77	25

1973-74

Boston United	46	27	11	8	69	32	65
Wigan Athletic	46	28	8	10	96	39	64
Altrincham	46	26	11	9	77	34	63
Stafford Rangers	46	27	9	10	101	45	63
Scarborough	46	22	14	10	62	43	58
South Shields	46	25	6	15	87	48	56
Runcorn	46	21	14	11	72	47	56
Macclesfield Town	46	18	15	13	48	47	51
Bangor City	46	19	11	16	65	56	49
Gainsborough Trinity	46	18	11	17	77	64	47
South Liverpool	46	16	15	15	55	47	47
Skelmersdale United	46	16	13	17	50	59	45
Goole Town	46	14	15	17	60	69	43
Fleetwood	46	14	15	17	48	68	43
Mossley	46	15	11	20	53	65	41
Northwich Victoria	46	14	13	19	68	75	41
Morecambe	46	13	13	20	62	84	39
Buxton	46	14	10	22	45	71	38
Matlock Town	46	11	14	21	50	79	36
Great Harwood	46	10	14	22	52	74	34
Bradford Park Avenue	46	9	15	22	42	84	33
Barrow	46	13	7	26	46	94	33
Lancaster City	46	10	12	24	52	67	32
Netherfield	46	11	5	30	42	88	27

1974-75

Wigan Athletic	46	33	6	7	94	38	72
Runcorn	46	30	8	8	102	42	68
Altrincham	46	26	12	8	87	43	64
Stafford Rangers	46	25	13	8	81	39	63
Scarborough	46	24	12	10	73	45	60
Mossley	46	23	11	12	78	52	57
Gateshead United	46	22	12	12	74	48	56
Goole Town	46	19	12	15	75	71	50
Northwich Victoria	46	18	12	16	83	71	48
Great Harwood	46	17	14	15	69	66	48
Matlock Town	46	19	8	19	87	79	46
Boston United	46	16	14	16	64	63	46
Morecambe	46	14	15	17	71	87	43
Worksop Town	46	14	14	18	69	66	42
South Liverpool	46	14	14	18	59	71	42
Buxton	46	11	17	18	50	77	39
Macclesfield Town	46	11	14	21	46	62	36
Lancaster City	46	13	10	23	53	76	36
Bangor City	46	13	9	24	56	67	35
Gainsborough Trinity	46	10	15	21	46	79	35
Skelmersdale United	46	13	7	26	63	93	33
Barrow	46	9	15	22	45	72	33
Netherfield	46	12	8	26	42	91	32
Fleetwood	46	5	10	31	26	97	20

1975-76

Runcorn	46	29	10	7	95	42	68
Stafford Rangers	46	26	15	5	81	41	67
Scarborough	46	26	10	10	84	43	62
Matlock Town	46	26	9	11	96	63	61
Boston United	46	27	6	13	95	58	60
Wigan Athletic	46	21	15	10	81	42	57
Altrincham	46	20	14	12	77	57	54
Bangor City	46	21	12	13	80	70	54
Mossley	46	21	11	14	70	58	53
Goole Town	46	20	13	13	58	49	53
Northwich Victoria	46	17	17	12	79	59	51
Lancaster City	46	18	9	19	61	70	45
Worksop Town	46	17	10	19	63	56	44
Gainsborough Trinity	46	13	17	16	58	69	43
Macclesfield Town	46	15	12	19	50	64	42
Gateshead United	46	17	7	22	64	63	41
Buxton	46	11	13	22	37	62	35
Skelmersdale United	46	12	10	24	45	74	34
Netherfield	46	11	11	24	55	76	33
Morecambe	46	11	11	24	47	67	33
Great Harwood	46	13	7	26	58	86	33
South Liverpool	46	12	9	25	45	78	33
Barrow	46	12	9	25	47	84	33
Fleetwood	46	3	9	34	36	131	15

1976-77

Boston United	44	27	11	6	82	35	65
Northwich Victoria	44	27	11	6	85	43	65
Matlock Town	44	26	11	7	108	57	63
Bangor City	44	22	11	11	87	52	55
Scarborough	44	21	12	11	77	66	54
Goole Town	44	23	6	15	64	50	52
Lancaster City	44	21	9	14	71	58	51
Gateshead United	44	18	12	14	80	64	48
Mossley	44	17	14	13	74	59	48
Altrincham	44	19	9	16	60	53	47
Stafford Rangers	44	16	14	14	60	55	46
Runcorn	44	15	14	15	57	49	44
Worksop Town	44	16	12	16	50	58	44
Wigan Athletic	44	14	15	15	62	54	43
Morecambe	44	13	11	20	59	75	37
Gainsborough Trinity	44	13	10	21	58	74	36
Great Harwood	44	11	14	19	63	84	36
Buxton	44	11	13	20	48	63	35
Macclesfield Town	44	8	15	21	41	68	31
Frickley Athletic	44	11	8	25	53	93	30
Barrow	44	11	6	27	56	87	28
South Liverpool	44	10	8	26	51	104	28
Netherfield	44	9	8	27	47	92	26

1977-78

Team	P	W	D	L	F	A	Pts
Boston United	46	31	9	6	85	35	71
Wigan Athletic	46	25	15	6	83	45	65
Bangor City	46	26	10	10	92	50	62
Scarborough	46	26	10	10	80	39	62
Altrincham	46	22	15	9	84	49	59
Northwich Victoria	46	22	14	10	83	55	50
Stafford Rangers	46	22	13	11	71	41	57
Runcorn	46	19	18	9	70	44	56
Mossley	46	22	11	13	85	73	55
Matlock Town	46	21	12	13	79	60	54
Lancaster City	46	15	14	17	66	82	44
Frickley Athletic	46	15	12	19	77	81	42
Barrow	46	14	12	20	50	61	40
Goole Town	46	15	9	22	60	68	39
Great Harwood	46	13	13	20	66	83	39
Gainsborough Trinity	46	14	10	22	61	74	38
Gateshead	46	16	5	25	65	74	37
Netherfield	46	11	13	22	50	80	35
Workington	46	13	8	25	48	80	34
Worksop Town	46	12	10	24	45	84	34
Morecambe	46	11	11	24	67	92	33
Macclesfield Town	46	12	9	25	60	92	33
Buxton	46	13	6	27	60	95	32
South Liverpool	46	9	7	30	53	111	25

1978-79

Team	P	W	D	L	F	A	Pts
Mossley	44	32	5	7	117	48	69
Altrincham	44	25	11	8	93	39	61
Matlock Town	44	24	8	12	100	59	56
Scarborough	44	19	14	11	61	44	52
Southport	44	19	14	11	62	49	52
Boston United	44	17	18	9	40	33	52
Runcorn	44	21	9	14	79	54	51
Stafford Rangers	44	18	14	12	67	41	50
Goole Town	44	17	15	12	56	61	49
Northwich Victoria	44	18	11	15	64	52	47
Lancaster City	44	17	12	15	62	54	46
Bangor City	44	15	14	15	65	66	44
Worksop Town	44	13	14	17	55	67	40
Workington	44	16	7	21	62	74	39
Netherfield	44	13	11	20	39	69	37
Barrow	44	14	9	21	47	78	37
Gainsborough Trinity	44	12	12	20	52	67	36
Morecambe	44	11	13	20	55	65	35
Frickley Athletic	44	13	9	22	58	70	35
South Liverpool	44	12	10	22	48	85	34
Gateshead	44	11	11	22	42	63	33
Buxton	44	11	9	24	50	84	31
Macclesfield Town	44	8	10	26	40	92	26

1979-80

Team	P	W	D	L	F	A	Pts
Mossley	42	28	9	5	96	41	65
Witton Albion	42	28	8	6	89	30	64
Frickley Athletic	42	24	13	5	93	48	61
Burton Albion	42	25	6	11	83	42	56
Matlock Town	42	18	17	7	87	53	53
Buxton	42	21	9	12	61	48	51
Worksop Town	42	20	10	12	65	52	50
Macclesfield Town	42	18	11	13	67	53	47
Grantham	42	18	8	16	71	65	44
Marine	42	16	10	16	65	57	42
Goole Town	42	14	13	15	61	63	41
Lancaster City	42	13	13	16	74	77	39
Oswestry Town	42	12	14	16	44	60	38
Gainsborough Trinity	42	14	8	20	64	75	36
Runcorn	42	11	11	20	46	63	33
Gateshead	42	11	11	20	50	77	33
Morecambe	42	10	12	20	40	59	32
Netherfield	42	7	15	20	37	66	29
Southport	42	8	13	21	30	75	29
South Liverpool	42	7	14	21	51	84	28
Workington	42	8	12	22	50	85	28
Tamworth	42	8	9	25	26	77	25

1980-81

Team	P	W	D	L	F	A	Pts
Runcorn	42	32	7	3	99	22	71
Mossley	42	24	7	11	95	55	55
Marine	42	22	10	10	60	41	54
Buxton	42	21	7	14	64	50	49
Gainsborough Trinity	42	17	13	12	50	57	47
Burton Albion	42	19	8	15	63	54	46
Witton Albion	42	19	8	15	70	62	46
Goole Town	42	14	16	12	56	50	44
South Liverpool	42	19	6	17	59	64	44
Workington	42	15	13	14	57	48	43
Gateshead	42	12	18	12	65	61	42
Worksop Town	42	15	11	16	66	61	41
Macclesfield Town	42	13	13	16	52	69	39
Grantham	42	14	9	19	57	74	37
Matlock Town	42	12	12	18	57	80	36
Lancaster City	42	13	9	20	48	70	35
Netherfield	42	11	12	19	73	81	34
Oswestry Town	42	13	8	21	54	67	34
King's Lynn	42	8	18	16	46	65	34
Southport	42	11	11	20	42	68	33
Morecambe	42	11	8	23	42	74	30
Tamworth	42	9	12	21	38	76	30

1981-82

Team	P	W	D	L	F	A	Pts
Bangor City	42	27	8	7	108	60	62
Mossley	42	24	11	7	76	43	59
Witton Albion	42	22	10	10	75	44	54
Gateshead	42	19	14	9	65	49	52
King's Lynn	42	19	12	11	61	36	50
Grantham	42	18	13	11	65	53	49
Burton Albion	42	19	9	14	71	62	47
Southport	42	16	14	12	63	55	46
Marine	42	17	12	13	64	57	46
Macclesfield Town	42	17	9	16	67	58	43
Workington	42	18	7	17	62	60	43
Worksop Town	42	15	13	14	52	60	43
South Liverpool	42	13	13	16	55	57	39
Goole Town	42	13	13	16	56	60	39
Oswestry Town	42	14	11	17	55	59	39
Buxton	42	14	11	17	48	56	39
Lancaster City	42	13	12	17	47	50	38
Gainsborough Trinity	42	10	13	19	60	69	33
Tamworth	42	10	9	23	31	56	29
Morecambe	42	9	11	22	43	86	29
Matlock Town	42	7	12	23	38	72	26
Netherfield	42	5	9	28	31	91	19

1982-83

Team	P	W	D	L	F	A	Pts
Gateshead	42	32	4	6	114	43	100
Mossley	42	25	9	8	77	42	84
Burton Albion	42	24	9	9	81	53	81
Chorley	42	23	11	8	77	49	80
Macclesfield Town	42	24	8	10	71	49	80
Marine	42	17	17	8	81	57	68
Workington	42	19	10	13	71	55	67
Hyde United	42	18	12	12	91	63	66
King's Lynn	42	17	13	12	62	44	64
Matlock Town	42	18	10	14	70	65	64
Witton Albion	42	17	12	13	82	52	63
Buxton	42	17	9	16	60	62	60
Morecambe	42	16	11	15	75	66	59
Grantham	42	15	13	14	49	50	58
Southport	42	11	14	17	58	65	47
Goole Town	42	13	7	22	52	66	46
Gainsborough Trinity	42	11	9	22	60	71	42
Oswestry Town	42	10	8	24	56	99	38
South Liverpool	42	7	15	20	57	91	36
Tamworth	42	7	8	27	44	97	29
Worksop Town	42	5	10	27	50	98	25
Netherfield	42	2	9	31	28	129	15

1983-84

Barrow	42	29	10	3	92	38	97
Matlock Town	42	23	8	11	72	48	77
South Liverpool	42	22	11	9	55	44	77
Grantham	42	20	8	14	64	51	68
Burton Albion	42	17	13	12	61	47	64
Macclesfield Town	42	18	10	14	65	55	64
Rhyl	42	19	6	17	64	55	63
Horwich	42	18	9	15	64	59	63
Gainsborough Trinity	42	17	11	14	82	66	62
Stafford Rangers	42	15	17	10	65	52	62
Hyde United	42	17	8	17	61	63	59
Marine	42	16	10	16	63	68	58
Witton Albion	42	14	14	14	64	57	56
Chorley	42	14	11	17	68	65	53
Workington	42	14	9	19	53	57	51
Southport	42	14	8	20	57	74	50
Worksop Town	42	13	8	21	57	74	47
Goole Town	42	12	10	20	59	80	46
Morecambe	42	11	12	19	59	75	45
Oswestry Town	42	11	8	23	66	97	41
Buxton	42	11	6	25	52	91	39
Mossley	42	9	9	24	47	74	33

Mossley had 3 points deducted

1984-85

Stafford Rangers	42	26	8	8	81	40	86
Macclesfield Town	42	23	13	6	67	39	82
Witton Albion	42	22	8	12	57	39	74
Hyde United	42	21	8	13	68	52	71
Marine	42	18	15	9	59	34	69
Burton Albion	42	18	15	9	70	49	69
Worksop Town	42	19	10	13	68	56	67
Workington	42	18	9	15	59	53	53
Horwich	42	16	14	12	67	50	62
Bangor City	42	17	9	16	70	61	60
Gainsborough Trinity	42	14	14	14	72	73	56
Southport	42	15	9	18	65	66	54
Matlock Town	42	14	9	19	56	66	51
Oswestry Town	42	14	9	19	59	75	51
Mossley	42	14	9	19	45	65	51
Goole Town	42	13	11	18	60	65	50
Rhyl	42	11	14	17	52	63	47
Morecambe	42	11	14	17	51	67	47
Chorley	42	12	10	20	47	63	46
South Liverpool	42	9	15	18	43	71	42
Grantham	42	8	13	21	41	69	36
Buxton	42	8	6	28	38	79	30

Grantham had 1 point deducted

1985-86

Gateshead	42	24	10	8	85	51	82
Marine	42	23	11	8	63	35	80
Morecambe	42	17	17	8	59	39	68
Gainsborough Trinity	42	18	14	10	66	52	68
Burton Albion	42	18	12	12	64	47	66
Southport	42	17	11	14	70	66	62
Worksop Town	42	17	10	15	51	48	61
Workington	42	14	18	10	54	46	59
Macclesfield Town	42	17	8	17	67	65	59
Hyde United	42	14	15	13	63	62	57
Witton Albion	42	15	13	14	56	59	57
Mossley	42	13	16	13	56	60	55
Bangor City	42	13	13	15	54	51	54
Rhyl	42	14	10	18	65	71	52
South Liverpool	42	11	17	14	43	44	50
Horwich	42	15	6	21	53	63	50
Caernarfon Town	42	11	17	14	51	63	50
Oswestry Town	42	12	13	17	51	60	49
Buxton	42	11	12	19	55	76	45
Chorley	42	9	15	18	56	64	42
Matlock Town	42	9	15	18	59	75	42
Goole Town	42	7	11	24	37	78	31

Workington, Witton Albion, Horwich and Goole Town all had 1 point deducted.

1986-87

Macclesfield Town	42	26	10	6	80	47	88
Bangor City	42	25	12	5	74	35	87
Caernarfon Town	42	20	16	6	67	40	76
Marine	42	21	10	11	70	43	73
South Liverpool	42	21	10	11	58	40	73
Morecambe	42	20	12	10	68	49	72
Matlock Town	42	20	10	12	81	67	70
Southport	42	19	11	12	67	49	68
Chorley	42	16	12	14	58	59	60
Mossley	42	15	12	15	57	52	57
Hyde United	42	15	10	17	81	70	55
Burton Albion	42	16	6	20	56	68	54
Buxton	42	13	14	15	71	68	53
Witton Albion	42	15	8	19	68	79	53
Barrow	42	15	7	20	42	57	52
Goole Town	42	13	12	17	58	62	51
Oswestry Town	42	14	8	20	55	83	50
Rhyl	42	10	15	17	56	74	45
Worksop Town	42	9	13	20	56	74	40
Gainsborough Trinity	42	9	10	23	53	77	37
Workington	42	5	14	23	38	70	28
Horwich RMI	42	3	12	27	36	85	20

Workington and Horwich RMI both had 1 point deducted.

1987-88

Premier Division

Chorley	42	26	10	6	78	35	88
Hyde United	42	25	10	7	91	52	85
Caernarfon Town	42	22	10	10	56	34	76
Morecambe	42	19	15	8	61	41	72
Barrow	42	21	8	13	70	41	71
Worksop Town	42	20	11	11	74	55	71
Bangor City	42	20	10	12	71	55	70
Rhyl	42	18	13	11	70	42	67
Marine	42	19	10	13	67	45	67
Frickley Athletic	42	18	11	13	61	55	65
Witton Albion	42	16	12	14	61	47	60
Goole Town	42	17	9	16	71	61	60
Horwich	42	17	9	16	46	42	60
Southport	42	15	12	15	43	48	57
South Liverpool	42	10	19	13	56	64	49
Buxton	42	11	14	17	72	76	47
Mossley	42	11	11	20	54	75	44
Gateshead	42	11	7	24	52	71	40
Matlock Town	42	10	8	24	58	89	38
Gainsborough Trinity	42	8	10	24	38	81	34
Oswestry Town	42	6	10	26	44	101	28
Workington	42	6	3	33	28	113	21

First Division

Fleetwood Town	36	22	7	7	85	45	73
Stalybridge Celtic	36	22	6	8	72	42	72
Leek Town	36	20	10	6	63	38	70
Accrington Stanley	36	21	6	9	71	39	69
Farsley Celtic	36	18	9	9	64	48	60
Droylsden	36	16	10	10	63	48	58
Eastwood Hanley	36	14	12	10	50	37	54
Winsford United	36	15	6	15	59	47	51
Congleton Town	36	12	16	8	43	39	51
Harrogate Town	36	13	9	14	51	50	48
Alfreton Town	36	13	8	15	53	54	47
Radcliffe Borough	36	11	13	12	62	62	46
Irlam Town	36	12	10	14	39	45	46
Penrith	36	11	11	14	46	51	44
Sutton Town	36	11	5	20	51	96	38
Lancaster City	36	10	6	20	45	72	36
Eastwood Town	36	8	10	18	45	65	34
Curzon Ashton	36	8	4	24	43	73	28
Netherfield	36	4	4	28	35	93	16

Congleton Town had 1 point deducted
Farsley Celtic had 3 points deducted

1988-89

Premier Division

Barrow	42	26	9	7	89	35	87
Hyde United	42	24	8	10	77	44	80
Witton Albion	42	22	13	7	67	39	79
Bangor City	42	22	10	10	77	48	76
Marine	42	23	7	12	69	48	76
Goole Town	42	22	7	13	75	60	73
Fleetwood Town	42	19	16	7	53	44	73
Rhyl	42	18	10	14	75	65	64
Frickley Athletic	42	17	10	15	64	53	61
Mossley	42	17	9	16	56	58	60
South Liverpool	42	15	13	14	65	57	58
Caernarfon Town	42	15	10	17	49	53	55
Matlock Town	42	16	5	21	65	73	53
Southport	42	13	12	17	66	52	51
Buxton	42	12	14	16	61	63	50
Morecambe	42	13	9	20	55	60	47
Gainsborough Trinity	42	12	11	19	56	73	47
Shepshed Charterhouse	42	14	8	20	19	80	44
Stalybridge Celtic	42	9	13	20	16	81	40
Horwich	42	7	14	21	12	70	35
Gateshead	42	7	13	22	36	70	34
Worksop Town	42	6	5	31	42	103	23

Morecambe had 1 point deducted
Shepshed Charterhouse had 6 points deducted

First Division

Colne Dynamo	42	30	11	1	102	21	98
Bishop Auckland	42	28	5	9	78	28	89
Leek Town	42	25	11	6	74	41	85
Droylsden	42	25	9	8	84	48	84
Whitley Bay	42	23	6	13	77	49	75
Accrington Stanley	42	21	10	11	81	60	73
Lancaster City	42	21	8	13	76	54	71
Harrogate Town	42	19	7	16	68	61	64
Newtown	42	15	12	15	65	59	57
Congleton Town	42	15	11	16	62	66	56
Workington	42	17	3	22	59	74	54
Eastwood Town	42	14	10	13	55	61	52
Curzon Ashton	42	13	11	18	74	72	50
Farsley Celtic	42	12	13	17	52	73	49
Irlam Town	42	11	14	17	53	63	47
Penrith	42	14	5	23	61	91	47
Radcliffe Borough	42	12	10	20	62	86	46
Eastwood Hanley	42	11	12	10	46	67	45
Winsford United	42	13	6	23	58	93	35
Alfreton Town	42	8	11	23	44	92	35
Netherfield	42	8	9	25	57	90	32
Sutton Town	42	7	6	29	70	109	23

Leek Town and Netherfield both had 1 point deducted
Colne Dynamo had 3 points deducted
Sutton Town had 4 points deducted

1989-90

Premier Division

Colne Dynamoes	42	32	6	4	86	40	102
Gateshead	42	22	10	10	78	58	76
Witton Albion	42	22	7	13	67	39	73
Hyde United	42	21	8	13	73	50	71
South Liverpool	42	20	9	13	89	79	69
Matlock Town	42	18	12	12	61	42	66
Southport	42	17	14	11	54	48	65
Fleetwood Town	42	17	12	13	73	66	63
Marine	42	16	14	12	59	55	62
Bangor City	42	15	15	12	64	58	60
Bishop Auckland	42	17	8	17	72	64	59
Frickley Athletic	42	16	8	18	56	61	56
Horwich	42	15	13	14	66	69	55
Morecambe	42	15	9	18	58	70	54
Gainsborough Trinity	42	16	8	18	59	55	53
Buxton	42	15	8	19	59	72	53
Stalybridge Celtic	42	12	9	21	48	61	45
Mossley	42	11	10	21	61	82	43
Goole Town	42	12	5	25	54	77	41
Shepshed	42	11	7	24	55	82	40
Caernarfon Town	42	10	8	24	56	86	38
Rhyl	42	7	10	25	43	77	30

Rhyl had 1 point deducted
Horwich and Gainsborough Trinity both had 3 points deducted

First Division

Leek Town	42	26	8	8	70	31	86
Droylsden	42	27	6	9	81	46	80
Accrington Stanley	42	22	10	10	80	53	76
Whitley Bay	42	21	11	10	93	59	74
Emley	42	20	9	13	70	42	69
Congleton Town	42	20	12	10	65	53	69
Winsford United	42	18	10	14	65	53	64
Curzon Ashton	42	17	11	14	66	60	62
Harrogate Town	42	17	9	16	68	62	60
Lancaster City	42	15	14	13	73	54	59
Eastwood Town	42	16	11	15	61	64	59
Farsley Celtic	42	17	6	19	71	75	57
Rossendale United	42	15	9	18	73	69	54
Newtown	42	14	12	16	49	62	54
Irlam Town	42	14	11	17	61	66	53
Workington	42	14	8	20	56	64	50
Radcliffe Borough	42	14	7	21	47	63	49
Alfreton Town	42	13	8	21	59	85	47
Worksop Town	42	13	5	24	56	95	44
Netherfield	42	11	6	25	56	89	39
Eastwood Hanley	42	10	6	26	45	76	36
Penrith	42	9	9	24	44	88	36

Congleton Town 3 points deducted. Droylsden 7 points deducted.

1990-91

Premier Division

Witton Albion	40	28	9	3	81	31	93
Stalybridge Celtic	40	22	11	7	44	26	77
Morecambe	40	19	16	5	72	44	73
Fleetwood Town	40	20	9	11	69	44	69
Southport	40	18	14	8	66	48	68
Marine	40	18	11	11	56	39	65
Bishop Auckland	40	17	10	13	62	56	61
Buxton	40	17	11	12	66	61	59
Leek Town	40	15	11	14	48	44	56
Frickley Athletic	40	16	6	18	64	62	54
Hyde United	40	14	11	15	73	63	53
Goole Town	40	14	10	16	68	74	52
Droylsden	40	12	11	17	67	70	47
Chorley	40	12	10	18	59	55	46
Mossley	40	13	10	17	55	68	45
Horwich	40	13	6	21	62	81	45
Matlock Town	40	12	7	21	52	70	43
Bangor City	40	9	12	19	52	70	39
South Liverpool	40	10	9	21	58	92	39
Gainsborough Trinity	40	9	11	20	57	84	38
Shepshed Charterhouse	40	6	7	27	38	83	25

First Division

Whitley Bay	42	25	10	7	95	38	85
Emley	42	24	12	6	78	37	84
Worksop Town	42	25	7	10	85	56	82
Accrington Stanley	42	21	13	8	83	57	76
Rhyl	42	21	7	14	62	63	70
Eastwood Town	42	17	11	14	70	60	62
Warrington Town	42	17	10	15	68	52	61
Lancaster City	42	19	8	15	58	56	61
Bridlington Town	42	15	15	12	72	52	60
Curzon Ashton	42	14	14	14	49	57	56
Congleton Town	42	14	12	16	57	71	54
Netherfield	42	14	11	17	67	66	53
Newtown	42	13	12	17	68	75	51
Caernarfon Town	42	13	10	19	51	64	49
Rossendale United	42	12	13	17	66	67	48
Radcliffe Borough	42	12	12	18	50	69	48
Irlam Town	42	12	11	19	55	76	47
Winsford United	42	11	13	18	51	66	46
Harrogate Town	42	11	13	18	55	73	46
Workington	42	11	11	20	54	67	41
Farsley Celtic	42	11	9	22	49	78	39
Alfreton Town	42	7	12	23	41	84	33

1991-92

Premier Division

Stalybridge Celtic	42	26	14	2	84	33	92
Marine	42	23	9	10	64	32	78
Morecambe	42	21	13	8	70	44	76
Leek Town	42	21	10	11	62	49	73
Buxton	42	21	9	12	65	47	72
Emley	42	18	11	13	69	47	65
Southport	42	16	17	9	57	48	65
Accrington Stanley	42	17	12	13	78	62	63
Hyde United	42	17	9	16	69	67	60
Fleetwood United	42	17	8	17	67	64	59
Bishop Auckland	42	16	9	17	48	58	57
Goole Town	42	15	9	18	60	72	54
Horwich	42	13	14	15	44	52	53
Frickley Athletic	42	12	16	14	61	57	52
Droylsden	42	12	14	16	62	72	50
Mossley	42	15	4	23	51	73	49
Whitley Bay	42	13	9	20	53	79	48
Gainsborough Trinity	42	11	13	18	48	63	46
Matlock Town	42	12	9	21	59	87	45
Bangor City	42	11	10	21	46	57	43
Chorley	42	11	9	22	61	82	42
Shepshed Albion	42	6	8	28	46	79	26

First Division

Colwyn Bay	42	30	4	8	99	49	94
Winsford United	42	29	6	7	96	41	93
Worksop Town	42	25	5	12	101	54	80
Guiseley	42	22	12	8	93	56	78
Caernarfon Town	42	23	9	10	78	47	78
Bridlington Town	42	22	9	11	86	46	75
Warrington Town	42	20	8	14	79	64	68
Knowsley United	42	18	10	14	69	52	64
Netherfield	42	18	7	17	54	61	61
Harrogate Town	42	14	16	12	73	69	58
Curzon Ashton	42	15	9	18	71	83	54
Farsley Celtic	42	15	9	18	79	101	53
Radcliffe Borough	42	15	9	18	67	72	51
Newtown	42	15	6	21	60	95	51
Eastwood Town	42	13	11	18	59	70	50
Lancaster City	42	10	19	13	55	62	49
Congleton Town	42	14	5	23	59	81	47
Rhyl	42	11	10	21	59	69	43
Rossendale United	42	9	11	22	61	90	38
Alfreton Town	42	12	2	28	63	98	38
Irlam Town	42	9	7	26	45	95	33
Workington	42	7	8	27	45	99	28

Farsley Celtic 1 point deducted. Radcliffe Borough 3 points deducted.

1992-93

Premier Division

Southport	42	29	9	4	103	31	96
Winsford United	42	27	9	6	91	43	90
Morecambe	42	25	11	6	93	51	86
Marine	42	26	8	8	83	47	86
Leek Town	42	21	11	10	86	51	74
Accrington Stanley	42	20	13	9	79	45	73
Frickley Athletic	42	21	6	15	62	52	62
Barrow	42	18	11	13	71	55	65
Hyde United	42	17	13	12	87	71	64
Bishop Auckland	42	17	11	14	63	52	62
Gainsborough Trinity	42	17	8	17	63	66	59
Colwyn Bay	42	16	6	20	80	79	54
Horwich	42	14	10	18	72	79	52
Buxton	42	13	10	19	60	75	49
Matlock Town	42	13	11	18	56	79	47
Emley	42	13	6	23	62	91	45
Whitley Bay	42	11	8	23	57	96	41
Chorley	42	10	10	22	52	93	40
Fleetwood Town	42	10	7	25	50	77	37
Droylsden	42	10	7	25	47	84	37
Mossley	42	7	8	27	53	95	29
Goole Town	42	6	9	27	47	105	27

Matlock Town had 3 points deducted

First Division

Bridlington Town	40	25	11	4	84	35	86
Knowsley United	40	23	7	10	86	48	76
Ashton United	40	22	8	10	81	54	74
Guiseley	40	20	10	10	90	64	70
Warrington Town	40	19	10	11	85	57	67
Gretna	40	17	12	11	64	47	63
Curzon Ashton	40	16	15	9	69	63	63
Great Harwood Town	40	17	9	14	66	57	60
Alfreton Town	40	15	9	16	80	80	54
Harrogate Town	40	14	12	14	77	81	54
Worksop Town	40	15	9	16	66	70	54
Radcliffe Borough	40	13	14	13	66	69	53
Workington	40	13	13	14	51	61	52
Eastwood Town	40	3	11	16	49	52	50
Netherfield	40	11	14	15	68	63	47
Caernarfon Town	40	13	8	19	66	74	47
Farsley Celtic	40	12	8	20	64	77	44
Lancaster City	40	10	12	18	49	76	42
Shepshed Albion	40	9	12	19	46	66	39
Congleton Town	40	10	7	23	58	95	37
Rossendale United	40	5	5	30	50	126	20

1993-94

Premier Division

Marine	42	27	9	6	106	62	90
Leek Town	42	27	8	7	79	50	89
Boston United	42	23	9	10	90	43	78
Bishop Auckland	42	23	9	10	73	58	78
Frickley Athletic	42	21	12	9	90	51	75
Colwyn Bay	42	18	14	10	74	51	68
Morecambe	42	20	7	15	90	56	67
Barrow	42	18	10	14	59	51	64
Hyde United	42	17	10	15	80	71	61
Chorley	42	17	10	15	70	67	61
Whitley Bay	42	17	9	16	61	72	60
Gainsborough Trinity	42	15	11	16	64	66	56
Emley	42	12	16	14	63	71	52
Matlock Town	42	13	12	17	71	76	51
Buxton	42	13	10	19	67	73	49
Accrington Stanley	42	14	7	21	63	85	49
Droylsden	42	11	14	17	57	82	47
Knowsley United	42	11	11	20	52	66	44
Winsford United	42	9	11	22	50	74	38
Horwich RMI	42	8	12	22	50	75	35
Bridlington Town	42	7	10	25	41	91	28
Fleetwood Town	42	7	7	28	55	114	28

Horwich RMI 1 point deducted. Bridlington Town 3 points deducted

First Division

Guiseley	40	29	6	5	87	37	93
Spennymoor United	40	25	6	9	95	50	81
Ashton United	40	24	7	9	85	41	79
Lancaster City	40	20	10	10	74	46	70
Netherfield	40	20	6	14	68	60	66
Alfreton Town	40	18	10	12	83	70	64
Warrington Town	40	17	11	12	52	48	62
Goole Town	40	16	11	13	72	58	59
Great Harwood Town	40	15	14	11	56	60	59
Gretna	40	16	7	17	64	65	55
Workington	40	14	10	16	70	74	52
Worksop Town	40	14	9	17	79	87	51
Bamber Bridge	40	13	11	16	62	59	50
Curzon Ashton	40	13	8	19	62	71	47
Congleton Town	40	12	9	19	53	68	45
Radcliffe Borough	40	10	14	16	62	75	44
Mossley	40	10	12	18	44	68	39
Caernarfon Town	40	9	11	20	54	88	38
Farsley Celtic	40	6	16	18	42	77	34
Harrogate Town	40	8	9	23	40	86	33
Eastwood Town	40	7	11	22	47	63	32

Mossley had 3 points deducted

1994-95

Premier Division

Marine	42	29	11	2	83	27	98
Morecambe	42	28	10	4	99	34	94
Guiseley	42	28	9	5	96	50	93
Hyde United	42	22	10	10	89	59	76
Boston United	42	20	11	11	80	43	71
Spennymoor United	42	20	11	11	66	52	71
Buxton	42	18	9	15	65	62	63
Gainsborough Trinity	42	16	13	13	69	61	61
Bishop Auckland	42	16	12	14	68	55	57
Witton Albion	42	14	14	14	54	56	56
Barrow	42	17	5	20	68	71	56
Colwyn Bay	42	16	8	18	71	80	56
Emley	42	14	13	15	62	68	55
Matlock Town	42	15	5	22	62	72	50
Accrington Stanley	42	12	13	17	55	77	49
Knowsley United	42	11	14	17	64	83	47
Winsford United	42	10	11	21	56	75	41
Chorley	42	11	7	24	64	87	40
Frickley Athletic	42	10	10	22	53	79	40
Droylsden	42	10	8	24	56	93	38
Whitley Bay	42	8	8	26	46	97	32
Horwich RMI	42	9	4	29	49	94	31

Bishop Auckland had 3 points deducted

First Division

Blyth Spartans	42	26	9	7	95	55	87
Bamber Bridge	42	25	10	7	101	51	85
Warrington Town	42	25	9	8	74	40	84
Alfreton Town	42	25	7	10	94	49	82
Lancaster City	42	23	10	9	81	44	79
Worksop Town	42	19	14	9	95	68	71
Radcliffe Borough	42	18	10	14	76	70	64
Ashton United	42	18	8	16	80	70	62
Netherfield	42	17	7	18	54	56	58
Eastwood Town	42	14	13	15	67	61	55
Gretna	42	14	13	15	64	66	55
Atherton Laurburn Rovers	42	14	8	20	60	67	50
Harrogate Town	42	14	8	20	57	78	50
Caernarfon Town	42	13	10	19	59	62	49
Curzon Ashton	42	10	16	16	64	80	46
Great Harwood Town	42	11	13	18	66	87	46
Congleton Town	42	11	13	18	52	75	46
Fleetwood	42	12	11	19	51	74	44
Farsley Celtic	42	12	7	23	66	100	43
Workington	42	12	6	24	61	91	42
Goole Town	42	11	7	24	46	81	40
Mossley	42	11	5	26	52	90	37

Mossley had 1 point deducted. Fleetwood had 3 points deducted

1995-96

Premier Division

Bamber Bridge	42	20	16	6	81	49	76
Boston United	42	23	6	13	86	59	75
Hyde United	42	21	11	10	86	51	74
Barrow	42	20	13	9	69	42	73
Gainsborough Trinity	42	20	13	9	60	41	73
Blyth Spartans	42	17	13	12	75	61	64
Accrington Stanley	42	17	14	11	62	54	62
Emley	42	17	10	15	57	53	61
Spennymoor United	42	14	18	10	67	61	60
Guiseley	42	15	14	13	62	57	59
Bishop Auckland	42	16	11	15	60	55	59
Marine	42	15	14	13	59	54	59
Witton Albion	42	17	8	17	60	62	59
Chorley	42	14	9	19	67	74	48
Knowsley United	42	14	6	22	61	89	48
Winsford United	42	10	16	16	56	79	46
Leek Town	42	10	15	17	52	55	45
Colwyn Bay	42	8	21	13	43	57	45
Frickley Athletic	42	11	14	17	63	87	44
Buxton	42	9	11	22	43	72	38
Droylsden	42	10	8	24	58	100	38
Matlock Town	42	8	11	23	71	86	35

Accrington Stanley, Chorley & Frickley Town all had 3 points deducted

First Division

Lancaster City	40	24	11	5	79	38	83
Alfreton Town	40	23	9	8	79	47	78
Lincoln United	40	22	7	11	80	56	73
Curzon Ashton	40	20	7	13	73	53	67
Farsley Celtic	40	19	9	12	66	61	66
Radcliffe Borough	40	17	13	10	70	48	64
Eastwood Town	40	18	9	13	60	47	63
Whitley Bay	40	18	8	14	72	62	62
Ashton United	40	19	7	14	73	65	60
Atherton Laburnum Rovers	40	15	12	13	60	61	57
Worksop Town	40	16	8	16	84	90	56
Gretna	40	13	13	14	75	65	52
Warrington Town	40	13	10	17	75	72	49
Leigh	40	14	7	19	53	59	49
Netherfield	40	13	10	17	64	73	49
Workington	40	11	12	17	50	62	45
Bradford Park Avenue	40	9	14	17	57	72	41
Congleton Town	40	11	11	18	36	59	41
Great Harwood Town	40	9	7	24	44	78	33
Fleetwood	40	7	10	23	41	81	31
Harrogate Town	40	7	10	23	54	96	31

Great Harwood Town had 1 point deducted, Congleton Town had 3 points deducted and Ashton United had 4 points deducted

1996-97

Premier Division

Leek Town	44	28	9	7	71	35	93
Bishop Auckland	44	23	14	7	88	43	83
Hyde United	44	22	16	6	93	46	82
Emley	44	23	12	9	89	54	81
Barrow	44	23	11	10	71	45	80
Boston United	44	22	13	9	74	47	79
Blyth Spartans	44	22	11	11	74	49	77
Marine	44	20	15	9	53	37	75
Guiseley	44	20	11	13	63	54	71
Gainsborough Trinity	44	18	12	14	65	46	66
Accrington Stanley	44	18	12	14	77	70	66
Runcorn	44	15	15	14	63	62	60
Chorley	44	16	9	19	69	66	57
Winsford United	44	13	14	17	50	56	53
Knowsley United	44	12	14	18	58	79	49
Colwyn Bay	44	11	13	20	60	76	46
Lancaster City	44	12	9	23	48	75	45
Frickley Athletic	44	12	8	24	62	91	44
Spennymoor United	44	10	10	24	52	68	40
Bamber Bridge	44	11	7	26	59	99	40
Alfreton Town	44	8	13	23	45	83	37
Witton Albion	44	5	14	25	41	91	29
Buxton	44	5	12	27	33	86	27

Knowsley United had 1 point deducted

First Division

Radcliffe Borough	42	26	7	9	77	33	85
Leigh	42	24	11	7	65	33	83
Lincoln United	42	25	8	9	78	47	83
Farsley Celtic	42	23	8	11	75	48	77
Worksop Town	42	20	12	10	68	38	69
Stocksbridge Park Steels	42	19	11	12	66	54	68
Bradford Park Avenue	42	20	8	14	58	50	68
Ashton United	42	17	14	11	73	52	65
Great Harwood Town	42	16	12	14	56	46	60
Droylsden	42	15	14	13	69	67	59
Matlock Town	42	16	10	16	61	69	58
Whitley Bay	42	14	12	16	47	54	54
Flixton	42	15	7	20	57	72	52
Netherfield	42	12	14	16	54	56	50
Eastwood Town	42	12	14	16	42	50	50
Gretna	42	10	18	14	55	68	48
Harrogate Town	42	13	8	21	55	76	47
Congleton Town	42	12	9	21	47	64	45
Workington	42	10	12	20	45	63	42
Curzon Ashton	42	8	10	24	48	79	34
Warrington Town	42	5	18	19	42	79	33
Atherton Laburnum Rovers	42	7	9	26	45	85	30

Worksop Town had 3 points deducted

1997-98

Premier Division

Barrow	42	25	8	9	61	29	83
Boston United	42	22	12	8	55	40	78
Leigh RMI	42	21	13	8	63	41	76
Runcorn	42	22	9	11	80	50	75
Gainsborough Trinity	42	22	9	11	60	39	75
Emley	42	22	8	12	81	61	74
Winsford United	42	19	12	11	54	43	69
Altrincham	42	18	11	13	76	44	65
Guiseley	42	16	16	10	61	53	64
Bishop Auckland	42	17	12	13	78	60	63
Marine	42	15	11	16	56	59	56
Hyde United	42	13	16	13	60	55	55
Colwyn Bay	42	15	9	18	53	57	54
Spennymoor United	42	14	11	17	58	72	52
Chorley	42	14	7	21	51	70	49
Frickley Athletic	42	12	12	18	45	62	48
Lancaster City	42	13	8	21	55	74	47
Blyth Spartans	42	12	13	17	52	63	39
Bamber Bridge	42	9	12	21	51	74	39
Accrington Stanley	42	8	14	20	49	68	38
Radcliffe Borough	42	6	12	24	39	70	30
Alfreton Town	42	3	13	26	32	86	22

Spennymoor United had 1 point deducted
Blyth Spartans had 10 points deducted

First Division

Whitby Town	42	30	8	4	99	48	98
Worksop Town	42	28	7	7	93	44	91
Ashton Town	42	26	9	7	93	43	87
Droylsden	42	24	8	10	70	49	80
Lincoln United	42	20	11	11	76	62	71
Farsley Celtic	42	20	10	12	72	66	70
Witton Albion	42	19	9	14	77	55	66
Eastwood Town	42	18	12	12	68	51	66
Bradford Park Avenue	42	18	11	13	62	46	65
Belper Town	42	18	7	17	68	66	61
Stocksbridge Park Steels	42	17	9	16	68	63	60
Trafford	42	16	6	20	59	61	54
Whitley Bay	42	14	12	16	60	63	54
Matlock Town	42	14	11	17	68	65	53
Gretna	42	13	9	20	58	64	48
Netherfield	42	12	11	19	55	75	47
Flixton	42	10	12	20	45	73	42
Congleton Town	42	11	8	23	65	101	41
Harrogate Town	42	8	14	20	57	80	38
Great Harwood Town	42	8	12	22	42	88	36
Workington	42	8	7	27	38	84	31
Buxton	42	7	3	32	41	87	24

1998-99

Premier Division

Altrincham	42	23	11	8	67	33	80
Worksop Town	42	22	10	10	66	48	76
Guiseley	42	21	9	12	64	47	72
Bamber Bridge	42	18	15	9	63	48	69
Gateshead	42	18	11	13	69	58	65
Gainsborough Trinity	42	19	8	15	65	59	65
Whitby Town	42	17	13	12	77	62	64
Leigh	42	16	15	11	63	54	63
Hyde United	42	16	11	15	61	48	59
Stalybridge Celtic	42	16	11	15	71	63	59
Winsford United	42	14	15	13	56	52	57
Runcorn	42	12	19	11	46	49	55
Emley	42	12	17	13	47	49	53
Blyth Spartans	42	14	9	19	56	64	51
Colwyn Bay	42	12	13	17	60	71	49
Frickley Athletic	42	11	15	16	55	71	48
Marine	42	10	17	15	61	69	47
Spennymoor United	42	12	11	19	52	71	47
Lancaster City	42	11	13	18	50	62	46
Bishop Auckland	42	10	15	17	49	67	45
Chorley	42	8	15	19	45	68	39
Accrington Stanley	42	9	9	24	47	77	36

First Division

Droylsden	42	26	8	8	97	55	86
Hucknall Town	42	26	11	5	80	38	86
Ashton United	42	22	12	8	79	46	78
Lincoln United	42	20	12	10	94	65	72
Eastwood Town	42	20	8	14	65	69	68
Radcliffe Borough	42	19	8	15	78	62	65
Burscough	42	19	8	15	67	61	65
Witton Albion	42	18	9	15	70	63	63
Bradford Park Avenue	42	17	11	14	64	55	62
Stocksbridge Park Steels	42	16	13	13	64	60	61
Harrogate Town	42	17	7	18	75	77	58
Gretna	42	16	10	16	73	80	58
Belper Town	42	15	11	16	58	57	56
Trafford	42	14	11	17	50	58	53
Netherfield Kendal	42	13	10	19	51	64	49
Flixton	42	12	12	18	50	64	48
Matlock Town	42	14	6	22	53	72	48
Farsley Celtic	42	11	13	18	56	73	46
Whitley Bay	42	10	9	23	53	77	39
Congleton Town	42	8	15	19	65	91	39
Great Harwood Town	42	10	8	24	51	73	38
Alfreton Town	42	9	8	25	53	86	35

Hucknall Town had 3 points deducted

1999-2000

Premier Division

Leigh	44	28	8	8	91	45	92
Hyde United	44	24	13	7	77	44	85
Gateshead	44	23	13	8	79	41	82
Marine	44	21	7	8	78	46	79
Emley	44	20	12	12	54	41	72
Lancaster City	44	20	11	13	65	55	71
Stalybridge Celtic	44	18	12	14	64	54	66
Bishop Auckland	44	18	11	15	63	61	65
Runcorn	44	18	10	16	64	55	64
Worksop Town	44	19	6	19	78	65	63
Gainsborough Trinity	44	16	15	13	59	49	63
Whitby Town	44	15	13	16	66	66	58
Barrow	44	14	15	15	65	59	57
Blyth Spartans	44	15	9	20	62	67	54
Droylsden	44	14	12	18	53	60	54
Frickley Athletic	44	15	9	20	64	85	54
Bamber Bridge	44	14	11	19	70	67	53
Hucknall Town	44	14	11	19	55	61	53
Leek Town	44	14	10	20	58	79	52
Colwyn Bay	44	12	12	20	46	85	48
Spennymoor United	44	10	13	21	41	71	42
Guiseley	44	8	17	19	52	72	41
Winsford United	44	3	7	34	40	116	16

Spennymoor United had 1 point deducted

First Division

Accrington Stanley	42	25	9	8	96	43	84
Burscough	42	22	18	2	81	35	84
Witton Albion	42	23	15	4	88	46	84
Bradford Park Avenue	42	23	9	10	77	48	78
Radcliffe Borough	42	22	12	8	71	48	78
Farsley Celtic	42	19	11	12	66	52	68
Matlock Town	42	17	16	9	72	55	67
Ossett Town	42	17	8	17	77	55	59
Stocksbridge Park Steels	42	16	8	18	55	70	56
Eastwood Town	42	15	11	16	64	65	55
Harrogate Town	42	14	12	16	65	67	54
Congleton Town	42	14	12	16	63	73	54
Chorley	42	13	15	14	53	64	54
Ashton United	42	12	16	14	65	67	52
Workington	42	13	13	16	49	55	52
Lincoln United	42	13	12	17	52	80	51
Belper Town	42	13	11	18	59	72	50
Trafford	42	11	12	19	55	63	45
Gretna	42	11	7	24	48	78	40
Netherfield Kendal	42	8	9	25	46	82	33
Flixton	42	7	9	26	47	85	30
Whitley Bay	42	7	9	26	41	87	30

Eastwood Town had 1 point deducted

2000-2001

Premier Division

Stalybridge Celtic	44	31	9	4	96	32	102
Emley	44	31	8	5	86	42	101
Bishop Auckland	44	26	7	11	89	53	85
Lancaster City	44	24	9	11	84	60	81
Worksop Town	44	20	13	11	102	60	73
Barrow	44	21	9	14	83	53	72
Altrincham	44	20	10	14	80	59	70
Gainsborough Trinity	44	17	14	13	59	56	65
Accrington Stanley	44	18	10	16	72	65	64
Hucknall Town	44	17	12	15	57	63	63
Gateshead	44	16	12	16	67	61	60
Bamber Bridge	44	17	8	19	63	65	59
Runcorn	44	15	10	19	56	71	55
Blyth Spartans	44	15	9	20	61	64	54
Burscough	44	14	10	20	59	68	52
Hyde United	44	13	12	19	72	79	51
Whitby Town	44	13	11	20	60	76	50
Marine	44	12	13	19	62	78	49
Colwyn Bay	44	12	10	22	68	102	46
Frickley Athletic	44	10	15	19	50	79	45
Droylsden	44	13	6	25	50	80	45
Leek Town	44	12	8	24	45	70	44
Spennymoor United	44	4	5	35	32	108	17

First Division

Bradford Park Avenue	42	28	5	9	83	40	89
Vauxhall Motors	42	23	10	9	95	50	79
Ashton United	42	23	9	10	91	49	78
Stocksbridge Park Steels	42	19	13	10	80	60	70
Trafford	42	20	9	13	70	62	68
Belper Town	42	18	11	13	71	62	65
Witton Albion	42	15	16	11	51	50	61
Ossett Town	42	16	12	14	66	58	60
Radcliffe Borough	42	17	8	17	72	71	59
Chorley	42	15	14	13	71	70	59
Harrogate Town	42	15	10	17	60	70	55
Matlock Town	42	14	10	18	70	74	52
North Ferriby United	42	14	10	18	64	73	52
Workington	42	13	12	17	53	60	51
Lincoln United	42	13	12	17	60	75	51
Gretna	42	12	12	18	72	82	48
Guiseley	42	11	15	16	37	50	48
Kendal Town	42	12	12	18	60	69	47
Farsley Celtic	42	12	11	19	53	71	47
Eastwood Town	42	12	8	21	40	63	44
Winsford United	42	13	11	18	61	70	44
Congleton Town	42	6	8	28	43	94	30

Trafford and Kendal Town both had 1 point deducted
Winsford United had 6 points deducted

2001-2002

Premier Division

Burton Albion	44	31	11	2	106	30	104
Vauxhall Motors	44	27	8	9	86	55	89
Lancaster City	44	23	9	12	80	57	78
Worksop Town	44	23	9	12	74	51	78
Emley	44	22	9	13	69	55	75
Accrington Stanley	44	21	9	14	89	64	72
Runcorn FC Halton	44	21	8	15	76	53	71
Barrow	44	19	10	15	75	59	67
Altrincham	44	19	9	16	66	58	66
Bradford Park Avenue	44	18	5	21	77	76	59
Droylsden	44	17	8	19	65	78	59
Blyth Spartans	44	14	16	14	59	62	58
Frickley Athletic	44	16	11	17	63	69	58
Gateshead	44	14	14	16	58	71	56
Whitby Town	44	15	8	21	61	76	53
Hucknall Town	44	14	9	21	50	68	51
Marine	44	11	17	16	62	71	50
Burscough	44	15	5	24	69	86	50
Gainsborough Trinity	44	13	10	21	61	76	49
Colwyn Bay	44	12	11	21	49	82	47
Bishop Auckland	44	12	8	24	46	68	44
Hyde United	44	10	10	24	61	87	40
Bamber Bridge	44	7	10	27	38	88	30

First Division

Harrogate Town	42	25	11	6	80	35	86
Ossett Town	42	21	13	8	73	44	76
Ashton United	42	21	12	9	90	63	75
Spennymoor United	42	22	6	14	75	73	72
Radcliffe Borough	42	20	8	14	73	51	68
Leek Town	42	20	8	14	67	51	68
Gretna	42	19	7	16	66	66	63
Eastwood Town	42	17	11	14	61	59	62
Rossendale United	42	17	10	15	69	58	61
Witton Albion	42	17	10	15	72	68	61
Guiseley	42	18	7	17	60	67	61
North Ferriby United	42	14	16	12	71	60	58
Chorley	42	16	9	17	59	57	57
Matlock Town	42	15	9	18	49	48	54
Trafford	42	14	9	19	64	80	51
Workington	42	12	12	18	51	57	48
Farsley Celtic	42	12	11	19	53	71	47
Belper Town	42	12	11	19	49	66	47
Lincoln United	42	11	14	17	62	80	47
Stocksbridge Park Steels	42	12	9	21	55	76	45
Kendal Town	42	9	9	24	52	76	36
Ossett Albion	42	8	8	26	43	92	32

2002-2003

Premier Division

Accrington Stanley	44	30	10	4	97	44	100
Barrow	44	24	12	8	84	52	84
Vauxhall Motors	44	22	10	12	81	46	76
Stalybridge Celtic	44	21	13	10	77	51	76
Worksop Town	44	21	9	14	82	67	72
Harrogate Town	44	21	8	15	75	63	71
Bradford Park Avenue	44	20	10	14	73	70	70
Hucknall Town	44	17	15	12	72	62	66
Droylsden	44	18	10	16	62	52	64
Whitby Town	44	17	12	15	80	69	63
Marine	44	17	10	17	63	60	61
Wakefield & Emley	44	14	18	12	46	49	60
Runcorn FC Halton	44	15	15	14	69	74	60
Altrincham	44	17	9	18	58	63	60
Gainsborough Trinity	44	16	11	17	67	66	59
Ashton United	44	15	13	16	71	79	58
Lancaster City	44	16	9	19	71	75	57
Burscough	44	14	9	21	44	51	51
Blyth Spartans	44	14	9	21	67	87	51
Frickley Athletic	44	13	8	23	45	78	47
Gateshead	44	10	11	23	60	81	41
Colwyn Bay	44	5	9	30	52	99	24
Hyde United	44	5	8	31	40	98	23

Division One

Alfreton Town	42	26	9	7	106	59	87
Spennymoor United	42	27	6	9	81	42	87
Radcliffe Borough	42	25	10	7	90	46	85
North Ferriby United	42	23	9	10	78	45	78
Chorley	42	21	10	11	80	51	73
Belper Town	42	20	13	9	53	42	73
Witton Albion	42	19	15	8	67	50	72
Matlock Town	42	20	10	12	67	48	70
Leek Town	42	20	9	13	63	46	69
Workington	42	19	10	13	73	60	67
Farsley Celtic	42	17	11	14	66	67	62
Kendal Town	42	18	7	17	68	58	61
Bamber Bridge	42	15	9	18	55	59	54
Guiseley	42	14	11	17	68	63	53
Bishop Auckland	42	13	10	19	58	83	49
Lincoln United	42	12	9	21	67	77	45
Stocksbridge PS	42	11	9	22	54	81	42
Rossendale United	42	12	5	25	58	88	41
Kidsgrove Athletic	42	9	11	22	49	71	38
Ossett Town	42	8	9	25	39	80	33
Eastwood Town	42	5	8	29	33	92	23
Trafford	42	5	6	31	34	99	21

2003-2004

Premier Division

Hucknall Town	44	29	8	7	83	38	95
Droylsden	44	26	8	10	96	64	86
Barrow	44	22	14	8	82	52	80
Alfreton Town	44	23	9	12	73	43	78
Harrogate Town	44	24	5	15	79	63	77
Southport	44	20	10	14	71	52	70
Worksop Town	44	19	13	12	69	50	70
Lancaster City	44	20	9	15	62	49	69
Vauxhall Motors	44	19	10	15	78	75	67
Gainsborough Trinity	44	17	13	14	70	52	64
Stalybridge Celtic	44	18	10	16	72	66	64
Altrincham	44	16	15	13	66	51	63
Runcorn FC Halton	44	16	13	15	67	63	61
Ashton United	44	17	8	19	59	79	59
Whitby Town	44	14	11	19	55	70	53
Marine	44	13	12	19	62	74	51
Bradford Park Avenue	44	12	14	18	48	62	50
Spennymoor United	44	14	6	24	55	93	48
Burscough	44	10	15	19	47	67	45
Radcliffe Borough	44	12	6	26	74	99	42
Blyth Spartans	44	10	10	24	54	74	40
Frickley Athletic	44	11	7	26	51	83	40
Wakefield & Emley	44	8	6	30	45	99	30

Division One

Hyde United	42	24	8	10	79	49	80
Matlock Town	42	23	7	12	78	51	76
Farsley Celtic	42	20	14	8	78	56	74
Lincoln United	42	20	11	11	73	53	71
Witton Albion	42	17	12	13	61	56	63
Gateshead	42	21	4	17	65	68	63
Workington	42	17	11	14	70	58	62
Leek Town	42	16	13	13	56	47	61
Guiseley	42	16	12	14	66	54	60
Bamber Bridge	42	16	12	14	64	53	60
Bridlington Town	42	16	10	16	70	68	58
Prescot Cables	42	16	10	16	63	65	58
Bishop Auckland	42	14	13	15	61	64	55
Ossett Town	42	15	10	17	62	73	52
Rossendale United	42	13	12	17	53	62	51
Colwyn Bay	42	14	9	19	56	82	51
North Ferriby United	42	13	11	18	64	70	50
Chorley	42	13	10	19	54	70	49
Stocksbridge Park Steels	42	12	12	18	57	69	48
Belper Town	42	9	15	18	44	58	42
Kendal Town	42	11	7	24	53	79	40
Kidsgrove Athletic	42	10	9	23	45	67	39

FOUNDATION

During the 1957-58 season a number of northern Football League clubs – led by Sunderland and Middlesbrough – decided to form their own league so that they could gain a more consistent level of opposition for their reserve teams. Although limited to reserve teams at first, a number of north-eastern semi-professional clubs later joined the league and played their first teams in it.

The league was originally formed with 19 founder members, all being Football League reserve sides. There were 7 clubs who had been playing in the North-Eastern League: Carlisle United, Darlington, Gateshead, Hartlepools United, Middlesbrough, Sunderland and Workington, and 8 clubs from the Midland League: Bradford (Park Avenue), Bradford City, Doncaster Rovers, Grimsby Town, Hull City, Lincoln City, Rotherham United and York City. The remaining four were Accrington Stanley from the Lancashire Combination, Halifax Town from the Yorkshire League, Stockport County from the Cheshire League and Barrow who are believed to have been playing in the Lancashire League.

CHANGES TO THE LEAGUE

1959   League extended to 22 clubs by the election of Crewe Alexandra and Port Vale from the Cheshire League and Scunthorpe United from the Midland League.

1960   Following Gateshead's failure to gain re-election to the Football League, Gateshead Reserves left, reducing the North Regional League to 21 clubs.

1961   Carlisle United, Darlington and Workington left to join the Northern Counties League; Barrow left to join the Lancashire Combination and Doncaster Rovers also left, reducing the league to 16 clubs. Accrington Stanley resigned during the season and their record was expunged.

1962   Port Vale left but the league was extended to 17 clubs by the election of Oldham Athletic from the Lancashire Combination, Doncaster Rovers and Gateshead who left the Northern Counties League to become the first club to play their first team in the North Regional League.

1963   Carlisle United, Darlington and Workington rejoined from the North-Eastern League and Port Vale also rejoined, extending the league to 21 clubs.

1964   Stockport County left and were replaced by South Shields who moved their first team from the North-Eastern League.

1965   Ashington joined by moving their first team from the Wearside League but the league was reduced to 17 clubs as Lincoln City and Scunthorpe United left to join the Midland League and Port Vale left to join the West Midlands League. Crewe Alexandra left and joined the Lancashire League while Grimsby Town also left.

1966   Bradford City and York City left to join the Yorkshire League, Oldham Athletic left to join the Lancashire Combination, Hartlepools United left to join the Wearside League and Halifax Town and Workington also left, reducing the league to 11 clubs.

1967   Darlington left to join the Wearside League while Rotherham United, Doncaster Rovers and Bradford (Park Avenue) also left. Workington rejoined and Stockton's first team joined from the Wearside League. League reduced to 9 clubs.

1968   South Shields, Ashington and Gateshead left to join the new Northern Premier League, Stockton left to join the Wearside League and Hull City also left and are believed to have concentrated on the Northern Intermediate League. League reduced to 4 clubs.

1969   With only four clubs – Carlisle United, Middlesbrough, Sunderland and Workington – remaining, the league closed down at the end of the season.

TABLE ERRORS

The North Regional League tables as published contained some errors. Additional research has corrected some of these leaving the following.

1959-60. Total goals scored 2 more than total goals conceded.

1960-61. Total goals scored 1 more than total goals conceded.

1961-62. Total goals scored 1 more than total goals conceded.

1967-68. Total goals scored 11 more than total goals conceded.

The North Regional League consisted principally of the reserve sides of Football League clubs. In the tables below, first teams are printed in CAPITALS all others are reserves.

1958-59

Middlesbrough	36	23	7	6	88	37	53
Sunderland	36	24	3	9	104	46	51
Hull City	36	21	6	9	89	61	48
Rotherham United	36	18	7	11	94	65	43
York City	36	18	6	12	70	56	42
Lincoln City	36	15	10	11	75	67	40
Stockport County	36	14	9	13	75	61	37
Hartlepools United	36	15	7	14	78	84	37
Carlisle United	36	14	9	13	49	55	37
Bradford City	36	13	10	13	64	71	36
Grimsby Town	36	12	10	14	58	58	34
Workington	36	14	5	17	78	75	33
Accrington Stanley	36	12	7	17	54	62	31
Doncaster Rovers	36	11	9	16	59	81	31
Darlington	36	10	9	17	51	66	29
Halifax Town	36	10	9	17	55	78	29
Bradford (Park Avenue)	36	9	9	18	49	73	27
Barrow	36	10	4	22	46	95	24
Gateshead	36	7	8	21	54	99	22

1959-60

Middlesbrough	42	28	6	8	115	46	62
Sunderland	42	23	8	11	103	60	54
Port Vale	42	25	4	13	101	70	54
Workington	42	22	8	12	112	76	52
Scunthorpe United	42	22	7	13	79	58	51
Hull City	42	22	6	14	85	69	50
York City	42	19	6	17	91	78	44
Darlington	42	16	11	15	75	79	43
Carlisle United	42	18	6	18	78	67	42
Rotherham United	42	16	10	16	79	69	42
Bradford (Park Avenue)	42	19	4	19	83	86	42
Gateshead	42	19	3	20	85	80	41
Halifax Town	42	15	10	17	73	89	40
Lincoln City	42	17	5	20	77	72	39
Crewe Alexandra	42	15	9	18	65	67	39
Bradford City	42	16	7	19	67	72	39
Doncaster Rovers	42	17	4	21	81	99	38
Accrington Stanley	42	16	5	21	60	95	37
Grimsby Town	42	13	8	21	58	67	34
Hartlepools United	42	11	10	21	82	125	32
Stockport County	42	10	8	24	56	103	28
Barrow	42	6	9	27	50	126	21

1960-61

Middlesbrough	40	28	8	4	126	46	64
Port Vale	40	30	2	8	132	63	62
Sunderland	40	23	7	10	100	60	53
Scunthorpe United	40	21	8	11	89	52	50
Hartlepools United	40	21	7	12	91	79	49
Hull City	40	20	7	13	92	66	47
Darlington	40	21	4	15	85	82	46
Lincoln City	40	19	6	15	84	79	44
Bradford (Park Avenue)	40	17	8	15	100	67	42
Rotherham United	40	19	4	17	98	77	42
Doncaster Rovers	40	16	10	14	67	75	42
Crewe Alexandra	40	16	6	18	83	81	38
Carlisle United	40	13	10	17	64	77	36
Grimsby Town	40	14	8	18	62	81	36
Bradford City	40	12	8	20	73	97	32
Halifax Town	40	12	8	20	66	88	32
York City	40	12	6	22	69	85	30
Workington	40	9	9	22	60	96	27
Accrington Stanley	40	11	3	26	55	106	25
Stockport County	40	9	6	25	46	122	24
Barrow	40	7	5	28	48	110	19

1961-62

Middlesbrough	28	18	4	6	79	36	40
Scunthorpe United	28	17	6	5	61	39	40
Sunderland	28	16	2	10	67	50	34
Bradford City	28	15	4	9	56	43	34
Lincoln City	28	13	7	8	57	40	33
Grimsby Town	28	14	3	11	70	50	31
Crewe Alexandra	28	12	4	12	42	49	28
Port Vale	28	9	9	10	56	58	27
Bradford (Park Avenue)	28	11	4	13	52	49	26
Rotherham United	28	9	7	12	50	60	25
Hartlepools United	28	11	3	14	48	60	25
York City	28	8	4	16	40	58	20
Stockport County	28	7	6	15	42	82	20
Hull City	28	7	5	16	33	51	19
Halifax Town	28	7	4	17	32	59	18

Accrington Stanley resigned during the season and their record was expunged.

1962-63

Rotherham United	32	23	5	4	89	32	51
Middlesbrough	32	20	4	8	80	49	44
Crewe Alexandra	32	16	9	7	69	45	41
Bradford (Park Avenue)	32	17	6	9	88	52	40
Scunthorpe United	32	16	8	8	58	43	40
Sunderland	32	17	6	9	65	54	40
Doncaster Rovers	32	16	5	11	62	55	37
Grimsby Town	32	16	3	13	68	53	35
Lincoln City	32	14	7	11	54	58	35
Oldham Athletic	32	12	6	14	49	60	30
GATESHEAD	32	10	9	13	60	55	29
Hull City	32	11	7	14	57	61	29
Hartlepools United	32	10	8	14	53	62	28
York City	32	6	6	20	35	80	18
Stockport County	32	6	5	21	33	64	17
Halifax Town	32	4	9	19	34	67	17
Bradford City	32	3	7	22	45	109	13

1963-64

GATESHEAD	32	21	3	8	79	47	45
Middlesbrough	32	19	6	7	74	37	44
Rotherham United	32	18	8	6	76	47	44
Hull City	32	20	4	8	67	43	44
Scunthorpe United	32	19	4	9	85	53	42
Grimsby Town	32	15	9	8	67	49	39
Lincoln City	32	15	7	10	77	69	37
Sunderland	32	12	11	9	69	62	35
Crewe Alexandra	32	16	3	13	51	51	35
Port Vale	32	13	7	12	63	65	33
Carlisle United	32	12	8	12	49	53	32
Oldham Athletic	32	12	5	15	85	65	29
Doncaster Rovers	32	11	7	14	50	63	29
Darlington	32	10	7	15	60	59	27
Bradford (Park Avenue)	32	11	5	16	63	74	27
Halifax Town	32	9	8	15	57	72	26
York City	32	8	10	14	38	59	26
Bradford City	32	8	7	17	63	88	23
Workington	32	8	6	18	53	76	22
Stockport County	32	4	10	18	34	79	18
Hartlepools United	32	3	9	20	44	93	15

1964-65

Hull City	32	24	4	4	95	26	52
Sunderland	32	23	5	4	105	33	51
Middlesbrough	32	19	8	5	102	45	46
GATESHEAD	32	17	7	8	80	43	41
SOUTH SHIELDS	32	18	4	10	79	61	40
Port Vale	31	15	8	8	60	39	38
Rotherham United	32	15	8	9	72	54	38
Lincoln City	32	15	6	11	61	54	36
Carlisle United	32	15	5	12	68	43	35
Scunthorpe United	32	14	7	11	65	58	35
Oldham Athletic	32	15	5	12	75	72	35
Grimsby Town	30	14	4	12	60	63	32
Doncaster Rovers	32	11	9	12	59	59	31
Bradford City	32	11	5	16	65	76	27
Workington	32	11	5	16	56	90	27
York City	32	8	6	18	48	69	22
Bradford (Park Avenue)	32	9	4	19	46	74	22
Crewe Alexandra	31	8	4	19	37	78	20
Darlington	32	5	6	21	45	99	16
Hartlepools United	32	4	7	21	32	95	15
Halifax Town	32	3	3	26	32	111	9

Two games were not played.

1965-66

Hull City	32	23	4	5	89	30	50
Middlesbrough	32	21	5	6	79	41	47
Carlisle United	32	22	3	7	75	39	47
SOUTH SHIELDS	32	21	4	7	115	46	46
Sunderland	32	20	2	10	99	64	42
ASHINGTON	32	15	8	9	70	55	38
Rotherham United	32	14	5	13	59	54	33
Oldham Athletic	32	10	7	15	50	66	27
Workington	32	10	7	15	66	92	27
GATESHEAD	32	10	6	16	48	67	26
Darlington	32	11	4	17	57	82	26
Doncaster Rovers	32	8	9	15	51	65	25
Hartlepools United	32	9	7	16	56	76	25
York City	32	9	6	17	58	78	24
Bradford City	32	10	4	18	36	68	24
Bradford (Park Avenue)	32	7	5	20	45	90	19
Halifax Town	32	6	6	20	37	77	18

1966-67

SOUTH SHIELDS	20	13	3	4	53	29	29
Hull City	20	11	6	3	37	22	28
Sunderland	20	11	2	7	57	33	24
ASHINGTON	20	9	6	5	53	34	24
Rotherham United	20	11	2	7	44	38	24
Middlesbrough	20	8	3	9	45	42	19
Carlisle United	20	8	3	9	27	44	19
Doncaster Rovers	20	6	4	10	31	36	16
GATESHEAD	20	6	3	11	29	41	15
Bradford (Park Avenue)	20	5	4	11	22	43	14
Darlington	20	3	2	15	30	66	8

1967-68

Hull City	15	11	3	1	42	17	25
Middlesbrough	16	10	3	3	47	27	23
Sunderland	16	9	4	3	45	27	22
SOUTH SHIELDS	16	9	3	4	39	18	21
ASHINGTON	16	6	4	6	28	26	16
GATESHEAD	16	5	6	5	26	37	16
Carlisle United	15	2	4	9	18	30	8
STOCKTON	16	1	4	11	21	44	6
Workington	16	1	3	12	17	46	5

One game was not played.

1968-69

Sunderland	6	4	2	0	17	8	10
Middlesbrough	6	4	1	1	20	5	9
Carlisle United	6	2	1	3	13	10	5
Workington	6	0	0	6	5	32	0

FORMATION — The North-Eastern League was formed because Mr. John Cameron – who was chairman of Newcastle United – wanted a better class of football for the second XI's of the region's Football League clubs. A meeting took place in the Newcastle United boardroom on 5th May 1906 and 10 clubs agreed to form the league. These ten consisted of six Football League clubs – Bradford City, Hull City, Leeds City, Middlesbrough, Newcastle United and Sunderland – plus Carlisle United, West Hartlepool, West Stanley and Workington. However Hull City placed their reserves in the Midland League instead and West Hartlepool chose to stay in the Northern League. These two were replaced in the North-Eastern League by Royal Rovers from Sunderland and Hebburn Argyle.

Middlesbrough Reserves, Newcastle United Reserves and Sunderland Reserves had played in the Northern League in 1905-06 although these sides were referred to as "A" teams at this time. Carlisle United and Workington had been playing in Division Two of the Lancashire Combination in 1905-06 and continued in that league as well. Officially both clubs fielded their first team in both leagues but as this would have meant 56 league fixtures, whether this actually happened must be open to doubt and the Lancashire Combination seems to have taken precedence.

Of the other five founder members, Bradford City's reserve side had been playing in the West Yorkshire League during 1905-06 but for 1906-07 they fielded teams in both the Midland League and the North-Eastern League as well as the Football League. Their North-Eastern League side was described as the "A" team but although the North-Eastern League was supposedly the club's third priority, as it turned out they frequently fielded their first team. Nearby Leeds City also fielded teams in the Football League and Midland League but their North-Eastern League side is thought to have been the third team. West Stanley had previously been playing in the Northern Alliance as Stanley and Royal Rovers moved from the Wearside League.

The last of the founders were Hebburn Argyle who had also been founder members of the Tyneside League in 1905 where they were described as Hebburn Argyle "A". However no Hebburn Argyle side was playing in any more senior league so it seems likely that this "A" team was the first team. In 1906-07 Hebburn Argyle fielded teams in both the Tyneside League and the North-Eastern League but as this only committed them to 44 league games, it is possible that the first team could have fulfilled all fixtures. In any case the North-Eastern League was the stronger of the two leagues so Hebburn Argyle would have played their strongest side in it.

The North-Eastern League's first season thus consisted of 10 clubs that could be broken down as follows:

- 3 North-Eastern Football League clubs' reserve sides.
- 2 ambitious but distant Cumberland clubs who probably could not field their first teams.
- 2 West Yorkshire Football League clubs who were planning to field their third teams.
- 3 ambitious local clubs who were not amongst first echelon of the region's non-League sides.

Despite this unpromising mixture, the league embarked on a history that was to last more than 50 years.

CHANGES TO THE LEAGUE

1907   League extended to 13 clubs by the election of Penrith, Shildon Athletic who moved from the Northern League and the reserves of the newly formed Bradford Park Avenue. Carlisle United and Workington officially fielded reserve sides rather than first teams.

1908   Penrith left and both Leeds City and Bradford City also stopped fielding teams in the North-Eastern League. However the league expanded to 18 by the election of 8 additional clubs. These included two newly formed clubs – Hartlepools United and Huddersfield Town while Darlington and Spennymoor United joined from the Northern League; North Shields Athletic, South Shield Adelaide and Wallsend Park Villa joined from the Northern Alliance and Seaham White Star joined from the Wearside League.

1909   Seaham White Star changed name to Seaham Harbour. Bradford Park Avenue Reserves & Huddersfield Town left to join the Midland League and Wingate Albion joined from the Wearside League. League reduced to 17 clubs.

1910   South Shields Adelaide changed name to South Shields and Royal Rovers changed name to Sunderland Rovers. League expanded to 18 clubs by the election of Jarrow Croft. Carlisle United and Workington were barred from the Lancashire Combination for geographical reasons and so moved their first teams in the North-Eastern League instead of their reserves.

1911   Workington went into liquidation and disbanded. League extended to 19 clubs by the election of Newcastle City from the Northern Alliance and Gateshead Town.

1912   Jarrow Croft changed name to Jarrow and Wallsend Park Villa changed name to Wallsend. Houghton Rovers joined thereby expanding the league to 20 clubs.

1913   Wingate Albion moved to the Wearside League and were replaced by Blyth Spartans from Northern Alliance.

1914   Seaham Harbour moved to the Wearside League and were replaced by Ashington from Northern Alliance.

1919   When the league resumed after the war, Gateshead Town did not re-form. Sunderland Rovers, Newcastle City and Hebburn Argyle also failed to re-appear and North Shields Athletic changed name to Preston Colliery and moved to the Tyneside League. South Shields were elected to the Football League and placed their reserves in the North-Eastern League instead of the first team. The league was made up to 18 clubs by the election of Scotswood from the Northern Alliance, Leadgate Park from the Northern League and Durham City who were a new club.

1920   League extended to 20 clubs by the election of Bedlington United from the Northern Alliance and Chester-le-Street.

1921   The Football League formed Division Three (North) and Ashington, Darlington, Durham City and Hartlepools United became founder members. Blyth Spartans and West Stanley also applied but were not elected. Darlington placed their reserves in the North-Eastern League and the league was maintained at 20 clubs by the election of Preston Colliery and Seaton Delaval from the Northern Alliance and Workington who had re-formed as a new club.

1922   Houghton Rovers left and joined the Wearside League and were replaced by Hartlepools United Reserves.

1923   Shildon Athletic changed name to Shildon.

1925   Wallsend left and joined the Northern Alliance and Leadgate Park disbanded. They were replaced by Annfield Plain and Durham City Reserves who both joined from the Northern Alliance.

1926   The league expanded to two divisions. The 20 existing members formed Division One while Division Two was formed by an amalgamation with the Northern Alliance, all 16 of its clubs joining the new division which was made up to 18 by the addition of Seaham Harbour from the Wearside League and Dipton United.

1927   Chester-le-Street and Seaton Delaval were relegated and Consett and Ashington Reserves promoted. Chilton Colliery R.A. left Division Two and joined the Northern League and Newburn also left. Usworth Colliery joined from the Tyneside League but Division Two was reduced to 17 clubs.

1928   Carlisle United were elected to Division Three (North) of the Football League, replacing Durham City who dropped down into the North-Eastern League. Durham City Reserves left the league. Washington Colliery and Wallsend were promoted and Preston Colliery were relegated and changed name to North Shields. Felling Colliery left and joined the Tyneside League but Division Two was increased to 18 clubs by the election of Carlisle United Reserves, White-le-Head Rangers and St. Peters Albion.

1929   Ashington Reserves and Durham City relegated and North Shields and Carlisle United Reserves promoted. Ashington later failed to gain re-election to the Football League and so the first team replaced the reserves in Division Two of the North-Eastern League. Seaham Harbour, High Fell and Ouston Rovers left reducing Division Two to 15 clubs.

1930   South Shields moved to Gateshead and so South Shields Reserves changed name to Gateshead Reserves. Bedlington United were relegated and Walker Celtic and Ashington were promoted. Crook Town joined Division One from the Northern League. Division One was increased to 22 clubs and Division Two reduced to 14.

1931   Consett and Scotswood were relegated and Chopwell Institute and Durham City promoted. White-le-Head Rangers and Seaton Delaval left and were replaced by Eden Colliery Welfare from the Northern League and Throckley Welfare.

1932   Shildon left and joined the Northern League and Washington Colliery were relegated. Division One reduced to 20 clubs. St. Peters Albion changed name to Newcastle East End. Craghead United left but Division Two was increased to 16 clubs by the election of Pegswood United and West Wylam Colliery Welfare.

1933   Durham City changed name to City of Durham. Newcastle United Reserves left to join the Central League. Wallsend were relegated and changed name to Wallsend Town. Eden Colliery Welfare and Consett were promoted. Spen Black & White left but Division Two was maintained at 16 clubs by the election of Stakeford Albion and Newbiggin West End.

1934   Chopwell Institute left but Division One was maintained at 20 clubs as Throckley Welfare were promoted. Hexham Town joined Division Two which was reduced to 13 clubs as Crawcrook Albion, Dipton United and Newcastle East End all left. Newcastle East End changed name back to St. Peters Albion and they and Crawcrook Albion joined the Tyneside League.

1935   The league reverted to a single division and all 13 Second Division clubs moved to different leagues. Birtley, Chester-le-Street, Usworth Colliery and Washington Colliery joined the Wearside League while the remaining 9 clubs joined the newly re-formed Northern Alliance. Consett from Division One of the North-Eastern League also moved to the Northern Alliance which re-started with 12 clubs by the addition of Amble and Whitley & Monkseaton. The remaining North-Eastern League clubs formed the single division for 1935-36 which was made up to 20 by the election of Horden Colliery Welfare from the Wearside League.

1936   Crook Town reverted to amateur status and left to join the Northern League but the league was increased to 21 clubs by the election of Hexham Town from the Northern Alliance and the newly formed South Shields. Eden Colliery Welfare resigned after their 23rd league match of the season at Spennymoor on February 6th and their record was expunged.

1937   Spennymoor United left to join the Wearside League and were replaced by Consett from Northern Alliance.

1938   City of Durham left and joined the Wearside League but disbanded in November 1938. Spennymoor United rejoined after one season in the Wearside League.

In the 1939-40 season the North-Eastern League operated a 10 club competition that included Blackhall Colliery Welfare and Stockton, neither of whom had previously played in the league. Before the war Blackhall Colliery Welfare had played in the Wearside League and Stockton in the Northern League. Consett were champions of this war-time competition and Blackhall Colliery Welfare were runners-up. The league then closed until 1944-45 when Spennymoor United were champions of the second war-time competition.

When the league resumed after the war, Jarrow, Hexham Town, Blyth Spartans and Walker Celtic did not immediately reform. Jarrow joined the Northern Alliance in 1946 together with a new club from Hexham called Hexham Hearts. Blyth Spartans reformed in 1947 but Walker Celtic failed to re-appear at a senior level. The four replacements were Murton Colliery Welfare who had played in the Wearside League before the war, Eppleton Colliery Welfare and the two clubs who had played in the league during the war – Stockton and Blackhall Colliery Welfare.

1947   Throckley Welfare left and joined the Northern Combination. Blyth Spartans rejoined.

1951   Workington were elected to the Football League and placed their reserves in the North-Eastern League instead of their first team. Eppleton Colliery Welfare and Murton Colliery Welfare left and joined the Wearside League. League reduced to 18 clubs.

1955   Blackhall Colliery Welfare left and joined the Wearside League and were replaced by Whitley Bay Athletic from the Northern Alliance.

1958   The end of the North-Eastern League.   In March 1958, Sunderland and Middlesbrough led a movement to form a new league whose membership would consist solely of reserve sides of Football League clubs. As a result the North Regional League was formed and the reserve sides of Carlisle United, Darlington, Gateshead, Hartlepools United, Middlesbrough, Sunderland and Workington all withdrew from the North-Eastern League and joined the new league. The North-Eastern League was unable to find sufficient suitable replacements and so eight of its clubs joined the Midland League which had also lost many reserve sides to the North Regional League. Thus Ashington, Blyth Spartans, Consett, Horden Colliery Welfare, North Shields, South Shields, Spennymoor United and Stockton all left and joined the Midland League. Annfield Plain and West Stanley joined the Northern Alliance and Whitley Bay Athletic joined the Northern League. The North-Eastern League thus closed down.

A new competition – also entitled the North-Eastern League – started in 1958-59 but this was at a much more junior level and disbanded after two seasons. Its membership consisted of just 12 clubs and included the "A" sides of some of the north-eastern Football League clubs and other clubs, a few of which were later admitted to the Wearside League.

1960   The formation of the Northern Counties League.   The additional travelling involved when the eight former North-Eastern League clubs joined the Midland League, quickly proved too much of a handicap for all Midland League clubs and after two years, all eight resigned. Spennymoor United chose to adopt amateur status and join the Northern League but the other seven decided to form a new senior league for north-eastern semi-professional clubs. The seven clubs – Ashington, Blyth Spartans, Consett, Horden Colliery Welfare, North Shields, South Shields and Stockton – were joined by Scarborough who had been members of the Midland League since 1927, Gateshead who had just lost their place in the Football League and Annfield Plain who moved from the Northern Alliance. As the title North-Eastern League was at that time still being used by a junior competition, the new league began life as the Northern Counties League with 10 founder members.

1961   League extended to 13 clubs by the election of the reserve sides of Carlisle United, Darlington and Workington from the North Regional League.

1962   Re-formation of the North-Eastern League.   Gateshead left and joined the North Regional League and were replaced by Redcar Albion who had been champions and league cup winners of the junior North-Eastern League in 1959-60. The Northern Counties League was disbanded and the 13 clubs re-formed the North-Eastern League.

1963   Redcar Albion resigned on 12th February 1963 and their record was expunged. Carlisle United, Darlington and Workington moved their reserve teams back to the North Regional League and Scarborough moved back to the Midland League reducing the North-Eastern League to 8 clubs.

1964   With only 8 clubs remaining, the North-Eastern League disbanded at the end of the season. Annfield Plain, Ashington, Consett, Horden Colliery Welfare and Stockton all joined the Wearside League, Blyth Spartans and North Shields joined the Northern League and South Shields joined the North Regional League.

TABLE ERRORS

The North-Eastern League tables as published contained a number of errors. Additional research has succeeded in correcting several of these, leaving those noted below.

1907-08   Total goals scored 10 more than total goals conceded.

1911-12   Total goals scored 10 less than total goals conceded.

1913-14   Total goals scored 1 more than total goals conceded.

1920-21   Total goals scored 23 less than total goals conceded.

1930-31   Total goals scored 13 more than total goals conceded.

1936-37   Total goals scored 1 more than total goals conceded.

1937-38   Total goals scored 1 more than total goals conceded.

1938-39   Total goals scored 1 less than total goals conceded.

1945-46   Total goals scored 2 less than total goals conceded.

1906-07

	P	W	D	L	F	A	Pts
Newcastle United Reserves	18	12	2	4	35	20	26
Sunderland Reserves	18	12	1	5	44	22	25
West Stanley	18	10	4	4	37	23	24
Leeds City "A"	18	9	4	5	33	20	22
Workington	18	6	6	6	34	33	18
Royal Rovers	18	4	9	5	23	30	17
Middlesbrough Reserves	18	5	6	7	34	34	16
Carlisle United	18	4	5	9	24	38	13
Bradford City "A"	18	5	1	12	26	34	11
Hebburn Argyle	18	2	4	12	16	52	8

1907-08

	P	W	D	L	F	A	Pts
Newcastle United Reserves	24	16	2	6	90	28	34
Sunderland Reserves	24	14	6	4	72	31	34
Shildon Athletic	24	14	3	7	43	35	31
Leeds City "A"	24	13	3	8	64	46	29
Sunderland Royal Rovers	24	11	4	9	44	47	26
Middlesbrough Reserves	24	9	6	9	43	53	24
West Stanley	24	9	4	11	53	52	22
Hebburn Argyle	24	9	4	11	37	65	22
Bradford Park Avenue Reserves	24	9	3	12	43	55	21
Bradford City "A"	24	7	6	11	47	56	20
Workington Reserves	24	7	6	11	40	57	20
Carlisle United Reserves	24	7	3	14	48	58	17
Penrith	24	4	4	16	34	65	12

1908-09

	P	W	D	L	F	A	Pts
Newcastle United Reserves	34	26	4	4	106	48	56
South Shields Adelaide	34	22	4	8	80	41	48
Bradford Park Avenue Reserves	34	19	5	10	84	49	43
Hartlepools United	34	16	9	9	79	51	41
Middlesbrough Reserves	34	17	6	11	82	45	40
Sunderland Reserves	34	18	3	13	81	54	39
West Stanley	34	18	3	13	73	56	39
Darlington	34	15	8	11	76	73	38
North Shields Athletic	34	14	6	14	63	48	34
Spennymoor United	34	13	7	14	55	63	33
Wallsend Park Villa	34	13	6	15	55	66	32
Workington Reserves	34	12	5	17	50	80	29
Seaham White Star	34	10	7	17	55	64	27
Hebburn Argyle	34	10	6	18	55	91	26
Carlisle United Reserves	34	10	4	20	61	84	24
Huddersfield Town	34	10	4	20	47	78	24
Shildon Athletic	34	7	6	21	51	101	20
Sunderland Royal Rovers	34	7	5	22	39	100	19

1909-10

	P	W	D	L	F	A	Pts
Spennymoor United	32	24	3	5	75	39	51
Newcastle United Reserves	32	21	6	5	134	31	48
Middlesbrough Reserves	32	21	5	6	90	51	47
Hartlepools United	32	17	11	4	82	37	45
Darlington	32	16	5	11	60	55	37
Sunderland Reserves	32	15	6	11	65	43	36
Shildon Athletic	32	13	8	11	61	61	34
South Shields Adelaide	32	14	5	13	77	63	33
North Shields Athletic	32	12	8	12	60	61	32
Seaham Harbour	32	14	3	15	56	57	31
Wallsend Park Villa	32	12	6	14	56	67	30
Carlisle United Reserves	32	11	4	17	52	62	26
Wingate Albion	32	8	8	16	43	80	24
West Stanley	32	9	5	18	56	85	23
Hebburn Argyle	32	8	4	20	33	103	20
Workington Reserves	32	7	4	21	41	98	18
Sunderland Royal Rovers	32	2	5	25	25	83	9

1910-11

	P	W	D	L	F	A	Pts
Newcastle United Reserves	34	25	4	5	88	25	54
Sunderland Reserves	34	20	6	8	81	38	46
Hartlepools United	34	18	8	8	71	40	44
Darlington	34	19	5	10	79	39	43
South Shields	33	18	5	10	99	52	41
North Shields Athletic	34	19	3	12	57	56	41
Middlesbrough Reserves	34	16	6	12	83	54	38
Wingate Albion	34	14	7	13	48	39	35
Wallsend Park Villa	34	15	3	16	49	59	33
Hebburn Argyle	34	13	6	15	38	62	32
Seaham Harbour	34	13	5	16	44	63	31
Spennymoor United	32	12	5	15	52	54	29
Workington	34	12	3	19	47	72	27
Shildon Athletic	34	11	3	20	50	64	25
Carlisle United	34	8	8	18	45	52	24
Jarrow Croft	34	11	2	21	34	70	24
West Stanley	33	10	3	20	39	84	23
Sunderland Rovers	34	8	2	24	37	94	18

Spennymoor United left two fixtures unplayed.

1911-12

	P	W	D	L	F	A	Pts
Middlesbrough Reserves	36	28	5	3	122	33	61
Newcastle United Reserves	36	28	2	6	113	33	58
Darlington	36	23	8	5	84	34	54
Sunderland Reserves	36	21	5	10	99	52	47
South Shields	36	21	4	11	73	43	46
Spennymoor United	36	18	6	12	62	57	42
Newcastle City	36	16	9	11	62	43	41
Gateshead Town	36	16	6	14	64	66	38
Hartlepools United	36	14	8	14	62	50	36
West Stanley	36	13	10	13	61	58	36
North Shields Athletic	36	13	9	14	59	72	35
Seaham Harbour	36	15	2	19	52	67	32
Hebburn Argyle	36	11	9	16	56	54	31
Wingate Albion	36	9	11	16	41	84	29
Jarrow Croft	36	10	7	19	52	87	27
Shildon Athletic	36	9	6	21	62	97	24
Carlisle United	36	7	6	23	27	98	20
Wallsend Park Villa	36	8	3	25	43	93	19
Sunderland Rovers	36	2	4	30	42	125	8

1912-13

Darlington	38	31	4	3	116	23	66
South Shields	38	27	7	4	103	30	61
Middlesbrough Reserves	38	26	6	6	102	40	58
Sunderland Reserves	38	26	5	7	100	48	57
Newcastle United Reserves	38	24	5	9	109	47	53
Spennymoor United	38	19	6	13	80	61	44
Shildon Athletic	38	17	9	12	79	69	43
Houghton Rovers	38	15	9	14	53	64	39
Wallsend	38	14	10	14	83	71	38
North Shields Athletic	38	15	7	16	72	78	37
Newcastle City	38	15	7	16	48	62	37
Hartlepools United	38	15	6	17	69	66	36
Hebburn Argyle	38	12	6	20	49	75	30
Carlisle United	38	12	5	21	61	98	29
Seaham Harbour	38	10	7	21	48	77	27
Jarrow	38	10	5	23	52	86	25
West Stanley	38	7	10	21	54	94	24
Sunderland Rovers	38	7	8	23	39	79	22
Gateshead Town	38	8	6	24	49	112	22
Wingate Albion	38	5	2	31	28	114	12

1913-14

South Shields	38	32	5	1	133	29	69
Middlesbrough Reserves	38	23	8	7	99	37	54
Newcastle United Reserves	38	24	5	9	91	40	53
Darlington	38	20	10	8	72	43	50
Sunderland Reserves	38	20	8	10	83	55	48
Blyth Spartans	38	19	7	12	71	51	45
Hartlepools United	38	17	10	11	68	37	44
Hebburn Argyle	38	14	11	13	55	50	39
Shildon Athletic	38	18	3	17	54	60	39
Gateshead Town	38	17	5	16	58	76	39
Jarrow	38	12	10	16	55	63	34
North Shields Athletic	38	11	10	17	57	81	32
Carlisle United	38	11	10	17	48	84	32
Spennymoor United	38	10	11	17	60	63	31
Sunderland Rovers	38	10	10	18	46	67	30
Newcastle City	38	7	16	15	34	57	30
West Stanley	38	13	3	22	54	87	29
Houghton Rovers	38	11	2	25	38	81	24
Seaham Harbour	38	7	8	23	30	73	22
Wallsend	38	5	6	27	44	115	16

1914-15

South Shields	38	31	4	3	160	34	66
Middlesbrough Reserves	38	28	5	5	151	34	61
Newcastle United Reserves	38	26	6	6	132	43	58
Darlington	38	25	4	9	109	37	54
West Stanley	38	24	4	10	79	44	52
Sunderland Reserves	38	18	9	11	86	50	45
Hartlepools United	38	16	11	11	74	57	43
North Shields Athletic	38	19	5	14	67	63	43
Ashington	38	15	11	12	60	63	41
Sunderland Rovers	38	17	4	17	74	79	38
Spennymoor United	38	12	9	17	40	82	33
Shildon Athletic	38	11	9	18	70	61	31
Blyth Spartans	38	11	9	18	49	72	31
Hebburn Argyle	38	12	6	20	49	73	30
Jarrow	38	10	10	18	45	95	30
Houghton Rovers	38	11	4	23	43	125	26
Carlisle United	38	8	7	23	51	120	23
Newcastle City	38	8	5	25	42	87	21
Gateshead Town	38	8	3	27	51	121	19
Wallsend	38	6	3	29	44	136	15

1919-20

Middlesbrough Reserves	34	22	7	5	86	30	51
Darlington	34	24	1	9	91	44	49
Newcastle United Reserves	34	22	5	7	82	41	49
Blyth Spartans	34	18	8	8	62	42	44
Durham City	34	17	6	11	52	41	40
Jarrow	34	16	6	12	55	52	38
Ashington	34	14	8	12	51	51	36
South Shields Reserves	34	14	7	13	67	57	35
Sunderland Reserves	34	15	4	15	67	49	34
Hartlepools United	34	12	10	12	45	36	34
Scotswood	34	13	6	15	47	55	32
West Stanley	34	12	7	15	45	63	31
Carlisle United	34	12	3	19	47	76	27
Shildon Athletic	34	10	6	18	50	75	26
Houghton Rovers	34	8	8	18	28	60	24
Spennymoor United	34	10	2	22	52	78	22
Leadgate Park	34	8	6	20	51	83	22
Wallsend	34	6	6	22	26	71	18

1920-21

Darlington	38	28	4	6	75	29	60
Middlesbrough Reserves	38	27	5	6	93	35	59
Newcastle United Reserves	38	23	7	8	96	39	53
Sunderland Reserves	38	21	10	7	73	49	52
Blyth Spartans	38	19	11	8	69	34	49
Carlisle United	38	18	10	10	79	46	46
West Stanley	38	14	14	10	54	42	42
Hartlepools United	38	18	6	14	64	50	42
Ashington	38	14	13	11	66	52	41
Jarrow	38	14	11	13	46	44	39
Durham City	38	16	5	17	31	60	37
Chester-le-Street	38	13	11	14	50	58	37
Leadgate Park	38	13	10	15	57	58	36
South Shields Reserves	38	12	11	15	51	66	35
Spennymoor United	38	10	10	18	51	79	30
Houghton Rovers	38	7	10	21	38	69	24
Shildon Athletic	38	8	7	23	41	75	23
Scotswood	38	8	5	25	35	76	21
Wallsend	38	6	8	24	39	98	20
Bedlington United	38	4	6	28	32	104	14

1921-22

Carlisle United	38	24	8	6	85	39	56
Newcastle United Reserves	38	24	7	7	80	30	55
Blyth Spartans	38	16	16	6	55	31	48
Chester-le-Street	38	20	7	11	53	35	47
South Shields Reserves	38	16	13	9	60	31	45
Shildon Athletic	38	20	5	13	65	44	45
Middlesbrough Reserves	38	18	8	12	61	45	44
Sunderland Reserves	38	16	11	11	66	43	43
Workington	38	17	8	13	52	49	42
Darlington Reserves	38	15	9	14	67	68	39
Jarrow	38	16	5	17	51	59	37
Leadgate Park	38	14	9	15	56	66	37
West Stanley	38	10	15	13	55	65	35
Spennymoor United	38	14	5	19	59	65	33
Wallsend	38	11	11	16	49	62	33
Preston Colliery	38	7	15	16	38	58	29
Bedlington United	38	8	11	19	32	56	27
Seaton Delaval	38	6	14	18	36	69	26
Scotswood	38	5	10	23	43	90	20
Houghton Rovers	38	4	11	23	27	85	19

1922-23

Newcastle United Reserves	38	30	8	0	109	24	68
Blyth Spartans	38	23	7	8	78	43	53
Sunderland Reserves	38	23	3	12	74	35	49
Middlesbrough Reserves	38	20	8	10	76	45	48
South Shields Reserves	38	21	5	12	74	44	47
Carlisle United	38	19	8	11	56	43	46
Workington	38	20	4	14	85	57	44
Shildon Athletic	38	17	10	11	74	55	44
Jarrow	38	17	6	15	56	63	40
Preston Colliery	38	16	7	15	48	47	39
Hartlepools United Reserves	38	14	9	15	64	56	37
Bedlington United	38	14	5	19	50	61	33
West Stanley	38	10	12	16	43	60	32
Darlington Reserves	38	13	5	20	46	57	31
Chester-le-Street	38	12	6	20	47	71	30
Seaton Delaval	38	10	7	21	40	68	27
Wallsend	38	8	9	21	43	89	25
Leadgate Park	38	8	8	22	38	82	24
Scotswood	38	6	10	22	40	91	22
Spennymoor United	38	6	9	23	42	92	21

1923-24

South Shields Reserves	38	29	5	4	106	32	63
Newcastle United Reserves	38	26	9	3	99	44	61
Middlesbrough Reserves	38	26	6	6	95	34	58
Sunderland Reserves	38	24	5	9	90	40	53
Workington	38	21	10	7	87	43	52
Blyth Spartans	38	21	7	10	68	35	49
West Stanley	38	18	11	9	66	43	47
Seaton Delaval	38	14	8	16	61	61	36
Hartlepools United Reserves	38	13	10	15	60	62	36
Shildon	38	15	4	19	60	63	34
Carlisle United	38	13	8	17	46	61	34
Darlington Reserves	38	13	6	19	55	64	32
Spennymoor United	38	10	10	18	41	65	30
Bedlington United	38	12	4	22	52	94	28
Scotswood	38	8	10	20	46	81	26
Leadgate Park	38	10	6	22	50	92	26
Preston Colliery	38	9	7	22	37	64	25
Chester-le-Street	38	9	6	23	36	80	24
Wallsend	38	6	11	21	44	91	23
Jarrow	38	10	3	25	46	96	23

1924-25

Sunderland Reserves	38	27	7	4	98	29	61
Darlington Reserves	38	25	7	6	97	40	57
Newcastle United Reserves	38	24	5	9	93	35	53
Middlesbrough Reserves	38	22	7	9	81	40	51
South Shields Reserves	38	19	11	8	79	55	49
Shildon	38	19	9	10	88	58	47
Workington	38	20	6	12	80	57	46
Blyth Spartans	38	17	9	12	69	46	43
West Stanley	38	14	14	10	51	53	42
Hartlepools United Reserves	38	16	7	15	63	54	39
Carlisle United	38	16	6	16	67	63	38
Jarrow	38	13	11	14	51	56	37
Spennymoor United	38	11	11	16	54	69	33
Seaton Delaval	38	12	3	23	39	79	27
Scotswood	38	9	9	20	36	78	27
Preston Colliery	38	10	6	22	41	73	26
Chester-le-Street	38	10	6	22	35	75	26
Leadgate Park	38	9	5	24	52	103	23
Bedlington United	38	6	8	24	41	84	20
Wallsend	38	5	5	28	33	101	15

1925-26

Newcastle United Reserves	38	31	4	3	147	43	66
Sunderland Reserves	38	26	6	6	133	50	58
South Shields Reserves	38	22	6	10	113	71	50
Workington	38	21	6	11	84	59	48
Carlisle United	38	19	9	10	83	70	47
Darlington Reserves	38	20	6	12	107	57	46
Middlesbrough Reserves	38	21	3	14	107	71	45
West Stanley	38	18	7	13	92	73	43
Jarrow	38	18	4	16	62	72	40
Preston Colliery	38	16	7	15	71	66	39
Shildon	38	16	5	17	93	86	37
Annfield Plain	38	15	7	16	77	78	37
Hartlepools United Reserves	38	16	5	17	77	108	37
Blyth Spartans	38	13	6	19	77	105	32
Chester-le-Street	38	14	1	23	68	97	29
Bedlington United	38	13	3	22	75	113	29
Scotswood	38	9	5	24	70	121	23
Durham City Reserves	38	11	1	26	58	109	23
Spennymoor United	38	6	8	24	76	134	20
Seaton Delaval	38	5	1	32	51	138	11

1926-27

Division One

Sunderland Reserves	38	27	2	9	115	54	56
Newcastle United Reserves	38	24	6	8	99	43	54
South Shields Reserves	38	24	6	8	103	65	54
Middlesbrough Reserves	38	22	7	9	133	69	51
Carlisle United	38	23	3	12	106	75	49
Jarrow	38	16	9	13	80	66	41
Hartlepools United Reserves	38	16	9	13	91	79	41
Darlington Reserves	38	15	11	12	88	82	41
Blyth Spartans	38	17	6	15	78	72	40
Annfield Plain	38	15	9	14	83	81	39
Shildon	38	13	10	15	83	87	36
Bedlington United	38	14	8	16	84	94	36
Durham City Reserves	38	15	5	18	72	91	35
Preston Colliery	38	14	6	18	89	101	34
Spennymoor United	38	11	10	17	82	89	32
Workington	38	12	8	18	60	76	32
Scotswood	38	9	10	19	77	106	28
West Stanley	38	10	8	20	66	113	28
Chester-le-Street	38	9	5	24	55	105	23
Seaton Delaval	38	4	2	32	40	134	10

Division Two

Consett	34	25	1	8	114	64	51
Ashington Reserves	34	22	6	6	129	53	50
Wallsend	34	21	4	9	92	65	46
Walker Celtic	34	20	6	8	93	67	46
Chilton Colliery Recreation Athletic	34	19	6	9	96	52	44
Chopwell Institute	34	16	9	9	98	81	41
Dipton United	34	16	6	12	92	62	38
Seaham Harbour	34	17	2	15	97	86	36
Craghead United	34	13	7	14	88	86	33
Washington Colliery	34	12	8	14	63	64	32
Spen Black & White	34	13	3	18	66	85	29
Birtley	34	11	7	16	66	95	29
High Fell	34	12	3	19	72	92	27
Ouston Rovers	34	10	7	17	65	90	27
Crawcrook Albion	34	11	5	18	54	81	27
Mickley	34	9	4	21	60	85	22
Felling Colliery	34	8	6	20	59	109	22
Newburn	34	6	0	28	54	141	12

1927-28

Division One

Sunderland Reserves	38	31	3	4	128	30	65
Carlisle United	38	25	5	8	111	61	55
Middlesbrough Reserves	38	22	8	8	126	59	52
West Stanley	38	22	6	10	106	82	50
Annfield Plain	38	21	5	12	96	61	47
Newcastle United Reserves	38	21	4	13	101	61	46
South Shields Reserves	38	20	4	14	98	74	44
Bedlington United	38	18	5	15	78	97	41
Workington	38	18	4	16	99	80	40
Spennymoor United	38	16	8	14	71	73	40
Hartlepools United Reserves	38	16	4	18	98	113	36
Darlington Reserves	38	16	2	20	92	90	34
Blyth Spartans	38	14	4	20	56	77	32
Ashington Reserves	38	12	6	20	71	106	30
Jarrow	38	12	5	21	76	122	29
Shildon	38	10	8	20	56	73	28
Consett	38	10	8	20	76	117	28
Scotswood	38	8	9	21	61	97	25
Preston Colliery	38	7	6	25	60	130	20
Durham City Reserves	38	7	4	27	48	105	18

Division Two

Washington Colliery	32	22	5	5	108	45	49
Wallsend	32	21	6	5	100	47	48
Dipton United	32	20	4	8	119	64	44
Usworth Colliery	32	18	6	8	73	49	42
Birtley	32	18	2	12	90	64	38
Seaham Harbour	32	16	6	10	68	50	38
Chopwell Institute	32	16	4	12	90	69	36
Spen Black & White	32	16	4	12	87	73	36
Walker Celtic	32	16	3	13	89	65	35
Seaton Delaval	32	15	3	14	72	77	33
Chester-le-Street	32	11	7	14	70	79	29
Mickley	32	12	2	18	61	103	26
Craghead United	32	7	11	14	77	96	25
Crawcrook Albion	32	11	2	19	59	75	24
Ouston Rovers	32	9	4	19	72	107	22
High Fell	32	4	4	24	51	128	12
Felling Colliery	32	3	1	28	44	139	7

1928-29

Division One

Sunderland Reserves	38	30	3	5	127	41	63
South Shields Reserves	38	23	8	7	110	49	54
Middlesbrough Reserves	38	21	7	10	113	66	49
Workington	38	19	8	11	100	74	46
Newcastle United Reserves	38	20	4	14	99	67	44
Spennymoor United	38	18	8	12	79	66	44
Annfield Plain	38	18	6	14	75	66	42
Hartlepools United Reserves	38	16	6	16	77	97	38
Jarrow	38	16	5	17	67	77	37
Wallsend	38	16	4	18	75	80	36
Blyth Spartans	38	13	10	15	66	75	36
Bedlington United	38	16	3	19	72	80	35
Shildon	38	12	10	16	74	77	34
Consett	38	14	6	18	65	91	34
Washington Colliery	38	14	5	19	81	103	33
Darlington Reserves	38	13	6	19	74	97	32
Scotswood	38	11	7	20	64	94	29
West Stanley	38	7	11	20	55	91	25
Ashington Reserves	38	9	7	22	47	89	25
Durham City	38	8	8	22	51	91	24

Division Two

North Shields	34	26	6	2	120	44	58
Carlisle United Reserves	34	26	0	8	130	40	52
Spen Black & White	34	19	9	6	105	61	47
Walker Celtic	34	16	10	8	84	56	42
White-le-Head Rangers	34	17	8	9	94	66	42
Usworth Colliery	34	16	8	10	78	53	40
Dipton United	34	16	7	11	85	76	39
St. Peters Albion	34	15	6	13	78	63	36
Chopwell Institute	34	15	6	13	83	88	36
Crawcrook Albion	34	16	3	15	73	85	35
Birtley	34	10	9	15	61	72	29
High Fell	34	9	9	16	62	83	27
Mickley	34	10	5	19	79	127	25
Seaham Harbour	34	10	5	19	58	103	25
Craghead United	34	9	5	20	73	96	23
Chester-le-Street	34	7	7	20	62	115	21
Ouston Rovers	34	6	6	22	61	99	18
Seaton Delaval	34	5	7	22	61	120	17

1929-30

Division One

Sunderland Reserves	38	26	6	6	157	58	58
Newcastle United Reserves	38	27	2	9	111	46	56
Darlington Reserves	38	21	8	9	103	79	50
Middlesbrough Reserves	38	22	4	12	118	53	48
West Stanley	38	20	6	12	89	79	46
Hartlepools United Reserves	38	20	5	13	97	80	45
North Shields	38	18	8	12	89	69	44
Jarrow	38	17	6	15	74	68	40
Workington	38	18	3	17	96	89	39
South Shields Reserves	38	16	4	18	80	85	36
Wallsend	38	14	8	16	73	88	36
Carlisle United Reserves	38	15	5	18	83	97	35
Spennymoor United	38	13	8	17	85	99	34
Annfield Plain	38	11	11	16	84	93	33
Consett	38	13	4	21	73	113	30
Scotswood	38	13	2	23	75	110	28
Shildon	38	11	6	21	65	101	28
Washington Colliery	38	11	4	23	79	126	26
Blyth Spartans	38	10	6	22	58	95	26
Bedlington United	38	9	4	25	65	126	22

Division Two

Walker Celtic	28	20	3	5	99	36	43
White-le-Head Rangers	28	21	0	7	85	50	42
Ashington	28	20	1	7	96	40	41
Spen Black & White	28	18	1	9	79	65	37
Usworth Colliery	28	15	3	10	85	61	33
Crawcrook Albion	28	13	3	12	83	70	29
Durham City	28	14	1	13	77	66	29
St. Peters Albion	28	11	7	10	57	65	29
Chopwell Institute	28	12	4	12	64	74	28
Birtley	28	10	4	14	83	78	24
Dipton United	28	10	2	16	51	74	22
Craghead United	28	8	3	17	66	82	19
Mickley	28	7	4	17	40	78	18
Seaton Delaval	28	6	2	20	34	92	14
Chester-le-Street	28	4	4	20	38	106	12

1930-31

Division One

Team	P	W	D	L	F	A	Pts
Middlesbrough Reserves	42	33	7	2	159	40	73
Newcastle United Reserves	42	33	6	3	159	39	72
Sunderland Reserves	42	28	5	9	130	65	61
Workington	42	23	9	10	105	57	55
Jarrow	42	23	6	13	111	69	52
Washington Colliery	42	20	11	11	82	62	51
Blyth Spartans	42	22	6	14	95	78	50
Walker Celtic	42	16	13	13	97	92	45
Hartlepools United Reserves	42	20	4	18	102	92	44
North Shields	42	17	9	16	102	87	43
Carlisle United Reserves	42	17	8	17	90	94	42
Wallsend	42	17	3	22	88	103	37
Darlington Reserves	42	13	10	19	97	116	36
Spennymoor United	42	15	5	22	85	84	35
Gateshead Reserves	42	12	10	20	59	74	34
Crook Town	42	14	6	22	85	114	34
West Stanley	42	14	6	22	65	106	34
Ashington	42	12	6	24	65	101	30
Annfield Plain	42	12	5	25	65	108	29
Shildon	42	12	5	25	65	128	29
Consett	42	10	8	24	58	126	28
Scotswood	42	3	4	35	45	161	10

Division Two

Team	P	W	D	L	F	A	Pts
Chopwell Institute	26	19	4	3	81	30	42
Durham City	26	18	4	4	77	38	40
Spen Black & White	26	12	7	7	64	36	31
Usworth Colliery	26	14	3	9	70	48	31
Dipton United	26	13	4	9	67	60	30
St. Peters Albion	26	10	8	8	58	47	28
Crawcrook Albion	26	11	6	9	52	48	28
White-le-Head Rangers	26	11	5	10	68	58	27
Craghead United	26	9	4	13	80	85	22
Mickley	26	10	2	14	55	77	22
Bedlington United	26	8	5	13	52	67	21
Birtley	26	7	4	15	47	69	18
Seaton Delaval	26	6	2	18	34	91	14
Chester-le-Street	26	4	2	20	44	95	10

1931-32

Division One

Team	P	W	D	L	F	A	Pts
Middlesbrough Reserves	42	29	7	6	128	45	65
Newcastle United Reserves	42	29	6	7	139	48	64
Sunderland Reserves	42	26	9	7	106	47	61
Workington	42	27	7	8	119	63	61
Blyth Spartans	42	24	9	9	129	75	57
Crook Town	42	23	6	13	100	63	52
Darlington Reserves	42	22	7	13	84	72	51
Spennymoor United	42	20	6	16	106	88	46
Hartlepools United Reserves	42	21	4	17	103	93	46
Jarrow	42	19	5	18	82	81	43
Wallsend	42	17	6	19	53	91	40
West Stanley	42	16	7	19	96	98	39
Gateshead Reserves	42	16	6	20	73	104	38
Chopwell Institute	42	14	9	19	80	104	37
Ashington	42	17	2	23	91	104	36
Carlisle United Reserves	42	13	8	21	65	80	34
North Shields	42	10	11	21	73	89	31
Durham City	42	13	5	24	56	89	31
Annfield Plain	42	12	5	25	72	123	29
Walker Celtic	42	11	6	25	82	109	28
Shildon	42	8	5	29	43	120	21
Washington Colliery	42	5	4	33	41	135	14

Division Two

Team	P	W	D	L	F	A	Pts
Crawcrook Albion	26	16	3	7	65	48	35
Dipton United	26	14	4	8	70	47	32
St. Peters Albion	26	14	3	9	73	51	31
Eden Colliery Welfare	26	14	3	9	67	56	31
Usworth Colliery	26	12	5	9	44	46	29
Throckley Welfare	26	11	6	9	49	42	28
Chester-le-Street	26	10	6	10	52	49	26
Spen Black & White	26	10	6	10	47	50	26
Consett	26	10	5	11	70	61	25
Mickley	26	9	6	11	56	58	24
Birtley	26	10	3	13	63	62	23
Scotswood	26	7	7	12	46	75	21
Bedlington United	26	6	5	15	46	77	17
Craghead United	26	7	2	17	43	69	16

1932-33

Division One

Team	P	W	D	L	F	A	Pts
Middlesbrough Reserves	38	32	0	6	146	55	64
Newcastle United Reserves	38	24	7	7	91	52	55
North Shields	38	23	7	8	107	59	53
Sunderland Reserves	38	23	4	11	87	56	50
Workington	38	22	5	11	101	53	49
Spennymoor United	38	22	4	12	71	43	48
Darlington Reserves	38	18	5	15	85	84	41
Carlisle United Reserves	38	17	6	15	80	72	40
Walker Celtic	38	14	7	17	70	85	35
Blyth Spartans	38	15	4	19	79	84	34
Crook Town	38	15	4	19	67	73	34
Chopwell Institute	38	14	6	18	83	91	34
Hartlepools United Reserves	38	14	6	18	63	87	34
Ashington	38	12	9	17	87	92	33
Annfield Plain	38	13	6	19	84	97	32
Gateshead Reserves	38	10	10	18	68	85	30
Durham City	38	10	10	18	63	86	30
West Stanley	38	11	5	22	62	118	27
Jarrow	38	10	3	25	65	121	23
Wallsend	38	6	2	30	43	109	14

Division Two

Team	P	W	D	L	F	A	Pts
Eden Colliery Welfare	30	19	4	7	97	50	42
Consett	30	20	2	8	87	50	42
Throckley Welfare	30	19	3	8	91	63	41
Scotswood	30	18	3	9	83	66	39
Usworth Colliery	30	17	3	10	82	55	37
Crawcrook Albion	30	13	9	8	53	46	35
Bedlington United	30	16	2	12	71	58	34
Birtley	30	15	4	11	76	65	34
Mickley	30	12	6	12	62	63	30
Pegswood United	30	10	8	12	80	71	28
Washington Colliery	30	10	4	16	52	68	24
West Wylam Colliery Welfare	30	8	6	16	55	84	22
Dipton United	30	6	8	16	52	86	20
Spen Black & White	30	7	5	18	46	85	19
Newcastle East End	30	7	4	19	41	80	18
Chester-le-Street	30	5	5	20	60	98	15

1933-34

Division One

	P	W	D	L	F	A	Pts
Sunderland Reserves	38	28	5	5	119	37	61
Jarrow	38	24	7	7	105	42	55
Spennymoor United	38	22	8	8	114	42	52
Blyth Spartans	38	23	5	10	81	58	51
Workington	38	24	2	12	147	68	50
Middlesbrough Reserves	38	17	8	13	89	59	42
North Shields	38	18	6	14	85	65	42
Gateshead Reserves	38	19	4	15	81	81	42
Hartlepools United Reserves	38	16	5	17	73	77	37
Crook Town	38	15	7	16	62	68	37
Carlisle United Reserves	38	14	5	19	81	64	33
Darlington Reserves	38	12	8	18	76	101	32
Ashington	38	13	5	20	58	100	31
Annfield Plain	38	13	5	20	55	110	31
Chopwell Institute	38	12	6	20	77	126	30
West Stanley	38	13	3	22	55	87	29
Consett	38	12	5	21	45	84	29
City of Durham	38	11	7	20	47	89	29
Eden Colliery Welfare	38	10	8	20	76	107	28
Walker Celtic	38	7	5	26	54	115	19

Division Two

	P	W	D	L	F	A	Pts
Throckley Welfare	30	21	7	2	94	35	49
Bedlington United	30	21	2	7	99	57	44
Wallsend Town	30	18	7	5	94	49	43
Stakeford Albion	30	17	5	8	82	56	39
Mickley	30	16	5	9	89	70	37
Birtley	30	14	4	12	73	57	32
Newbiggin West End	30	13	3	14	72	64	29
Pegswood United	30	12	5	13	78	73	29
Usworth Colliery	30	12	5	13	61	71	29
Washington Colliery	30	10	7	13	61	82	27
Chester-le-Street	30	12	1	17	84	88	25
Scotswood	30	10	5	15	63	81	25
West Wylam Colliery Welfare	30	9	5	16	58	79	23
Dipton United	30	8	5	17	58	99	21
Crawcrook Albion	30	4	10	16	44	82	18
Newcastle East End	30	3	4	23	43	110	10

1934-35

Division One

	P	W	D	L	F	A	Pts
Middlesbrough Reserves	38	26	9	3	129	51	61
Sunderland Reserves	38	28	3	7	126	37	59
Walker Celtic	38	27	3	8	109	53	57
Jarrow	38	24	5	9	93	60	53
Blyth Spartans	38	23	4	11	95	55	50
Eden Colliery Welfare	38	19	10	9	92	62	48
Spennymoor United	38	18	9	11	84	59	45
Workington	38	18	5	15	76	81	41
North Shields	38	17	6	15	90	69	40
Gateshead Reserves	38	17	4	17	67	72	38
Hartlepools United Reserves	38	15	6	17	91	86	36
Darlington Reserves	38	15	5	18	95	90	35
Throckley Welfare	38	13	5	20	75	94	31
Carlisle United Reserves	38	13	4	21	73	83	30
Crook Town	38	12	5	21	84	111	29
Ashington	38	10	9	17	57	96	27
Annfield Plain	38	10	6	22	74	117	26
City of Durham	38	10	2	26	56	142	22
Consett	38	5	7	26	44	118	17
West Stanley	38	6	3	29	58	132	15

Division Two

	P	W	D	L	F	A	Pts
Newbiggin West End	24	20	2	2	79	28	42
Bedlington United	24	13	4	7	58	45	30
West Wylam Colliery Welfare	24	13	3	8	70	61	29
Hexham	24	11	5	8	53	49	27
Stakeford Albion	24	10	5	9	65	50	25
Scotswood	24	11	3	10	53	48	25
Wallsend Town	24	10	4	10	49	50	24
Usworth Colliery	24	10	3	11	59	59	23
Pegswood United	24	9	4	11	56	65	22
Birtley	24	8	5	11	56	48	21
Washington Colliery	24	7	6	11	51	75	20
Mickley	24	5	5	14	38	56	15
Chester-le-Street	24	3	3	18	33	86	9

1935-36

	P	W	D	L	F	A	Pts
Blyth Spartans	38	26	4	8	104	60	56
Walker Celtic	38	23	8	7	87	45	54
North Shields	38	22	8	8	95	52	52
Sunderland Reserves	38	22	4	12	115	65	48
Workington	38	20	5	13	87	53	45
Middlesbrough Reserves	38	21	2	15	123	78	44
Gateshead Reserves	38	18	7	13	86	73	43
Horden Colliery Welfare	38	18	6	14	84	64	42
Spennymoor United	38	19	4	15	83	81	42
Jarrow	38	17	7	14	78	68	41
Darlington Reserves	38	18	4	16	93	86	40
Throckley Welfare	38	16	5	17	80	78	37
Annfield Plain	38	16	5	17	86	96	37
Hartlepools United Reserves	38	14	6	18	77	81	34
Carlisle United Reserves	38	13	6	19	65	104	32
West Stanley	38	12	4	22	73	127	28
Eden Colliery Welfare	38	12	3	23	59	89	27
Ashington	38	10	6	22	48	74	26
City of Durham	38	8	3	27	57	115	19
Crook Town	38	5	3	30	50	141	13

1936-37

	P	W	D	L	F	A	Pts
Sunderland Reserves	38	29	5	4	155	55	63
Spennymoor United	38	23	8	7	107	55	54
Middlesbrough Reserves	38	21	9	8	117	48	51
Workington	38	22	7	9	114	54	51
Blyth Spartans	38	21	7	10	103	68	49
North Shields	38	21	5	12	115	56	47
Ashington	38	21	4	13	93	72	46
Annfield Plain	38	18	9	11	99	84	45
Throckley Welfare	38	19	7	12	99	90	45
Darlington Reserves	38	19	6	13	88	83	44
Horden Colliery Welfare	38	17	5	16	88	79	39
South Shields	38	16	7	15	88	97	39
Hartlepools United Reserves	38	15	7	16	65	81	37
Carlisle United Reserves	38	11	7	20	79	93	29
Walker Celtic	38	12	5	21	74	102	29
Jarrow	38	10	6	22	55	115	26
Hexham Town	38	9	6	23	64	99	24
City of Durham	38	6	6	26	67	131	18
Gateshead Reserves	38	7	3	28	67	122	17
West Stanley	38	2	3	33	37	189	7

Eden Colliery Welfare resigned after playing their 23rd league match of the season at Spennymoor on February 6th and their record was expunged.

1937-38

	P	W	D	L	F	A	Pts
Horden Colliery Welfare	38	24	8	6	99	39	56
Sunderland Reserves	38	26	3	9	106	39	55
South Shields	38	26	3	9	119	54	55
Blyth Spartans	38	21	6	11	113	70	48
Carlisle United Reserves	38	19	8	11	112	73	46
Ashington	38	19	8	11	87	63	46
Workington	38	20	6	12	111	86	46
Gateshead Reserves	38	19	6	13	87	74	44
Middlesbrough Reserves	38	18	4	16	97	63	40
North Shields	38	14	9	15	81	81	37
Annfield Plain	38	16	5	17	76	77	37
Walker Celtic	38	11	13	14	68	75	35
Darlington Reserves	38	13	8	17	67	91	34
Throckley Welfare	38	16	1	21	86	93	33
Hartlepools United Reserves	38	13	6	19	73	81	32
West Stanley	38	11	9	18	60	91	31
Hexham Town	38	13	2	23	73	130	28
Jarrow	38	10	5	23	71	105	25
Consett	38	8	7	23	64	118	23
City of Durham	38	3	3	32	43	189	9

1938-39

	P	W	D	L	F	A	Pts
South Shields	38	28	4	6	141	50	60
Workington	38	26	5	7	121	59	57
North Shields	38	25	7	6	111	62	57
Sunderland Reserves	38	23	5	10	121	55	51
Middlesbrough Reserves	38	21	5	12	128	76	47
Gateshead Reserves	38	21	5	12	109	71	47
Ashington	38	20	6	12	107	87	46
Horden Colliery Welfare	38	16	11	11	69	43	43
Blyth Spartans	38	15	9	14	82	97	39
Darlington Reserves	38	14	8	16	95	92	36
Consett	38	12	11	15	84	113	35
Spennymoor United	38	12	7	19	91	104	31
Hartlepools United Reserves	38	12	6	20	77	92	30
Carlisle United Reserves	38	12	4	22	98	101	28
West Stanley	38	11	6	21	75	104	28
Jarrow	38	11	5	22	69	104	27
Walker Celtic	38	11	5	22	56	103	27
Throckley Welfare	38	10	7	21	63	133	27
Hexham Town	38	8	8	22	66	143	24
Annfield Plain	38	7	6	25	55	130	20

1939-1945

The league operated war-time competitions in 1939-40 and 1944-45 but with a limited membership.

1945-46

	P	W	D	L	F	A	Pts
Spennymoor United	38	24	3	11	146	74	51
Murton Colliery Welfare #	38	24	6	8	105	59	50
Ashington	38	23	4	11	116	89	50
North Shields	38	21	7	10	97	67	49
Annfield Plain	38	23	2	13	97	68	48
Consett	38	18	8	12	92	62	44
South Shields	38	19	6	13	107	87	44
Gateshead Reserves	38	17	3	18	83	90	37
Eppleton Colliery Welfare	38	15	7	16	66	92	37
Middlesbrough Reserves	38	15	6	17	76	82	36
Sunderland Reserves	38	14	7	17	84	79	35
Stockton	38	15	5	18	88	105	35
West Stanley	38	15	4	19	97	106	34
Horden Colliery Welfare	38	15	4	19	93	105	34
Darlington Reserves	38	14	6	18	76	88	34
Blackhall Colliery Welfare	38	13	6	19	76	101	32
Workington	38	12	6	20	71	75	30
Hartlepools United Reserves	38	12	4	22	62	116	28
Carlisle United Reserves	38	10	5	23	77	117	25
Throckley Welfare	38	7	9	22	60	109	23

Murton Colliery Welfare had 4 points deducted.

1946-47

	P	W	D	L	F	A	Pts
Middlesbrough Reserves	38	23	6	9	104	56	52
Sunderland Reserves	38	23	5	10	111	61	51
South Shields	38	19	10	9	103	79	48
Ashington	38	19	6	13	98	93	44
Darlington Reserves	38	19	5	14	81	64	43
Gateshead Reserves	38	18	6	14	105	87	42
Consett	38	18	5	15	97	83	41
Carlisle United Reserves	38	18	5	15	101	87	41
Stockton	38	18	5	15	75	73	41
Annfield Plain	38	17	7	14	90	88	41
West Stanley	38	17	6	15	112	99	40
North Shields	38	17	4	17	97	91	38
Workington	38	14	9	15	80	69	37
Hartlepools United Reserves	38	15	7	16	70	75	37
Blackhall Colliery Welfare	38	13	10	15	57	76	36
Eppleton Colliery Welfare	38	12	7	19	63	98	31
Spennymoor United	38	11	6	21	70	81	28
Horden Colliery Welfare	38	11	6	21	71	101	28
Throckley Welfare	38	13	2	23	78	132	28
Murton Colliery Welfare	38	4	5	29	43	113	13

1947-48

	P	W	D	L	F	A	Pts
Sunderland Reserves	38	24	9	5	102	51	57
Gateshead Reserves	38	25	6	7	105	48	56
Middlesbrough Reserves	38	24	6	8	91	46	54
North Shields	38	21	7	10	89	65	49
Hartlepools United Reserves	38	17	9	12	62	62	43
West Stanley	38	18	5	15	87	74	41
Consett	38	18	4	16	87	75	40
Blyth Spartans	38	15	10	13	62	60	40
Ashington	38	16	7	15	81	70	39
Horden Colliery Welfare	38	17	3	18	60	66	37
Stockton	38	13	10	15	57	59	36
Spennymoor United	38	14	7	17	70	69	35
Darlington Reserves	38	15	5	18	65	68	35
Carlisle United Reserves	38	14	7	17	61	65	35
South Shields	38	17	1	20	65	79	35
Workington	38	14	6	18	80	98	34
Murton Colliery Welfare	38	12	7	19	65	85	31
Annfield Plain	38	11	9	18	72	96	31
Blackhall Colliery Welfare	38	7	6	25	70	115	20
Eppleton Colliery Welfare	38	3	6	29	41	121	12

1948-49

	P	W	D	L	F	A	Pts
Middlesbrough Reserves	38	26	6	6	126	47	58
South Shields	38	18	13	7	80	60	49
Gateshead Reserves	38	20	7	11	77	62	47
Spennymoor United	38	19	8	11	88	66	46
Sunderland Reserves	38	18	9	11	90	53	45
Consett	38	18	9	11	80	72	45
Ashington	38	18	8	12	96	83	44
Blyth Spartans	38	18	7	13	71	56	43
Carlisle United Reserves	38	19	5	14	62	68	43
Hartlepools United Reserves	38	16	7	15	85	97	39
West Stanley	38	15	8	15	82	79	38
Horden Colliery Welfare	38	14	9	15	67	54	37
Annfield Plain	38	15	7	16	74	65	37
Stockton	38	12	10	16	67	75	34
North Shields	38	15	4	19	74	94	34
Eppleton Colliery Welfare	38	11	9	18	64	101	31
Darlington Reserves	38	11	5	22	67	83	27
Workington	38	12	3	23	84	105	27
Murton Colliery Welfare	38	8	3	27	55	106	19
Blackhall Colliery Welfare	38	4	9	25	39	102	17

1949-50

	P	W	D	L	F	A	Pts
North Shields	38	24	6	8	95	60	54
West Stanley	38	23	6	9	65	45	52
Middlesbrough Reserves	38	22	7	9	124	53	51
Stockton	38	21	7	10	69	52	49
Sunderland Reserves	38	20	5	13	90	54	45
Blyth Spartans	38	18	8	12	87	69	44
Carlisle United Reserves	38	16	10	12	59	49	42
Horden Colliery Welfare	38	16	9	13	75	64	41
Workington	38	16	8	14	84	83	40
Spennymoor United	38	15	9	14	73	53	39
Hartlepools United Reserves	38	15	9	14	85	77	39
Consett	38	14	10	14	65	86	38
Murton Colliery Welfare	38	14	6	18	72	95	34
South Shields	38	11	11	16	61	78	33
Ashington	38	13	5	20	74	93	31
Gateshead Reserves	38	11	8	19	77	79	30
Annfield Plain	38	9	10	19	69	91	28
Darlington Reserves	38	11	5	22	63	91	27
Blackhall Colliery Welfare	38	9	5	24	63	115	23
Eppleton Colliery Welfare	38	8	4	26	51	114	20

1950-51

Stockton	38	25	6	7	79	37	56
Middlesbrough Reserves	38	25	5	8	100	51	55
Carlisle United Reserves	38	21	4	13	105	60	46
Horden Colliery Welfare	38	21	4	13	78	53	46
Workington	38	18	9	11	79	68	45
Sunderland Reserves	38	16	12	10	80	49	44
North Shields	38	16	12	10	80	64	44
Ashington	38	16	11	11	83	67	43
Spennymoor United	38	18	7	13	80	65	43
Blyth Spartans	38	15	9	14	67	76	39
Darlington Reserves	38	15	8	15	69	64	38
Blackhall Colliery Welfare	38	16	3	19	63	81	35
Consett	38	14	6	18	76	84	34
Hartlepools United Reserves	38	14	5	19	74	91	33
West Stanley	38	12	9	17	55	68	33
South Shields	38	12	8	18	48	81	32
Gateshead Reserves	38	10	6	22	60	82	26
Annfield Plain	38	11	4	23	64	95	26
Eppleton Colliery Welfare	38	6	11	21	51	95	23
Murton Colliery Welfare	38	5	9	24	49	109	19

1951-52

Middlesbrough Reserves	34	23	4	7	96	38	50
North Shields	34	21	3	10	95	43	45
Sunderland Reserves	34	18	8	8	82	50	44
Gateshead Reserves	34	17	6	11	86	64	40
Ashington	34	15	8	11	84	78	38
Blackhall Colliery Welfare	34	14	8	12	67	51	36
Hartlepools United Reserves	34	16	4	14	69	66	36
West Stanley	34	16	3	15	74	72	35
Spennymoor United	34	14	6	14	78	70	34
Blyth Spartans	34	11	10	13	53	68	32
Stockton	34	11	8	15	60	77	30
Horden Colliery Welfare	34	13	4	17	54	80	30
Carlisle United Reserves	34	11	6	17	66	63	28
South Shields	34	9	10	15	53	74	28
Consett	34	11	6	17	70	101	28
Annfield Plain	34	10	8	16	59	90	28
Darlington Reserves	34	9	9	16	58	84	27
Workington Reserves	34	7	9	18	69	104	23

1952-53

Sunderland Reserves	34	28	2	4	102	27	58
Middlesbrough Reserves	34	23	4	7	95	46	50
Carlisle United Reserves	34	19	7	8	88	55	45
Blyth Spartans	34	20	5	9	93	61	45
Darlington Reserves	34	16	8	10	76	64	40
Spennymoor United	34	10	14	10	68	71	34
Workington Reserves	34	13	7	14	74	68	33
North Shields	34	14	3	17	81	85	31
Gateshead Reserves	34	12	6	16	68	68	30
Ashington	34	12	6	16	71	76	30
Stockton	34	13	4	17	48	66	30
Consett	34	10	9	15	45	66	29
South Shields	34	10	8	16	41	55	28
West Stanley	34	9	10	15	54	85	28
Hartlepools United Reserves	34	9	9	16	61	85	27
Blackhall Colliery Welfare	34	9	8	17	50	80	26
Horden Colliery Welfare	34	9	6	19	55	80	24
Annfield Plain	34	9	6	19	56	88	24

1953-54

Middlesbrough Reserves	34	20	7	7	92	45	47
Sunderland Reserves	34	21	5	8	92	50	47
Spennymoor United	34	20	4	10	80	45	44
Horden Colliery Welfare	34	18	7	9	66	52	43
Hartlepools United Reserves	34	18	6	10	84	74	42
Gateshead Reserves	34	17	4	13	85	69	38
Annfield Plain	34	16	4	14	71	71	36
Consett	34	17	2	15	63	75	36
Carlisle United Reserves	34	17	1	16	100	78	35
South Shields	34	12	7	15	66	68	31
Darlington Reserves	34	12	5	17	76	78	29
Workington Reserves	34	12	5	17	63	69	29
Blackhall Colliery Welfare	34	12	5	17	50	66	29
Blyth Spartans	34	11	6	17	48	82	28
Ashington	34	11	5	18	61	79	27
North Shields	34	10	5	19	65	100	25
Stockton	34	10	4	20	56	86	24
West Stanley	34	8	6	20	59	90	22

1954-55

Middlesbrough Reserves	34	25	5	4	97	27	55
Sunderland Reserves	34	23	3	8	112	42	49
Spennymoor United	34	20	7	7	80	48	47
Workington Reserves	34	19	5	10	76	42	43
Horden Colliery Welfare	34	17	5	12	72	61	39
North Shields	34	14	9	11	76	73	37
South Shields	34	13	10	11	74	67	36
Darlington Reserves	34	14	7	13	81	64	35
Blyth Spartans	34	13	7	14	64	78	33
Gateshead Reserves	34	14	4	16	71	74	32
Carlisle United Reserves	34	14	3	17	85	70	31
Annfield Plain	34	11	9	14	67	86	31
Ashington	34	10	9	15	61	74	29
Hartlepools United Reserves	34	11	5	18	65	82	27
Consett	34	12	3	19	57	98	27
Stockton	34	8	7	19	48	77	23
Blackhall Colliery Welfare	34	8	4	22	33	95	20
West Stanley	34	6	6	22	45	106	18

1955-56

Middlesbrough Reserves	34	28	3	3	112	34	59
South Shields	34	20	7	7	96	51	47
Ashington	34	19	7	8	92	59	45
Workington Reserves	34	18	8	8	81	42	44
Sunderland Reserves	34	20	3	11	87	54	43
Gateshead Reserves	34	13	11	10	69	65	37
Blyth Spartans	34	17	3	14	68	80	37
Stockton	34	15	5	14	68	65	35
Carlisle United Reserves	34	14	6	14	74	56	34
Darlington Reserves	34	13	7	14	76	71	33
Annfield Plain	34	12	8	14	54	65	32
Spennymoor United	34	12	5	17	59	63	29
Consett	34	11	6	17	58	88	28
North Shields	34	10	6	18	54	78	26
Hartlepools United Reserves	34	10	6	18	48	78	26
Whitley Bay Athletic	34	8	8	18	62	92	24
Horden Colliery Welfare	34	8	5	21	50	94	21
West Stanley	34	4	4	26	34	107	12

1956-57

Spennymoor United	34	22	7	5	79	42	51
South Shields	34	22	5	7	88	39	49
North Shields	34	21	6	7	92	39	48
Ashington	34	20	8	6	117	55	48
Middlesbrough Reserves	34	20	7	7	92	43	47
Sunderland Reserves	34	20	5	9	97	46	45
Workington Reserves	34	16	7	11	74	57	39
Blyth Spartans	34	17	5	12	90	71	39
Hartlepools United Reserves	34	18	3	13	80	71	39
Darlington Reserves	34	14	6	14	78	75	34
Gateshead Reserves	34	13	6	15	62	79	32
Annfield Plain	34	10	7	17	66	86	27
Horden Colliery Welfare	34	11	4	19	54	84	26
Consett	34	8	4	22	51	86	20
Stockton	34	10	0	24	59	107	20
Carlisle United Reserves	34	5	8	21	35	83	18
West Stanley	34	6	4	24	32	100	16
Whitley Bay Athletic	34	6	2	26	44	127	14

1957-58

South Shields	34	27	3	4	107	42	57
Middlesbrough Reserves	34	22	5	7	92	33	49
Ashington	34	22	5	7	79	48	49
North Shields	34	16	9	9	66	44	41
Workington Reserves	34	17	5	12	73	59	39
Sunderland Reserves	34	17	4	13	84	50	38
Gateshead Reserves	34	15	8	11	82	72	38
Carlisle United Reserves	34	16	4	14	66	57	36
Blyth Spartans	34	14	7	13	66	66	35
Horden Colliery Welfare	34	13	9	12	58	59	35
Hartlepools United Reserves	34	15	4	15	72	61	34
Spennymoor United	34	13	8	13	70	72	34
Consett	34	13	6	15	68	63	32
Annfield Plain	34	9	7	18	57	96	25
Darlington Reserves	34	7	8	19	56	92	22
Stockton	34	7	5	22	60	107	19
West Stanley	34	8	2	24	47	97	18
Whitley Bay Athletic	34	3	5	26	35	120	11

1963-64

Horden Colliery Welfare	14	10	2	2	34	11	22
South Shields	14	11	0	3	37	20	22
Ashington	14	7	2	5	33	19	16
Blyth Spartans	14	7	2	5	43	33	16
Stockton	14	4	4	6	32	35	12
Annfield Plain	14	4	2	8	22	37	10
North Shields	14	2	3	9	25	40	7
Consett	14	2	3	9	14	45	7

1958-1960

The League did not operate but was reformed in 1960 as the Northern Counties League.

1960-61 Northern Counties League

North Shields	18	11	5	2	59	28	27
Ashington	18	12	2	4	50	22	26
Blyth Spartans	18	8	6	4	29	22	22
Gateshead	18	8	4	6	35	26	20
Consett	18	9	1	8	46	42	19
Scarborough	18	9	1	8	32	30	19
South Shields	18	7	4	7	31	32	18
Stockton	18	5	4	9	39	55	14
Horden Colliery Welfare	18	6	2	10	25	43	14
Annfield Plain	18	0	1	17	15	61	1

1961-62

Consett	24	16	3	5	77	44	35
South Shields	24	16	2	6	67	30	34
Ashington	24	14	5	5	63	36	33
Horden Colliery Welfare	24	13	4	7	57	50	30
Gateshead	24	13	3	8	42	34	29
Scarborough	24	11	5	8	48	31	27
North Shields	24	10	5	9	61	42	25
Darlington Reserves	24	8	5	11	55	57	21
Blyth Spartans	24	7	6	11	52	61	20
Carlisle United Reserves	24	6	7	11	31	43	19
Stockton	24	6	3	15	41	82	15
Annfield Plain	24	5	3	16	34	72	13
Workington Reserves	24	5	1	18	36	82	11

1962

The League reverted to title of the North-Eastern League.

1962-63

Scarborough	22	14	4	4	71	34	32
South Shields	22	13	5	4	48	27	31
North Shields	22	11	4	7	54	43	26
Blyth Spartans	22	11	3	8	49	39	25
Ashington	22	7	7	8	47	46	21
Darlington Reserves	22	10	1	11	35	37	21
Horden Colliery Welfare	22	8	5	9	33	36	21
Stockton	22	8	3	11	39	57	19
Consett	22	7	4	11	40	49	18
Workington Reserves	22	8	2	12	32	49	18
Annfield Plain	22	7	3	12	27	46	17
Carlisle United Reserves	22	6	3	13	35	47	15

Redcar Albion resigned on February 12th 1963 and their record was expunged.

FORMATION

Whereas in the north-west of England there were for many years two senior non-League competitions of roughly equal status – the Cheshire League and the Lancashire Combination, the position on the other side of the Pennines was more complex. The north-east had two senior competitions, the Northern League which after WWII was strictly amateur, and the North-Eastern League which was semi-professional. Moving south, there was the long established Midland League which was one of the strongest semi-professional leagues in the country and the Yorkshire League. The Yorkshire League though was not as strong as its north-western counterpart the Lancashire Combination and in reality acted almost as an unofficial feeder to the Midland League, with its better clubs sometimes moving up to the more widely based competition.

The collapse of the North-Eastern League in 1958 left its clubs to choose between the long journeys south to play in the Midland League or abandoning professionalism and joining the Northern League. In 1968 the formation of the Northern Premier League saw the best sides from all leagues in the northern third of the country creamed off into this new competition and in 1974 the distinction between amateur and professional players was abandoned. This meant that there were now three leagues east of the Pennines, all of which could theoretically provide clubs who could move up into the NPL. However there was a feeling that the better clubs were too thinly spread and that they could benefit from taking part in a merged, more competitive league that was part of a formal pyramid structure. Thus the Midland League and Yorkshire League agreed on such a merger and in 1982 became part of the new northern pyramid but the Northern League chose not to join in and remained independent. The new league was at first informally referred to as the "Northern Combination" but this title was already in use for a lower level competition and so the title Northern Counties (East) League (NCEL) was agreed.

CHANGES TO THE LEAGUE (NPL = Northern Premier League, CML = Central Midlands League)

1983   Shepshed Charterhouse left and joined the Southern League and Long Eaton Grange and Rolls Royce Welfare left and joined the CML. Skegness Town left and joined the Lincolnshire League and Leeds Ashley Road and Creswell Colliery also left. Premier Division reduced to 18 clubs. Retford Town joined from the Derbyshire Premier League, Armthorpe Welfare joined from the Doncaster Senior League and Yorkshire Main Colliery joined from the Sheffield & Hallamshire County Senior League. Collingham & Linton changed name to Collingham. Division Two (South) reduced to 13 clubs.

1984   Three points awarded for a win. Premier Division increased to 19 clubs. Sutton Trinity left and joined the CML and Winterton Rangers disbanded with financial problems. Scarborough Reserves, Brook Sports and Retford Rail also left. Divisions One and Two reorganised into three regional First Divisions – North with 17 clubs and Central and South with 16 clubs each. Norton Woodseats changed name to Dronfield United.

1985   Guisborough Town left and joined the Northern League and Retford Town also left. Premier Division increased to 20 clubs and the three regional first divisions re-organised into Divisions One and Two with 16 clubs each and Division Three with 15 clubs. Phoenix Park (Bradford) changed name to Eccleshill United and Garforth Miners changed name to Garforth Town. Glasshoughton Welfare joined from the West Yorkshire League. Blidworth Welfare left during the 1985-86 season and their record was expunged. They joined the CML in 1986.

1986   The national strike called in March 1984 by the then president of the National Union of Mineworkers Arthur Scargill, proved to be one of the most divisive events in modern British history. The strike lasted almost exactly a year and caused great bitterness and enmity between the mining communities of Yorkshire who were solidly behind the strike, and those of Derbyshire and Nottinghamshire where most continued to work. This bitterness continued for some time even after all miners returned to work and with no regional divisions in the 1985-86 season, fixtures between clubs from the two areas became much more common. Almost certainly this residue of bad feeling was a factor behind the decision of Arnold, Arnold Kingswell, Borrowash Victoria, Graham Street Prims, Harworth Colliery Institute, Heanor Town, Ilkeston Town, Kimberley Town, Lincoln United and Oakham United to leave and join the CML which set up a new Supreme Division to help accommodate the influx of clubs. Spalding United left and joined the United Counties League, Thorne Colliery left and joined the Doncaster & District League and Appleby-Frodingham Athletic and also left. Immingham Town and Winterton Rangers joined the NCEL but the Premier Division was reduced to 19 clubs, while Division Three was disbanded to allow Divisions One and Two both to increase to 18 clubs. B.S.C. Parkgate changed name to Parkgate and Stocksbridge Works changed name to Stocksbridge Park Steels.

1987   Alfreton Town, Eastwood Town, Farsley Celtic, Harrogate Town and Sutton Town left to become founder members of the new First Division of the NPL. Boston left and joined the CML and Bentley Victoria Welfare also left. The Premier Division was reduced to 17 clubs, Division One to 16 clubs and Division Two to 15 clubs.

1988   Staveley Works and Wombwell Sporting Association left and joined the CML. Brodsworth Miners Welfare joined from the Doncaster Senior League. Division Two reduced to 14 clubs.

1989   Emley left and joined the NPL and Long Eaton United left and joined the CML. The Premier Division increased to 18 clubs by the addition of North Shields from the Northern League and Sutton Town who were relegated from the NPL. Division One was reduced to 15 clubs.

1990   Bridlington Town left and joined the NPL and Bridlington Trinity disbanded. Spennymoor United joined the Premier Division from the Northern League. A number of clubs were promoted or relegated based on the standard of their ground facilities. As a result the Premier Division was reduced to 16 clubs, Division One to 14 clubs and Division Two to 13 clubs. Frecheville Community Association left and joined the Sheffield County Senior League and Collingham and Woolley Miners Welfare also left. Parkgate changed name to R.E.S. Parkgate. Grimethorpe Miners Welfare resigned from Division One on 20th October, 1990 and their record was expunged.

1991   Guiseley left and joined the NPL. Divisions One and Two amalgamated and a new Division One formed with 16 clubs while the Premier Division increased to 19 clubs. Rossington Main joined from the CML. Fryston Colliery Welfare, Kiveton Park and Mexborough Town Athletic left and joined the CML and Yorkshire Main Colliery left and joined the Sheffield County Senior League. Rowntree Mackintosh left and joined the Teesside League and Dronfield United and Pilkington Recreation also left.

1992   North Shields left to join the NPL but were in administration and unable to give the financial guarantees the league demanded. With new backers, they reformed and joined the Wearside League. York Railway Institute left and joined the York & District League. Sutton Town changed name to Ashfield United. Hucknall Town and Lincoln United joined from the CML. Premier Division increased to 20 clubs and Division One reduced to 15 clubs. Bradley Rangers failed to complete their fixtures in the 1992-93 season and their record was expunged.

1993   Spennymoor United left and joined the NPL. Arnold Town and Louth United joined from the CML.

1994   Blidworth Welfare joined from the CML. Division One increased to 16 clubs. R.E.S. Parkgate changed name to Parkgate.

1995   Lincoln United left and joined the NPL. Goole Town joined the Premier Division from the NPL and Borrowash Victoria joined Division One from the CML. Division One increased to 17 clubs. Immingham Town disbanded in December 1995 and their record was expunged.

1996   Goole Town disbanded and Stocksbridge Park Steels left and joined the NPL. Maltby Miners Welfare changed name to Maltby Main. Glapwell joined from the CML. Division One reduced to 15 clubs.

1997   Belper Town left and joined the NPL and Ashfield United stopped playing temporarily until their new ground was ready. However this never happened and the club disbanded. Curzon Ashton joined the Premier Division from the NPL and Staveley Miners Welfare joined Division One from the CML.

1998   Hucknall Town left and joined the NPL, Curzon Ashton left and joined the North-West Counties League and Blidworth Welfare left and joined the CML. Buxton joined the Premier Division from the NPL. Division One reduced to 13 clubs.

1999   Ossett Town left and joined the NPL and Alfreton Town joined the Premier Division from the NPL. Goole and Mickleover Sports joined from the CML and Bridlington Town joined from the East Riding County League. Division One increased to 16 clubs.

2000   North Ferriby United left and joined the NPL and Gedling Town joined from the CML.

2001   Ossett Albion left and joined the NPL and Lincoln Moorlands joined from the CML.

2002   Alfreton Town left and joined the NPL and Denaby United disbanded. Ossett Albion joined the Premier Division from the NPL and Long Eaton United and Shirebrook Town joined Division One from the CML.

2003   Bridlington Town left and joined the NPL and Eastwood Town joined the Premier Division from the NPL. Hatfield Main left and joined the Doncaster Senior League. Carlton Town, South Normanton Athletic and Sutton Town (formed in 2000 and known as North Notts until 2002) joined from the CML.

Table errors – None.

The previous leagues and divisions of the founder members are shown below in the first season's tables with M referring to ex-Midland League clubs and Y to ex-Yorkshire League clubs. Of the Midland League members, the only first teams who did join the NCEL were Ashby of the Premier Division and Attenborough of Division One who joined the Derbyshire Premier League which became the Central Midlands League in 1983. Folk House Old Boys changed name to Blidworth Welfare in 1982, between leaving the Midland League and joining the NCEL. The only Yorkshire League club not to join the NCEL was Rawmarsh Welfare whose next league has not been traced. Rowntree Mackintosh were the only founder member of the NCEL not to have come from the Midland League or Yorkshire League, having joined the NCEL direct from the York & District League.

1982-83

Premier Division

Shepshed Charterhouse (M-P)	38	24	8	6	109	34	56
Eastwood Town (M-P)	38	21	11	6	71	41	53
Belper Town (M-P)	38	21	10	7	75	32	52
Spalding United (M-P)	38	19	14	5	69	44	52
Guiseley (Y-1)	38	21	9	8	72	35	51
Winterton Rangers (Y-1)	38	20	9	9	55	32	49
Thackley (Y-1)	38	18	11	9	62	42	47
Arnold (M-P)	38	17	12	9	77	56	46
Heanor Town (M-P)	38	17	12	9	50	43	46
Emley (Y-1)	38	14	11	13	74	58	39
Appleby-Frodingham Ath. (M-P)	38	15	9	14	59	61	39
Guisborough Town (M-P)	38	16	6	16	59	59	38
Alfreton Town (M-P)	38	16	3	19	47	55	35
Sutton Town (M-P)	38	12	10	16	59	64	34
Ilkeston Town (M-P)	38	10	11	17	50	73	31
Boston (M-P)	38	10	11	17	53	91	31
Bridlington Trinity (M-P)	38	10	3	25	39	89	23
Skegness Town (M-P)	38	5	8	25	46	82	18
Bentley Victoria Welfare (Y-1)	38	6	2	30	44	107	14
Mexborough Town Ath. (M-P)	38	2	2	34	32	104	6

Division One (North)

Scarborough Reserves (Y-1)	26	17	6	3	53	20	40
North Ferriby United (Y-1)	26	14	10	2	48	24	38
Farsley Celtic (Y-1)	26	13	8	5	53	30	34
Harrogate Town (Y-2)	26	12	10	4	42	23	34
Garforth Miners (Y-2)	26	13	6	7	38	30	32
Ossett Town (Y-2)	26	13	5	8	43	30	31
Ossett Albion (Y-1)	26	8	10	8	41	38	26
Liversedge (Y-1)	26	8	9	9	35	35	25
Bradley Rangers (Y-2)	26	8	7	11	41	51	23
Leeds Ashley Road (Y-1)	26	7	6	13	30	44	20
Hatfield Main (Y-2)	26	6	5	15	31	50	17
Bridlington Town (Y-2)	26	3	10	13	28	49	16
York Railway Institute (Y-1)	26	4	6	16	39	64	14
Hall Road Rangers (Y-2)	26	4	6	16	22	56	14

Division One (South)

Lincoln United (Y-1)	26	16	7	3	55	25	39
Staveley Works (M-1)	26	16	4	6	50	30	36
Sheffield (Y-1)	26	12	8	6	48	34	32
Frecheville Commun. Assoc. (Y-1)	26	12	7	7	35	28	31
Denaby United (Y-3)	26	11	8	7	54	41	30
Maltby Miners (Y-2)	26	10	9	7	50	43	29
B.S.C. Parkgate (Y-2)	26	9	6	11	37	37	24
Arnold Kingswell (M-1)	26	8	8	10	43	46	24
Norton Woodseats (Y-2)	26	10	3	13	32	37	23
Hallam (Y-1)	26	9	5	12	31	44	23
Harworth Colliery Institute (Y-2)	26	5	12	9	34	35	22
Long Eaton United (M-P)	26	8	6	12	33	40	22
Brigg Town (M-P)	26	4	7	15	26	59	15
Kimberley Town (M-1)	26	3	8	15	29	58	14

Division Two (North)

Rowntree Mackintosh (Y & D)	26	18	6	2	73	29	42
Pontefract Collieries (Y-3)	26	18	4	4	63	29	40
Tadcaster Albion (Y-3)	26	15	5	6	48	34	35
Yorkshire Amateurs (Y-2)	26	9	9	8	48	38	27
Pilkington Recreation (Y-2)	26	10	7	9	44	44	27
Grimethorpe MWES (Y-2)	26	8	10	8	36	32	26
Collingham & Linton (Y-3)	26	10	6	10	40	43	26
Phoenix Park (Bradford) (Y-3)	26	11	3	12	43	44	25
Fryston Colliery Welfare (Y-2)	26	9	5	12	45	47	23
Thorne Colliery (Y-3)	26	9	5	12	37	57	23
Brook Sports (Y-3)	26	8	6	12	32	47	22
Selby Town (Y-3)	26	8	5	13	38	46	21
Pickering Town (Y-3)	26	7	6	13	26	40	20
Harrogate Railway Ath. (Y-3)	26	2	3	21	19	62	7

Division Two (South)

Woolley Miners Welfare (Y-3)	26	19	4	3	61	13	42
Borrowash Victoria (M-1)	26	16	8	2	57	20	40
Worsborough Bridge MW (Y-3)	26	15	3	8	47	40	33
Oakham United (M-1)	26	14	4	8	51	44	32
Stocksbridge Works S.S. (Y-3)	26	12	6	8	41	26	30
Graham Street Prims (M-1)	26	12	5	9	49	33	29
Kiveton Park (Y-2)	26	11	6	9	52	40	28
Long Eaton Grange (M-1)	26	9	6	11	40	45	24
Blidworth Welfare # (M-1)	26	10	3	13	40	46	23
Rolls Royce Welfare (M-1)	26	7	9	10	45	59	23
Creswell Colliery (M-1)	26	8	3	15	37	60	19
Retford Rail (M-1)	26	6	4	16	29	57	16
Wombwell Sporting Ass. (Y-3)	26	3	8	15	18	44	14
Sutton Trinity (M-1)	26	3	5	18	19	59	11

Formerly known as Folk House Old Boys

1983-84

Premier Division

Spalding United	34	20	8	6	76	43	48
Arnold	34	22	3	9	82	37	47
Emley	34	20	7	7	59	32	47
Alfreton Town	34	18	6	10	56	32	42
Eastwood Town	34	17	7	10	75	49	41
Ilkeston Town	34	14	11	9	49	38	39
Guiseley	34	14	11	9	54	48	39
Guisborough Town	34	16	6	12	58	54	38
Thackley	34	14	6	14	61	54	34
Winterton Rangers	34	13	7	14	48	42	33
Belper Town	34	12	8	14	47	46	32
Boston	34	10	12	12	46	57	32
Sutton Town	34	10	7	17	36	63	27
Appleby-Frodingham Athletic	34	8	9	17	51	75	25
Mexborough Town Athletic	34	6	12	16	34	68	24
Bridlington Trinity	34	7	9	18	40	60	23
Heanor Town	34	7	9	18	31	68	23
Bentley Victoria Welfare	34	6	6	22	45	82	18

Division One (North)

Pontefract Collieries	26	17	5	4	43	24	39
Rowntree Mackintosh	26	16	2	8	59	43	34
Farsley Celtic	26	12	6	8	51	33	30
Bradley Rangers	26	12	6	8	35	36	30
Ossett Albion	26	10	9	7	44	30	29
Garforth Miners	26	10	8	8	45	33	28
Harrogate Town	26	12	4	10	43	31	28
Scarborough Reserves	26	9	7	10	42	43	25
North Ferriby United	26	8	10	8	33	35	24
York Railway Institute	26	9	6	11	35	45	24
Bridlington Town	26	7	9	10	30	50	23
Hatfield Main	26	6	7	13	38	45	19
Liversedge	26	5	7	14	29	53	17
Ossett Town	26	4	6	16	34	60	14

Division One (South)

Borrowash Victoria	26	18	3	5	61	24	39
Denaby United	26	16	4	6	58	28	36
Woolley Miners Welfare	26	14	6	6	61	33	34
Sheffield	26	12	6	8	44	38	30
Lincoln United	26	11	7	8	39	30	29
Maltby Miners #	26	11	7	8	36	29	27
B.S.C. Parkgate	26	11	5	10	29	29	27
Staveley Works	26	10	5	11	41	34	25
Hallam	26	8	7	11	28	39	23
Long Eaton United	26	7	8	11	24	38	22
Frecheville Community Assoc.	26	6	10	10	33	48	22
Arnold Kingswell	26	7	7	12	30	44	21
Norton Woodseats	26	5	4	17	23	59	14
Harworth Colliery Institute	26	5	3	18	19	53	13

Maltby Miners had 2 points deducted

Division Two (North)

Harrogate Railway Athletic	26	19	6	1	72	23	44
Armthorpe Welfare	26	17	5	4	48	26	39
Yorkshire Amateurs	26	14	7	5	42	21	35
Selby Town	26	12	7	7	48	30	31
Phoenix Park (Bradford)	26	12	7	7	49	36	31
Pickering Town	26	13	2	11	36	34	28
Fryston Colliery Welfare	26	10	6	10	48	41	26
Thorne Colliery	26	10	6	10	43	41	26
Grimethorpe MWES	26	8	9	9	38	39	25
Hall Road Rangers	26	5	8	13	36	57	18
Collingham	26	5	6	15	26	47	16
Pilkington Recreation	26	4	7	15	33	55	15
Tadcaster Albion	26	3	9	14	23	56	15
Brook Sports	26	5	5	16	27	63	15

Division Two (South)

Retford Town	24	18	3	3	63	22	39
Kimberley Town	24	16	4	4	39	21	36
Graham Street Prims	24	15	3	6	58	37	33
Brigg Town	24	13	6	5	44	30	32
Oakham United	24	12	3	9	44	28	27
Yorkshire Main Colliery	24	12	3	9	44	37	27
Worsborough Bridge MW	24	12	3	9	51	46	27
Wombwell Sporting Association	24	7	6	11	28	37	20
Blidworth Welfare	24	8	3	13	32	52	19
Kiveton Park	24	7	4	13	31	41	18
Stocksbridge Works S.S.	24	6	5	13	40	44	17
Retford Rail	24	5	4	15	27	53	14
Sutton Trinity	24	0	3	21	21	74	3

Division One (Central)

Armthorpe Welfare	30	21	5	4	68	26	68
Brigg Town	30	19	7	4	68	36	64
Woolley Miners Welfare	30	19	6	5	67	38	63
Ossett Albion	30	16	7	7	55	28	55
Hatfield Main	30	16	7	7	56	35	55
Pilkington Recreation	30	14	4	12	41	42	46
Thorne Colliery	30	13	6	11	54	45	45
Ossett Town	30	12	6	12	51	37	42
B.S.C. Parkgate	30	12	6	12	52	41	42
Grimethorpe MW	30	12	6	12	59	53	42
Maltby Miners	30	13	3	14	49	46	42
Yorkshire Main Colliery	30	11	8	11	53	56	41
Worsborough Bridge MW	30	8	7	15	48	67	31
Stocksbridge Works	30	6	2	22	31	76	20
Wombwell Sporting Association	30	3	5	22	23	70	14
Fryston Colliery Welfare	30	2	1	27	26	105	7

Division One (South)

Long Eaton United	30	21	5	4	58	23	68
Borrowash Victoria	30	20	5	5	64	32	65
Dronfield United #	30	18	4	8	55	35	58
Retford Town	30	17	5	8	60	36	56
Harworth Colliery Institute	30	14	7	9	42	33	49
Sheffield	30	13	8	9	58	39	47
Staveley Works	30	13	5	12	42	39	44
Arnold Kingswell	30	12	6	12	48	42	42
Hallam	30	10	9	11	46	41	39
Frecheville Community Assoc.	30	10	9	11	47	45	39
Lincoln United	30	10	8	12	37	35	38
Kiveton Park	30	10	5	15	29	49	35
Oakham United	30	8	8	14	30	44	32
Graham Street Prims	30	9	4	17	28	45	31
Blidworth Welfare	30	7	1	22	32	87	22
Kimberley Town	30	2	3	25	21	72	9

Formerly known as Norton Woodseats

1984-85

Premier Division

Belper Town	36	25	6	5	74	30	81
Eastwood Town	36	23	3	10	98	59	72
Guiseley	36	21	7	8	78	47	70
Alfreton Town	36	20	6	10	69	39	66
Guisborough Town	36	18	8	10	71	49	62
Denaby United	36	18	8	10	71	51	62
Arnold	36	17	9	10	72	49	60
Emley	36	16	7	13	67	52	55
Bridlington Trinity	36	16	5	15	71	67	53
Thackley	36	15	6	15	55	61	51
Spalding United	36	14	8	14	55	48	50
Sutton Town	36	14	5	17	45	69	47
Ilkeston Town	36	14	4	18	49	54	46
Pontefract Collieries	36	11	10	15	45	54	43
Bentley Victoria Welfare	36	11	6	19	47	67	39
Appleby-Frodingham Athletic	36	8	9	19	46	73	33
Boston	36	8	6	22	35	88	30
Heanor Town	36	8	5	23	50	89	29
Mexborough Town Athletic	36	2	8	26	32	84	14

Division One (North)

Farsley Celtic	32	18	10	4	66	28	64
Harrogate Town	32	17	9	6	61	35	60
Bradley Rangers	32	16	11	5	61	35	59
Harrogate Railway Athletic	32	17	7	8	65	41	58
Bridlington Town	32	16	6	10	57	46	54
Rowntree Mackintosh	32	15	8	9	62	37	53
North Ferriby United	32	16	5	11	54	42	53
Liversedge	32	14	6	12	55	50	48
Garforth Miners	32	11	9	12	53	57	42
York Railway Institute	32	11	9	12	51	55	42
Pickering Town	32	11	8	13	37	43	41
Phoenix Park (Bradford)	32	10	8	14	57	59	38
Selby Town	32	10	7	15	43	59	37
Hall Road Rangers	32	9	6	17	45	70	33
Yorkshire Amateurs	32	7	7	18	34	60	28
Collingham	32	5	12	15	42	71	27
Tadcaster Albion	32	3	4	25	23	78	13

1985-86

Premier Division

Arnold #	38	24	8	6	83	36	79
Emley	38	22	11	5	77	47	77
Guiseley	38	22	6	10	81	52	72
Long Eaton United	38	19	11	8	70	39	68
Eastwood Town #	38	21	5	12	73	62	67
Alfreton Town	38	21	2	15	66	47	65
Sutton Town	38	18	6	14	69	57	60
Farsley Celtic	38	14	12	12	71	55	54
Belper Town	38	15	9	14	54	45	54
Thackley	38	14	11	13	52	58	53
Denaby United #	38	13	14	11	63	56	52
Pontefract Collieries	38	15	7	16	55	54	52
Armthorpe Welfare	38	15	7	16	57	58	52
Bentley Victoria Welfare	38	12	11	15	61	65	47
Heanor Town #	38	11	9	18	61	69	41
Spalding United	38	9	12	17	41	62	39
Boston	38	10	6	22	42	79	36
Appleby-Frodingham Athletic	38	6	12	20	40	83	30
Bridlington Trinity	38	4	14	20	34	85	26
Ilkeston Town	38	5	7	26	31	72	22

The four clubs marked each had 1 point deducted for breach of rule.

Division One

North Ferriby United	30	18	5	7	54	31	59
Sheffield	30	16	8	6	54	39	56
Harrogate Town	30	16	6	8	65	42	54
Rowntree Mackintosh	30	16	5	9	67	45	53
Ossett Albion	30	13	11	6	54	39	50
Bridlington Town	30	11	13	6	49	41	46
Borrowash Victoria	30	12	10	8	53	48	46
Harworth Colliery Institute	30	12	6	12	51	50	42
Woolley Miners Welfare #	30	12	7	11	59	59	42
Bradley Rangers	30	12	4	14	51	51	40
Hatfield Main	30	8	13	9	57	43	37
Brigg Town	30	8	8	14	31	42	32
Mexborough Town Athletic #	30	8	7	15	39	68	30
Harrogate Railway Athletic #	30	6	6	18	47	70	23
Dronfield United #	30	6	6	18	32	61	23
Pilkington Recreation	30	4	9	17	32	66	21

The four clubs marked each had 1 point deducted for breach of rule.

Division Two

Lincoln United	30	20	5	5	73	29	65
Garforth Town @	30	20	4	6	66	29	64
York Railway Institute	30	17	5	8	58	39	56
Staveley Works	30	17	4	9	52	33	55
Hallam	30	15	2	13	48	42	47
Maltby Miners	30	12	7	11	44	48	43
Grimethorpe MW *	30	12	7	11	50	48	40
Kiveton Park	30	11	6	13	42	48	39
B.S.C. Parkgate #	30	11	7	12	43	50	39
Liversedge	30	11	5	14	46	56	38
Frecheville Community Assoc.	30	9	8	13	43	61	35
Arnold Kingswell	30	10	4	16	48	57	34
Yorkshire Main Colliery #	30	10	5	15	38	53	34
Ossett Town	30	8	7	15	40	53	31
Pickering Town #	30	5	10	15	33	52	24
Thorne Colliery #	30	7	4	19	31	57	24

The four clubs marked each had 1 point deducted for breach of rule.
* Grimethorpe Miners Welfare had 3 points deducted for breach of rule.
@ Garforth Town previously known as Garforth Miners

Division Three

Collingham	26	16	7	3	66	23	55
Worsborough Bridge MW	26	14	5	7	60	32	47
Eccleshill United @	26	13	6	7	43	34	45
Glasshoughton Welfare	26	12	7	7	42	33	43
Yorkshire Amateurs #	26	11	10	5	38	29	42
Hall Road Rangers	26	9	9	8	37	33	36
Oakham United	26	10	6	10	38	35	36
Graham Street Prims	26	10	5	11	43	41	35
Tadcaster Albion	26	9	7	10	44	39	34
Stocksbridge Works	26	9	6	11	42	43	33
Selby Town	26	8	7	11	47	59	31
Fryston Colliery Welfare	26	5	6	15	32	72	21
Wombwell Sporting Association *	26	6	5	15	28	49	20
Kimberley Town	26	4	6	16	26	64	18

Blidworth Welfare left during the season – their record was expunged.
Yorkshire Amateurs had 1 point deducted for breach of rule.
* Wombwell Sporting Association had 3 points deducted.
@ Formerly known as Phoenix Park (Bradford)

1986-87

Premier Division

Alfreton Town	36	25	6	5	74	29	81
Farsley Celtic	36	24	6	6	74	41	78
North Ferriby United	36	20	10	6	57	26	70
Emley	36	17	10	9	60	41	61
Sutton Town	36	17	10	9	54	45	61
Denaby United	36	15	10	11	59	43	55
Thackley	36	14	13	9	47	45	55
Pontefract Collieries	36	16	6	14	54	44	54
Harrogate Town	36	14	10	12	48	48	52
Bridlington Town	36	12	14	10	57	49	50
Long Eaton United	36	12	11	13	41	43	47
Armthorpe Welfare	36	13	6	17	55	60	45
Eastwood Town	36	11	9	16	45	57	42
Bentley Victoria Welfare	36	10	9	17	64	77	39
Belper Town	36	8	12	16	49	47	36
Guiseley	36	9	8	19	46	76	35
Bridlington Trinity	36	6	11	19	46	76	29
Brigg Town	36	6	9	21	35	73	27
Boston	36	6	4	26	23	68	22

Division One

Ossett Albion	34	22	4	8	65	43	70
Rowntree Mackintosh	34	20	4	10	101	54	64
Hatfield Main	34	19	7	8	69	47	64
Harrogate Railway Athletic	34	19	7	8	65	44	64
Bradley Rangers	34	17	8	9	64	51	59
Hallam	34	16	8	10	49	37	56
Staveley Works	34	14	9	11	51	46	51
York Railway Institute	34	15	5	14	49	56	50
Maltby Miners	34	13	7	14	53	57	46
Pilkington Recreation	34	13	6	15	51	49	45
Garforth Town	34	11	10	13	44	48	43
Grimethorpe MW	34	13	4	17	60	65	43
Woolley Miners Welfare	34	11	9	14	57	61	42
Kiveton Park	34	11	6	17	41	64	39
Parkgate	34	10	8	16	51	57	38
Mexborough Town Athletic	34	8	10	16	38	64	34
Sheffield	34	9	6	19	41	55	33
Dronfield United	34	4	4	26	33	84	16

Division Two

Frecheville Community Assoc.	34	24	7	3	57	27	79
Eccleshill United	34	22	6	6	75	36	72
Immingham Town	34	18	4	12	53	43	58
Hall Road Rangers	34	16	9	9	72	48	57
Collingham	34	14	13	7	67	34	55
Worsborough Bridge MW	34	15	7	12	61	48	52
Stocksbridge Park Steels #	34	12	15	7	50	38	51
Selby Town	34	14	8	12	47	42	50
Yorkshire Amateurs	34	12	10	12	47	36	46
Ossett Town	34	12	10	12	42	52	46
Liversedge	34	10	13	11	40	45	43
Glasshoughton Welfare	34	11	9	14	50	52	42
Tadcaster Albion	34	11	7	16	38	46	40
Pickering Town	34	8	15	11	39	57	39
Yorkshire Main Colliery	34	8	13	13	43	60	37
Winterton Rangers	34	7	7	20	30	53	28
Wombwell Sporting Association	34	7	7	20	39	75	28
Fryston Colliery Welfare	34	2	6	26	18	76	12

formerly known as Stocksbridge Works

1987-88

Premier Division

Emley	32	20	8	4	57	21	68
Armthorpe Welfare	32	21	5	6	56	36	68
Denaby United	32	19	4	9	61	46	61
Bridlington Town	32	18	5	9	63	25	59
Thackley	32	16	8	8	50	37	56
North Ferriby United	32	12	11	9	49	41	47
Guiseley	32	14	5	13	52	51	47
Pontefract Collieries	32	11	11	10	42	42	43
Grimethorpe MW	32	11	9	12	46	49	42
Hallam	32	11	6	15	48	53	39
Hatfield Main	32	11	6	15	52	59	39
Harrogate Railway Athletic	32	9	9	14	40	56	36
Bridlington Trinity	32	8	9	15	52	68	33
Long Eaton United	32	9	6	17	24	44	33
Brigg Town	32	8	8	16	40	57	32
Belper Town	32	5	12	15	32	52	27
Ossett Albion	32	4	9	19	31	58	21

Division One

York Railway Institute	30	22	2	6	66	29	68
Rowntree Mackintosh	30	20	5	5	74	35	65
Maltby Miners Welfare	30	18	6	6	61	32	60
Parkgate	30	18	4	8	52	34	58
Bradley Rangers	30	15	9	6	45	45	54
Woolley Miners Welfare	30	14	8	8	69	39	50
Eccleshill United	30	13	8	9	49	50	47
Sheffield	30	13	4	13	38	34	43
Immingham Town	30	9	10	11	41	40	37
Frecheville Community Assoc.	30	8	10	12	40	51	34
Kiveton Park	30	10	4	16	29	51	34
Staveley Works	30	9	5	16	42	65	32
Pilkington Recreation	30	6	7	17	30	65	25
Garforth Town	30	6	6	18	29	51	24
Mexborough Town Athletic	30	6	5	19	38	62	23
Dronfield United	30	3	7	20	36	75	16

Division Two

Pickering Town	28	18	6	4	66	33	60
Collingham	28	16	9	3	63	26	57
Yorkshire Amateurs	28	16	9	3	44	23	57
Ossett Town	28	16	7	5	78	37	55
Worsborough Bridge MW	28	14	4	10	54	43	46
Liversedge	28	13	5	10	51	40	44
Yorkshire Main Colliery	28	11	8	9	53	58	41
Stocksbridge Park Steels	28	11	7	10	50	37	40
Winterton Rangers	28	10	7	11	47	47	37
Selby Town	28	9	4	15	39	48	31
Hall Road Rangers	28	9	4	15	35	63	31
Glasshoughton Welfare	28	6	12	10	29	35	30
Fryston Colliery Welfare	28	6	4	18	30	60	22
Wombwell Sporting Association	28	5	5	18	27	60	20
Tadcaster Albion	28	1	7	20	19	75	10

1988-89

Premier Division

Emley	32	25	5	2	80	18	80
Hatfield Main	32	21	9	2	67	24	72
Bridlington Town	32	21	5	6	67	26	68
North Ferriby United	32	17	9	6	63	31	60
Guiseley	32	16	10	6	50	27	58
Denaby United	32	13	7	12	52	50	46
Pontefract Collieries	32	10	11	11	37	34	41
Harrogate Railway Athletic	32	10	11	11	41	43	41
Thackley	32	11	6	15	43	59	39
Belper Town	32	9	10	13	45	51	37
Armthorpe Welfare	32	9	9	14	44	60	36
Hallam	32	9	5	18	47	77	32
Long Eaton United	32	8	7	17	32	54	31
Brigg Town	32	8	7	17	43	66	31
Grimethorpe MW	32	8	5	19	38	59	29
Bridlington Trinity	32	6	7	19	40	72	25
Ossett Albion	32	5	9	18	33	71	24

Division One

Sheffield	30	21	5	4	76	25	68
Rowntree Mackintosh	30	18	6	6	68	36	60
Woolley Miners Welfare	30	16	11	3	49	28	59
Maltby Miners Welfare	30	17	5	8	68	38	56
Pickering Town	30	16	4	10	58	54	52
Garforth Town	30	15	5	10	56	34	50
Eccleshill United	30	15	4	11	47	39	49
Collingham	30	14	5	11	38	30	47
Immingham Town	30	12	10	8	39	31	46
Kiveton Park	30	11	1	18	30	44	34
Mexborough Town Athletic	30	8	7	15	28	40	31
Parkgate	30	8	6	16	29	54	30
Frecheville Community Assoc.	30	6	11	13	31	44	29
York Railway Institute	30	6	10	14	25	37	28
Bradley Rangers	30	6	3	21	22	62	21
Pilkington Recreation	30	3	3	24	18	86	12

Division Two

Ossett Town	26	19	3	4	76	17	60
Liversedge	26	16	4	6	52	24	52
Selby Town	26	15	5	6	54	35	50
Worsborough Bridge MW	26	14	5	7	64	41	47
Glasshoughton Welfare	26	14	3	9	52	36	45
Dronfield United	26	11	7	8	39	36	40
Hall Road Rangers	26	10	4	12	44	60	34
Yorkshire Main Colliery	26	9	5	12	45	46	32
Stocksbridge Park Steels	26	8	6	12	37	52	30
Tadcaster Albion	26	8	6	12	30	46	30
Winterton Rangers	26	8	6	12	37	63	30
Brodsworth Miners Welfare	26	6	8	12	21	43	26
Yorkshire Amateurs	26	6	3	17	30	55	21
Fryston Colliery Welfare	26	3	5	18	23	50	14

1989-90

Premier Division

Bridlington Town	34	22	9	3	72	24	75
North Shields	34	21	6	7	63	31	69
Denaby United	34	19	5	10	55	40	62
Bridlington Trinity	34	18	6	10	82	44	60
Harrogate Railway Athletic	34	17	9	8	59	50	60
North Ferriby United	34	18	5	11	66	43	59
Armthorpe Welfare	34	18	4	12	53	39	58
Sutton Town	34	16	9	9	52	38	57
Sheffield	34	15	10	9	44	33	55
Brigg Town	34	13	7	14	57	50	46
Guiseley	34	12	7	15	54	46	43
Belper Town	34	11	6	17	39	50	39
Pontefract Collieries	34	10	7	17	43	67	37
Hallam	34	9	8	17	45	64	35
Thackley	34	7	9	18	43	64	30
Ossett Albion	34	6	7	21	27	69	25
Grimethorpe MW	34	7	3	24	40	90	24
Hatfield Main	34	6	5	23	27	79	23

Division One

Rowntree Mackintosh	28	18	7	3	63	23	61
Liversedge	28	17	3	8	57	29	54
Ossett Town	28	15	9	4	49	22	54
Woolley Miners Welfare	28	15	5	8	51	33	50
Maltby Miners Welfare	28	12	11	5	51	29	47
Garforth Town	28	13	7	8	42	23	46
Eccleshill United	28	11	9	8	50	45	42
Kiveton Park	28	13	2	13	35	31	41
Immingham Town	28	10	7	11	28	37	37
Collingham	28	10	3	15	29	41	33
Frecheville Community Assoc.	28	8	7	13	41	45	31
Parkgate	28	7	10	11	33	42	31
York Railway Institute	28	9	3	16	34	66	30
Pickering Town	28	6	5	17	39	64	23
Mexborough Town Athletic	28	1	2	25	17	89	5

Division Two

Winterton Rangers	26	15	6	5	46	28	51
Selby Town	26	13	8	5	51	29	47
Bradley Rangers	26	12	9	5	48	34	45
Fryston Colliery Welfare	26	12	8	6	39	29	44
Yorkshire Main Colliery	26	13	3	10	41	46	42
Glasshoughton Welfare	26	10	7	9	40	35	37
Stocksbridge Park Steels	26	9	9	8	36	28	36
Yorkshire Amateurs	26	8	9	9	41	34	33
Brodsworth Miners Welfare	26	7	11	8	35	41	32
Tadcaster Albion	26	8	6	12	31	38	30
Worsborough Bridge MW	26	7	8	11	36	40	29
Hall Road Rangers	26	5	9	12	25	47	24
Dronfield United	26	5	8	13	30	47	23
Pilkington Recreation	26	4	7	15	20	43	19

Winterton Rangers were promoted to the Premier Division.

1990-91

Premier Division

Guiseley	30	24	4	2	78	25	76
North Shields	30	23	2	5	75	29	71
Spennymoor United	30	19	4	7	55	29	61
North Ferriby United	30	14	8	8	55	42	50
Brigg Town	30	13	8	9	40	40	47
Maltby Miners Welfare	30	13	7	10	44	46	46
Harrogate Railway Athletic	30	12	9	9	49	40	45
Ossett Town	30	10	10	10	42	38	40
Armthorpe Welfare	30	10	6	14	52	55	36
Winterton Rangers	30	9	9	12	49	65	36
Thackley	30	9	7	14	43	46	34
Sutton Town	30	9	6	15	53	60	33
Belper Town	30	7	10	13	37	52	31
Ossett Albion	30	3	12	15	34	51	21
Denaby United	30	5	6	19	33	81	21
Pontefract Collieries	30	4	4	22	34	74	16

Division One

Sheffield	24	21	1	2	60	16	64
Hallam	24	18	1	5	61	27	55
Liversedge	24	15	2	7	61	35	47
Pickering Town	24	15	2	7	54	41	47
Eccleshill United	24	14	2	8	58	36	44
Garforth Town	24	11	7	6	45	33	40
Selby Town	24	10	3	11	60	41	33
Hatfield Main	24	9	5	10	38	42	32
R.E.S. Parkgate	24	7	6	11	40	49	27
York Railway Institute	24	7	3	14	32	47	24
Glasshoughton Welfare	24	4	5	15	18	50	17
Yorkshire Main Colliery	24	2	3	19	16	61	9
Mexborough Town Athletic	24	3	0	21	16	81	9

Grimethorpe Miners Welfare resigned on 20th October and their record was expunged.

Division Two

Hall Road Rangers	24	15	5	4	42	25	50
Worsborough Bridge MW	24	14	5	5	45	22	47
Rowntree Mackintosh	24	12	8	4	46	25	44
Bradley Rangers	24	13	5	6	45	32	44
Yorkshire Amateurs	24	13	3	8	47	37	42
Tadcaster Albion	24	11	3	10	39	34	36
Stocksbridge Park Steels	24	9	8	7	41	35	35
Fryston Colliery Welfare	24	9	4	11	44	44	31
Immingham Town	24	7	7	10	29	43	28
Kiveton Park	24	7	4	13	30	43	25
Dronfield United	24	5	6	13	29	40	21
Brodsworth Miners Welfare	24	4	5	15	25	51	17
Pilkington Recreation	24	3	5	16	25	56	14

1991-92

Premier Division

North Shields	36	31	3	2	109	14	96
Sutton Town	36	21	9	6	79	41	72
Denaby United #	36	22	3	11	78	47	68
North Ferriby United	36	19	8	9	63	45	65
Spennymoor United	36	17	8	11	61	45	59
Sheffield	36	16	9	11	71	48	57
Maltby Miners Welfare	36	16	8	12	61	61	56
Brigg Town	36	15	7	14	44	42	52
Thackley	36	14	9	13	45	45	51
Ossett Albion	36	14	8	14	40	51	50
Belper Town	36	12	11	13	48	50	47
Ossett Town	36	11	12	13	48	57	45
Armthorpe Welfare	36	12	9	15	57	67	45
Liversedge	36	11	8	17	54	72	41
Winterton Rangers	36	10	5	21	53	78	35
Pontefract Collieries	36	9	7	20	36	71	34
Eccleshill United	36	7	10	19	38	83	31
Harrogate Railway Athletic	36	5	8	23	31	60	23
Glasshoughton Welfare	36	5	8	23	35	74	23

Denaby United had 1 point deducted.

Division One

Stocksbridge Park Steels	30	19	5	6	71	34	62
Pickering Town	30	19	4	7	84	46	61
Bradley Rangers	30	18	7	5	59	26	61
Yorkshire Amateurs	30	18	3	9	56	27	57
Hallam	30	17	6	7	57	36	57
Hall Road Rangers	30	17	5	8	68	36	56
Rossington Main	30	13	5	12	44	48	44
R.E.S. Parkgate	30	12	5	13	41	59	41
Immingham Town	30	12	4	14	48	64	40
Worsborough Bridge MW	30	11	6	13	44	43	39
Garforth Town	30	10	5	15	48	44	35
Tadcaster Albion	30	8	4	18	37	62	28
Selby Town	30	8	4	18	32	67	28
York Railway Institute	30	6	7	17	32	77	25
Brodsworth Miners Welfare	30	6	6	18	45	72	24
Hatfield Main #	30	7	2	21	36	71	22

Hatfield Main had 1 point deducted

1992-93

Premier Division

Spennymoor United	38	26	7	5	102	33	85
Pickering Town	38	27	4	7	90	48	85
North Ferriby United	38	23	7	8	90	40	76
Maltby Miners Welfare	38	21	11	6	69	40	74
Thackley	38	20	7	11	62	39	67
Brigg Town	38	16	14	8	55	39	62
Denaby United	38	15	11	12	71	63	56
Ossett Albion	38	16	7	15	68	60	55
Eccleshill United	38	16	6	16	65	65	54
Winterton Rangers	38	14	7	17	61	72	49
Ashfield United #	38	12	11	15	69	88	47
Ossett Town	38	13	7	18	69	71	46
Belper Town	38	11	12	15	56	62	45
Liversedge	38	12	8	18	56	77	44
Sheffield	38	12	6	20	55	70	42
Stocksbridge Park Steels	38	10	11	17	54	70	41
Pontefract Collieries	38	11	8	19	62	88	41
Glasshoughton Welfare	38	9	9	20	46	77	36
Armthorpe Welfare	38	8	8	22	49	81	32
Harrogate Railway Athletic	38	3	9	26	49	115	18

Formerly known as Sutton Town

Division One

Lincoln United	26	17	5	4	62	31	56
Hucknall Town	26	15	6	5	54	32	51
Hallam	26	15	5	6	50	23	50
Yorkshire Amateurs	26	14	3	9	42	29	45
R.E.S. Parkgate	26	12	9	5	39	38	45
Tadcaster Albion	26	12	5	9	51	43	41
Rossington Main	26	9	7	10	33	31	34
Hall Road Rangers	26	9	6	11	48	43	33
Garforth Town	26	8	8	10	34	38	32
Worsborough Bridge MW	26	7	8	11	33	48	29
Hatfield Main	26	6	6	14	40	63	24
Immingham Town	26	5	8	13	38	51	23
Brodsworth Miners Welfare	26	6	4	16	41	65	22
Selby Town	26	5	4	17	34	64	19

Bradley Rangers failed to complete their fixtures and their record was expunged.

1993-94

Premier Division

Stocksbridge Park Steels	38	23	5	10	82	39	74
Thackley	38	21	11	6	57	32	74
Lincoln United	38	21	9	8	82	44	72
Sheffield	38	22	5	11	69	49	71
Brigg Town	38	18	8	12	77	54	62
Pickering Town	38	17	10	11	76	61	61
Maltby Miners Welfare	38	18	6	14	77	62	60
Ossett Albion	38	16	12	10	73	59	60
North Ferriby United	38	18	5	15	57	43	59
Armthorpe Welfare	38	14	15	9	55	42	57
Liversedge	38	17	4	17	63	65	55
Glasshoughton Welfare	38	13	11	14	51	58	50
Denaby United	38	13	7	18	66	66	46
Hucknall Town	38	13	5	20	48	64	44
Belper Town	38	12	7	19	57	75	43
Ossett Town	38	10	11	17	43	71	41
Pontefract Collieries	38	10	10	18	52	71	40
Ashfield United	38	9	8	21	50	85	35
Eccleshill United	38	8	9	21	44	75	33
Winterton Rangers	38	6	4	28	40	103	22

Division One

Team	P	W	D	L	F	A	Pts
Arnold Town	28	20	1	7	88	34	61
Hallam	28	18	5	5	64	26	59
Louth United	28	17	4	7	72	38	55
Hatfield Main	28	17	4	7	61	33	55
Yorkshire Amateurs	28	16	4	8	51	25	52
Garforth Town	28	15	6	7	39	28	51
Rossington Main	28	12	4	12	43	47	40
Worsborough Bridge MW	28	11	3	14	49	47	36
Harrogate Railway Athletic	28	10	5	13	47	56	35
Hall Road Rangers	28	9	6	13	57	63	33
Selby Town #	28	10	5	13	44	66	29
Tadcaster Albion	28	8	2	18	38	73	26
R.E.S. Parkgate	28	6	5	17	43	69	23
Immingham Town	28	6	5	17	33	76	23
Brodsworth Miners Welfare	28	3	5	20	26	74	14

Selby Town had 6 points deducted

1994-95

Premier Division

Team	P	W	D	L	F	A	Pts
Lincoln United	38	29	5	4	116	49	92
Arnold Town	38	25	7	6	98	46	82
Stocksbridge Park Steels	38	21	6	11	74	46	69
Belper Town	38	19	8	11	78	44	65
Ashfield United	38	18	11	9	65	48	65
Pickering Town	38	19	7	12	89	63	64
North Ferriby United	38	18	8	12	68	60	62
Armthorpe Welfare	38	13	18	7	56	41	57
Thackley	38	15	11	12	76	56	56
Ossett Albion	38	15	9	14	48	57	54
Brigg Town	38	14	10	14	49	57	52
Ossett Town	38	12	10	16	50	56	46
Maltby Miners Welfare	38	13	7	18	59	71	46
Denaby United	38	12	9	17	48	77	45
Hucknall Town	38	9	13	16	47	60	40
Glasshoughton Welfare	38	10	9	19	60	68	39
Hallam	38	9	8	21	46	76	35
Sheffield	38	6	12	20	45	87	30
Liversedge	38	7	8	23	48	81	29
Pontefract Collieries	38	3	10	25	30	107	19

Division One

Team	P	W	D	L	F	A	Pts
Hatfield Main	30	25	2	3	88	32	77
Worsborough Bridge MW	30	19	4	7	66	40	61
Selby Town	30	16	9	5	62	38	57
Immingham Town #	30	18	4	8	66	43	56
Yorkshire Amateurs	30	15	8	7	53	29	53
Hall Road Rangers	30	15	7	8	57	44	52
Harrogate Railway Athletic	30	16	4	10	64	52	52
Eccleshill United	30	13	5	12	62	47	44
Garforth Town	30	11	8	11	58	49	41
Louth United	30	9	8	13	39	50	35
Rossington Main	30	9	7	14	48	63	34
Tadcaster Albion	30	6	8	16	36	59	26
Blidworth Welfare	30	7	5	18	39	63	26
Winterton Rangers	30	7	3	20	44	72	24
Parkgate	30	5	5	20	47	84	20
Brodsworth Miners Welfare	30	2	7	21	15	79	13

Immingham Town had 2 points deducted

1995-96   Premier Division

Team	P	W	D	L	F	A	Pts
Hatfield Main	38	22	9	7	77	45	75
Stocksbridge Park Steels	38	21	10	7	59	36	73
North Ferriby United	38	21	9	8	78	33	72
Belper Town	38	20	10	8	66	39	70
Thackley	38	20	9	9	60	40	69
Denaby United	38	19	5	14	63	56	62
Brigg Town	38	17	8	13	65	50	59
Ashfield United	38	17	5	16	56	50	56
Liversedge	38	16	7	15	52	49	55
Ossett Albion	38	13	12	13	56	55	51
Armthorpe Welfare	38	13	11	14	53	47	50
Pickering Town	38	14	5	19	73	86	47
Goole Town	38	13	8	17	53	74	47
Arnold Town	38	13	7	18	51	57	46
Ossett Town	38	12	9	17	48	61	45
Hucknall Town	38	12	6	20	52	67	42
Hallam	38	11	7	20	41	68	40
Glasshoughton Welfare	38	10	9	19	45	62	39
Maltby Miners Welfare	38	11	5	22	58	83	38
Sheffield	38	6	7	25	46	94	25

Division One

Team	P	W	D	L	F	A	Pts
Selby Town	30	19	6	5	79	34	63
Pontefract Collieries	30	19	6	5	76	33	63
Garforth Town	30	18	7	5	63	27	61
Yorkshire Amateurs	30	18	6	6	51	30	60
Hall Road Rangers	30	17	5	8	65	34	56
Eccleshill United	30	18	1	11	74	53	55
Borrowash Victoria	30	13	5	12	59	46	44
Harrogate Railway Athletic	30	12	5	13	48	52	41
Winterton Rangers	30	11	6	13	44	51	39
Rossington Main	30	10	7	13	43	55	37
Worsborough Bridge MW	30	9	5	16	48	60	32
Louth United	30	8	7	15	54	66	31
Blidworth Welfare	30	9	3	18	47	83	30
Tadcaster Albion	30	6	5	19	25	61	23
Parkgate	30	6	4	20	36	81	22
Brodsworth Miners Welfare	30	2	12	16	23	69	18

Immingham Town disbanded in December 1995 and their record was expunged.

1996-97   Premier Division

Team	P	W	D	L	F	A	Pts
Denaby United	38	25	10	3	82	33	85
Belper Town	38	24	7	7	78	41	79
Brigg Town	38	23	8	7	80	43	77
North Ferriby United	38	21	9	8	86	36	72
Ossett Albion	38	21	8	9	73	36	71
Hucknall Town	38	19	8	11	84	48	65
Hallam	38	17	7	14	56	69	58
Ossett Town	38	14	11	13	52	53	53
Arnold Town	38	12	15	11	48	43	51
Glasshoughton Welfare	38	13	12	13	58	58	51
Selby Town	38	14	9	15	63	69	51
Armthorpe Welfare	38	12	9	17	42	48	45
Thackley	38	12	9	17	43	58	45
Maltby Main	38	12	8	18	58	81	44
Pickering Town	38	11	8	19	45	72	41
Pontefract Collieries	38	8	11	19	44	73	35
Hatfield Main	38	8	10	20	40	75	34
Sheffield	38	7	11	20	50	70	32
Ashfield United	38	7	11	20	51	80	32
Liversedge	38	5	9	24	40	87	24

Division One

Team	P	W	D	L	F	A	Pts
Eccleshill United	28	21	4	3	81	30	67
Garforth Town	28	20	4	4	57	22	64
Harrogate Railway Athletic	28	15	7	6	54	32	52
Yorkshire Amateurs	28	15	4	9	52	52	49
Glapwell	28	14	4	10	52	41	46
Borrowash Victoria	28	12	6	10	47	39	42
Hall Road Rangers	28	12	5	11	48	46	41
Louth United	28	9	9	10	47	37	36
Rossington Main	28	10	6	12	44	46	36
Worsborough Bridge MW	28	9	8	11	41	49	35
Parkgate	28	8	7	13	38	46	31
Winterton Rangers	28	7	9	12	39	51	30
Tadcaster Albion	28	4	10	14	20	51	22
Brodsworth Miners Welfare	28	4	5	19	22	58	17
Blidworth Welfare	28	4	4	20	31	73	16

1997-98

Premier Division

Hucknall Town	38	26	8	4	90	34	86
North Ferriby United	38	25	6	7	89	37	81
Ossett Albion	38	21	11	6	59	25	74
Brigg Town	38	20	10	8	76	40	70
Glasshoughton Welfare	38	17	9	12	66	64	60
Maltby Main	38	17	8	13	51	40	59
Ossett Town	38	17	7	14	67	53	58
Eccleshill United	38	16	9	13	64	58	57
Armthorpe Welfare	38	16	8	14	60	44	56
Selby Town	38	15	6	17	60	75	51
Thackley	38	12	12	14	48	55	48
Denaby United	38	14	6	18	55	68	48
Pontefract Collieries	38	13	9	16	60	76	48
Arnold Town	38	10	16	12	55	52	46
Sheffield	38	13	7	18	62	72	46
Pickering Town	38	12	8	18	56	68	44
Hallam	38	10	10	18	52	77	40
Liversedge	38	7	9	22	41	88	30
Curzon Ashton	38	7	8	23	42	75	29
Hatfield Main	38	6	5	27	46	98	23

Division One

Garforth Town	28	23	3	2	77	17	72
Staveley Miners Welfare	28	15	9	4	51	30	54
Hall Road Rangers	28	16	4	8	68	34	52
Glapwell	28	14	4	10	59	50	46
Parkgate	28	14	3	11	61	47	45
Louth United	28	14	2	12	73	50	44
Worsborough Bridge MW	28	13	4	11	58	57	43
Borrowash Victoria	28	11	8	9	67	50	41
Rossington Main	28	11	4	13	41	46	37
Winterton Rangers	28	11	3	14	41	55	36
Harrogate Railway Athletic	28	10	4	14	58	52	34
Brodsworth Miners Welfare	28	8	9	11	53	43	33
Tadcaster Albion	28	8	6	14	56	46	30
Yorkshire Amateurs	28	8	5	15	49	57	29
Blidworth Welfare	28	0	0	28	8	186	0

1998-99

Premier Division

Ossett Albion	38	23	5	10	86	50	74
Ossett Town	38	22	7	9	76	44	73
Brigg Town	38	20	12	6	78	43	72
Hallam	38	22	5	11	95	63	71
North Ferriby United	38	19	12	7	92	50	69
Liversedge	38	21	4	13	87	63	67
Arnold Town	38	19	7	12	78	56	64
Denaby United	38	15	12	11	66	60	57
Garforth Town	38	15	9	14	74	70	54
Buxton	38	14	10	14	54	53	52
Selby Town	38	15	7	16	59	61	52
Sheffield	38	15	6	17	55	58	51
Armthorpe Welfare	38	13	11	14	46	50	50
Glasshoughton Welfare	38	13	9	16	58	71	48
Thackley	38	14	5	19	65	77	47
Eccleshill United	38	12	6	20	56	74	42
Staveley Miners Welfare #	38	9	11	18	50	84	36
Maltby Main *	38	8	6	24	51	87	26
Pontefract Collieries #	38	7	7	24	37	86	26
Pickering Town	38	5	7	26	44	107	22

Staveley Miners Welfare & Pontefract Collieries had 2 points deducted
* Maltby Main had 4 points deducted

Division One

Harrogate Railway Athletic	24	15	6	3	58	29	51
Brodsworth Miners Welfare	24	13	3	8	52	42	42
Glapwell	24	12	6	6	47	39	42
Parkgate	24	12	5	7	61	32	41
Borrowash Victoria	24	12	5	7	48	38	41
Worsborough Bridge MW	24	9	6	9	49	42	33
Hall Road Rangers	24	9	6	9	44	49	33
Hatfield Main #	24	10	3	11	27	47	31
Louth United	24	9	3	12	37	33	30
Yorkshire Amateurs	24	6	7	11	41	49	25
Tadcaster Albion	24	6	6	12	33	51	24
Rossington Main	24	6	4	14	37	51	22
Winterton Rangers	24	3	8	13	22	54	17

Hatfield Main had 2 points deducted

1999-2000   Premier Division

North Ferriby United	38	25	10	3	87	31	85
Brigg Town	38	25	6	7	73	38	81
Glasshoughton Welfare	38	20	6	12	68	57	66
Liversedge	38	20	5	13	76	45	65
Alfreton Town	38	17	11	10	73	49	62
Brodsworth Miners Welfare	38	15	10	13	66	69	55
Ossett Albion	38	15	9	14	70	60	54
Arnold Town	38	14	11	13	60	47	53
Selby Town	38	13	14	11	53	49	53
Eccleshill United	38	15	8	15	59	65	53
Armthorpe Welfare	38	14	10	14	45	50	52
Hallam	38	14	9	15	72	67	51
Denaby United	38	13	11	14	46	41	50
Sheffield	38	12	13	13	62	55	49
Garforth Town	38	10	11	17	53	65	41
Harrogate Railway Athletic	38	11	6	21	54	95	39
Maltby Main	38	8	12	18	36	58	36
Buxton #	38	11	6	21	35	67	36
Staveley Miners Welfare	38	9	8	21	53	83	35
Thackley	38	6	10	22	39	89	28

Buxton had 3 points deducted

Division One

Goole	30	22	5	3	66	19	71
Glapwell	30	18	6	6	74	36	60
Borrowash Victoria	30	14	8	8	48	35	50
Mickleover Sports	30	14	7	9	52	44	49
Bridlington Town	30	15	4	11	43	36	49
Winterton Rangers	30	13	9	8	52	31	48
Yorkshire Amateurs	30	14	5	11	55	37	47
Hall Road Rangers	30	14	5	11	58	49	47
Louth United	30	12	4	14	51	62	40
Worsborough Bridge MW	30	11	6	13	44	46	39
Pickering Town	30	11	5	14	46	36	38
Parkgate	30	11	5	14	58	59	38
Pontefract Collieries	30	8	9	13	34	50	33
Tadcaster Albion	30	7	3	20	33	84	24
Rossington Main	30	5	7	18	27	62	22
Hatfield Main	30	5	4	21	36	91	19

2000-01   Premier Division

Brigg Town	38	29	5	4	87	36	92
Ossett Albion	38	25	7	6	84	33	82
Alfreton Town	38	23	4	11	71	44	73
Goole	38	19	9	10	65	46	66
Hallam	38	19	7	12	61	51	64
Arnold Town	38	16	14	8	67	46	62
Sheffield	38	15	15	8	59	38	60
Thackley	38	16	9	13	59	57	57
Selby Town	38	16	7	15	71	71	55
Glapwell	38	13	11	14	62	58	50
Denaby United	38	15	4	19	54	63	49
Buxton	38	12	9	17	38	57	45
Harrogate Railway Athletic	38	11	9	18	59	65	42
Eccleshill United	38	9	13	16	48	58	40
Liversedge	38	9	13	16	50	63	40
Glasshoughton Welfare	38	9	11	18	57	64	38
Garforth Town	38	9	10	19	56	75	37
Brodsworth Miners Welfare #	38	11	7	20	41	86	37
Armthorpe Welfare	38	9	7	22	53	81	34
Staveley Miners Welfare	38	6	7	25	42	92	25

Brodsworth Miners Welfare had 3 points deducted

Division One

Borrowash Victoria	30	22	4	4	74	28	70
Pickering Town	30	21	6	3	67	24	69
Mickleover Sports	30	18	5	7	65	39	59
Bridlington Town	30	15	7	8	48	41	52
Gedling Town	30	14	7	9	47	37	49
Hall Road Rangers	30	14	6	10	43	37	48
Parkgate	30	13	6	11	60	52	45
Hatfield Main	30	13	4	13	54	49	43
Maltby Main	30	11	6	13	36	48	39
Yorkshire Amateurs	30	9	5	16	33	53	32
Worsborough Bridge MW	30	9	4	17	31	54	31
Louth United	30	8	6	16	48	58	30
Pontefract Collieries	30	6	9	15	37	56	27
Winterton Rangers #	30	8	6	16	30	53	27
Rossington Main	30	7	5	18	39	54	26
Tadcaster Albion	30	6	6	18	29	58	24

Winterton Rangers had 3 points deducted

2001-02

Premier Division

	P	W	D	L	F	A	Pts
Alfreton Town	38	27	5	6	94	36	86
Brigg Town	38	25	5	8	90	46	80
Hallam	38	21	6	11	72	62	69
Pickering Town	38	20	8	10	70	38	68
Harrogate Railway Athletic	38	17	10	11	83	61	61
Armthorpe Welfare	38	17	7	14	56	58	58
Selby Town	38	14	12	12	47	47	54
Thackley	38	14	11	13	48	47	53
Sheffield	38	14	10	14	54	62	52
Arnold Town	38	13	10	15	53	55	49
Liversedge	38	14	6	18	59	66	48
Goole	38	13	9	16	43	51	48
Eccleshill United	38	13	9	16	60	72	48
Glapwell	38	12	10	16	66	71	46
Brodsworth Miners Welfare #	38	13	9	16	68	74	45
Borrowash Victoria	38	10	13	15	49	67	43
Glasshoughton Welfare	38	10	10	18	49	62	40
Denaby United	38	11	5	22	47	78	38
Buxton	38	8	13	17	43	61	37
Garforth Town	38	8	4	26	46	83	28

Brodsworth Miners Welfare had 3 points deducted

Division One

	P	W	D	L	F	A	Pts
Gedling Town	30	21	5	4	75	42	68
Bridlington Town	30	20	4	6	73	25	64
Worsborough Bridge MW	30	18	8	4	70	37	62
Lincoln Moorlands	30	15	6	9	52	41	51
Mickleover Sports	30	16	2	12	51	42	50
Maltby Main	30	15	3	12	54	44	48
Winterton Rangers	30	14	6	10	44	36	48
Rossington Main	30	12	7	11	44	46	43
Hall Road Rangers	30	12	7	11	54	57	43
Hatfield Main	30	10	7	13	50	47	37
Louth United	30	10	5	15	36	46	35
Yorkshire Amateur	30	8	6	16	32	47	30
Tadcaster Albion	30	9	3	18	40	62	30
Parkgate	30	8	3	19	53	80	27
Staveley Miners Welfare	30	4	12	14	32	60	24
Pontefract Collieries	30	4	4	22	23	71	16

2002-03

Premier Division

	P	W	D	L	F	A	Pts
Bridlington Town	38	29	5	4	92	33	92
Brigg Town	38	22	6	10	75	42	72
Goole	38	20	11	7	68	36	71
Buxton	38	21	7	10	84	56	70
Ossett Albion	38	21	7	10	70	52	70
Thackley	38	17	11	10	53	39	62
Sheffield	38	17	8	13	74	55	59
Eccleshill United	38	16	7	15	61	57	55
Liversedge	38	16	6	16	59	65	54
Harrogate Railway Athletic	38	15	7	16	87	71	52
Glapwell	38	14	7	17	52	59	49
Glasshoughton Welfare	38	13	9	16	65	74	48
Pickering Town	38	14	5	19	49	51	47
Brodsworth Miners Welfare	38	13	7	18	64	84	46
Arnold Town	38	12	8	18	58	53	44
Selby Town	38	11	7	20	44	73	40
Hallam	38	10	9	19	50	75	39
Armthorpe Welfare	38	10	6	22	53	85	36
Borrowash Victoria	38	9	5	24	41	97	32
Garforth Town	38	9	4	25	47	89	31

Division One

	P	W	D	L	F	A	Pts
Mickleover Sports	32	24	3	5	62	26	75
Shirebrook Town	32	21	5	6	79	38	68
Long Eaton United	32	17	7	8	66	52	58
Pontefract Collieries	32	16	7	9	68	56	55
Hatfield Main	32	17	4	11	49	42	55
Gedling Town	32	15	8	9	70	48	53
Lincoln Moorlands	32	14	6	12	56	42	48
Parkgate	32	12	10	10	66	52	46
Hall Road Rangers	32	12	8	12	55	67	44
Winterton Rangers	32	10	8	14	48	54	38
Yorkshire Amateur	32	10	8	14	39	45	38
Rossington Main	32	9	10	13	45	59	37
Louth United	32	10	6	16	48	62	36
Worsborough Bridge MW	32	10	5	17	41	56	35
Maltby Main	32	10	3	19	51	80	33
Tadcaster Albion	32	6	4	22	30	59	22
Staveley Miners Welfare	32	5	6	21	34	69	21

2003-04

Premier Division

	P	W	D	L	F	A	Pts
Ossett Albion	38	22	10	6	76	37	76
Eastwood Town	38	23	7	8	73	34	76
Brigg Town	38	20	11	7	73	40	71
Sheffield	38	19	12	7	64	40	69
Pickering Town	38	19	10	9	67	44	67
Goole	38	18	10	10	67	44	64
Buxton	38	17	12	9	69	50	63
Selby Town	38	16	11	11	86	57	59
Liversedge	38	17	8	13	72	58	59
Glapwell	38	14	10	14	53	45	52
Thackley	38	14	9	15	61	67	51
Harrogate Railway	38	12	13	13	63	64	49
Mickleover Sports	38	14	5	19	52	66	47
Armthorpe Welfare	38	14	4	20	48	67	46
Hallam	38	13	5	20	56	76	44
Eccleshill United	38	12	8	18	52	74	44
Glasshoughton Welfare	38	10	7	21	58	83	37
Arnold Town	38	10	6	22	45	67	36
Borrowash Victoria	38	8	7	23	35	84	31
Broadsworth Miners Welfare	38	3	5	30	38	111	14

Division One

	P	W	D	L	F	A	Pts
Shirebrook Town	34	22	5	7	59	26	71
Long Eaton United	34	22	2	10	63	40	68
* Maltby Main	34	21	7	6	81	49	67
Sutton Town	34	19	8	7	79	37	65
Gedling Town	34	18	9	7	81	49	63
Garforth Town	34	17	7	10	60	47	58
Yorkshire Amateur	34	15	8	11	57	44	53
Lincoln Moorlands	34	14	10	10	53	40	52
Carlton Town	34	14	7	13	52	51	49
Parkgate	34	12	11	11	52	53	47
Winterton Rangers	34	13	8	13	52	56	47
Rossington Main	34	13	5	16	56	62	44
South Normanton Athletic	34	11	3	20	49	61	36
Hall Road Rangers	34	9	5	20	42	70	32
Worsborough Bridge	34	9	2	23	31	75	29
Staveley Miners Welfare	34	7	6	21	41	75	27
Pontefract Collieries	34	5	10	19	30	60	25
Tadcaster Albion	34	6	5	23	32	75	23

Maltby Main had 3 points deducted.

FORMATION

The explosive growth in the popularity of football in the last quarter of the 19th century meant that by about 1890 there was hardly a village of any size in England without its own club. However there were a few regional exceptions and the most significant of these was Yorkshire which – apart from the Sheffield area – had adopted rugby as its principal game. Gradually the major cities and towns in the county formed their own professional football clubs, most of whom were quickly elected to the Football League, but the formation of a successful county league took longer. There was a Yorkshire League in the 1890s and a Yorkshire Combination formed in 1910 but both of these lasted for only a very short time and it was not until 1920 that a viable Yorkshire League was formed with the following 13 founder members : Acomb, Bradford Park Avenue Reserves, Dewsbury & Savile, Fryston Colliery Welfare, Goole Shipyards, Harrogate, Rowntrees, Selby Town from the York & District League, Wakefield City, Wath Athletic, Wombwell, York Y.M.C.A. and Yorkshire Amateurs who were a new club.

CHANGES TO THE LEAGUE

1921   Harrogate, Wakefield City, Wath Athletic and Wombwell all left and joined the Midland League, placing their reserves in the Yorkshire League. Dewsbury & Savile also left. Houghton Main, Brodsworth Main, Halifax Town Reserves, Doncaster Rovers Reserves and Castleford Town Reserves joined. Goole Shipyards became known as Hook Shipyards (Goole). League increased to 17 clubs.

1922   York Y.M.C.A., Castleford Town Reserves, Wath Athletic Reserves, Hook Shipyards (Goole) and Rowntrees left. Bentley Colliery and Frickley Colliery joined from the Sheffield Association League and Castleford & Allerton United and Rothwell Athletic also joined. Harrogate and Wakefield City returned from the Midland League replacing their reserves with their first teams. League reduced to 16 clubs.

1923   Doncaster Rovers Reserves left and joined the Midland League and Houghton Main and Acomb also left. Leeds Harehills, York City Reserves, Methley Perseverance, Monckton Athletic and Altofts West Riding Colliery joined. League increased to 18 clubs.

1924   Bradford Park Avenue Reserves and Halifax Town Reserves left and joined the Midland Combination. Wombwell Reserves, Leeds Harehills, Rothwell Athletic and Yorkshire Amateurs also left. Goole Town, Leeds City, Bridlington Town and Bullcroft joined. Frickley Colliery joined the Midland League and replaced their first team with their reserves in the Yorkshire League. League reduced to 16 clubs.

1925   Bentley Colliery left and joined the Doncaster & District Senior League and Frickley Colliery Reserves and Bullcroft also left. Scarborough Penguins joined from the Scarborough & District League and O.C.O. Selby also joined. League reduced to 15 clubs.

1926   Fryston Colliery Welfare left. Castleford Town joined from the Midland League and Scarborough joined from the Northern League. League increased to 16 clubs.

1927   Scarborough left and joined the Midland League and Leeds City and Monckton Athletic also left. League reduced to 13 clubs.

1928   Scarborough Penguins merged with Scarborough on 26th October 1928 and so Scarborough Penguins continued in the league as Scarborough Reserves. Castleford & Allerton United and Wakefield City left. Bradford Park Avenue Reserves and Halifax Town Reserves joined from the Midland Combination. Bradford City Reserves joined from the Central League and Hull City "A" and Pontefract Borough also joined. League increased to 16 clubs.

1929   Bradford Park Avenue Reserves left and joined the Midland League and Castleford Town also left. Leeds United "A" joined. Methley Perseverance became Huddersfield Town "A" in mid-season. League reduced to 15 clubs. Pontefract Borough left in the middle of the 1929-30 season and their record was expunged.

1930   Bradford City Reserves left and joined the Midland League and Scarborough Reserves, Hull City "A" and Altofts West Riding Colliery also left. Yorkshire Amateurs and East Riding Amateurs joined. League reduced to 12 clubs and a subsidiary competition was run.

1931   York City Reserves left and joined the Midland League, Harrogate left and joined the Northern League and O.C.O. Selby, Brodsworth Main and East Riding Amateurs also left. League reduced to 7 clubs. It was decided to run two separate league competitions with the two clubs who were top of the tables playing each other to decide the league championship.

1932   Brodsworth Main, Thorne Colliery and Sheffield University joined. League increased to 10 clubs. Once again two separate competitions were run but Brodsworth Main, Sheffield University and Yorkshire Amateurs were not included in the final table for the second competition.

1933   South Kirkby Colliery, Upton Colliery and Bradford City "A" joined. League increased to 13 clubs and reverted to normal single league competition.

1934   York City Reserves joined from the Midland League and Sheffield Wednesday "A", Sheffield United "A", Castleford Town and Altofts West Riding Colliery also joined. League increased to 18 clubs.

1935   Brodsworth Main left. Worksop Town joined from the Central Combination and Bradford Park Avenue "A" and Barnoldswick Town also joined. League increased to 20 clubs.

1936   Barnoldswick Town, Castleford Town and Sheffield University left. Dinnington Athletic joined from the Sheffield Association League and Ollerton Colliery Reserves also joined. League reduced to 19 clubs.

1937   Bradford City "A" left. Bolsover Colliery joined from the Central Combination and Barnsley "A" also joined. Ollerton Colliery withdrew their reserves and moved their first team into the league from the Central Combination. League increased to 20 clubs.

1938   Bradford Park Avenue "A" left. Chesterfield "A" joined.

1939   Dinnington Athletic left and joined the Sheffield Association League and Altofts West Riding Colliery and Bolsover Colliery also left. Gainsborough Trinity Reserves, Ransome & Marles (Newark) and Scunthorpe United Reserves joined. However the 1939-40 season was abandoned when war was declared on September 3rd, 1939 and the league was unable to restart until 1945.

1945   When the league resumed after the war Ollerton Colliery and Ransome & Marles (Newark) joined the Midland League and Bridlington Town, Gainsborough Trinity Reserves, Upton Colliery, Worksop Town, Sheffield United "A", Chesterfield "A", Barnsley "A", Leeds United "A" and Sheffield Wednesday "A" also failed to rejoin. Ossett Town joined from the West Yorkshire League and Bradford United, Firbeck Main Colliery, Hull Amateurs, Wombwell Athletic and Bradford City "A" also joined. League reduced to 15 clubs.

1946   Bradford City "A" and Firbeck Main Colliery left. Chesterfield "A", Sheffield Wednesday "A", Leeds United "A", Gainsborough Trinity Reserves, Keighley Town, Harworth Colliery and Upton Colliery joined. League increased to 20 clubs.

1947   York City Reserves left and joined the Midland League and Hull Amateurs and Upton Colliery also left. Brodsworth Main, Barnsley "A" and Sheffield United "A" joined.

1948   Bradford United and Keighley Town left. Rotherham United "A" and Bradford Park Avenue "A" joined. Goole Town left and joined the Midland League and replaced their first team with their reserves in the Yorkshire League.

1949   Halifax Town Reserves left and joined the Midland League and were replaced by Halifax Town "A". South Kirkby Colliery and Bradford Park Avenue "A" relegated to new Second Division. Remaining 18 clubs formed Division One. Division Two formed with 18 clubs by the election of 16 new members: – Beighton Miners Welfare, Bentley Colliery, Dinnington Athletic, Sheffield and Stocksbridge Works who were all from the Sheffield Association League, plus Doncaster Rovers "A", Farsley Celtic, Frickley Colliery Reserves, Hull City "A", Kiveton Park, Maltby Main, Norton Woodseats, Retford Town Reserves (a new club), Scarborough Reserves, Worksop Town Reserves and York City "A".

1950   Scunthorpe United Reserves left and joined the Midland League and Harworth Colliery also left. Bradford United joined. Division Two reduced to 17 clubs.

1951   Bradford United, Dinnington Athletic, Kiveton Park and York City "A" left. Division Two reduced to 13 clubs.

1952   Gainsborough Trinity Reserves and Halifax Town "A" left. Briggs Sports Club, Hallam and Hampton Sports Club joined. Division Two increased to 14 clubs.

1953   Retford Town joined from the Central Alliance, replacing their reserves. Dunscroft Welfare and Rawmarsh Miners Welfare joined. Division Two increased to 16 clubs.

1954   Goole Town Reserves left. Halifax Town Reserves joined from the Midland League.

1955   Dunscroft Welfare, Maltby Main, Chesterfield "A" and Doncaster Rovers "A" left. Salts (Saltaire) joined from the West Riding County Amateur League and Harrogate Railway Athletic joined from the West Yorkshire League. Hatfield Main and York City "A" also joined.

1956   Goole Town Reserves joined. Wombwell Athletic changed name to Wombwell & Darfield. Division Two increased to 17 clubs.

1957   Hull City "A", Rotherham United "A", Barnsley "A", Bradford Park Avenue "A", Brodsworth Main and Briggs Sports Club left. Ossett Albion joined from the West Yorkshire League and Harrogate Town and East End Park W.M.C. also joined. Division Two reduced to 14 clubs.

1958   Halifax Town Reserves left and joined the North Regional League and Huddersfield Town "A" and Leeds United "A" also left. British Ropes (of Retford) joined from the Central Alliance and Dodworth Miners Welfare also joined. Wombwell & Darfield changed name to Wombwell. Division Two reduced to 13 clubs.

1959   Worksop Town Reserves left. Grimethorpe Miners Welfare, Bridlington Town and Doncaster United joined. Division Two increased to 15 clubs.

1960   Swillington Miners Welfare joined from the West Riding County Amateur League and Bridlington Trinity, Gainsborough Trinity Reserves and Swallownest Miners Welfare also joined. Division Two increased to 19 clubs.

1961   Retford Town left and joined the Midland League. Bentley Victoria abandoned senior football and joined Division Three of the Bentley & District League and Gainsborough Trinity Reserves, Hampton Sports Club, Sheffield Wednesday "A", Sheffield United "A", Beighton Miners Welfare, British Ropes and Dodworth Miners Welfare also left. Division One reduced to 16 clubs. Wombwell changed name to Wombwell Sporting. Hull Brunswick joined from the East Riding Amateur League and Brodsworth Main also joined. Division Two reduced to 14 clubs. Division Three formed with the following 9 new members: The reserves of Farsley Celtic, Harrogate Town and Salts (Saltaire)from the West Riding County Amateur League, plus Leeds United "A" and the reserves of East End Park W.M.C., Harrogate Railway Athletic, Ossett Albion, Ossett Town and Yorkshire Amateurs.

1962   East End Park W.M.C. withdrew their first team and reserves. Mexborough Town and Dodworth Miners Welfare joined Division Two which increased to 15 clubs. Leeds United "A" left. Division Three reduced to 7 clubs.

1963   Kiveton Park joined Division Two. Keighley Central and Slazengers joined Division Three. York City "A" left. Division Three increased to 9 clubs.

1964   Division Three disbanded and all members left the league, of those Keighley Central joined the West Yorkshire League. Dodworth Miners Welfare and South Kirkby Colliery also left. Barton Town joined from the Lincolnshire League and Retford Town Reserves also joined.

1965   Salts (Saltaire) left and joined the West Yorkshire League and Swillington Miners Welfare and Grimethorpe Miners Welfare also left. Denaby United joined from the Midland League and Heeley Amateurs and Leeds Ashley Road also joined.

1966   Both divisions increased to 17 clubs. Goole Town Reserves left. York City Reserves and Bradford City Reserves joined from the North Regional League, Micklefield Welfare joined from the West Yorkshire League and Hampton Sports also joined.

1967   Frickley Colliery Reserves and Bradford City Reserves left. Lincoln United joined from the Lincolnshire League and Thackley joined from the West Yorkshire League.

1968   Barton Town left and joined the Midland League and York City Reserves also left. Division One increased to 18 clubs. Guiseley joined from the West Yorkshire League and Hall Road Rangers joined from the East Riding County League. Frecheville Community Association also joined.

1969   Retford Town Reserves, Doncaster United and Micklefield Welfare left. Emley joined from the Huddersfield League and North Ferriby United joined from the East Riding Amateur League. Dinnington Athletic and Firth Vickers also joined. Division Two increased to 18 clubs.

1970   Barton Town from the Midland League and Winterton Rangers from the Lincolnshire League joined Division One. League split into three divisions. The bottom six in Division One were all relegated and no clubs promoted. Divisions One and Two reduced to 14 clubs each. Division Three formed of 15 clubs by relegating 9 clubs from Division Two who were joined by 6 new clubs: Bradford Park Avenue Reserves from the Northern Intermediate League, Brook Sports, International Harvesters, Leeds & Carnegie College, Sheffield Water Works and St. John College (York). Hampton Sports left.

1971   Division One increased to 16 clubs. Division Two increased to 15 clubs. Swallownest Miners Welfare and Firth Vickers left. Worsborough Bridge joined from the Sheffield & Hallamshire Senior League and Blackburn Welfare, Woolley Miners Welfare and Retford Town Reserves also joined. Division Three reduced to 14 clubs.

1972   Bridlington Trinity left and joined the Midland League. Divisions Two and Three increased to 16 clubs. Liversedge, Pickering Town, Sheffield Polytechnic and Worksop Town Reserves joined.

1973   Hull Brunswick disbanded and Bradford Park Avenue Reserves, Harrogate Railway Athletic and Retford Town Reserves also left. Maltby Miners Welfare joined from the Sheffield Senior League and Bentley Victoria Welfare, Redfearn National Glass and Tadcaster Albion also joined.

1974   Mexborough Town joined the Midland League and placed their reserves in the Yorkshire League. Dinnington Athletic left and joined the Rotherham Association League and Worksop Town Reserves and Sheffield Polytechnic also left. Division Two reduced to 15 clubs. B.S.C. Parkgate joined from the Sheffield & Hallamshire League and York Railway Institute also joined.

1975   Mexborough Town Reserves, International Harvesters and Blackburn Welfare left. Rossington Miners Welfare joined from the Doncaster & District League and Collingham and Dodworth Miners Welfare also joined.

1976   Division Two increased to 16 clubs. Brodsworth Main left. Fryston Colliery Welfare and Pilkington Recreation joined.

1977   Redfearn National Glass and Heeley left. Division Two reduced to 15 clubs. Harworth Colliery Institute joined.

1978   Division Two increased to 16 clubs and Division Three reduced to 15 clubs. St. John College (York) left and Garforth Miners joined from the West Yorkshire League.

1979   Dodworth Miners Welfare and Leeds & Carnegie College left. Pontefract Collieries joined. Division Three reduced to 14 clubs.

1980   Rossington Miners Welfare left and joined the Sheffield Senior League and Sheffield Water Works also left. Bradley Rangers joined from the West Yorkshire League and Grimethorpe Miners Welfare, Harrogate Railway Athletic and Y.W.A. (Southern) also joined. Division Three increased to 16 clubs.

1981   Barton Town left and joined the Lincolnshire League and Y.W.A. (Southern) also left. Phoenix Park joined. Division Three reduced to 15 clubs.

1982   The Yorkshire League merged with the Midland League (see *Non-League Football Tables 1889-2002* for complete set of tables) to form the Northern Counties East League (NCEL) and all clubs with the exception of Rawmarsh Welfare joined the new league. Bentley Victoria, Emley, Guiseley, Thackley and Winterton Rangers joined its Premier Division; Bradley Rangers, Bridlington Town, Farsley Celtic, Garforth Miners, Hall Road Rangers, Harrogate Town, Hatfield Main, Leeds Ashley Road, Liversedge, North Ferriby United, Ossett Albion, Ossett Town, Scarborough Reserves and York Railway Institute joined Division One (North); B.S.C. Parkgate, Denaby United, Frecheville Community Association, Hallam, Harworth Colliery Institute, Lincoln United, Maltby Miners Welfare, Norton Woodseats and Sheffield joined Division One (South); Brook Sports, Collingham, Fryston Colliery Welfare, Grimethorpe Miners Welfare, Harrogate Railway Athletic, Phoenix Park, Pickering Town, Pilkington Recreation, Pontefract Collieries, Selby Town, Tadcaster Albion, Thorne Colliery and Yorkshire Amateurs joined Division Two (North) and Kiveton Park, Stocksbridge Works, Wombwell Sporting, Woolley Miners Welfare and Worsborough Bridge joined Division Two (South). Rawmarsh Welfare played in the Sheffield and Hallamshire Cup in 1982-83 but the league they played in has not been traced.

The Yorkshire League tables as published contained a number of errors. Additional research has succeeded in correcting several of these, leaving those noted below.

1920-21 Total goals scored 1 less than total goals conceded.

1921-22 Total goals scored 3 more than total goals conceded.

1922-23 Total goals scored 1 more than total goals conceded.

1923-24 Total goals scored 1 less than total goals conceded.

1924-25 Total goals scored 8 more than total goals conceded.

1925-26 Total goals scored 14 more than total goals conceded.

1926-27 Total goals scored 1 more than total goals conceded.

1927-28 Total goals scored 5 more than total goals conceded.

1928-29 Total goals scored 13 more than total goals conceded.

1929-30 Total goals scored 6 more than total goals conceded.

1961-62 Division Two – Total goals scored 2 less than total goals conceded.

1962-63 Division One –Total goals scored 1 less than total goals conceded.

1962-63 Division Two – Goal record traced for only the top two clubs.

1963-64 Division Two – Total goals scored 6 less than total goals conceded.

1965-66 Division Two – Total goals scored 3 more than total goals conceded.

1966-67 Division One – Total goals scored 3 less than total goals conceded.

1966-67 Division Two – Total goals scored 10 less than total goals conceded.

1967-68 Division One – Total goals scored 21 more than total goals conceded.

1967-68 Division Two – Total goals scored 4 less than total goals conceded.

1968-69 Division One – Total goals scored 2 less than total goals conceded.

1968-69 Division Two – Total goals scored 7 less than total goals conceded.

1969-70 Division Two – Total goals scored 8 more than total goals conceded.

1970-71 Division Two – Total goals scored 12 less than total goals conceded.

1970-71 Division Three – Total goals scored 2 more than total goals conceded.

1920-21

Bradford Park Avenue Reserves	24	18	3	3	85	28	39
Wombwell	24	16	4	4	67	18	36
Wath Athletic	24	15	4	5	56	29	34
Harrogate	24	15	3	6	66	41	33
Selby Town	24	11	5	8	55	47	27
Wakefield City	24	10	6	8	41	33	26
Goole Shipyards	24	10	4	10	52	48	24
Rowntrees	24	9	2	13	42	45	20
Acomb	24	8	3	13	43	66	19
Fryston Colliery Welfare	24	7	5	12	35	59	19
Dewsbury & Savile	24	7	2	15	35	63	16
Yorkshire Amateurs	24	6	3	15	42	66	15
York Y.M.C.A.	24	2	0	22	18	95	4

1921-22

Houghton Main	32	24	4	4	86	25	52
Bradford Park Avenue Reserves	32	23	4	5	119	36	50
Brodsworth Main	32	20	7	5	81	34	47
Wombwell Reserves	32	21	4	7	86	45	46
Halifax Town Reserves	32	18	5	9	87	40	41
Doncaster Rovers Reserves	32	17	4	11	84	40	38
Selby Town	32	15	7	10	94	51	37
Rowntrees	32	14	9	9	60	44	37
Acomb	32	18	1	13	61	86	37
Wath Athletic Reserves	32	14	5	13	80	59	33
Fryston Colliery Welfare	32	13	2	17	76	65	28
Harrogate Reserves	32	10	5	17	62	74	25
Yorkshire Amateurs	32	9	4	19	69	72	22
Castleford Town Reserves	32	7	6	19	49	86	20
Hook Shipyards (Goole) #	32	7	4	21	40	51	18
Wakefield City Reserves	32	3	4	25	33	140	10
York Y.M.C.A.	32	1	1	30	23	239	3

Formerly known as Goole Shipyards

1922-23

Bradford Park Avenue Reserves	30	24	2	4	119	43	50
Halifax Town Reserves	30	22	3	5	90	37	47
Frickley Colliery	30	18	3	9	58	35	39
Castleford & Allerton United	30	17	4	9	58	40	38
Doncaster Rovers Reserves	30	14	8	8	52	38	36
Wakefield City	30	11	11	8	53	39	33
Selby Town	30	14	5	11	56	52	33
Wombwell Reserves	30	11	9	10	55	44	31
Brodsworth Main	30	11	9	10	51	56	31
Bentley Colliery	30	12	5	13	57	52	29
Fryston Colliery Welfare	30	9	6	15	45	48	24
Yorkshire Amateurs	30	8	7	15	49	78	23
Harrogate	30	8	6	16	30	50	22
Rothwell Athletic	30	6	5	19	27	81	17
Houghton Main	30	5	5	20	36	76	15
Acomb	30	4	4	22	42	108	12

1923-24

Methley Perseverance	34	24	6	4	84	24	54
Frickley Colliery	34	22	8	4	96	41	52
Bradford Park Avenue Reserves	34	22	5	7	96	38	49
Monckton Athletic	34	17	8	9	71	41	42
Altofts West Riding Colliery	34	17	5	12	67	47	39
Halifax Town Reserves	34	16	6	12	66	56	38
Brodsworth Main	34	15	7	12	62	65	37
Leeds Harehills	34	14	7	13	51	54	35
Wakefield City	34	15	5	14	51	54	35
Castleford & Allerton United	34	13	7	14	51	52	33
Harrogate	34	14	3	17	69	73	31
York City Reserves	34	10	9	15	36	58	29
Bentley Colliery	34	10	8	16	46	56	28
Wombwell Reserves	34	10	6	18	46	77	26
Fryston Colliery Welfare	34	10	5	19	46	60	25
Selby Town	34	10	4	20	65	81	24
Yorkshire Amateurs	34	8	4	22	50	99	20
Rothwell Athletic	34	6	3	25	28	106	15

1924-25

Brodsworth Main	30	21	4	5	73	28	46
Selby Town	30	17	6	7	77	57	40
Castleford & Allerton United	30	16	6	8	66	37	38
Fryston Colliery Welfare	30	17	3	10	58	41	37
Goole Town	30	15	6	9	49	46	36
Leeds City	30	13	7	10	59	44	33
Harrogate	30	12	7	11	46	49	31
Methley Perseverance	30	10	8	12	59	64	28
Bridlington Town	30	11	6	13	55	67	28
Altofts West Riding Colliery	30	9	8	13	30	44	26
Frickley Colliery Reserves	30	11	3	16	45	48	25
Bullcroft	30	11	3	16	49	66	25
Bentley Colliery	30	9	7	14	40	61	25
Wakefield City	30	7	9	14	38	48	23
York City Reserves	30	7	6	17	48	65	20
Monckton Athletic	30	8	3	19	40	59	19

1925-26

Methley Perseverance	28	20	4	4	99	36	44
Selby Town	28	20	4	4	73	46	44
Altofts West Riding Colliery	28	17	3	8	76	54	37
Leeds City	28	15	4	9	84	55	34
Harrogate	28	14	5	9	62	52	33
Brodsworth Main	28	13	5	10	81	66	31
Monckton Athletic	28	11	7	10	84	82	29
Scarborough Penguins	28	12	3	13	56	68	27
Castleford & Allerton United	28	11	2	15	62	61	24
Bridlington Town	28	9	6	13	55	69	24
Goole Town	28	9	6	13	49	72	24
O.C.O. Selby	28	8	5	15	66	75	21
York City Reserves	28	7	4	17	53	76	18
Wakefield City	28	6	4	18	35	71	16
Fryston Colliery Welfare	28	4	6	18	39	77	14

1926-27

Harrogate	30	21	6	3	102	51	48
Castleford Town	30	20	5	5	87	37	45
Selby Town	30	19	5	6	94	48	43
Goole Town	30	17	3	10	92	71	37
Scarborough Penguins	30	17	1	12	72	63	35
O.C.O. Selby	30	15	4	11	67	46	34
Castleford & Allerton United	30	14	6	10	66	56	34
York City Reserves	30	10	8	12	73	54	28
Brodsworth Main	30	12	4	14	63	77	28
Scarborough	30	10	7	13	74	69	27
Leeds City	30	11	4	15	69	59	26
Monckton Athletic	30	11	2	17	58	94	24
Methley Perseverance	30	10	3	17	69	111	23
Altofts West Riding Colliery	30	10	3	17	42	74	23
Bridlington Town	30	9	3	18	52	70	21
Wakefield City	30	0	4	26	24	123	4

1927-28

Goole Town	24	17	3	4	88	47	37
Selby Town	24	16	4	4	88	35	36
Altofts West Riding Colliery	24	16	4	4	73	31	36
Castleford Town	24	17	2	5	89	47	36
Harrogate	24	15	3	6	85	46	33
Bridlington Town	23	14	2	7	74	55	30
Brodsworth Main	24	9	4	11	57	59	22
O.C.O. Selby	24	9	2	13	49	60	20
York City Reserves	22	8	2	12	38	63	18
Castleford & Allerton United	24	6	4	14	62	83	16
Scarborough Penguins	23	5	2	16	56	82	12
Methley Perseverance	20	2	2	16	24	67	6
Wakefield City	24	1	0	23	31	134	2

Methley Perseverance were unable to complete their fixtures.

1928-29

Bradford Park Avenue Reserves	30	28	2	0	191	23	58
Selby Town	30	18	5	7	73	74	41
Bradford City Reserves	30	18	2	10	108	52	38
Halifax Town Reserves	30	15	7	8	87	47	37
Goole Town	30	15	3	12	81	82	33
Methley Perseverance	30	14	3	13	76	88	31
York City Reserves	30	13	5	12	61	85	31
Bridlington Town	30	13	2	15	93	71	28
Altofts West Riding Colliery	30	11	5	14	95	98	27
O.C.O. Selby	30	9	7	14	77	96	25
Scarborough Reserves #	30	11	3	16	60	81	25
Hull City "A"	30	11	2	17	73	85	24
Castleford Town	30	8	7	15	77	100	23
Harrogate	30	9	5	16	56	90	23
Brodsworth Main	30	9	2	19	63	114	20
Pontefract Borough	30	7	2	21	76	148	16

Scarborough and Scarborough Penguins merged on 26th October
1928 and Scarborough Penguins became Scarborough Reserves.

1929-30

Bradford City Reserves	26	19	4	3	100	44	42
Leeds United "A"	26	17	6	3	86	29	40
Harrogate	26	15	4	7	73	49	34
Scarborough Reserves	26	15	4	7	52	35	34
Goole Town	26	12	5	9	60	45	29
Selby Town	26	13	1	12	76	69	27
Bridlington Town	26	11	4	11	54	56	26
Halifax Town Reserves	25	9	5	11	53	53	23
York City Reserves	26	9	4	13	69	72	22
Huddersfield Town "A" #	26	5	9	12	39	57	19
Brodsworth Main	26	7	5	14	35	57	19
Hull City "A"	25	8	2	15	58	93	18
O.C.O. Selby	26	5	5	16	41	70	15
Altofts West Riding Colliery	26	6	2	18	42	103	14

Halifax Town Reserves v. Hull City "A" was not played.
Pontefract Borough left in mid-season and their record was expunged

when it was	18	1	2	15	17	14	4

Methley Perseverance became Huddersfield Town "A" in mid-season.

1930-31

Main Competition

Leeds United "A"	22	19	1	2	103	29	39
York City Reserves	22	18	0	4	87	40	36
Selby Town	22	13	5	4	81	50	31
Goole Town	22	13	3	6	68	40	29
Yorkshire Amateurs	22	10	2	10	52	51	22
Huddersfield Town "A"	22	10	1	11	59	51	21
Halifax Town Reserves	22	7	3	12	49	77	17
Harrogate	22	8	0	14	71	87	16
Bridlington Town	22	6	4	12	48	72	16
O.C.O. Selby	22	7	1	14	51	75	15
Brodsworth Main	22	7	1	14	44	83	15
East Riding Amateurs	22	3	1	18	37	95	7

Subsidiary Competition – Section A

York City Reserves	10	9	0	1	46	17	18
Selby Town	10	5	1	4	28	27	11
Bridlington Town	9	4	1	4	27	25	9
Goole Town	9	4	0	5	22	22	8
East Riding Amateurs	10	2	3	5	23	39	7
O.C.O. Selby	10	2	1	7	15	31	5

One game was not played

Subsidiary Competition – Section B

Leeds United "A"	10	9	1	0	47	14	19
Yorkshire Amateurs	10	6	3	1	28	16	15
Huddersfield Town "A"	10	5	1	4	22	23	11
Halifax Town Reserves	10	2	2	6	25	35	6
Harrogate	10	2	1	7	15	41	5
Brodsworth Main	10	2	0	8	20	28	4

Subsidiary Competition – Final

Leeds United "A" v York City Reserves   5-4

1931-32

First Competition

Huddersfield Town "A"	12	7	1	4	28	18	15
Selby Town	12	6	3	3	30	23	15
Leeds United "A"	12	6	2	4	28	18	14
Halifax Town Reserves	12	6	0	6	29	26	12
Yorkshire Amateurs	12	6	0	6	35	35	12
Goole Town	12	4	2	6	18	37	10
Bridlington Town	12	2	2	8	24	35	6

Second Competition

Yorkshire Amateurs	12	6	4	2	26	18	16
Halifax Town Reserves	12	7	0	5	31	25	14
Selby Town	12	5	4	3	25	21	14
Leeds United "A"	12	4	4	4	33	20	12
Huddersfield Town "A"	12	3	5	4	22	29	11
Goole Town	12	3	4	5	19	18	10
Bridlington Town	12	3	1	8	23	48	7

Championship Decider

Huddersfield Town "A" v Yorkshire Amateurs   1-0
(played at South Kirkby Colliery, 04/05/1932)

1932-33

First Competition

Selby Town	18	13	3	2	58	20	29
Leeds United "A"	18	12	3	3	45	25	27
Huddersfield Town "A"	18	10	5	3	55	31	25
Goole Town	18	11	2	5	41	24	24
Yorkshire Amateurs	18	9	5	4	46	26	23
Halifax Town Reserves	18	7	2	9	41	46	16
Brodsworth Main	18	5	5	8	36	46	15
Thorne Colliery	18	3	2	13	28	60	8
Bridlington Town	18	3	2	13	31	65	8
Sheffield University	18	2	1	15	28	66	5

Second Competition

Huddersfield Town "A"	12	8	1	3	38	13	17
Goole Town	12	7	1	4	31	21	15
Leeds United "A"	12	6	2	4	32	25	14
Selby Town	12	6	1	5	23	19	13
Bridlington Town	12	5	1	6	25	37	11
Halifax Town Reserves	12	4	2	6	21	29	10
Thorne Colliery	12	1	2	9	11	37	4

Championship Decider

Selby Town v Huddersfield Town "A"   3-2
(played at Huddersfield, 25/04/1933)

1933-34

Huddersfield Town "A"	24	16	3	5	62	25	35
South Kirkby Colliery	24	14	6	4	42	24	34
Selby Town	24	15	3	6	71	36	33
Upton Colliery	24	11	6	7	63	54	28
Leeds United "A"	24	12	3	9	57	45	27
Bridlington Town	24	11	4	9	42	33	26
Halifax Town Reserves	24	10	5	9	45	41	25
Yorkshire Amateurs	24	10	4	10	42	43	24
Goole Town	24	11	1	12	68	55	23
Bradford City "A"	24	9	5	10	55	64	23
Thorne Colliery	24	7	5	12	53	58	19
Sheffield University	24	2	4	18	30	87	8
Brodsworth Main	24	3	1	20	26	91	7

1934-35

	P	W	D	L	F	A	Pts
Selby Town	34	25	2	7	127	58	52
Upton Colliery	34	24	4	6	88	46	52
Sheffield Wednesday "A"	34	23	4	7	125	60	50
Leeds United "A"	34	19	8	7	90	59	46
Yorkshire Amateurs	34	19	5	10	85	66	43
Huddersfield Town "A"	34	17	8	9	79	53	42
Halifax Town Reserves	34	18	4	12	110	66	40
South Kirkby Colliery	34	13	9	12	83	66	35
York City Reserves	34	16	2	16	82	79	34
Bradford City "A"	34	11	10	13	73	74	32
Sheffield United "A"	34	12	4	18	87	104	28
Thorne Colliery	34	11	5	18	79	92	27
Castleford Town	34	11	3	20	74	114	25
Bridlington Town	34	10	4	20	77	108	24
Altofts West Riding Colliery	34	9	6	19	69	111	24
Goole Town	34	9	6	19	69	119	24
Brodsworth Main	34	7	5	22	52	115	19
Sheffield University	34	5	5	24	49	108	15

1935-36

	P	W	D	L	F	A	Pts
Selby Town	38	25	5	8	144	67	55
Sheffield Wednesday "A"	38	26	3	9	124	62	55
Worksop Town	38	23	7	8	116	60	53
Thorne Colliery	38	24	5	9	113	65	53
Bradford City "A"	38	21	8	9	111	66	50
Leeds United "A"	38	20	6	12	112	70	46
Huddersfield Town "A"	38	19	6	13	88	59	44
Upton Colliery	38	19	5	14	78	75	43
South Kirkby Colliery	38	16	10	12	102	83	42
Goole Town	38	17	8	13	88	76	42
Halifax Town Reserves	38	17	6	15	91	70	40
York City Reserves	38	14	6	18	99	103	34
Bridlington Town	38	13	6	19	76	104	32
Yorkshire Amateurs	38	13	6	19	75	102	32
Altofts West Riding Colliery	38	14	4	20	101	123	32
Barnoldswick Town	38	11	8	19	83	125	30
Bradford Park Avenue "A"	38	10	9	19	83	119	29
Sheffield United "A"	38	12	5	21	95	91	29
Castleford Town	38	4	5	29	61	157	13
Sheffield University	38	2	2	34	30	193	6

1936-37

	P	W	D	L	F	A	Pts
Goole Town	36	23	8	5	101	49	54
York City Reserves	36	23	3	10	99	59	49
Upton Colliery	36	20	9	7	108	69	49
South Kirkby Colliery	36	19	8	9	109	74	46
Worksop Town	36	17	12	7	86	60	46
Huddersfield Town "A"	36	18	7	11	75	55	43
Sheffield Wednesday "A"	36	17	6	13	94	73	40
Leeds United "A"	36	17	5	14	114	75	39
Dinnington Athletic	36	15	7	14	90	79	37
Selby Town	36	14	6	16	92	87	34
Bridlington Town	36	14	5	17	76	81	33
Halifax Town Reserves	36	14	5	17	77	84	33
Bradford City "A"	36	13	4	19	83	92	30
Sheffield United "A"	36	12	5	19	93	104	29
Thorne Colliery	36	11	6	19	73	103	28
Bradford Park Avenue "A"	36	9	10	17	72	112	28
Yorkshire Amateurs	36	10	6	20	61	89	26
Altofts West Riding Colliery	36	6	8	22	70	145	20
Ollerton Colliery Reserves	36	9	2	25	65	148	20

1937-38

	P	W	D	L	F	A	Pts
York City Reserves	38	26	7	5	118	60	59
Ollerton Colliery	38	23	5	10	101	53	51
Selby Town	38	23	4	11	114	62	50
Dinnington Athletic	38	21	7	10	91	72	49
Worksop Town	38	19	5	14	82	59	43
Bridlington Town	38	17	9	12	74	61	43
Leeds United "A"	38	18	6	14	83	54	42
Huddersfield Town "A"	38	15	10	13	74	66	40
Sheffield Wednesday "A"	38	17	4	17	100	91	38
Halifax Town Reserves	38	17	4	17	84	85	38
Goole Town	38	17	4	17	61	83	38
Bolsover Colliery	38	15	6	17	78	84	36
Thorne Colliery	38	15	5	18	75	76	35
Yorkshire Amateurs	38	13	8	17	65	82	34
Barnsley "A"	38	15	3	20	72	81	33
Sheffield United "A"	38	12	7	19	76	85	31
South Kirkby Colliery	38	11	7	20	61	82	29
Upton Colliery	38	11	5	22	59	91	27
Bradford Park Avenue "A"	38	11	5	22	63	108	27
Altofts West Riding Colliery	38	7	3	28	39	135	17

1938-39

	P	W	D	L	F	A	Pts
Sheffield Wednesday "A"	38	31	3	4	138	44	65
Leeds United "A"	38	30	1	7	125	47	61
York City Reserves	38	24	8	6	121	44	56
Ollerton Colliery	38	21	5	12	83	64	47
Huddersfield Town "A"	38	19	8	11	91	71	46
Bridlington Town	38	17	11	10	99	71	45
Worksop Town	38	18	8	12	92	64	44
Chesterfield "A"	38	15	9	14	77	69	39
Upton Colliery	38	16	6	16	78	76	38
Dinnington Athletic	38	14	8	16	85	78	36
Sheffield United "A"	38	13	9	16	103	85	35
Barnsley "A"	38	12	11	15	87	87	35
Thorne Colliery	38	15	5	18	80	90	35
South Kirkby Colliery	38	13	8	17	90	94	34
Goole Town	38	14	4	20	74	91	32
Halifax Town Reserves	38	11	8	19	81	112	30
Bolsover Colliery	38	11	8	19	82	125	30
Yorkshire Amateurs	38	10	6	22	58	103	26
Selby Town	38	9	6	23	84	118	24
Altofts West Riding Colliery	38	0	2	36	30	225	2

1939-45

League did not operate.

1945-46

	P	W	D	L	F	A	Pts
Wombwell Athletic	28	24	0	4	103	36	48
Thorne Colliery	28	17	5	6	67	50	39
Huddersfield Town "A"	28	16	6	6	82	58	38
Goole Town	28	11	7	10	81	54	29
Bradford United	28	12	5	11	72	60	29
Yorkshire Amateurs	28	13	3	12	72	61	29
Scunthorpe United Reserves	28	11	6	11	57	71	28
Firbeck Main Colliery	28	11	5	12	78	74	27
Bradford City "A"	28	11	5	12	71	71	27
Selby Town	28	9	8	11	65	76	26
York City Reserves	28	8	10	10	48	57	26
Halifax Town Reserves	28	8	7	13	52	83	23
Ossett Town	28	8	4	16	52	77	20
South Kirkby Colliery	28	5	6	17	51	74	16
Hull Amateurs	28	6	3	19	51	100	15

1946-47

Thorne Colliery	38	25	6	7	117	56	56
Bradford United	38	25	5	8	151	68	55
Huddersfield Town "A"	38	21	7	10	125	64	49
York City Reserves	38	22	5	11	115	74	49
Ossett Town	38	20	9	9	96	87	49
Selby Town	38	20	6	12	106	75	46
Halifax Town Reserves	38	18	9	11	109	77	45
Wombwell Athletic	38	20	4	14	114	95	44
Scunthorpe United Reserves	38	20	3	15	105	74	43
Chesterfield "A"	38	15	9	14	101	83	39
Goole Town	38	16	5	17	88	87	37
Harworth Colliery	38	14	8	16	82	76	36
Sheffield Wednesday "A"	38	14	7	17	69	88	35
South Kirkby Colliery	38	13	8	17	79	85	34
Leeds United "A"	38	15	4	19	83	99	34
Yorkshire Amateurs	38	16	2	20	94	130	34
Gainsborough Trinity Reserves	38	9	9	20	63	107	27
Keighley Town	38	9	5	24	63	87	23
Hull Amateurs	38	6	6	26	49	155	18
Upton Colliery	38	2	3	33	46	188	7

1947-48

Goole Town	38	29	5	4	118	48	63
Gainsborough Trinity Reserves	38	24	3	11	99	53	51
Selby Town	38	20	10	8	92	73	50
Harworth Colliery	38	22	4	12	92	70	48
Bradford United	38	20	6	12	104	56	46
Ossett Town	38	17	11	10	91	95	45
Barnsley "A"	38	18	8	12	68	59	44
Thorne Colliery	38	19	2	17	90	83	40
Scunthorpe United Reserves	38	15	9	14	83	90	39
Wombwell Athletic	38	17	4	17	85	92	38
Chesterfield "A"	38	15	5	18	82	70	35
Halifax Town Reserves	38	13	9	16	77	72	35
Sheffield Wednesday "A"	38	15	5	18	81	83	35
South Kirkby Colliery	38	14	6	18	82	92	34
Yorkshire Amateurs	38	15	2	21	89	97	32
Leeds United "A"	38	12	8	18	78	93	32
Sheffield United "A"	38	11	7	20	61	105	29
Brodsworth Main	38	11	5	22	80	98	27
Huddersfield Town "A"	38	6	7	25	53	118	19
Keighley Town	38	6	6	26	53	111	18

1948-49

Sheffield United "A"	38	26	4	8	98	49	56
Goole Town Reserves	38	26	3	9	114	55	55
Gainsborough Trinity Reserves	38	22	6	10	99	60	50
Selby Town	38	20	4	14	93	69	44
Ossett Town	38	19	6	13	94	73	44
Rotherham United "A"	38	17	9	12	79	62	43
Halifax Town Reserves	38	18	7	13	86	82	43
Huddersfield Town "A"	38	15	9	14	65	72	39
Leeds United "A"	38	17	5	16	85	93	39
Wombwell Athletic	38	15	8	15	74	81	38
Chesterfield "A"	38	14	9	15	68	92	37
Scunthorpe United Reserves	38	12	12	14	83	82	36
Barnsley "A"	38	13	9	16	79	86	35
Sheffield Wednesday "A"	38	13	8	17	70	78	34
Harworth Colliery	38	10	13	15	90	98	33
Yorkshire Amateurs	38	11	9	18	62	74	31
Thorne Colliery	38	12	5	21	68	91	29
Brodsworth Main	38	9	8	21	65	106	26
South Kirkby Colliery	38	11	3	24	85	107	25
Bradford Park Avenue "A"	38	10	3	25	65	112	23

1949-50   Division One

Goole Town Reserves	34	27	3	4	91	37	57
Wombwell Athletic	34	22	6	6	73	29	50
Ossett Town	34	22	4	8	120	61	48
Scunthorpe United Reserves	34	17	11	6	75	44	45
Yorkshire Amateurs	34	19	5	10	85	55	43
Gainsborough Trinity Reserves	34	15	10	9	79	57	40
Rotherham United "A"	34	15	7	12	64	54	37
Selby Town	34	15	6	13	82	63	36
Sheffield United "A"	34	15	4	15	75	52	34
Barnsley "A"	34	13	7	14	53	49	33
Sheffield Wednesday "A"	34	12	7	15	52	55	31
Huddersfield Town "A"	34	12	6	16	58	65	30
Brodsworth Main	34	11	8	15	53	68	30
Leeds United "A"	34	11	7	16	62	67	29
Halifax Town "A"	34	11	4	19	52	71	26
Chesterfield "A"	34	6	7	21	48	90	19
Thorne Colliery	34	7	5	22	62	124	19
Harworth Colliery	34	2	1	31	31	174	5

Division Two

Retford Town Reserves	34	23	5	6	91	55	51
Beighton Miners Welfare	34	21	7	6	103	60	49
Scarborough Reserves	34	20	8	6	95	47	48
Dinnington Athletic	34	21	6	7	82	53	48
Norton Woodseats	34	20	4	10	86	49	44
Bentley Colliery	34	19	6	9	96	69	44
Stocksbridge Works	34	20	3	11	78	68	43
Farsley Celtic	34	16	5	13	100	76	37
Bradford Park Avenue "A"	34	15	6	13	71	65	36
Sheffield	34	14	4	16	89	79	32
Hull City "A"	34	14	4	16	99	89	32
Worksop Town Reserves	34	12	6	16	78	86	30
Doncaster Rovers "A"	34	11	8	15	60	78	30
South Kirkby Colliery	34	9	6	19	61	86	24
Frickley Colliery Reserves	34	8	7	19	71	109	23
Maltby Main	34	4	8	22	48	117	16
York City "A"	34	4	7	23	54	94	15
Kiveton Park	34	3	4	27	47	129	10

1950-51   Division One

Sheffield Wednesday "A"	34	24	4	6	101	47	52
Selby Town	34	22	2	10	103	68	46
Beighton Miners Welfare	34	21	3	10	95	58	45
Scarborough Reserves	34	20	4	10	86	57	44
Goole Town Reserves	34	19	4	11	77	51	42
Ossett Town	34	20	2	12	93	65	42
Gainsborough Trinity Reserves	34	13	10	11	87	86	36
Retford Town Reserves	34	15	5	14	60	44	35
Yorkshire Amateurs	34	15	4	15	67	68	34
Barnsley "A"	34	13	7	14	56	44	33
Wombwell Athletic	34	12	8	14	71	82	32
Rotherham United "A"	34	13	5	16	72	61	31
Sheffield United "A"	34	10	10	14	61	64	30
Leeds United "A"	34	12	2	20	68	104	26
Huddersfield Town "A"	34	11	3	20	61	87	25
Dinnington Athletic	34	7	9	18	55	107	23
Brodsworth Main	34	6	8	20	52	96	20
Halifax Town "A"	34	6	4	24	44	120	16

Division Two

Stocksbridge Works	32	23	5	4	106	30	51
Worksop Town Reserves	32	22	5	5	94	51	49
Hull City "A"	32	20	5	7	77	50	45
Norton Woodseats	32	19	5	8	75	33	43
Bentley Colliery	32	20	3	9	105	63	43
Chesterfield "A"	32	17	7	8	102	51	41
Sheffield	32	16	5	11	85	55	37
Farsley Celtic	32	16	4	12	77	67	36
Bradford United	32	15	3	14	78	58	33
Doncaster Rovers "A"	32	13	7	12	66	58	33
Thorne Colliery	32	15	3	14	74	89	33
Frickley Colliery Reserves	32	10	8	14	50	60	28
Bradford Park Avenue "A"	32	8	2	22	39	99	18
South Kirkby Colliery	32	7	3	22	49	84	17
Kiveton Park	32	5	3	24	48	109	13
York City "A"	32	5	3	24	43	125	13
Maltby Main	32	3	5	24	32	118	11

1951-52

Division One

Stocksbridge Works	34	22	9	3	94	36	53
Retford Town Reserves	34	23	7	4	99	39	53
Beighton Miners Welfare	34	19	9	6	92	48	47
Goole Town Reserves	34	20	7	7	75	50	47
Selby Town	34	19	8	7	99	57	46
Hull City "A"	34	19	7	8	90	54	45
Sheffield Wednesday "A"	34	17	4	13	84	64	38
Leeds United "A"	34	14	6	14	77	77	34
Norton Woodseats	34	12	7	15	64	60	31
Rotherham United "A"	34	13	5	16	73	82	31
Ossett Town	34	13	5	16	61	71	31
Barnsley "A"	34	12	3	19	55	76	27
Sheffield United "A"	34	10	5	19	59	91	25
Wombwell Athletic	34	9	6	19	64	86	24
Gainsborough Trinity Reserves	34	8	5	21	61	102	21
Yorkshire Amateurs	34	7	7	20	46	99	21
Scarborough Reserves	34	8	4	22	56	120	20
Worksop Town Reserves	34	6	6	22	39	76	18

Division Two

Farsley Celtic	24	17	1	6	78	37	35
Bentley Colliery	24	14	5	5	55	43	33
Sheffield	24	13	5	6	85	41	31
Doncaster Rovers "A"	24	14	3	7	73	43	31
Chesterfield "A"	24	14	3	7	58	39	31
Huddersfield Town "A"	24	11	3	10	61	43	25
Bradford Park Avenue "A"	24	11	2	11	48	49	24
South Kirkby Colliery	24	11	2	11	55	61	24
Thorne Colliery	24	10	4	10	47	56	24
Brodsworth Main	24	8	2	14	52	54	18
Frickley Colliery Reserves	24	7	4	13	45	61	18
Halifax Town "A"	24	3	3	18	35	91	9
Maltby Main	24	3	3	18	26	100	9

1952-53

Division One

Selby Town	34	26	2	6	106	54	54
Beighton Miners Welfare	34	21	6	7	93	52	48
Stocksbridge Works	34	19	4	11	104	54	42
Retford Town Reserves	34	17	8	9	106	69	42
Hull City "A"	34	16	4	14	74	55	36
Bentley Colliery	34	13	10	11	79	74	36
Ossett Town	34	14	8	12	85	85	36
Sheffield	34	15	6	13	72	76	36
Rotherham United "A"	34	14	7	13	79	69	35
Barnsley "A"	34	13	8	13	54	66	34
Norton Woodseats	34	15	3	16	53	63	33
Sheffield Wednesday "A"	34	11	10	13	59	69	32
Goole Town Reserves	34	10	10	14	77	95	30
Farsley Celtic	34	12	5	17	77	84	29
Leeds United "A"	34	12	5	17	65	80	29
Wombwell Athletic	34	10	3	21	53	102	23
Doncaster Rovers "A"	34	8	3	23	45	91	19
Sheffield United "A"	34	6	6	22	50	93	18

Division Two

Huddersfield Town "A"	26	22	1	3	106	27	45
Yorkshire Amateurs	26	15	3	8	64	33	33
Scarborough Reserves	26	15	1	10	72	50	31
South Kirkby Colliery	26	13	4	9	76	64	30
Worksop Town Reserves	26	13	2	11	62	56	28
Bradford Park Avenue "A"	26	9	10	7	56	62	28
Frickley Colliery Reserves	26	9	7	10	60	67	25
Thorne Colliery	26	10	3	13	54	59	23
Chesterfield "A"	26	10	3	13	50	69	23
Briggs Sports Club	26	10	3	13	57	83	23
Hallam	26	9	4	13	59	57	22
Brodsworth Main	26	8	4	14	45	77	20
Hampton Sports Club	26	6	7	13	49	62	19
Maltby Main	26	4	6	16	38	82	14

1953-54

Division One

Selby Town	34	23	6	5	99	50	52
Huddersfield Town "A"	34	22	4	8	88	57	48
Rotherham United "A"	34	16	9	9	90	70	41
Norton Woodseats	34	17	6	11	85	55	40
Stocksbridge Works	34	12	15	7	76	50	39
Bentley Colliery	34	17	5	12	83	82	39
Barnsley "A"	34	15	7	12	94	68	37
Retford Town	34	15	6	13	78	74	36
Sheffield Wednesday "A"	34	11	10	13	67	65	32
Scarborough Reserves	34	15	2	17	79	105	32
Beighton Miners Welfare	34	13	5	16	82	92	31
Farsley Celtic	34	10	10	14	75	72	30
Ossett Town	34	10	10	14	61	81	30
Yorkshire Amateurs	34	9	11	14	56	64	29
Sheffield	34	12	5	17	73	88	29
Goole Town Reserves	34	11	5	18	62	93	27
Hull City "A"	34	7	12	15	54	68	26
South Kirkby Colliery	34	4	6	24	59	127	14

Division Two

Rawmarsh Welfare	30	23	3	4	76	35	49
Sheffield United "A"	30	20	7	3	103	35	47
Chesterfield "A"	30	18	9	3	86	44	45
Thorne Colliery	30	19	5	6	77	34	43
Leeds United "A"	30	19	3	8	97	40	41
Wombwell Athletic	30	13	8	9	62	53	34
Doncaster Rovers "A"	30	11	8	11	56	50	30
Hallam	30	12	5	13	68	62	29
Briggs Sports Club	30	11	7	12	61	66	29
Hampton Sports Club	30	11	4	15	60	81	26
Frickley Colliery Reserves	30	8	8	14	52	69	24
Worksop Town Reserves	30	8	5	17	49	66	21
Bradford Park Avenue "A"	30	6	8	16	53	85	20
Maltby Main	30	6	4	20	40	111	16
Brodsworth Main	30	4	5	21	46	95	13
Dunscroft Welfare	30	6	1	23	49	109	13

1954-55

Division One

Stocksbridge Works	34	22	4	8	78	46	48
Norton Woodseats	34	19	9	6	72	50	47
Sheffield United "A"	34	17	9	8	77	53	43
Barnsley "A"	34	16	9	9	97	59	41
Bentley Colliery	34	18	5	11	90	69	41
Selby Town	34	15	8	11	82	67	38
Beighton Miners Welfare	34	13	11	10	75	76	37
Huddersfield Town "A"	34	16	3	15	87	65	35
Sheffield Wednesday "A"	34	15	5	14	56	64	35
Chesterfield "A"	34	13	8	13	64	72	34
Ossett Town	34	13	6	15	70	90	32
Retford Town	34	11	8	15	66	73	30
Farsley Celtic	34	10	9	15	68	68	29
Yorkshire Amateurs	34	10	9	15	58	71	29
Rotherham United "A"	34	9	9	16	66	73	27
Scarborough Reserves	34	10	6	18	58	88	26
Thorne Colliery	34	9	3	22	50	90	21
Rawmarsh Welfare	34	6	7	21	53	93	19

Division Two

Hull City "A"	30	22	4	4	113	28	48
Halifax Town Reserves	30	23	0	7	110	50	46
Sheffield	30	19	6	5	96	38	44
Leeds United "A"	30	20	3	7	86	38	43
South Kirkby Colliery	30	19	4	7	93	51	42
Worksop Town Reserves	30	16	4	10	69	52	36
Hampton Sports Club	30	13	10	7	69	53	36
Wombwell Athletic	30	17	1	12	65	60	35
Frickley Colliery Reserves	30	9	7	14	55	84	25
Hallam	30	9	5	16	51	60	23
Doncaster Rovers "A"	30	8	5	17	53	80	21
Briggs Sports Club	30	8	3	19	57	94	19
Brodsworth Main	30	8	2	20	70	99	18
Bradford Park Avenue "A"	30	8	2	20	55	102	18
Dunscroft Welfare	30	6	2	22	50	126	14
Maltby Main	30	4	4	22	37	114	12

1955-56

Division One

Stocksbridge Works	34	18	10	6	85	58	46
Selby Town	34	19	4	11	78	54	42
Sheffield Wednesday "A"	34	16	8	10	86	57	40
Halifax Town Reserves	34	18	4	12	71	57	40
Farsley Celtic	34	18	4	12	60	58	40
Sheffield	34	18	4	12	84	85	40
Huddersfield Town "A"	34	18	3	13	75	58	39
Hull City "A"	34	16	7	11	69	58	39
Beighton Miners Welfare	34	18	3	13	80	70	39
Sheffield United "A"	34	14	10	10	81	71	38
Ossett Town	34	14	4	16	64	80	32
Barnsley "A"	34	10	9	15	56	68	29
Norton Woodseats	34	12	4	18	80	83	28
Rotherham United "A"	34	13	2	19	71	75	28
Yorkshire Amateurs	34	12	3	19	68	96	27
Retford Town	34	10	4	20	76	95	24
Leeds United "A"	34	9	6	19	52	77	24
Bentley Colliery	34	7	3	24	60	96	17

Division Two

Retford Town	32	20	7	5	113	55	47
Hallam	32	21	5	6	87	43	47
Bentley Colliery #	32	22	3	7	91	45	45
Frickley Colliery Reserves	32	20	3	9	97	54	43
South Kirkby Colliery	32	19	5	8	75	64	43
Worksop Town Reserves	32	17	6	9	88	53	40
Leeds United "A"	32	16	5	11	86	49	37
Goole Town Reserves	32	17	2	13	71	66	36
Hampton Sports Club	32	16	1	15	68	68	33
Yorkshire Amateurs	32	14	5	13	68	72	33
Harrogate Railway Athletic	32	13	4	15	82	75	30
Brodsworth Main	32	9	7	16	60	80	25
Scarborough Reserves	32	8	5	19	55	85	21
Bradford Park Avenue "A"	32	9	2	21	57	94	20
Hatfield Main	32	7	3	22	41	103	17
Briggs Sports Club	32	5	3	24	44	104	13
Wombwell & Darfield	32	4	4	24	52	125	12

Bentley Colliery had two points deducted for fielding an ineligible player.

Division Two

Rawmarsh Welfare	30	21	3	6	87	52	45
Thorne Colliery	30	20	2	8	95	53	42
York City "A"	30	17	7	6	91	48	41
Salts (Saltaire)	30	18	4	8	93	46	40
Hallam	30	18	4	8	70	47	40
Scarborough Reserves	30	16	3	11	88	60	35
Worksop Town Reserves #	30	12	10	8	63	52	34
Harrogate Railway Athletic	30	12	5	13	78	87	29
South Kirkby Colliery	30	12	5	13	70	80	29
Bradford Park Avenue "A"	30	9	7	14	70	77	25
Hampton Sports Club	30	9	6	15	66	84	24
Brodsworth Main	30	10	3	17	68	92	23
Frickley Colliery Reserves	30	10	2	18	66	82	22
Wombwell Athletic	30	7	8	15	55	81	22
Hatfield Main	30	8	3	19	46	88	19
Briggs Sports Club #	30	4	2	24	38	115	10

Worksop Town Reserves were awarded a win after their game with Briggs Sports was not played.

1957-58

Division One

Stocksbridge Works	34	23	5	6	98	45	51
Farsley Celtic	34	19	6	9	85	42	44
Sheffield Wednesday "A"	34	17	9	8	97	49	43
Selby Town	34	19	5	10	86	53	43
Halifax Town Reserves	34	18	5	11	93	66	41
Norton Woodseats	34	17	7	10	75	58	41
Bentley Colliery	34	16	7	11	73	68	39
Beighton Miners Welfare	34	16	7	11	77	73	39
Sheffield United "A"	34	16	6	12	90	68	38
Sheffield	34	15	6	13	58	63	36
Frickley Colliery Reserves	34	15	5	14	65	71	35
Ossett Town	34	14	6	14	86	86	34
Retford Town	34	11	8	15	75	76	30
Hallam	34	11	6	17	50	76	28
Salts (Saltaire)	34	12	2	20	70	93	26
Rawmarsh Welfare	34	10	6	18	58	79	26
Huddersfield Town "A"	34	6	3	25	54	83	15
Thorne Colliery	34	1	1	32	34	175	3

1956-57

Division One

Stocksbridge Works	34	20	8	6	100	55	48
Sheffield Wednesday "A"	34	18	8	8	86	42	44
Selby Town	34	19	5	10	99	57	43
Farsley Celtic	34	17	7	10	68	43	41
Halifax Town Reserves	34	17	6	11	70	46	40
Sheffield United "A"	34	17	6	11	90	65	40
Norton Woodseats	34	17	6	11	66	54	40
Huddersfield Town "A"	34	18	4	12	79	76	40
Beighton Miners Welfare	34	16	7	11	74	73	39
Sheffield	34	18	1	15	81	67	37
Barnsley "A"	34	16	4	14	74	70	36
Ossett Town	34	13	5	16	73	83	31
Salts (Saltaire)	34	12	7	15	68	86	31
Rawmarsh Welfare	34	9	6	19	48	83	24
Rotherham United "A"	34	7	8	19	67	96	22
Thorne Colliery	34	9	3	22	68	107	21
York City "A"	34	8	2	24	49	93	18
Hull City "A"	34	5	7	22	43	107	17

Division Two

East End Park W.M.C.	26	20	2	4	76	28	42
Scarborough Reserves	26	17	4	5	65	32	38
Harrogate Railway Athletic	26	15	6	5	71	41	36
Worksop Town Reserves	26	11	8	7	65	53	30
Yorkshire Amateurs	26	14	1	11	58	45	29
South Kirkby Colliery	26	12	4	10	81	69	28
Ossett Albion	26	11	4	11	50	50	26
Goole Town Reserves #	26	10	7	9	58	58	25
York City "A"	26	9	5	12	42	54	23
Leeds United "A"	26	8	5	13	42	60	21
Hatfield Main	26	7	6	13	46	89	20
Hampton Sports Club	26	5	8	13	37	55	18
Harrogate Town	26	4	7	15	43	62	15
Wombwell & Darfield	26	4	3	19	42	80	11

Goole Town Reserves had two points deducted for fielding an ineligible player.

1958-59

Division One

Retford Town	34	24	1	9	94	52	49
Farsley Celtic	34	19	9	6	74	39	47
East End Park W.M.C.	34	19	6	9	73	53	44
Sheffield Wednesday "A"	34	18	7	9	62	35	43
Stocksbridge Works	34	17	5	12	79	58	39
Scarborough Reserves	34	15	8	11	79	58	38
Beighton Miners Welfare	34	17	4	13	90	76	38
Sheffield United "A"	34	15	6	13	62	56	36
Frickley Colliery Reserves	34	17	2	15	83	85	36
Bentley Colliery	34	14	7	13	77	75	35
Norton Woodseats	34	15	3	16	72	74	33
Sheffield	34	11	8	15	70	78	30
Selby Town	34	11	7	16	69	75	29
Hallam	34	11	4	19	57	78	26
Worksop Town Reserves	34	9	8	17	45	78	26
Ossett Town	34	10	5	19	79	81	25
Harrogate Railway Athletic	34	6	7	21	48	84	19
Salts (Saltaire)	34	7	5	22	45	123	19

Division Two

Yorkshire Amateurs	24	19	4	1	79	23	42
Ossett Albion	24	16	2	6	77	37	34
Goole Town Reserves	24	14	6	4	79	39	34
Rawmarsh Welfare	24	14	3	7	60	48	31
South Kirkby Colliery	24	13	2	9	72	52	28
Harrogate Town	24	12	4	8	74	61	28
Dodworth Miners Welfare	24	9	6	9	62	44	24
York City "A"	24	10	4	10	41	47	24
Thorne Colliery	24	9	3	12	69	79	21
Hampton Sports Club	24	7	1	16	34	57	15
British Ropes	24	5	5	14	36	87	15
Wombwell	24	3	3	18	41	75	9
Hatfield Main	24	2	3	19	44	119	7

1959-60

Division One

Farsley Celtic	34	21	10	3	77	30	52
Ossett Albion	34	19	7	8	76	47	45
Sheffield United "A"	34	18	8	8	86	51	44
Sheffield Wednesday "A"	34	18	6	10	77	53	42
Retford Town	34	16	7	11	85	66	39
Norton Woodseats	34	14	10	10	70	62	38
Scarborough Reserves	34	14	10	10	69	70	38
Yorkshire Amateurs	34	13	11	10	67	53	37
Frickley Colliery Reserves	34	13	10	11	65	53	36
East End Park W.M.C.	34	13	9	12	54	53	35
Selby Town	34	16	3	15	62	68	35
Stocksbridge Works	34	13	6	15	58	50	32
Bentley Colliery	34	9	11	14	59	69	29
Sheffield	34	11	6	17	59	80	28
Beighton Miners Welfare	34	8	8	18	57	83	24
Goole Town Reserves	34	9	6	19	68	101	24
Hallam	34	5	7	22	51	96	17
Rawmarsh Welfare	34	4	9	21	42	97	17

Division Two

Grimethorpe Miners Welfare	28	22	1	5	109	37	45
Bridlington Town	28	21	3	4	86	37	45
Ossett Town	28	18	3	7	112	53	39
Doncaster United	28	15	9	4	76	44	39
Harrogate Town	28	15	6	7	62	34	36
South Kirkby Colliery	28	13	5	10	76	69	31
Hampton Sports Club	28	12	5	11	59	42	29
York City "A"	28	10	7	11	59	59	27
Salts (Saltaire)	28	9	7	12	54	60	25
Thorne Colliery	28	10	4	14	67	77	24
Harrogate Railway Athletic	28	10	2	16	68	91	22
Hatfield Main #	28	9	1	18	59	102	17
Wombwell	28	7	1	20	49	106	15
Dodworth Miners Welfare	28	4	6	18	33	84	14
British Ropes	28	3	4	21	35	109	10

Hatfield Main had 2 points deducted for playing an ineligible man

1960-61

Division One

Sheffield Wednesday "A"	34	27	4	3	90	32	58
Stocksbridge Works	34	25	4	5	89	39	54
Farsley Celtic	34	24	4	6	68	30	52
Retford Town	34	17	11	6	90	51	45
Grimethorpe Miners Welfare	34	15	10	9	85	64	40
Frickley Colliery Reserves	34	15	9	10	62	47	39
Ossett Albion	34	17	5	12	61	61	39
Scarborough Reserves	34	17	3	14	67	53	37
Selby Town	34	16	5	13	69	60	37
Bridlington Town	34	16	5	13	57	51	37
Sheffield United "A"	34	16	4	14	68	49	36
Norton Woodseats	34	14	5	15	69	71	33
Yorkshire Amateurs	34	10	6	18	50	76	26
East End Park W.M.C.	34	10	5	19	49	66	25
Ossett Town	34	7	5	22	63	113	19
Doncaster United	34	4	6	24	37	86	14
Sheffield	34	4	5	25	40	94	13
Bentley Colliery	34	1	6	27	23	94	8

Division Two

Hallam	36	26	8	2	132	42	60
Swillington Miners Welfare	36	26	3	7	132	55	55
Harrogate Town	36	24	6	6	96	42	54
Goole Town Reserves	36	23	7	6	126	66	53
Bridlington Trinity	36	18	10	8	80	53	46
Thorne Colliery	36	17	10	9	107	77	44
South Kirkby Colliery	36	16	4	16	68	78	36
Hatfield Main	36	16	3	17	81	78	35
Harrogate Railway Athletic	36	14	7	15	82	81	35
Gainsborough Trinity Reserves	36	16	3	17	78	83	35
Hampton Sports Club	36	16	3	17	80	87	35
Rawmarsh Welfare	36	13	8	15	88	89	34
Salts (Saltaire)	36	13	8	15	79	81	34
Swallownest Miners Welfare	36	11	6	19	60	77	28
Dodworth Miners Welfare	36	9	7	20	66	110	25
York City "A"	36	10	5	21	50	87	25
Beighton Miners Welfare	36	10	3	23	61	111	23
Wombwell	36	4	6	26	52	130	14
British Ropes	36	3	7	26	37	128	13

1961-62

Division One

Stocksbridge Works	30	22	4	4	90	28	48
Ossett Albion	30	21	5	4	84	40	47
Bridlington Town	30	19	7	4	61	25	45
Farsley Celtic	30	15	5	10	40	35	35
Yorkshire Amateurs	30	14	5	11	69	58	33
Harrogate Town	30	13	6	11	56	45	32
Norton Woodseats	30	14	3	13	59	59	31
Hallam	30	12	5	13	65	59	29
Selby Town	30	12	5	13	51	53	29
East End Park W.M.C.	30	9	9	12	45	55	27
Scarborough Reserves	30	12	2	16	66	76	26
Goole Town Reserves	30	10	5	15	56	66	25
Grimethorpe Miners Welfare	30	9	6	15	60	86	24
Swillington Miners Welfare	30	7	7	16	59	85	21
Frickley Colliery Reserves	30	5	8	17	35	65	18
Ossett Town	30	4	2	24	39	99	10

Division Two

Bridlington Trinity	26	19	4	3	73	23	42
Doncaster United	26	17	4	5	75	37	38
Swallownest Miners Welfare	26	18	2	6	81	42	38
Hatfield Main	26	17	2	7	86	47	36
Wombwell Sporting	26	14	2	10	70	51	30
Rawmarsh Welfare	26	12	5	9	69	52	29
Sheffield	26	11	5	10	61	48	27
Harrogate Railway Athletic	26	11	3	12	63	74	25
Hull Brunswick	26	10	4	12	59	52	24
Thorne Colliery	26	6	8	12	52	60	20
Brodsworth Main	26	8	3	15	49	71	19
Salts (Saltaire)	26	9	1	16	47	72	19
York City "A"	26	6	2	18	27	64	14
South Kirkby Colliery	26	0	3	23	24	145	3

Division Three

Farsley Celtic Reserves	16	13	1	2	68	10	27
Ossett Albion Reserves	16	7	3	6	44	43	17
Leeds United "A"	16	8	0	8	39	35	16
Yorkshire Amateurs Reserves	16	6	3	7	32	37	15
Salts (Saltaire) Reserves	16	7	1	8	33	40	15
Harrogate Town Reserves	16	5	4	7	21	36	14
Ossett Town Reserves	16	7	0	9	41	56	14
East End Park W.M.C. Reserves	16	5	3	8	43	39	13
Harrogate Railway Athletic Reserves	16	5	3	8	25	50	13

1962-63

Division One

Stocksbridge Works	30	19	7	4	83	28	45
Harrogate Town	30	18	4	8	70	34	40
Farsley Celtic	30	15	6	9	60	37	36
Ossett Albion	30	13	9	8	63	49	35
Bridlington Town	30	14	7	9	47	44	35
Bridlington Trinity	30	12	7	11	69	70	31
Norton Woodseats	30	11	8	11	52	51	30
Swallownest Miners Welfare	30	12	4	14	56	55	28
Scarborough Reserves	30	10	8	12	50	55	28
Selby Town	30	12	4	14	45	58	28
Doncaster United	30	9	10	11	35	49	28
Hallam	30	11	5	14	60	60	27
Hatfield Main	30	10	5	15	55	69	25
Goole Town Reserves	30	9	6	15	49	61	24
Yorkshire Amateurs	30	8	6	16	44	70	22
Grimethorpe Miners Welfare	30	6	6	18	40	89	18

Division Two

Wombwell Sporting	28	21	4	3	67	20	46
Mexborough Town	28	15	11	2	64	28	41
Swillington Miners Welfare	28	16	7	5	***	***	39
Hull Brunswick	28	17	4	7	***	***	38
Sheffield	28	18	0	10	***	***	36
Ossett Town	28	13	7	8	***	***	33
Salts (Saltaire)	28	13	4	11	***	***	30
Harrogate Railway Athletic	28	12	6	10	***	***	30
Rawmarsh Welfare	28	13	4	11	***	***	30
Frickley Colliery Reserves	28	10	5	13	***	***	25
Brodsworth Main	28	10	4	14	***	***	24
Thorne Colliery	28	6	2	20	***	***	14
York City "A"	28	5	4	19	***	***	14
South Kirkby Colliery	28	4	3	21	***	***	11
Dodworth Miners Welfare	28	4	1	23	***	***	9

*** Final goal record not traced.

Division Three

Farsley Celtic Reserves	12	10	1	1	37	13	21
Ossett Albion Reserves	12	7	1	4	32	19	15
Yorkshire Amateurs Reserves	12	6	1	5	26	23	13
Salts (Saltaire) Reserves	12	5	2	5	24	29	12
Harrogate Railway Athletic Reserves	12	5	1	6	25	32	11
Harrogate Town Reserves	12	3	2	7	19	31	8
Ossett Town Reserves	12	2	0	10	20	36	4

1963-64

Division One

Bridlington Trinity	30	18	6	6	76	42	42
Mexborough Town	30	19	2	9	79	53	40
Harrogate Town	30	15	6	9	53	29	36
Bridlington Town	30	14	6	10	50	37	34
Ossett Albion	30	12	10	8	47	37	34
Scarborough Reserves	30	16	2	12	70	64	34
Farsley Celtic	30	13	7	10	51	35	33
Wombwell Sporting	30	13	5	12	40	35	31
Hull Brunswick	30	9	9	12	47	62	27
Hallam	30	12	3	15	40	61	27
Selby Town	30	10	6	14	55	71	26
Swillington Miners Welfare	30	10	6	14	45	64	26
Swallownest Miners Welfare	30	9	6	15	50	57	24
Stocksbridge Works	30	7	8	15	38	48	22
Norton Woodseats	30	9	4	17	44	67	22
Doncaster United	30	8	6	16	37	60	22

Division Two

Rawmarsh Welfare	28	19	2	7	88	51	40
Hatfield Main	28	19	1	8	71	35	39
Harrogate Railway Athletic	28	18	3	7	69	39	39
Brodsworth Main	28	17	4	7	86	49	38
Yorkshire Amateurs	28	16	4	8	66	48	36
Sheffield	28	15	6	7	65	48	36
Goole Town Reserves	28	15	4	9	57	48	34
Kiveton Park	28	13	3	12	69	43	29
Salts (Saltaire)	28	10	8	10	45	40	28
Grimethorpe Miners Welfare	28	13	2	13	61	64	28
Ossett Town	28	8	6	14	55	62	22
Frickley Colliery Reserves	28	7	6	15	47	67	20
Thorne Colliery	28	5	6	17	53	78	16
Dodworth Miners Welfare	28	3	5	20	40	106	11
South Kirkby Colliery	28	2	0	26	36	136	4

Division Three

Keighley Central	16	12	3	1	47	13	27
Farsley Celtic Reserves	16	10	4	2	38	16	24
Harrogate Town Reserves	16	8	5	3	26	24	21
Ossett Albion Reserves	16	8	1	7	29	26	17
Yorkshire Amateurs Reserves	16	6	2	8	34	32	14
Harrogate Railway Athletic Reserves	16	5	4	7	24	34	14
Salts (Saltaire) Reserves	16	4	3	9	21	33	11
Ossett Town Reserves	16	4	2	10	28	55	10
Slazengers	16	2	2	12	25	39	6

1964-65

Division One

Wombwell Sporting	30	18	8	4	82	28	44
Swillington Miners Welfare	30	20	3	7	89	51	43
Ossett Albion	30	17	6	7	68	29	40
Hatfield Main	30	16	6	8	68	50	38
Bridlington Town	30	14	9	7	69	41	37
Bridlington Trinity	30	16	5	9	70	62	37
Farsley Celtic	30	14	8	8	60	44	36
Scarborough Reserves	30	14	5	11	71	57	33
Mexborough Town	30	11	8	11	58	57	30
Rawmarsh Welfare	30	13	4	13	64	74	30
Hallam	30	11	4	15	55	56	26
Harrogate Town	30	9	7	14	46	55	25
Selby Town	30	7	6	17	50	85	20
Harrogate Railway Athletic	30	6	5	19	44	70	17
Hull Brunswick	30	7	2	21	42	92	16
Brodsworth Main	30	3	2	25	44	129	8

Division Two

Stocksbridge Works	28	20	4	4	85	29	44
Barton Town	28	18	4	6	88	35	40
Frickley Colliery Reserves	28	17	4	7	56	37	38
Goole Town Reserves	28	15	5	8	65	37	35
Kiveton Park	28	14	5	9	51	32	33
Retford Town Reserves	28	11	8	9	54	41	30
Yorkshire Amateurs	28	13	3	12	54	61	29
Sheffield	28	12	4	12	47	41	28
Doncaster United	28	9	8	11	41	46	26
Swallownest Miners Welfare	28	10	5	13	47	55	25
Grimethorpe Miners Welfare	28	10	3	15	45	60	23
Norton Woodseats	28	9	5	14	45	62	23
Thorne Colliery	28	7	7	14	43	72	21
Salts (Saltaire)	28	6	4	18	30	75	16
Ossett Town	28	4	2	22	26	94	10

1965-66

Division One

Wombwell Sporting	30	18	7	5	62	37	43
Hatfield Main	30	19	2	9	100	54	40
Selby Town	30	15	10	5	67	37	40
Ossett Albion	30	19	2	9	64	40	40
Bridlington Town	30	16	6	8	62	44	38
Bridlington Trinity	30	16	2	12	85	60	34
Farsley Celtic	30	15	4	11	49	36	34
Barton Town	30	15	4	11	83	68	34
Mexborough Town	30	14	4	12	66	51	32
Goole Town Reserves	30	13	4	13	50	52	30
Scarborough Reserves	30	11	5	14	51	52	27
Hallam	30	11	4	15	50	59	26
Frickley Colliery Reserves	30	7	7	16	41	77	21
Harrogate Town	30	8	3	19	49	65	19
Rawmarsh Welfare	30	4	5	21	34	98	13
Stocksbridge Works	30	2	5	23	41	124	9

Division Two

Norton Woodseats	28	18	5	5	85	35	41
Thorne Colliery	28	17	5	6	90	49	39
Sheffield	28	15	5	8	61	33	35
Kiveton Park	28	15	4	9	73	57	34
Denaby United	28	14	5	9	84	40	33
Hull Brunswick	28	15	3	10	70	60	33
Heeley Amateurs	28	13	6	9	56	62	32
Retford Town Reserves	28	11	8	9	66	48	30
Harrogate Railway Athletic	28	12	2	14	64	51	26
Swallownest Miners Welfare	28	11	4	13	55	70	26
Yorkshire Amateurs	28	8	7	13	46	57	23
Doncaster United	28	10	3	15	54	68	23
Ossett Town	28	8	4	16	44	104	20
Leeds Ashley Road	28	7	4	17	47	61	18
Brodsworth Main	28	2	3	23	32	129	7

1966-67

Division One

Bridlington Trinity	32	22	3	7	101	43	47
Bridlington Town	32	21	5	6	83	43	47
Wombwell Sporting	32	15	12	5	57	35	42
Thorne Colliery	32	16	9	7	68	53	41
Hatfield Main	32	17	4	11	70	46	38
Barton Town	32	16	2	14	69	69	34
Farsley Celtic	32	14	6	12	44	44	34
Mexborough Town	32	15	4	13	61	65	34
Kiveton Park	32	15	4	13	53	60	34
Hallam	32	13	6	13	50	50	32
Selby Town	32	13	5	14	60	60	31
Norton Woodseats	32	13	5	14	53	55	31
Ossett Albion	32	11	9	12	52	54	31
Frickley Colliery Reserves	32	10	2	20	56	73	22
Scarborough Reserves	32	9	4	19	51	78	22
Sheffield	32	7	2	23	49	76	16
Harrogate Town	32	1	6	25	34	110	8

Division Two

Hull Brunswick	32	25	3	4	105	40	53
Denaby United	32	23	2	7	91	40	48
York City Reserves	32	21	3	8	96	42	45
Stocksbridge Works	32	17	7	8	79	53	41
Bradford City Reserves	32	18	4	10	72	41	40
Doncaster United	32	17	6	9	55	38	40
Retford Town Reserves	32	17	4	11	66	54	38
Hampton Sports	32	12	7	13	53	54	31
Harrogate Railway Athletic	32	14	3	15	54	58	31
Leeds Ashley Road	32	13	4	15	53	67	30
Micklefield Welfare	32	12	4	16	37	57	28
Rawmarsh Welfare	32	10	7	15	60	69	27
Yorkshire Amateurs	32	9	4	19	39	60	22
Ossett Town	32	8	6	18	51	79	22
Heeley Amateurs	32	7	6	19	53	97	20
Swallownest Miners Welfare	32	5	6	21	38	82	16
Brodsworth Main	32	4	4	24	30	111	12

1967-68

Division One

Bridlington Trinity	32	24	4	4	90	42	52
Denaby United	32	18	10	4	67	29	46
Bridlington Town	32	20	6	6	74	47	46
Hatfield Main	32	18	7	7	69	39	43
Kiveton Park	32	15	9	8	54	40	39
Farsley Celtic	32	15	7	10	48	34	37
Hull Brunswick	32	14	9	9	60	45	37
Wombwell Sporting	32	14	8	10	56	40	36
Selby Town	32	14	8	10	65	61	36
Barton Town	32	13	5	14	67	65	31
Ossett Albion	32	9	10	13	40	58	28
York City Reserves	32	11	3	18	71	46	25
Mexborough Town	32	8	8	16	54	74	24
Norton Woodseats	32	6	10	16	51	71	22
Hallam	32	5	8	19	48	86	18
Thorne Colliery	32	6	4	22	49	94	16
Stocksbridge Works	32	2	4	26	28	99	8

Division Two

Lincoln United	32	23	5	4	96	23	51
Hampton Sports	32	20	6	6	79	35	46
Retford Town Reserves	32	19	8	5	75	38	46
Thackley	32	17	9	6	54	28	43
Heeley Amateurs	32	20	3	9	62	49	43
Leeds Ashley Road	32	16	5	11	55	51	37
Micklefield Welfare	32	15	6	11	58	47	36
Sheffield	32	14	7	11	56	44	35
Harrogate Railway Athletic	32	12	9	11	44	62	33
Scarborough Reserves	32	12	7	13	62	66	31
Yorkshire Amateurs	32	9	7	16	37	62	25
Swallownest Miners Welfare	32	7	10	15	45	60	24
Doncaster United	32	8	5	19	41	51	21
Rawmarsh Welfare	32	7	7	18	54	70	21
Brodsworth Main	32	6	8	18	38	71	20
Ossett Town	32	6	6	20	36	86	18
Harrogate Town	32	5	4	23	31	83	14

1968-69

Division One

Farsley Celtic	34	21	9	4	60	21	51
Mexborough Town	34	24	2	8	69	29	50
Kiveton Park	34	23	4	7	69	35	50
Selby Town	34	18	12	4	78	44	48
Bridlington Trinity	34	19	7	8	68	41	45
Bridlington Town	34	19	6	9	63	42	44
Wombwell Sporting	34	18	6	10	72	39	42
Denaby United	34	15	3	16	63	49	33
Thackley	34	12	9	13	41	46	33
Lincoln United	34	12	8	14	59	55	32
Hatfield Main	34	12	8	14	53	51	32
Ossett Albion	34	10	6	18	58	80	26
Hallam	34	10	6	18	53	84	26
Retford Town Reserves	34	9	5	20	56	74	23
Norton Woodseats	34	8	5	21	43	98	21
Hull Brunswick	34	6	7	21	51	78	19
Thorne Colliery	34	7	5	22	51	100	19
Hampton Sports	34	8	2	24	54	97	18

Division Two

Rawmarsh Welfare	32	23	5	4	110	35	51
Heeley Amateurs	32	21	5	6	81	25	47
Swallownest Miners Welfare	32	21	5	6	101	43	47
Frecheville Community Association	32	21	4	7	83	27	46
Scarborough Reserves	32	18	4	10	84	54	40
Yorkshire Amateurs	32	16	3	13	64	68	35
Guiseley	32	15	4	13	79	74	34
Harrogate Railway Athletic	32	15	4	13	54	64	34
Sheffield	32	13	7	12	62	61	33
Leeds Ashley Road	32	11	10	11	55	65	32
Brodsworth Main	32	11	6	15	68	68	28
Ossett Town	32	10	7	15	53	72	27
Stocksbridge Works	32	9	6	17	78	106	24
Hall Road Rangers	32	7	8	17	68	107	22
Doncaster United	32	7	2	23	50	96	16
Harrogate Town	32	7	2	23	42	85	16
Micklefield Welfare	32	4	4	24	39	128	12

1969-70

Division One

Rawmarsh Welfare	34	26	2	6	90	39	54
Bridlington Trinity	34	20	8	6	70	44	48
Mexborough Town	34	20	6	8	66	41	46
Farsley Celtic	34	17	10	7	55	28	44
Selby Town	34	18	8	8	69	47	44
Wombwell Sporting	34	16	9	9	69	50	41
Denaby United	34	15	8	11	58	40	38
Bridlington Town	34	14	9	11	68	50	37
Lincoln United	34	16	5	13	58	47	37
Hallam	34	13	6	15	72	76	32
Ossett Albion	34	12	7	15	44	46	31
Frecheville Community Association	34	12	4	18	52	54	28
Thackley	34	11	5	18	37	43	27
Swallownest Miners Welfare	34	10	5	19	46	70	25
Norton Woodseats	34	8	9	17	46	87	25
Hatfield Main	34	7	6	21	41	73	20
Kiveton Park	34	6	6	22	39	100	18
Heeley Amateurs	34	5	7	22	45	90	17

Division Two

Dinnington Athletic	34	24	7	3	91	37	55
Emley	34	23	4	7	79	29	50
North Ferriby United	34	20	9	5	95	46	49
Hull Brunswick	34	20	6	8	103	52	46
Scarborough Reserves	34	17	7	10	76	47	41
Yorkshire Amateurs	34	14	9	11	57	54	37
Brodsworth Main	34	15	5	14	60	59	35
Thorne Colliery	34	15	5	14	76	84	35
Stocksbridge Works	34	14	6	14	67	66	34
Harrogate Town	34	12	10	12	40	54	34
Sheffield	34	9	12	13	41	51	30
Guiseley	34	10	8	16	68	83	28
Hampton Sports	34	11	5	18	60	82	27
Harrogate Railway Athletic	34	10	7	17	39	55	27
Firth Vickers	34	11	4	19	54	83	26
Leeds Ashley Road	34	9	5	20	47	84	23
Hall Road Rangers	34	8	6	20	45	79	22
Ossett Town	34	3	7	24	29	74	13

1970-71

Division One

Lincoln United	26	16	7	3	56	26	39
Farsley Celtic	26	13	9	4	41	25	35
Rawmarsh Welfare	26	13	8	5	49	30	34
Mexborough Town	26	12	7	7	56	40	31
Hallam	26	13	5	8	49	42	31
Bridlington Town	26	10	7	9	43	35	27
Denaby United	26	11	4	11	44	37	26
Ossett Albion	26	8	8	10	30	36	24
Bridlington Trinity	26	9	4	13	43	50	22
Winterton Rangers	26	8	6	12	40	48	22
Frecheville Community Association	26	8	6	12	41	51	22
Selby Town	26	7	5	14	42	54	19
Barton Town	26	5	9	12	41	65	19
Wombwell Sporting	26	3	7	16	20	56	13

Division Two

North Ferriby United	26	17	6	3	69	19	40
Thackley	26	16	6	4	55	21	38
Scarborough Reserves	26	16	3	7	67	38	35
Emley	26	14	7	5	51	29	35
Hull Brunswick	26	13	7	6	46	36	33
Hatfield Main	26	14	4	8	46	36	32
Dinnington Athletic	26	11	3	12	42	37	25
Norton Woodseats	26	9	3	14	45	51	21
Kiveton Park	26	9	3	14	41	62	21
Yorkshire Amateurs	26	7	4	15	42	51	18
Heeley Amateurs	26	6	6	14	33	64	18
Thorne Colliery	26	5	6	15	35	69	16
Brodsworth Main	26	7	2	17	24	55	16
Swallownest Miners Welfare	26	6	4	16	31	71	16

Division Three

Stocksbridge Works	28	19	5	4	74	38	43
Brook Sports	28	16	8	4	60	46	40
Leeds & Carnegie College	28	15	5	8	69	32	35
Guiseley	28	14	5	9	68	52	33
Harrogate Railway Athletic	28	13	5	10	42	40	31
Sheffield	28	12	6	10	61	52	30
St. John College (York)	28	9	10	9	45	37	28
Ossett Town	28	10	8	10	48	44	28
Leeds Ashley Road	28	10	7	11	48	41	27
Hall Road Rangers	28	11	4	13	49	66	26
International Harvesters	28	9	7	12	50	52	25
Harrogate Town	28	8	6	14	34	45	22
Bradford Park Avenue Reserves	28	8	5	15	39	53	21
Firth Vickers	28	8	3	17	43	72	19
Sheffield Water Works	28	3	6	19	23	81	12

1971-72

Division One

Winterton Rangers	30	20	5	5	60	30	45
Farsley Celtic	30	16	7	7	43	28	39
Bridlington Town	30	12	9	9	35	28	33
Mexborough Town	30	14	5	11	49	43	33
Denaby United	30	12	9	9	52	47	33
North Ferriby United	30	14	5	11	53	49	33
Selby Town	30	12	6	12	41	45	30
Emley	30	12	5	13	38	40	29
Hallam	30	12	4	14	48	68	28
Lincoln United	30	10	6	14	39	41	26
Frecheville Community Association	30	10	6	14	36	46	26
Rawmarsh Welfare	30	9	7	14	42	43	25
Thackley	30	6	13	11	35	38	25
Scarborough Reserves	30	10	5	15	44	49	25
Ossett Albion	30	9	7	14	34	44	25
Bridlington Trinity	30	9	7	14	33	43	25

Division Two

Barton Town	28	20	5	3	89	28	45
Yorkshire Amateurs	28	17	8	3	60	28	42
Kiveton Park	28	16	10	2	70	34	42
Brook Sports	28	13	7	8	53	47	33
Leeds & Carnegie College	28	12	7	9	46	35	31
Hull Brunswick	28	11	7	10	48	32	29
Hatfield Main	28	12	5	11	42	36	29
Guiseley	28	10	6	12	45	43	26
Stocksbridge Works	28	9	8	11	35	40	26
Wombwell Sporting	28	8	8	12	37	41	24
Thorne Colliery	28	8	6	14	46	79	22
Dinnington Athletic	28	7	7	14	34	67	21
Norton Woodseats	28	6	7	15	33	56	19
Heeley	28	7	5	16	32	66	19
Brodsworth Main	28	4	4	20	26	64	12

Division Three

Leeds Ashley Road	26	16	7	3	58	21	39
Harrogate Town	26	15	6	5	54	27	36
Worsborough Bridge	26	17	1	8	75	38	35
Woolley Miners Welfare	26	15	5	6	63	42	35
St. John College (York)	26	16	2	8	49	49	34
Ossett Town	26	12	4	10	44	35	28
Sheffield	26	12	4	10	39	39	28
Bradford Park Avenue Reserves	26	11	4	11	44	36	26
International Harvesters	26	8	7	11	46	42	23
Hall Road Rangers	26	8	6	12	40	41	22
Harrogate Railway Athletic	26	8	5	13	29	40	21
Retford Town Reserves	26	5	4	17	36	65	14
Blackburn Welfare	26	5	4	17	35	64	14
Sheffield Water Works	26	4	1	21	26	99	9

1972-73

Division One

Mexborough Town	30	17	10	3	65	32	44
Emley	30	14	11	5	52	29	39
Barton Town	30	18	2	10	54	33	38
Denaby United	30	16	5	9	56	37	37
Farsley Celtic	30	15	7	8	53	37	37
Lincoln United	30	13	7	10	39	37	33
Winterton Rangers	30	10	11	9	59	57	31
Yorkshire Amateurs	30	11	8	11	30	33	30
Frecheville Community Association	30	9	10	11	37	37	28
Hallam	30	11	6	13	60	67	28
Kiveton Park	30	11	6	13	50	71	28
Rawmarsh Welfare	30	10	7	13	51	53	27
North Ferriby United	30	9	6	15	52	46	24
Brook Sports	30	7	7	16	51	82	21
Selby Town	30	7	6	17	33	63	20
Bridlington Town	30	4	7	19	45	73	15

Division Two

Leeds & Carnegie College	30	21	1	8	73	30	43
Woolley Miners Welfare	30	19	4	7	85	57	42
Worsborough Bridge	30	18	5	7	74	39	41
Hatfield Main	30	18	2	10	66	37	38
Leeds Ashley Road	30	15	5	10	57	37	35
Harrogate Town	30	16	3	11	55	44	35
Ossett Albion	30	14	3	13	55	49	31
Scarborough Reserves	30	14	2	14	64	52	30
Hull Brunswick	30	12	6	12	33	43	30
Thackley	30	9	9	12	35	37	27
Wombwell Sporting	30	9	9	12	41	55	27
Guiseley	30	10	7	13	43	62	27
Norton Woodseats	30	11	3	16	54	75	25
Dinnington Athletic	30	7	9	14	41	48	23
Stocksbridge Works	30	8	5	17	36	54	21
Thorne Colliery	30	1	3	26	30	123	5

Division Three

Hall Road Rangers	30	15	11	4	56	37	41
Liversedge	30	18	4	8	63	35	40
Ossett Town	30	16	6	8	49	35	38
Bradford Park Avenue Reserves	30	16	5	9	68	43	37
Pickering Town	30	15	7	8	61	45	37
Worksop Town Reserves	30	15	6	9	55	42	36
Blackburn Welfare	30	13	9	8	62	48	35
Sheffield	30	13	9	8	55	45	35
Harrogate Railway Athletic	30	11	11	8	36	30	33
International Harvesters	30	11	7	12	55	48	29
Sheffield Water Works	30	8	7	15	43	63	23
St. John College (York)	30	8	5	17	39	70	21
Retford Town Reserves	30	9	2	19	44	66	20
Brodsworth Main	30	5	9	16	32	50	19
Heeley	30	8	2	20	44	77	18
Sheffield Polytechnic	30	6	6	18	32	60	18

1973-74

Division One

Lincoln United	30	19	4	7	61	33	42
Emley	30	19	4	7	54	35	42
Farsley Celtic	30	16	7	7	60	37	39
Mexborough Town	30	14	9	7	72	44	37
Hallam	30	13	8	9	66	64	34
Denaby United	30	13	7	10	44	42	33
Hatfield Main	30	11	8	11	62	56	30
Worsborough Bridge	30	12	6	12	53	58	30
Winterton Rangers	30	11	6	13	51	53	28
Frecheville Community Association	30	10	8	12	34	39	28
Leeds & Carnegie College	30	11	6	13	49	66	28
Yorkshire Amateurs	30	11	5	14	44	45	27
Kiveton Park	30	9	5	16	43	53	23
Barton Town	30	9	3	18	38	57	21
Rawmarsh Welfare	30	7	6	17	37	54	20
Woolley Miners Welfare	30	8	2	20	44	76	18

Division Two

Thackley	30	21	5	4	58	19	47
Ossett Albion	30	19	9	2	66	27	47
North Ferriby United	30	17	8	5	61	34	42
Guiseley	30	16	7	7	52	33	39
Liversedge	30	15	7	8	45	33	37
Scarborough Reserves	30	13	5	12	43	41	31
Leeds Ashley Road	30	12	6	12	41	47	30
Hall Road Rangers	30	8	11	11	40	45	27
Harrogate Town	30	9	9	12	37	43	27
Bridlington Town	30	10	6	14	46	53	26
Dinnington Athletic	30	10	5	15	37	53	25
Ossett Town	30	9	6	15	47	53	24
Selby Town	30	7	10	13	33	48	24
Brook Sports	30	8	6	16	37	44	22
Wombwell Sporting	30	7	3	20	24	61	17
Norton Woodseats	30	5	5	20	30	63	15

Division Three

Pickering Town	30	22	4	4	96	34	48
Maltby Miners Welfare	30	17	10	3	60	27	44
Bentley Victoria Welfare	30	19	6	5	76	39	44
Redfearn National Glass	30	17	8	5	73	40	42
Heeley	30	16	4	10	75	45	36
St. John College (York)	30	16	4	10	64	51	36
International Harvesters	30	13	7	10	56	42	33
Stocksbridge Works	30	13	4	13	73	49	30
Sheffield Water Works	30	11	7	12	47	57	29
Sheffield	30	12	4	14	62	52	28
Tadcaster Albion	30	13	2	15	54	54	28
Worksop Town Reserves	30	11	3	16	46	63	25
Brodsworth Main	30	5	8	17	33	66	18
Sheffield Polytechnic	30	3	10	17	33	67	16
Blackburn Welfare	30	4	4	22	33	108	12
Thorne Colliery	30	3	5	22	41	128	11

1974-75

Division One

Ossett Albion	30	19	5	6	59	34	43
Frecheville Community Association	30	18	6	6	50	29	42
Thackley	30	13	13	4	35	21	39
Farsley Celtic	30	14	9	7	32	31	37
Emley	30	11	11	8	55	39	33
Lincoln United	30	12	7	11	45	33	31
Hallam	30	12	7	11	50	45	31
Winterton Rangers	30	10	9	11	49	60	29
Leeds & Carnegie College	30	10	8	12	52	57	28
North Ferriby United	30	10	7	13	48	48	27
Hatfield Main	30	9	8	13	53	53	26
Worsborough Bridge	30	8	9	13	41	58	25
Guiseley	30	8	9	13	35	54	25
Mexborough Town Reserves	30	6	12	12	41	51	24
Denaby United	30	4	14	12	44	55	22
Yorkshire Amateurs	30	5	8	17	29	50	18

Division Two

Bridlington Town	28	15	9	4	43	26	39
Pickering Town	28	14	9	5	55	32	37
Redfearn National Glass	28	14	7	7	43	31	35
Maltby Miners Welfare	28	15	4	9	43	32	34
Liversedge	28	14	5	9	56	32	33
Barton Town	28	11	6	11	41	41	28
Kiveton Park	28	9	9	10	37	37	27
Bentley Victoria Welfare	28	9	8	11	38	44	26
Hall Road Rangers	28	7	11	10	33	45	25
Harrogate Town	28	8	8	12	41	37	24
Woolley Miners Welfare	28	6	12	10	34	47	24
Leeds Ashley Road	28	9	5	14	32	37	23
Scarborough Reserves	28	7	9	12	29	44	23
Rawmarsh Welfare	28	6	9	13	37	55	21
Ossett Town #	28	6	9	13	27	49	19

Ossett Town had two points deducted

Division Three

Stocksbridge Works	30	25	2	3	91	28	52
Selby Town	30	20	6	4	77	31	46
Tadcaster Albion	30	20	6	4	70	37	46
Norton Woodseats	30	19	6	5	82	38	44
Sheffield	30	15	5	10	58	45	35
Thorne Colliery	30	13	7	10	59	47	33
St. John College (York)	30	13	6	11	62	47	32
Wombwell Sporting	30	13	4	13	44	61	30
B.S.C. Parkgate	30	10	9	11	58	49	29
Heeley	30	8	7	15	47	65	23
Brook Sports	30	9	4	17	41	59	22
International Harvesters	30	6	9	15	29	48	21
Sheffield Water Works	30	7	7	16	27	62	21
York Railway Institute	30	7	4	19	42	78	18
Brodsworth Main	30	7	1	22	45	82	15
Blackburn Welfare	30	5	3	22	31	86	13

1975-76

Division One

Emley	30	21	7	2	68	25	49
North Ferriby United	30	21	4	5	70	25	46
Hallam	30	15	4	11	58	44	34
Bridlington Town	30	14	6	10	41	38	34
Leeds & Carnegie College	30	14	5	11	52	40	33
Thackley	30	10	13	7	28	26	33
Hatfield Main	30	11	10	9	48	45	32
Redfearn National Glass	30	11	10	9	45	47	32
Ossett Albion	30	12	6	12	46	43	30
Winterton Rangers	30	10	8	12	44	44	28
Lincoln United	30	10	7	13	41	50	27
Pickering Town	30	9	8	13	36	49	26
Farsley Celtic	30	7	9	14	28	46	23
Maltby Miners Welfare	30	9	3	18	45	70	21
Worsborough Bridge	30	8	1	21	41	60	17
Frecheville Community Association	30	6	3	21	44	83	15

Division Two

Guiseley	28	19	7	2	69	26	45
Leeds Ashley Road	28	18	7	3	58	23	43
Liversedge	28	14	10	4	47	25	38
Denaby United	28	16	3	9	44	32	35
Kiveton Park	28	15	4	9	50	28	34
Woolley Miners Welfare	28	13	6	9	54	49	32
Tadcaster Albion	28	13	5	10	55	55	31
Barton Town	28	9	12	7	40	32	30
Selby Town	28	9	8	11	28	34	26
Norton Woodseats	28	11	3	14	47	48	25
Yorkshire Amateurs	28	4	11	13	29	56	19
Harrogate Town	28	5	8	15	30	51	18
Bentley Victoria Welfare	28	4	10	14	29	50	18
Hall Road Rangers	28	5	5	18	29	62	15
Stocksbridge Works	28	3	5	20	31	69	11

Division Three

Rawmarsh Welfare	30	20	5	5	62	21	45
Scarborough Reserves	30	20	5	5	74	40	45
Ossett Town	30	20	5	5	60	34	45
Sheffield	30	14	9	7	50	29	37
B.S.C. Parkgate	30	13	9	8	53	52	35
Thorne Colliery	30	13	6	11	55	42	32
Brook Sports	30	14	2	14	51	38	30
Wombwell Sporting	30	12	6	12	43	42	30
Collingham	30	11	8	11	46	45	30
Dodworth Miners Welfare	30	9	11	10	46	44	29
Sheffield Water Works	30	11	6	13	44	51	28
St. John College (York)	30	7	10	13	49	54	24
Heeley	30	10	4	16	43	63	24
Rossington Miners Welfare	30	6	9	15	24	42	21
York Railway Institute	30	5	5	20	40	73	15
Brodsworth Main	30	4	2	24	26	96	10

1976-77

Division One

Winterton Rangers	30	17	10	3	77	31	44
Emley	30	18	8	4	66	38	44
Ossett Albion	30	17	5	8	51	28	39
Guiseley	30	18	3	9	55	37	39
Leeds Ashley Road	30	16	6	8	48	35	38
Thackley	30	14	9	7	44	26	37
Hallam	30	14	9	7	47	33	37
North Ferriby United	30	14	8	8	62	38	36
Bridlington Town	30	9	10	11	45	43	28
Leeds & Carnegie College	30	11	3	16	45	42	25
Lincoln United	30	8	9	13	45	51	25
Denaby United	30	8	7	15	40	60	23
Redfearn National Glass	30	7	9	14	40	64	23
Liversedge	30	7	6	17	37	57	20
Hatfield Main	30	3	7	20	30	87	13
Pickering Town	30	4	1	25	23	85	9

Division Two

Sheffield	30	15	10	5	42	26	40
Tadcaster Albion	30	15	7	8	53	33	37
Frecheville Community Association	30	14	9	7	50	33	37
Farsley Celtic	30	16	4	10	42	24	36
Ossett Town	30	14	8	8	48	31	36
Barton Town	30	10	14	6	48	38	34
Kiveton Park	30	11	10	9	45	45	32
Norton Woodseats	30	11	9	10	48	41	31
Worsborough Bridge	30	11	9	10	49	45	31
Harrogate Town	30	9	12	9	45	50	30
Maltby Miners Welfare	30	9	11	10	47	55	29
Scarborough Reserves	30	10	8	12	43	48	28
Yorkshire Amateurs	30	6	15	9	34	39	27
Rawmarsh Welfare	30	5	10	15	32	49	20
Woolley Miners Welfare	30	7	4	19	42	71	18
Selby Town	30	3	8	19	26	66	14

Division Three

Bentley Victoria Welfare	30	19	6	5	70	38	44
Fryston Colliery Welfare	30	16	6	8	64	39	38
Brook Sports	30	15	6	9	54	33	36
Collingham	30	13	10	7	51	34	36
Hall Road Rangers	30	14	7	9	50	35	35
Thorne Colliery	30	13	7	10	47	38	33
York Railway Institute	30	12	8	10	68	64	32
Dodworth Miners Welfare	30	11	9	10	50	57	31
Wombwell Sporting	30	11	9	10	36	44	31
Sheffield Water Works	30	10	8	12	41	41	28
St. John College (York)	30	11	6	13	58	61	28
Rossington Miners Welfare	30	9	6	15	46	55	24
Stocksbridge Works	30	10	4	16	40	60	24
B.S.C. Parkgate	30	8	5	17	41	59	21
Heeley #	30	7	9	14	38	63	19
Pilkington Recreation	30	4	8	18	30	63	16

Heeley had four points deducted

1977-78

Division One

Emley	30	20	7	3	63	33	47
Winterton Rangers	30	15	12	3	62	35	42
Thackley	30	13	11	6	41	27	37
North Ferriby United	30	12	11	7	50	40	35
Guiseley	30	13	8	9	59	41	34
Hallam	30	14	6	10	47	42	34
Sheffield	30	12	9	9	42	35	33
Frecheville Community Association	30	10	9	11	41	41	29
Tadcaster Albion	30	9	10	11	42	51	28
Bridlington Town	30	11	5	14	41	49	27
Lincoln United	30	8	9	13	42	61	25
Leeds Ashley Road	30	9	6	15	35	45	24
Ossett Albion	30	6	10	14	49	58	22
Leeds & Carnegie College	30	9	3	18	38	46	21
Farsley Celtic	30	5	11	14	41	63	21
Denaby United	30	8	5	17	39	65	21

Division Two

Kiveton Park	28	17	3	8	52	27	37
Ossett Town	28	14	7	7	43	27	35
Bentley Victoria Welfare	28	13	8	7	53	34	34
Scarborough Reserves	28	15	4	9	43	28	34
Liversedge	28	12	10	6	41	34	34
Norton Woodseats	28	13	6	9	45	33	32
Maltby Miners Welfare	28	11	9	8	47	33	31
Barton Town	28	13	3	12	43	36	29
Worsborough Bridge	28	10	9	9	45	47	29
Brook Sports	28	11	6	11	46	48	28
Hatfield Main	28	11	4	13	43	47	26
Fryston Colliery Welfare	28	7	8	13	29	45	22
Harrogate Town	28	7	6	15	38	55	20
Pickering Town	28	8	3	17	38	73	19
Collingham	28	2	6	20	22	61	10

Division Three

Yorkshire Amateurs	30	18	7	5	59	23	43
Wombwell Sporting	30	17	7	6	45	28	41
Rawmarsh Welfare	30	16	8	6	66	40	40
Thorne Colliery	30	15	9	6	60	40	39
Sheffield Water Works	30	15	8	7	52	25	38
Dodworth Miners Welfare	30	13	12	5	71	43	38
York Railway Institute	30	15	7	8	71	41	37
Hall Road Rangers	30	10	11	9	52	47	31
Pilkington Recreation	30	12	6	12	54	47	30
Harworth Colliery Institute	30	12	5	13	53	61	29
Stocksbridge Works	30	13	2	15	42	50	28
B.S.C. Parkgate	30	10	4	16	40	59	24
Selby Town	30	7	8	15	47	60	22
Woolley Miners Welfare	30	7	7	16	45	68	21
St. John College (York)	30	3	7	20	40	86	13
Rossington Miners Welfare	30	1	4	25	22	101	6

1978-79

Division One

Winterton Rangers	30	19	5	6	54	21	43
Emley	30	18	5	7	58	31	41
North Ferriby United	30	16	9	5	55	31	41
Guiseley	30	11	9	10	35	32	31
Thackley	30	13	5	12	41	39	31
Ossett Town	30	14	2	14	42	37	30
Scarborough Reserves	30	10	10	10	34	36	30
Sheffield	30	9	11	10	26	28	29
Leeds Ashley Road	30	10	8	12	34	37	28
Hallam	30	12	4	14	33	42	28
Bridlington Town	30	11	6	13	36	48	28
Frecheville Community Association	30	7	13	10	33	42	27
Tadcaster Albion	30	9	8	13	33	39	26
Bentley Victoria Welfare	30	9	7	14	34	38	25
Kiveton Park	30	8	7	15	44	54	23
Lincoln United	30	5	9	16	28	65	19

Division Two

Ossett Albion	30	17	9	4	37	18	43
Fryston Colliery Welfare	30	15	6	9	56	36	36
Thorne Colliery	30	12	12	6	45	34	36
Liversedge	30	13	9	8	39	33	35
Brook Sports	30	12	8	10	45	48	32
Farsley Celtic	30	10	11	9	49	38	31
Hatfield Main	30	11	9	10	39	36	31
Maltby Miners Welfare	30	8	12	10	37	38	28
Denaby United	30	10	7	13	47	51	27
Norton Woodseats	30	10	7	13	38	47	27
Yorkshire Amateurs	30	9	9	12	34	46	27
Barton Town	30	10	6	14	43	47	26
Rawmarsh Welfare	30	8	10	12	45	51	26
Worsborough Bridge	30	11	4	15	39	48	26
Leeds & Carnegie College	30	11	3	16	55	58	25
Wombwell Sporting	30	9	6	15	33	52	24

Division Three

York Railway Institute	28	17	5	6	70	41	39
Stocksbridge Works	28	16	6	6	46	31	38
Harworth Colliery Institute #	28	17	5	6	49	23	37
B.S.C. Parkgate	28	15	6	7	57	42	36
Hall Road Rangers *	28	15	4	9	62	42	33
Pickering Town	28	13	7	8	67	47	33
Selby Town	28	14	4	10	37	30	32
Dodworth Miners Welfare #	28	12	6	10	54	47	28
Woolley Miners Welfare	28	10	3	15	45	52	23
Collingham	28	8	7	13	42	51	23
Pilkington Recreation	28	9	5	14	36	45	23
Sheffield Water Works	28	8	7	13	32	45	23
Harrogate Town	28	7	6	15	27	55	20
Garforth Miners	28	5	7	16	30	62	17
Rossington Miners Welfare	28	3	4	21	29	70	10

Harworth Colliery Institute and Dodworth Miners Welfare each had two points deducted for breach of rules.
* Hall Road Rangers had one point deducted for breach of rules.

1979-80

Division One

Emley	30	22	6	2	62	21	50
Guiseley	30	20	7	3	62	23	47
Thackley	30	13	9	8	43	35	35
Scarborough Reserves	30	14	6	10	43	37	34
Sheffield	30	11	11	8	34	24	33
Winterton Rangers	30	15	2	13	49	39	32
Hallam	30	13	5	12	42	46	31
North Ferriby United	30	9	12	9	32	30	30
Liversedge	30	10	9	11	34	33	29
Leeds Ashley Road	30	10	8	12	39	36	28
Frecheville Community Association	30	10	7	13	30	37	27
Bridlington Town	30	9	7	14	42	50	25
Thorne Colliery	30	8	7	15	35	52	23
Ossett Town	30	7	8	15	31	47	22
Fryston Colliery Welfare	30	7	6	17	22	49	20
Ossett Albion	30	4	6	20	26	67	14

Division Two

Barton Town	30	22	4	4	62	20	48
Bentley Victoria Welfare	30	19	6	5	70	38	44
Kiveton Park	30	17	8	5	61	38	42
Maltby Miners Welfare	30	15	9	6	50	30	39
Hatfield Main	30	14	8	8	54	29	36
B.S.C. Parkgate	30	15	4	11	44	37	34
York Railway Institute	30	12	9	9	47	49	33
Farsley Celtic	30	13	6	11	49	43	32
Norton Woodseats	30	11	10	9	43	39	32
Lincoln United	30	10	7	13	46	64	27
Harworth Colliery Institute	30	8	10	12	32	40	26
Yorkshire Amateurs	30	6	9	15	31	48	21
Brook Sports	30	6	9	15	32	55	21
Denaby United	30	6	5	19	29	51	17
Tadcaster Albion	30	4	9	17	23	49	17
Stocksbridge Works	30	1	9	20	25	68	11

Division Three

Hall Road Rangers	26	15	6	5	62	29	36
Garforth Miners	26	14	6	6	40	25	34
Rawmarsh Welfare	26	14	6	6	43	33	34
Pilkington Recreation	26	13	7	6	41	28	33
Pontefract Collieries	26	11	8	7	39	29	30
Harrogate Town	26	11	6	9	44	36	28
Worsborough Bridge	26	9	7	10	31	31	25
Woolley Miners Welfare	26	7	11	8	35	36	25
Selby Town	26	8	9	9	32	41	25
Pickering Town	26	11	2	13	44	34	24
Collingham	26	9	6	11	26	36	24
Sheffield Water Works	26	9	5	12	41	44	23
Rossington Miners Welfare	26	4	4	18	25	70	12
Wombwell Sporting	26	3	5	18	25	56	11

1980-81

Division One

Leeds Ashley Road	30	18	8	4	58	25	44
Emley	30	17	8	5	61	36	42
North Ferriby United	30	16	8	6	40	23	40
Thackley	30	14	7	9	48	39	35
Guiseley	30	10	12	8	48	41	32
Winterton Rangers	30	12	8	10	35	31	32
Scarborough Reserves	30	13	5	12	55	49	31
Frecheville Community Assoc.	30	10	11	9	41	38	31
Hallam	30	11	7	12	42	39	29
Liversedge	30	11	7	12	35	49	29
Barton Town	30	8	10	12	39	41	26
Sheffield	30	9	8	13	24	41	26
Bentley Victoria Welfare	30	9	7	14	47	47	25
Maltby Miners Welfare	30	9	7	14	37	41	25
Kiveton Park	30	9	7	14	40	50	25
Bridlington Town	30	1	6	23	12	72	8

Division Two

Ossett Albion	30	15	8	7	46	30	38
York Railway Institute	30	13	10	7	52	46	36
Lincoln United	30	10	14	6	48	40	34
Farsley Celtic	30	12	10	8	36	28	34
Garforth Miners	30	12	9	9	49	42	33
Pilkington Recreation	30	12	9	9	48	42	33
B.S.C. Parkgate	30	11	9	10	31	35	31
Harworth Colliery Institute	30	10	10	10	46	40	30
Norton Woodseats	30	11	7	12	34	31	29
Yorkshire Amateurs	30	8	13	9	36	40	29
Hall Road Rangers	30	7	14	9	37	44	28
Ossett Town	30	11	5	14	37	41	27
Fryston Colliery Welfare	30	11	5	14	34	40	27
Hatfield Main	30	8	11	11	36	43	27
Thorne Colliery	30	9	5	16	44	53	23
Rawmarsh Welfare	30	4	13	13	27	46	21

Division Three

Bradley Rangers	30	20	4	6	68	33	44
Harrogate Town	30	20	4	6	64	31	44
Y.W.A. (Southern)	30	18	5	7	59	29	41
Grimethorpe Miners Welfare	30	14	9	7	54	29	37
Stocksbridge Works	30	16	5	9	56	44	37
Denaby United	30	14	8	8	55	36	36
Worsborough Bridge	30	14	8	8	57	49	36
Pickering Town	30	12	10	8	43	34	34
Pontefract Collieries	30	13	8	9	48	41	34
Harrogate Railway Athletic	30	10	5	15	30	38	25
Tadcaster Albion	30	9	6	15	46	52	24
Wombwell Sporting	30	7	10	13	33	49	24
Brook Sports	30	6	9	15	30	51	21
Woolley Miners Welfare	30	6	5	19	34	61	17
Collingham	30	4	6	20	21	56	14
Selby Town	30	4	4	22	26	91	12

1981-82

Division One

Emley	30	16	9	5	57	27	41
Guiseley	30	17	5	8	52	33	39
Leeds Ashley Road	30	15	9	6	44	30	39
Scarborough Reserves	30	15	7	8	51	38	37
Bentley Victoria Welfare	30	13	9	8	46	37	35
Lincoln United	30	13	8	9	47	35	34
Winterton Rangers	30	13	8	9	37	30	34
Thackley	30	13	7	10	51	35	33
Ossett Albion	30	10	11	9	28	26	31
North Ferriby United	30	10	7	13	46	46	27
Sheffield	30	10	7	13	33	46	27
Hallam	30	10	6	14	46	53	26
Frecheville Community Association	30	11	3	16	39	48	25
Farsley Celtic	30	10	2	18	38	54	22
Liversedge	30	6	5	19	24	52	17
York Railway Institute	30	5	3	22	28	77	13

Division Two

Harrogate Town	30	16	8	6	56	29	40
Ossett Town	30	17	6	7	51	29	40
Garforth Miners	30	14	11	5	44	27	39
Bradley Rangers	30	14	10	6	42	31	38
Maltby Miners Welfare	30	13	8	9	48	39	34
B.S.C. Parkgate	30	13	8	9	43	40	34
Norton Woodseats	30	14	5	11	35	28	33
Hatfield Main	30	10	10	10	42	41	30
Hall Road Rangers	30	11	8	11	32	37	30
Harworth Colliery Institute	30	11	7	12	40	37	29
Bridlington Town	30	9	6	15	35	55	24
Grimethorpe Miners Welfare	30	7	9	14	39	42	23
Pilkington Recreation	30	5	12	13	29	41	22
Yorkshire Amateurs	30	9	4	17	27	53	22
Kiveton Park	30	7	7	16	37	52	21
Fryston Colliery Welfare	30	5	11	14	37	56	21

Division Three

Pontefract Collieries	28	24	2	2	62	23	50
Denaby United	28	16	5	7	44	29	37
Woolley Miners Welfare	28	16	4	8	51	28	36
Worsborough Bridge	28	13	9	6	54	35	35
Tadcaster Albion	28	13	7	8	52	37	33
Stocksbridge Works	28	11	8	9	51	35	30
Phoenix Park	28	12	5	11	37	37	29
Wombwell Sporting	28	10	9	9	29	31	29
Pickering Town	28	11	4	13	38	41	26
Selby Town	28	9	6	13	34	39	24
Brook Sports	28	10	4	14	33	41	24
Collingham	28	8	7	13	27	36	23
Harrogate Railway Athletic	28	6	6	16	24	53	18
Rawmarsh Welfare	28	4	7	17	22	64	15
Thorne Colliery	28	4	3	21	39	68	11

FOUNDATION

The Central Amateur League was founded in 1935 to provide senior football for the few midlands based clubs who were strictly amateur. The 8 founder members were Banbury Spencer from the Oxfordshire Senior League who also joined the Birmingham Combination, Ibstock Penistone Rovers from the Leicestershire Senior League, Leicester Nomads from the Midland Amateur Alliance, North Derbyshire Ramblers, Northampton Mount Pleasant, Northampton Nomads from the United Counties League, R.A.F. Cranwell from the Central Combination and R.A.F. Upper Heyford.

CHANGES TO THE LEAGUE

1936   North Derbyshire Ramblers left for the Central Combination and Banbury Spencer and R.A.F. Upper Heyford also left. However the league increased to 11 clubs as 6 new clubs joined. They were Moor Green from the Birmingham A.F.A., Coalville Town, Badsey Rangers, Bedworth Town, Loughborough College and Coventry Morris Motors.

1937   Bedworth Town left but the league increased to 12 clubs as Boldmere St. Michaels joined from the Birmingham A.F.A. and Nuneaton Borough joined as a new club.

1938   League reduced to 11 clubs as Nuneaton Borough left for the Birmingham Combination.

1946   When the league restarted after the war Moor Green had already joined the Birmingham Combination and Badsey Rangers, Loughborough College, Leicester Nomads, Northampton Nomads, Northampton Mount Pleasant and R.A.F. Cranwell also did not rejoin. However the league was maintained at 11 clubs as Lye Town joined from the Worcestershire Combination, along with 6 other new clubs – Rugby Town Amateurs, Coventry Amateurs, Bournville Athletic, Smethwick Highfield, Northampton Amateurs and Leicester Y.M.C.A.

1947   Lye Town left and joined the Birmingham League and Coventry Morris Motors and Leicester Y.M.C.A. also left. They were replaced by Lockheed Leamington, Redditch High Duty Alloys and Oakham Rovers.

1948   Bournville Athletic, Redditch High Duty Alloys and Smethwick Highfield left for the Worcestershire Combination, Rugby Town left for the United Counties League and Coalville Town left and took their reserves place in the Leicestershire Senior League. Whitwick Colliery joined from the Leicestershire Senior League and Bedford Avenue and Warwick Town also joined. League reduced to 9 clubs.

1949   Lockheed Leamington left and joined the Birmingham Combination and Whitwick Colliery and Boldmere St. Michaels left and joined the Birmingham League. Oakham Rovers also left but the league increased to 10 clubs with the election of Birmingham Paget Rangers, Huntingdon United, St. Ives Town, Leicester University College and Evesham Town Amateurs.

1950   League disbanded. Bedford Avenue, Huntingdon United and St. Ives Town joined the United Counties League, Paget Rangers joined the Worcestershire Combination and Leicester University College and Ibstock Penistone Rovers joined the Leicestershire Senior League. The next league of Warwick Town, Coventry Amateurs, Northampton Amateurs and Evesham Town Amateurs has not been traced.

TABLE NOTES

Central Amateur League tables as published contained some errors as noted below:

1935-36   Total goals for 1 more than total goals against.
1936-37   Total goals for 2 less than total goals against.
1937-38   Total goals for 2 less than total goals against.
1938-39   Total goals for 1 more than total goals against.

1935-36

Northampton Mount Pleasant	14	12	1	1	53	16	25
Leicester Nomads	14	9	3	2	48	28	21
North Derbyshire Ramblers	14	7	2	5	55	35	16
Ibstock Penistone Rovers	14	7	2	5	43	31	16
R.A.F. Cranwell	14	5	2	7	27	37	12
Banbury Spencer	14	5	1	8	27	44	11
R.A.F. Upper Heyford	14	3	1	10	27	56	7
Northampton Nomads	14	2	0	12	26	58	4

1936-37

Moor Green	20	17	1	2	87	26	35
R.A.F. Cranwell	20	13	2	5	83	36	28
Leicester Nomads	20	12	1	7	67	49	25
Coalville Town	20	11	2	7	75	53	24
Ibstock Penistone Rovers	20	10	4	6	53	58	24
Northampton Mount Pleasant	20	9	3	8	46	52	21
Badsey Rangers	20	9	2	9	57	52	20
Bedworth Town	20	4	7	9	53	84	15
Loughborough College	20	4	3	13	45	66	11
Coventry Morris Motors	20	3	3	14	34	78	9
Northampton Nomads	20	3	2	15	43	91	8

1937-38

Moor Green	22	13	5	4	58	27	31
Coventry Morris Motors	22	14	3	5	65	40	31
Coalville Town	22	13	3	6	60	46	29
Nuneaton Borough	22	11	5	6	45	31	27
Badsey Rangers	22	12	1	9	67	50	25
Ibstock Penistone Rovers	22	9	5	8	54	64	23
Loughborough College	22	9	3	10	64	62	21
Boldmere St. Michaels	22	8	4	10	52	43	20
Northampton Mount Pleasant	22	7	5	10	42	47	19
R.A.F. Cranwell	22	6	6	10	48	67	18
Leicester Nomads	22	7	2	13	40	59	16
Northampton Nomads	22	1	2	19	38	99	4

1938-39

Moor Green	20	17	1	2	93	28	35
Ibstock Penistone Rovers	20	13	2	5	69	37	28
Coventry Morris Motors	20	10	3	7	49	40	23
Badsey Rangers	20	11	0	9	52	70	22
Boldmere St. Michaels	20	8	4	8	51	37	20
Coalville Town	20	9	1	10	49	50	19
Loughborough College	20	7	4	9	51	53	18
Leicester Nomads	20	7	4	9	47	51	18
Northampton Nomads	20	6	2	12	39	81	14
Northampton Mount Pleasant	20	5	3	12	29	50	13
R.A.F. Cranwell	20	4	2	14	29	60	10

1946-47

Boldmere St. Michaels	20	12	6	2	56	16	30
Coventry Amateurs	20	14	2	4	73	29	30
Rugby Town Amateurs	20	14	1	5	72	38	29
Lye Town	20	13	2	5	79	39	28
Coalville Town	20	11	2	7	59	38	24
Bournville Athletic	20	10	3	7	73	50	23
Coventry Morris Motors	20	10	3	7	57	48	23
Ibstock Penistone Rovers	20	4	2	14	37	93	10
Smethwick Highfield	20	4	1	15	45	72	9
Northampton Amateurs	20	3	2	15	40	77	8
Leicester Y.M.C.A.	20	2	2	16	25	116	6

1947-48

Rugby Town	20	15	1	4	77	24	31
Boldmere St. Michaels	20	14	2	4	60	21	30
Lockheed Leamington	20	13	2	5	67	36	28
Coalville Town	20	12	0	8	76	45	24
Smethwick Highfield	20	10	2	8	55	48	22
Redditch High Duty Alloys	20	9	2	9	40	46	20
Bournville Athletic	20	8	2	10	47	35	18
Coventry Amateurs	20	6	4	10	40	41	16
Northampton Amateurs	20	7	1	12	55	72	15
Ibstock Penistone Rovers	20	5	3	12	35	60	13
Oakham Rovers	20	1	1	18	22	146	3

1948-49

Boldmere St. Michaels	16	13	1	2	51	19	27
Ibstock Penistone Rovers	16	12	1	3	58	26	25
Lockheed Leamington	16	9	1	6	46	32	19
Coventry Amateurs	16	8	2	6	41	21	18
Warwick Town	16	7	2	7	42	41	16
Whitwick Colliery	16	4	5	7	37	47	13
Bedford Avenue	16	4	4	8	37	37	12
Northampton Amateurs	16	4	4	8	28	33	12
Oakham Rovers	16	1	0	15	19	103	2

1949-50

Ibstock Penistone Rovers	18	15	0	3	69	15	30
Coventry Amateurs	18	14	2	2	78	18	30
Birmingham Paget Rangers	18	9	5	4	57	24	23
Bedford Avenue	18	9	3	6	46	33	21
Huntingdon United	18	9	1	8	70	44	19
St. Ives	18	6	5	7	58	45	17
Leicester University College	18	5	5	8	52	34	15
Warwick Town	18	5	4	9	37	41	14
Northampton Amateurs	18	5	1	12	57	59	11
Evesham Town Amateurs	18	0	0	18	10	221	0

FOUNDATION

The Central Combination was founded in 1933 principally by clubs whose first teams had been playing in the Derbyshire Senior League (DSL) but wanted a stronger league with a wider area. Eight of the 17 founder members – Sutton Town, Heanor Town, Ilkeston, Matlock Town, Ripley Town and Athletic, Sutton Junction, Bolsover Colliery and Chesterfield "A" – moved straight from the DSL. Gresley Rovers and Loughborough Corinthians had been fielding their reserves in the DSL but moved their first teams to the Central Combination, Gresley from the Birmingham Combination and Loughborough from the Midland League. Mansfield Town had been fielding their "A" side in the DSL but moved their reserves into the Central Combination from the Midland League.

The other six founder members had not been fielding a side in the DSL and were –

Grantham and Newark Town who both moved from the Midland League, Kettering Town from the Northamptonshire League, Worksop Town who are thought to have moved from the Sheffield League and Nottingham Forest Reserves and R.A.F. Cranwell whose leagues the previous season have not been traced.

CHANGES TO THE LEAGUE

1934   Loughborough Corinthians disbanded, Grantham returned to the Midland League and Sutton Junction also left. Ollerton Colliery joined but the league was reduced to 15 clubs.

1935   Kettering Town left for the United Counties League, Worksop Town left for the Yorkshire League, Gresley Rovers left for the Leicestershire Senior League, R.A.F. Cranwell left for the Central Amateur League and Nottingham Forest Reserves, Matlock Town and Bolsover Colliery also left. Burton Town Reserves joined but the league was reduced to 9 clubs.

1936   Newark Town and Mansfield Town Reserves left for the Midland League and Burton Town Reserves also left. North Derbyshire Ramblers joined from the Central Amateur League and Bolsover Colliery, Danesmoor Welfare and Staveley Welfare also joined. League increased to 10 clubs.

1937   League disbanded. Ollerton Colliery and Bolsover Colliery joined the Yorkshire League while Chesterfield "A", Staveley Miners Welfare, Danesmoor Welfare, Sutton Town and Heanor Town helped to re-form the DSL. The next leagues of Ilkeston, Ripley and North Derbyshire Ramblers have not been traced.

TABLE NOTES

Central Combination tables as published contained some errors. Additional research has corrected some of these but note that in 1934-35 the total goals for are 1 more than the total goals against.

1933-34

Nottingham Forest Reserves	32	24	4	4	131	34	52
Heanor Town	32	24	2	6	117	58	50
Chesterfield "A"	32	23	3	6	97	42	49
Sutton Town	32	18	4	10	88	58	40
Kettering Town	32	17	4	11	122	83	38
Mansfield Town Reserves	32	14	7	11	106	75	35
Ilkeston	32	13	7	12	105	68	33
Ripley Town and Athletic	32	14	5	13	64	79	33
Worksop Town	32	13	6	13	77	76	32
Loughborough Corinthians	32	14	3	15	73	76	31
R.A.F. Cranwell	32	10	6	16	69	99	26
Bolsover Colliery	32	10	4	18	72	121	24
Newark Town	32	8	7	17	81	101	23
Gresley Rovers	32	10	3	19	67	129	23
Matlock Town	32	9	4	19	84	123	22
Grantham	32	7	6	19	58	99	20
Sutton Junction	32	5	3	24	59	149	13

1934-35

Heanor Town	28	23	2	3	100	34	48
Nottingham Forest Reserves	28	17	5	6	98	40	39
Mansfield Town Reserves	28	16	5	7	80	58	37
Ripley Town and Athletic	28	15	6	7	79	58	36
Ollerton Colliery	28	16	2	10	70	48	34
Worksop Town	28	11	8	9	57	39	30
Kettering Town	28	13	4	11	90	62	30
Ilkeston	28	14	1	13	72	60	29
Newark Town	28	13	2	13	94	88	28
Chesterfield "A"	28	12	2	14	72	68	26
Matlock Town	28	11	3	14	75	82	25
Sutton Town	28	10	3	15	61	79	23
Gresley Rovers	28	7	4	17	59	123	18
Bolsover Colliery	28	2	5	21	41	134	9
R.A.F. Cranwell	28	1	6	21	22	96	8

1935-36

Ollerton Colliery	16	11	3	2	43	25	25
Ripley Town and Athletic	16	10	3	3	56	28	23
Newark Town	16	8	3	5	46	41	19
Mansfield Town Reserves	16	7	3	6	43	39	17
Heanor Town	16	6	4	6	61	37	16
Sutton Town	16	6	4	6	28	39	16
Chesterfield "A"	16	4	5	7	44	54	13
Ilkeston	16	4	2	10	28	49	10
Burton Town Reserves	16	2	1	13	28	65	5

1936-37

Ollerton Colliery	18	14	2	2	62	23	30
Ripley Town	18	9	5	4	62	38	23
Bolsover Colliery	18	10	3	5	56	44	23
Chesterfield "A"	18	6	5	7	53	45	17
Heanor Town	18	7	2	9	32	30	16
Danesmoor Welfare	18	7	2	9	33	42	16
Staveley Welfare	18	7	2	9	42	74	16
Ilkeston	18	6	3	9	43	51	15
North Derbyshire Ramblers	18	7	1	10	48	64	15
Sutton Town	18	3	3	12	31	51	9

FOUNDATION

The United League was founded in 1896 principally to give clubs who were playing in other leagues more first team fixtures. As a lot of these clubs had only turned professional a few years earlier it will have been important to them to keep the revenue coming in so that they could afford to pay their players. There were eight founder members of the United League whose other leagues were as follows :

Football League Division Two – Woolwich Arsenal and Loughborough.

Southern League – Tottenham Hotspur and Millwall Athletic.

Midland League – Kettering Town, Rushden and Wellingborough (all from Northamptonshire).

The eighth club were Luton Town, who had been members of the Southern League in the previous season but played only in the United League in 1896-97.

Although the members did not consider United League games as quite so important as the games in their other leagues, they still played their strongest sides in them. This was made possible because most United League games were played in mid-week.

CHANGES TO THE LEAGUE

1897   Luton Town were elected to the Football League but continued also to play first team games in the United League. The league was extended to 9 clubs by the election of Southampton whose first team also played in the Southern League.

1898   Loughborough resigned from the United League to concentrate on the Football League but the league was extended to 11 clubs by the election of three more clubs who were also members of the Southern League – Bristol City, Reading and Brighton United. Brighton United were a newly formed club.

1899   Brighton United disbanded and Luton Town resigned to concentrate on the Football League. A new league called the Southern District Combination was formed to fulfil the same function as the United League but was more southerly based. Woolwich Arsenal, Reading, Millwall Athletic, Bristol City, Southampton and Tottenham Hotspur all left the United League to join the new league. Northampton Town joined the United League with their first team also joining the Midland League. They had previously been playing in the Northamptonshire League. Desborough Unity, Finedon Revellers and Rothwell Town Swifts all joined while continuing in the Northamptonshire League and thus the United League became solely Northamptonshire based with seven members.

1900   Desborough Unity left but continued in the Northamptonshire League. They were replaced by Luton Town who had left the Football League and returned to both the United League and the Southern League.

1901   Luton Town resigned and entered their reserves in the newly formed South-Eastern League instead. Northampton Town also resigned as they decided to concentrate on the Southern League following their move from the Midland League. Irthlingborough joined while continuing in the Northamptonshire League.

1902   Finedon Revellers failed to complete their fixtures and are believed to have disbanded at the end of the season. The United League closed down with Irthlingborough, Rothwell Town Swifts and Rushden Town continuing in the Northamptonshire League and Kettering Town and Wellingborough continuing in the Southern League which they had to moved to from the Midland League in 1900 (Kettering) and 1901 (Wellingborough).

1905   The league was revived with 10 clubs, 9 of whom also played in the Southern League. The exception was Clapton Orient whose other league was the Football League Division Two.

1906   Southern United were disbanded by the F.A. and Clapton Orient, Swindon Town and Grays United resigned. Two more Southern League clubs – Norwich City and Hastings & St. Leonards United – joined but the league was reduced to 8 clubs.

1907   6 of the 8 clubs resigned, the exceptions being Hastings & St. Leonards and New Brompton. They were joined by 3 more Southern League clubs – Brentford, Croydon Common and Southend United. League reduced to 5 clubs.

1908   The 5 existing members played in the Southern Section while 7 new clubs played in a newly formed Northern Section. The new clubs were Norwich City and Coventry City of the Southern League, Rotherham Town and Lincoln City of the Midland League, Walsall of the Birmingham League and Peterborough City of the Northamptonshire League. Grantham Avenue were the other club but they played only in the United League having left the Midland League.

1909   The United League disbanded and its clubs continued in their other leagues with the exception of Peterborough City who moved from the Northamptonshire League to the Southern League, Lincoln City who moved from the Midland League to the Football League and Grantham Avenue who are thought to have disbanded.

TABLE NOTES

United League tables as published contained some errors. Additional research has corrected these but note that very few tables were published for 1899-1900. It has been found that Rushden beat Kettering 3-0 on 9th December 1899 but the result was not included in published tables probably because Kettering objected. However no record has been found that the game was ever replayed and so the original result has been included. Also it is known that Wellingborough beat Desborough near to the end of the season but neither the score or a table including the result have been traced. The clubs have thus been credited with a win and a loss as applicable but no addition for this game has been made to the goals for and against.

1896-97

Millwall Athletic	14	11	1	2	43	22	23
Luton Town	14	10	1	3	52	16	21
Woolwich Arsenal	14	6	3	5	28	34	15
Loughborough	14	6	1	7	29	31	13
Rushden	14	6	1	7	25	42	13
Kettering Town	14	4	4	6	23	24	12
Wellingborough	14	3	3	8	17	39	9
Tottenham Hotspur	14	1	4	9	25	34	6

1897-98

Luton Town	16	13	2	1	49	11	28
Tottenham Hotspur	16	8	5	3	40	27	21
Woolwich Arsenal	16	8	5	3	35	24	21
Kettering Town	16	9	1	6	28	24	19
Rushden	16	7	1	8	24	26	15
Southampton #	16	6	3	7	23	28	13
Millwall Athletic	16	4	4	8	27	27	12
Wellingborough	16	3	3	10	17	42	9
Loughborough	16	1	2	13	8	42	4

Southampton had two points deducted for fielding an ineligible player

1898-99

Millwall Athletic	20	14	3	3	42	19	31
Southampton	20	12	1	7	53	32	25
Tottenham Hotspur	20	11	2	7	36	25	24
Woolwich Arsenal	20	10	4	6	40	30	24
Bristol City	20	11	0	9	43	31	22
Reading	20	8	5	7	36	25	21
Brighton United	20	10	1	9	41	42	21
Wellingborough	20	7	1	12	32	40	15
Kettering Town #	20	8	1	11	25	38	15
Rushden	20	6	1	13	26	45	13
Luton Town	20	2	3	15	24	71	7

Kettering Town had two points deducted for fielding an ineligible player

1899-1900

Wellingborough	12	8	2	2	35	12	18
Northampton Town	12	7	3	2	43	16	17
Rushden	12	8	1	3	33	20	17
Kettering Town	12	8	0	4	30	11	16
Rothwell Town Swifts	12	4	0	8	25	34	8
Finedon Revellers	12	3	1	8	13	41	7
Desborough Unity	12	0	1	11	3	48	1

1900-1901

Rothwell Town Swifts	12	10	0	2	36	11	20
Luton Town	12	7	4	1	30	18	18
Kettering Town	12	6	3	3	23	18	15
Wellingborough	12	6	0	6	24	28	12
Northampton Town	12	2	4	6	16	27	8
Rushden Town	12	2	3	7	16	24	7
Finedon Revellers	12	0	4	8	10	29	4

1901-1902

Irthlingborough	8	4	3	1	9	5	11
Rothwell Town Swifts	9	4	2	3	13	13	10
Kettering Town	9	3	3	3	11	7	9
Rushden Town	8	2	3	3	13	14	7
Wellingborough	8	1	4	3	11	15	6
Finedon Revellers	4	1	1	2	4	7	3

Finedon Revellers failed to complete their fixtures

1905-1906

Watford	18	13	4	1	49	15	30
Crystal Palace	18	13	1	4	51	21	27
Leyton	18	8	4	6	33	31	20
Luton Town	18	7	4	7	47	27	18
Clapton Orient	18	5	8	5	24	27	18
Swindon Town	18	7	3	8	33	29	17
Brighton & Hove Albion	18	6	4	8	28	28	16
New Brompton	18	7	2	9	26	27	16
Grays United	18	4	2	12	21	64	10
Southern United	18	3	2	13	21	64	8

1906-1907

Crystal Palace	14	8	5	1	39	20	21
Brighton & Hove Albion	14	6	6	2	33	26	18
Luton Town	14	8	1	5	23	27	17
Norwich City	14	6	4	4	34	22	16
Hastings & St. Leonards United	14	6	2	6	27	24	14
Leyton	14	3	4	7	24	27	10
New Brompton	14	3	3	8	24	35	9
Watford	14	3	1	10	15	38	7

1907-1908

Brentford	8	6	1	1	19	8	13
Southend United	8	3	2	3	16	16	8
New Brompton	8	2	3	3	10	11	7
Croydon Common	8	3	1	4	9	18	7
Hastings & St. Leonards United	8	1	3	4	13	14	5

1908-1909

Southern Section

New Brompton	8	5	1	2	27	14	11
Hastings & St. Leonards United	8	4	1	3	13	12	9
Croydon Common	8	4	0	4	13	17	8
Southend United	8	2	3	3	15	18	7
Brentford	8	2	1	5	13	20	5

Northern Section

Rotherham Town	12	8	1	3	39	15	17
Lincoln City	12	7	2	3	32	18	16
Norwich City	12	7	2	3	33	20	16
Walsall	12	5	2	5	23	25	12
Coventry City	12	5	1	6	27	31	11
Peterborough City	12	4	1	7	18	34	9
Grantham Avenue	12	1	1	10	12	41	3

Championship Play-Off

New Brompton 4   Rotherham Town 1

Supporters' Guides & Other Titles

This top-selling series has been published annually since 1982 and contains 2003/2004 Season's results and tables, Directions, Photographs, Phone numbers, Parking information, Admission details, Disabled information and much more.

THE SUPPORTERS' GUIDE TO PREMIER & FOOTBALL LEAGUE CLUBS 2005

The 21st edition featuring all Premiership and Football League clubs. *Price £6.99*

THE SUPPORTERS' GUIDE TO NON-LEAGUE FOOTBALL 2005 – STEP 1 & STEP 2 CLUBS

Following the reorganisation of Non-League Football this 13th edition covers all 66 Step 1 & Step 2 clubs – effectively the Football Conference and it's feeder Leagues. *Price £6.99*

THE SUPPORTERS' GUIDE TO NON-LEAGUE FOOTBALL 2005 – STEP 3 CLUBS

Following the reorganisation of Non-League Football the 1st edition of this book features all 66 clubs which feed into the Football Conference. *Price £6.99*

THE SUPPORTERS' GUIDE TO SCOTTISH FOOTBALL 2005

The 13th edition featuring all Scottish Premier League, Scottish League and Highland League clubs. *Price £6.99*

THE SUPPORTERS' GUIDE TO WELSH FOOTBALL GROUNDS 2005

The 9th edition featuring all League of Wales, Cymru Alliance & Welsh Football League Clubs + results, tables & much more. *Price £6.99*

FOOTBALL LEAGUE TABLES 1888-2004

The 7th edition contains every Football League, Premier League, Scottish League and Scottish Premier League Final Table from 1888-2004 together with Cup Final Information. *Price £9.99*

These books are available UK & Surface post free from –

Soccer Books Limited (Dept. SBL)
72 St. Peter's Avenue
Cleethorpes
N.E. Lincolnshire
DN35 8HU

Also available –

DEFUNCT FOOTBALL LEAGUES of the SOUTH-EAST 1939-2000

Compiled by:
Mick Blakeman
Bob Perkins
Dave Twydell

Priced £ 7.95 + £ 1.25 postage.   *Order from:*

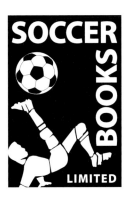